THE POSSESSION OF MAN

THE SOCIETAL EFFECT THAT INFLUENCES THE LIFE AND SOUL OF MAN

JOHN BROKAAR

BY THE SAME AUTHOR

The Way of the Pilgrim:
BOOK I – The Inner Evolution of Man
BOOK II – The Outer World of Man
BOOK III – Merging the Inner and Outer World of Man

Divine Orchestrations surrounding Phil Cerami

Contemplations and Deliberations,
between Swami Vidyananda and John Brokaar

Copyright

The Possession of Man

Copyright @ 2025 by John Brokaar

Some rights are reserved.
With exception of the cover and licensed images, any other part of this book may be freely reproduced in physical or digital format for non-commercial purposes, provided the author and title of this book are cited as the source.

Cover Painting:
The Fall of Man, by William Blake, 1807.
Reproduced with permission of the Victoria and Albert Museum, London.

Backpage:
The Carolingian Family Tree, by Frutolf von Michelsberg, 1107.
Reproduced from Thuringian University and State Library Jena,
Cod. Bose q. 19, fol. 152v

Edited by: Steve Rush   Graphics support: Ricky van der Walt

ISBN: 978-1-0492-0621-9 (print)   978-1-0492-0622-6 (e-book)

This book is dedicated to all the children.

*Each of whom is born pure, innocent and good,
at least until our clever societies, agencies and things take them,
and opt to condition them accordingly.*

*However, until then their Essence remains
without judgment or opinion,
seeking only that which is inherently known:*

Love and compassion, through attention and touch.

II

PREFACE

The conveyance of information that provides a multi-dimensional context in layers of understanding, on topics that are both physical and metaphysical, is complex. It is even more so when we attempt to do so by writing, being a one-dimensional form of transmission in which the beginning of a sentence is often only understood at its end. It is for this reason that this book is written in paragraphs, within which each paragraph aims at providing a particular impression. A complex paragraph may therefore become clearer if it is read a second or even a third time, when an impression of its content is already present. The reader may further note that, for the sake of emphasis or elucidation, the structure of sentences, including the use of italics, quotation marks, commas and semi-colons, differ from section to section.

The difficulty of projecting a conceptual understanding is exacerbated when emphasis on the meaning of something specific is required. For this we may use a combination of words, making sure that we then do not alter their meaning. Take for example the 'world of man', which uses two physical elements to create a metaphysical concept, and in addition, it is not necessarily about the 'world' or 'humankind', but a conceptual or behavioral phenomenon. Hence within these writings, such words are often hyphenated into phrases such as the 'world-of-man' and 'deep-state'.

Then, besides capitalizing the obvious references to generally recognized Divine Beings, such as God, Christ, and the Buddha, we also capitalized the names of conscious entities and beings from a dimensional (or vibrational) origin that is higher than that of mankind. Amongst others these include Time, Life, Great Nature, Earth, Biosphere, Sun, Cosmos, Universe and Consciousness in itself.

Last but not least, it must be noted that the masculine referral such as 'man', 'him' or 'his' throughout these writings, unless otherwise described, does not refer to gender but 'humankind' or 'humanity'.

IV

CONTENTS

DEDICATION	I
PREFACE	II
CONTENTS	V

FOREWORD I:	**IN SEARCH OF THE SEEKER**	**1**
o	Realizing the Conundrum of Being	1
o	Defining the Quest	2
o	Finding the Seeker	2
o	Becoming the Knower	3
o	The Purpose of this Book	4

FOREWORD II:	**THE CORRELATION OF GOD AND THE CONCEPT OF EXCHANGE**	**5**
o	The Contemporary Individual and his Society	5
o	The Power of Coexistence	6
o	The Possession of man	7

DIAGRAM 1: THE PYRAMIDS OF OPPOSITE REALITIES	9

A TALISMAN FOR THE JOURNEY	**10**

INTRODUCTION		**11**
o	The Paradox of our Reality	11
o	Revisiting the Pilgrim	12
o	The World of Man	14
o	The Microcosm and its Source	15
o	The macrocosm and its Purpose	16
o	The Concluding Emergence	17

1. THE FALLACY OF PARADOXICAL PARADIGMS		**19**
o	The Big Bang – From Emptiness to the All and Everything	19
o	The Merger of Science and Spirituality	21
o	Concluding Paradoxes	22

2. THE NATURAL BUT INVISIBLE INFLUENCES ON OUR STATES OF BEING		**23**
o	The Nature and Effects of Influence and Interference	23

3. THE MAGICAL EARTH, PART I
THE PHENOMENON OF GEOGRAPHY — 26

- A. Cities Cursed by Geography: Jerusalem — 27
  - History — 27
  - The Geopolitics of Weaponized Religion — 28
  - Geology and Geometry — 29
- B. Cities on the Earth's Natural Energy centers: Giza — 33
  - The irrefutable but Ignored feature of Time — 34
  - The irrefutable but Ignored feature of Design — 34
  - The irrefutable but Ignored feature of Location — 35
  - Indelible Evidence in the Veil of Myth and Legend — 36
  - Evidence underneath the veils of Record and Logic — 42
  - The Departure of the Gods, and the Fall of Egypt — 43
- C. Cities on Artificial Energy Centers: Manhattan — 45
  - The City that never Rests — 45
  - Ending the Monster — 48
- D. Natural Centers of Creation and Destruction: Germania — 49
  - Defining Germania — 49
  - The Occult Pursuit to either Contain and Control, or Scatter and Destroy the Germanic Race — 51
  - The Germanic Race of Afrikaners — 53
  - The Recovery of Africa, by Germanic Means — 55
  - The Return of German Might — 56
  - Determining the Source of Germanic Power — 58
  - Other Regions with Comparable Power — 60
- E. The Sacrificial Land Chosen and Doomed by the gods named Isis, Rah and El: Israel — 61
  - Separate Entities — 62
  - Defining the Roots of an Entity — 63

4. THE MAGICAL EARTH, PART II
MAGICAL STRUCTURES — 65

- Contemplating the Why and How — 66
- The Emergence of Magic — 68
- The Correspondence of Snowflakes with Humans and Pyramids — 69
- Physical Geodesy and the Magic of Emergence — 71
- Defining the Source and its Ultimate Purpose — 72
- The Unnatural and Occult Influences in States — 74

5. THE MAGICAL EARTH, PART III
CONSCIOUSNESS AND ITS OMNISCIENT
OMNIPRESENCE — 76

- Contemplating the Subject of Consciousness along the Spectra of the Differing Human Realities — 76
- Defining Reality by defining the Illusory — 78
- Defining Consciousness by What it is Not — 79
- Defining Consciousness along the Contemporary Perspective — 81

DIAGRAM 2: THE CENTERS OF MAN — 82

- Science and Technology's Perspective on Consciousness — 82
- Defining Consciousness via Religion and Spirituality — 84
- Defining Consciousness via the Trance and Psychedelic Path — 85
- Defining Consciousness as a Medium — 86
- Water, Earth, Air, Fire and Aether — 87
- Water as a Medium of Consciousness — 87
- Earth as a Medium of Consciousness — 88
- Air as a Medium of Consciousness — 88
- Aether as a Medium of Consciousness — 89
- The Purpose of Fire — 90

6. THE PERCEIVED REALITIES OF MAN, PART I
PERCEIVING REALITY IN LAYERS AND SPHERES — 92

- The Reality of Perception versus the Power of Belief — 92
- The Fundamental Basis of Reality — 95
- Reality in Layers — 96
- Reality Based on Layers of Time — 97
- Contemplating the Why and How in a Layered Reality — 100
- Reality in Spheres — 101
- The Co-existence of Realities in Spheres and Layers — 103
- The Existence of Realities Outside of Layers and Spheres — 104

7. THE PERCEIVED REALITIES OF MAN, PART II
PERCEIVING REALITY IN DIVERSE REALMS — 106

- The comparative Reality of the Soldier and the Monk — 107
- The Social Conditioning and Coercion that form the Soldier and the Monk — 109
- Duty and Idealism — 110
- Power and Ego — 111
- Realities in Flux — 112
- The Rules and laws that Manifest and Maintain Dimensions — 113
- Comparing the Spiritual Realities of the Monk and the Soldier — 117
- Comparing the Physical Realities of the Monk and the Soldier — 117
- Contemplating the Reality of the Devoted — 118
- The Realities of the Corporate, Judiciary and Academic Realms — 120

8. THE PERCEIVED REALITIES OF MAN, PART III
TRUTH AND ITS INEVITABLE CALLED HOPE — 121

- The Necessity of Falsehood — 122
- The Perceived as Necessary 'Absence of Truth', in the Collectives of Man — 124
- The Necessity of Hope — 127

9. THE PERCEIVED REALITIES OF MAN, PART IV THE ILLUSION OF POLITICAL CORRECTNESS AND EQUALITY — 130

- The Reason and Logic of Absurdity — 131
  - A Review of Contemporary campaigns: The End of Poverty — 131
  - A Review of Contemporary campaigns: The End of Illiteracy — 132
  - A Review of Contemporary campaigns: The End of Sadness — 134
- The Necessity of Conscious Giving and Receiving — 135
- Equality within a Politically Correct System of Belief — 136

10. UNDERSTANDING THE DAEMON, PART I THE SPIRITUAL POSSESSION OF THE UNCONSCIOUS MAN — 138

- Power Corrupts, and Absolute Power Corrupts Absolutely — 138
- The Manifestation of Entities — 140
- Comparing Conjurors of Darkness with the Bearers of Light — 142
- The Possession's Disguises and ways of Transmission — 143
- Understanding the Possession's nature — 144
- Defining the Possession as an Entity or Structure of Thought — 147
- Evading the Possession by Understanding its Cosmic Harmony — 149
  - The First Observation: Metaphysical Causes with Physical Effects — 150
  - The Second Observation: The Law of Opposites — 150
  - The Third Observation: The Effect of Purpose — 151
  - The Fourth Observation: The Law of Causality — 152
  - The Fifth Observation: The Law of Vibration — 152
  - The Sixth Observation: The Law of Rhythm — 163

11. UNDERSTANDING THE DAEMON, PART II THE PREDICTABLE EFFECT OF SPIRIT ON THE UNCONSCIOUS MAN — 155

- Defining the Unawakened or Unconscious Man — 155
- The Influences or Effects of an Astral World of Duality — 156
- The Consequential Cycles of Choice — 158
- Justifying Artificial Intelligence, along the Law of Causality — 160
- The Possession that Transcends across Generations — 163
  - A Track-record of Entities — 163
  - The Entity versus the Id-entity — 164
- Exorcism through Awareness, by Crossing the Threshold — 166
- The Cyclic Patterns of a Possession — 168
- The Rise of an Entity called 'Technology' — 169

12. UNDERSTANDING THE DAEMON, PART III GOVERNING THE COLLECTIVE POSSESSIONS OF MAN — 171

- Acknowledging the Dimensional Difference of Egos — 171
- The Three Parts of the Sum of Man — 172
  - The Universal Spirit — 172
  - The Physical Man — 172
  - The Ego of Man — 172
- The Workings of the Sum of Man — 173
- The Possession of Man — 174
- The Effects of Geography, Causality and Inevitability — 176
- The Unnatural and Invisible or Occult Influences on States — 181

13. DETERMINING PURPOSE AND BEING, THROUGH REASON AND LOGIC — 184

- What is the Human-being, wherein lies its Purpose? — 184
- The Differing of Reason and Logic among Differing People — 185

14. DETERMINING PURPOSE AND BEING, THROUGH THE CONCEPT OF MORALITY — 190

- The Question of Morality — 190
- The Effects of Technology on the Logic of Societal Morals — 192
- The Opposing but Occult Political and Geopolitical Logic — 194
- Morality as Defined by Those who Speak and Those that Act — 196
- Fact and Rule based Morality — 197
- The Purpose of Morality — 198

15. THE POWER AND PURPOSE OF PRAYER AND MEDITATION — 199

- The Flow — 199
- Defining the Purpose of Prayer — 201
- Observing the Power of Prayer — 201
- Defining the Power of Meditation — 203
- Observing the Purpose of Meditation — 203
- The Synergy in Prayer and Meditation — 204

16. CONTEMPLATING TAT SVAM ASI; "THOU ART THAT" — 206

- What Art Thou? — 206
- Who Art Thou? — 208
- Thou Art That — 209

AN INTRODUCTION INTO THE CLOSING CHAPTERS OF THIS BOOK — 211

- The Value of Knowledge — 211
- To Know the Future by Knowing Ourselves — 212

17. THE GREAT MECHANISM THAT DRIVES THE POSSESSION OF MAN — 215

- The Causal Force of Influence behind the Possession — 215
- Realizing the Divine Mechanism or Great Cycle — 216
- The Design of the Great Mechanism — 217
- The Laws or Principles of the Great Mechanism — 218
  - The Principle of Motion — 218
  - The Principle of Trajectory or Shape — 219
  - The Principle of Magnetism — 220
- The Anomalies in our Civilization, that are Fruitless and Destructive to People, Society and the Earth — 221
- Turning Points that Link Events with Precessional Time — 223
- The Anomalies in Ancient Civilizations, that were harmonious to People, Society and the Earth — 224
- Observing a Turn of the Tide, a Return to the Light — 225
  - The Phenomenon of Population-growth — 225
  - The Phenomenon of changes in Right and Left-brain Perception — 225
  - The Phenomenon of Desperate Times and Desperate Men — 227
  - The Phenomenon of Reincarnating non-transcended Souls — 227
  - The Phenomenon of Resource and Energy Depletion — 227
- The Picture that Emerges from the Collation of Phenomena — 228

18. THE PURPOSE OF MAN — 230

- Purpose — 230
- Possession versus Purpose — 232
- The Power of Purpose — 234
- The Purpose of Guardians — 235
- In Closing — 236

EPILOGUE — 237

APPENDIX A - THE RISE AND FALL OF CIVILIZATIONS — 239

- The Opposites of Man — 239
- Defining the demonic Possession of Man — 240
- The Mark of the Possession, in Signs and Symbols — 242
- The Effects and Purpose of the Possession — 243
- A view on Co-existing with the Possession — 244
- Containing and Limiting the Possession — 247
- The Consequence of Restraining the Possession — 251

APPENDIX B; EVADING THE POSSESSION THROUGH GOVERNANCE BY THE PRINCIPLES OF TWELVE   253

- Purpose   253
- Introduction   254
- Part I: The Principles of a Sustainable Pyramidical System   255
- Part II: Defining a harmonious System of Governance   257
  - In Harmony with the essence of Man   257
  - In Harmony with the Cosmos, Earth and Great Nature   259
  - The Internal Sustainability, by its Component or Affiliated Parts   259

DIAGRAM 3: The Layers of Participation for Public Affairs   260

- Part III: The Principles of Governance by Twelves   261
  - The Structure   261
  - The Constitutional Principles in Circes of Twelve   261
- Part IV: The Philosophy behind the System of Twelve's Multidimensional and Natural Structure   264
  - Comparing a Top-down with bottom-up Governance   265
  - The Momentary Problem of Productivity   266
  - The Automated Effects of the System's Natural Structure   267
- Part V: The Formation and Functional Structure of Circles   267
  - The Household Circle   267
  - The Street Circle   268
  - The Block Circle   269
  - The District Circle   269
  - The Town Circle   269
  - The State Circle   269
  - The Country Circle   270
  - The Federation Circle   270
  - The Civilization Circle   270
- Part VI: The Nature of an Inherent Limitation on Power   270
  - The Effects of the Principles in Geo-politics   271
  - The Effects of the Principles in Politics   272
  - The Effects of the Principles in Economics and Finance   272
- On Taxation and Contribution   273
- The Inevitable Cycles of Order and Chaos   273

APPENDIX C; THE LAST WORD   276

A SUGGESTED BIBLIOGRAPHY   277

FOREWORD I

IN SEARCH OF THE SEEKER

Realizing the Conundrum of Being

When we consider the known and observable starry systems of our Great Cosmos, we observe that somehow, within her[1] seemingly disconnected chaos, there is a clear measure of order. There are different theories that attempt to explain this, be it electrical, gravitational, mathematical or mythical. But what most will agree is that this order makes room for *purpose*, which can be labelled as a form of Divine Influence or God. It is from this that logic and reason can be formulated, and although this too is debated and fought over, the underlying presence of an all-imposing order is not.

If next we bear focus on the Earth and our species of human beings in particular, we cannot but note how the Cosmos' lawful mathematical and mechanical logic becomes blurred. Where Great Nature[2] is studied and formulated in her immense but finite micro- and macrocosmic contexts, the ultimate mystery that surfaces is the presence, within this finite organism, of the infinitely inexplicable man[3]. To put this another way: The laws that regulate Great Nature cease to apply to mankind. If we wished to predict what man will do next, then we'd have a greater chance of success by looking at what goes counter to such law.

If we then zoom in further, and see man as an individual within the human species, the next riddle appears. The problem with the individual being is that he abides to neither the laws of Great Nature nor those of humanity as a civilized species. As such, he either remains reactive, asleep and un-creative, or he awakens and seeks to become proactively creative. Among these then, the ones who are relatively healthy, intelligent, cognitive, curious and sincere, become aware of the conundrum that he says "I" to. At this, he may begin his quest of realization, being the knowing, understanding and accepting what, who and why he or she is, individually.

---

[1] The use of feminine to the Cosmos and Great Nature, like the use of masculine in the referral to man, does not imply to gender but context.
[2] Great Nature (capitalized in these writings) refers to the conscious organism also known as Mother Nature or the earth's biosphere, which includes all that is animate and inanimate that supports the noumenon of Life. This differs from the reference to the 'nature' of things, which describes the phenomena that comes off the noumena (a phenomenon being what it appears as, noumenon being the thing as it is).
[3] The masculine referral such as 'man', 'him' or 'his' throughout these writings, unless otherwise described, does not refer to gender but 'humankind' or 'humanity'.

Defining the Quest

As with everything in our known Creation, the higher dimensional or vibrational gives manifest to the lower dimensional and vibrational forms, and not the other way around. Although a collection of lesser evolved forms may appear to make up a more complex one, when the higher form is removed, the lesser delves into chaos and non-existence. Taking this further, if all the lesser cease to be, the higher forms will continue to exist.

In the same way, we can look at our civilization's various collectives. Although as such, they seem to be the more complex or evolved, the fact is that they are still made up of individuals. The societal collectives may facilitate the individual's existence, but do not give rise to him, and when it tries to do so, it merely produces grotesque versions. Hence, in our assessment, we must consider the value of the individual above that of his collectives. In other words; to analyze a holistic or sum 'whole' of human existence, we must, at all times, firstly consider its individual components. But this becomes exceedingly complex because, when we study the individual, we see that we can only do so by incorporating the higher dimensional or meta-physical influences that not only govern him, but from whence he came!

Due to the lower vibrational state of the material world, there are no means to measure or otherwise verify these higher vibrational or dimensional influences. Hence, all we've got to work from is *man's experience of it*, but here too we encounter a perplexing state. We see that this experience consists of that which stimulates him to think, feel or do certain things But, this cannot easily be defined either as nothing is ever random or unrelated, as in being the cause of its own beginning or end. This problem is exacerbated if we consider that we sense and react to the physical, mechanical, and energetical world using our 5 basic senses, without which, to us, our perceived reality does not exist.

To summarize: For us as such, nothing can exist on or of its own accord, or in fact, without our 5 basic senses. To define our quest of understanding therefore, we must begin the quest by referring to 'our life' as an *experiential reality*.

Finding the Seeker

When we enter our quest to understand the substance and higher purpose of ourselves, we may find that the reality we individually experience during the course of life, is both unique and sovereign. It (our *experiential reality*) is to each of us our God-the-All, because from our respective perspective as observers, it is all that is. And yet, collectively our various and vastly differing egos co-create the one- two- and three-dimensional worlds we all individually perceive and consider as *our* reality.

Still, if this confusing every-one-and-no-one is what you, I and all in our respective realities are, then the holy-grail of the *experiential journey* is learning *who* and *why* we are. And this not just as the individual "I" that is made up of around 50 trillion cells[1], but also the organism each of us forms a part of, which encapsulates an ever-existent collective of around 100 billion human lives?[2]

Thus, when the somewhat paradoxical nature of our personal grail-quest is realized, the first veil that limits our perspective dissolves. We now begin to see that which gave rise to us, *and not from underneath this veil, but from above*. We seemingly arose out of a higher vibrational state, by a process of reduced vibration, not unlike a vapor becoming tangible, making the invisible visible.

The meaning of our birth and life, with all its encounters, interactions, sufferings and tribulations, followed by its inevitable death, is therefore not just some pointless, disconnected and random event. Instead, it is a unique component within the greatest of mechanisms, within which everything connects and correlates along very specific laws that define the level of vibrations or dimensions. Yet outside of these laws there is consciousness, otherwise described as our conscious awareness, that is separated from this machine only by our vibrationally limited egos.

It is upon this *consequential but eventual* realization, that those who wish to be free from this mechanical construct, will, by asking questions, find the Seeker.

Becoming the Knower

When the Seeker perseveres, he may discover that it is because of its cyclic nature, that the world he knows is not finite and his journey in it is not outcome based. However, to find what transcends his consciousness to that of the Knower, he must cease his egoic pursuit. In its stead, he has to contemplate the many facets of what he thinks he is and can be, both good and evil, and know to discern to enhance his heart.

And yet, as unorthodox as this undertaking may seem, it is just one of the many profoundly paradoxical yet wonderful parts of the human experience. If, however, we can learn to understand the miraculous or magic that surrounds the illusion of our perceived reality, only then can we know how to fearlessly and fully appreciate living it.

---

[1] Estimates vary the human body to contain between 30 and 100 Trillion cells, which include a large percentage of (vitally important) bacteria.

[2] Estimates of the "total number of Homo Sapiens who have ever lived, since they appeared in their present order 50,000 years ago, is in the order of 100 billion, according to the Population Reference Bureau

The Purpose of this Book

The Knower must reside within the design of his immediate surroundings, and learn to recognize that which affects his perspectives. Blinded by his sensory demands, the influences of his societal and religious identifications, his providers of mis-information, and deceived by his kakistocracy[1], he must return to the mechanical components of the Great Machine[2].

Through an unbiased analysis the Knower must return to his roots, but not with a sentimental wish for joy, happiness or some sort of salvation. Instead, it must be with a resolute intention to identify and if needs be, shed all that does not belong and that weighs down the self.

The biblical comparison of the ability of a rich man finding salvation with a camel passing through the key-hole[3] is not what this book is about though. This is because material wealth is as limiting to mindfulness as is the lack of material wealth. Neither is it about building temples, eradicating hunger or following organized religious doctrine. Instead, it is about watching the heart, that most precious of components in our being. Where the mind and its thoughts can be mischievous, and where the body is demanding, the heart is akin to a small child. Born in pure goodness and innocence, but naïve and easily swayed to follow those in whom it has misplaced its valued trust.

The purpose of this book therefore, is to assist the reader by training his eyes, ears, and senses to recognize that which has captured or attempts to capture their consciousness[4]. The purpose is also to enable him to identify those who are deceived by power and fear, and whose only resolve now is to mutate the environment in an ever enlarging habitat, to suit their beliefs, deeds and dark ways of life. Keeping a watch over the heart requires one to learn and know that these deceived ones will recruit as many as possible, by capturing the psyche of their minds, regardless of the physical, mental, emotional or spiritual consequences.

---

[1] Governed by the worst, least qualified and unscrupulous persons.
[2] The Great Machine being synonymous or in reference to the workings of the lawful mechanism of Creation by its Grand Architect or Creator.
[3] The New Testament, Matthew 19:24
[4] The meaning of the term 'consciousness' will differ among varying perspectives, but in this case it is simply the aware observer who is not identified by only the thinking mind, reactive emotions and demanding body, but by all three as well as that 'spiritual' intuitive and impartial self.

FOREWORD II
THE CORRELATION OF GOD
AND
THE CONCEPT OF EXCHANGE

The Contemporary Individual and his Society

As human beings, biologically speaking, we are generally the same in appearance, but from the perspective of our reality awareness or consciousness, we differ vastly. This is because the bulk or about 80%[1] of humanity is *cognitively* limited, in that their conscious awareness is stuck in either the first or second dimension. If, for example, we compare these masses to those whose consciousness is of a higher vibrational (or dimensional state) we find that the one or two dimensional perspective on reality, and its applicable sense of reason and logic, is dramatically incomplete, to all but themselves.

The resultant phenomenon of absurd focus or nonsensical activity among the bulk of our civilization is not just observable from a higher level of awareness, but also when we consider the interaction between opposing sectors within this contemporary group. We need but to observe how the masses support militant authority and pointless wars amongst each other. Some of these wars are against nations they have no reason to be in conflict with, and yet, they willingly sacrifice their most valuable generations, possessions and resources to them, only to repeat the same a few years later.

If we were to perceive this from a more holistic but impartial three-dimensional perspective, this contemporary way of life and focus of attention will appear naïve and one-sided. From the contemporary's perspective however, the objectives and lifestyle of a higher vibrational nature will appear iconic, unobtainable or illusory. This explains the unnatural co-existence of opposites in some regions where, for example, the adherence to hereditary royal authority persists without question, and why the republican or democratic systems, in areas with large populations and resources, are playgrounds for political manipulators.

But, in the absence of laziness, happiness and productivity can still be found in all dimensional states of awareness. The limited levels of consciousness among humanity's dominant population would not be a problem, were it not

---

[1] This ratio will vary, but on average follows the mathematically verified and documented Pareto Principle (or Effect), of 80/20, where 80% of something is applied to 20% of people (and visa-versa). In the collective societies of man, it is applied to all contemporary trends, ranging from entertainment, property ownership, buying patterns, voting averages, to other psychological patterns and statistics.

for one major side-effect: *Suggestibility*. To the contemporary person, the acts of perceiving, thinking and doing occur along a one-dimensional line, and usually with a desirous two dimensional or picture-like purpose or outcome. This results in their total obedience to entities with the greatest forms of wealth, power, idol-like fame, or key to heaven, even if it is at the risk of their own destruction. History has shown that these limited lines of thought are inevitably fatal to civilizations as a whole, and with that, the fate of the individual inner evolution, as the latter is largely dependent on the former's stability and resourcefulness.

It is therefore inevitable that, as a result of this *Suggestibility*, following the passage of certain devolutionary phases, including the loss of purpose for which it was established, all civilizations with their empires and dynasties within will decay and fall. Depending on elements such as geography, cosmic related occurrences as well as related climatic and economic events, the cycles of civilizations may differ in many aspects, except for the fact that they are finite. This means that *the ability* for the inner evolution of man[1] is equally finite as, regardless of myth and scripture, an individual cannot live long or contextual enough to evolve in a life of subsistence without societal support.

The Power of Coexistence

When we subsequently consider the necessity for an integrated *physical* existence of the individual within his society, it is clear that a measure of coexistence is also necessary on the emotional and psychic planes.

Ultimately, coexistence is what defines both the macro- and microcosms; from the Solar System that requires coexistence of both the sun and the planetary spheres, to the existence of Life that requires both the biosphere and the sun. as such, we can also see the obvious correlation of the animal and the plant, the plant and the mineral, and so on. In humanity we see the meaninglessness of wealth without products and services (forms of labor), or cities without infrastructure. In all aspects to do with man, both large and small, the ultimate source of power does not lie in one part or the other, or even within the actual existence of anything. It resides in the ability to exchange.

Hence, even the theory of a heavenly god who is separate of both the individual and mankind would make little sense. If man did not exist, then from his perspective, neither would God! Even for God to exist as such, a harmonious exchange of conscious recognition would be necessary. In the end, it is in the process of exchange between opposites that man can find his Creator, as long as this occurs within the spectrum of Truth.

---

[1] In reference to Book I of The Way of the Pilgrim; *The Inner Evolution of Man*

The Possession of Man

For us to exist harmoniously and productively, unaffected by the rise or fall of civilizations, and within our Cosmos of opposites, it is critical for us to find the synthesis between them. For this, we must be realistic. If we can acknowledge the existence of a higher vibrational source of creation and light, then we must also accept the reality of its opposite, a low vibrational force that brings destruction and darkness. This darkness, or the evil it may give rise to, is not defined by what it is but by what it does; therefore: No person can ever be born evil, and it is only natural for man to exist in harmony with the elements. The seeds of corruption and evil reside in our attachment to things, ideas and even others. To prevent these seeds from germinating, and to avoid them from influencing our respective life-journeys, we must also understand how the outer world of man[1] works, has worked and will continue to work.

Although the world may seem cruel and filled with unnecessary suffering, it is important to fully understand how this is still part of a divine design. To see this, we need to learn to know the world and our place in it. Ultimately, regardless of where our bouquet of choices have led us, it is in our ability to unreservedly accept the consequences of our choices, that we can evolve. Without the inherent challenges and distractions that the world brings, mankind will find no purpose. And without some sort of purpose, a complacent humanity quickly descends into states of pointless neglect, and devolves to a vegetative state. To prevent this from happening to us, it is necessary for us to familiarize ourselves with these challenges and distractions, including those that originate from entities in our equally dual omnipresent astral world.

This world, that some see as magical and helpful, but most consider imaginary or relatively harmless, can be all that; it all depends on the amount and kind of attention one pays to it! The astral world namely, as stated in the Hermetic law 'as above so below', mirrors the physical one in many ways. This includes things such as having light and dark elements, and a hierarchical nature. But this also includes a desire to capture and control the psyches of people, which it does by permeating and influencing the systems that govern our physical and psychological world.

The correlation of God and the concept of Exchange thus refers to a desired state of harmony between opposites. This may be a complex idea to digest, especially if one has a specific bias for or against something, or someone, and yet, it is veritably one of dominant the keys to Being. And not just the individual human being, but also the greater Being that manifests in our societal structures, organizations, and our species as a whole.

---

[1] In reference to Book II of The Way of the Pilgrim; *The Outer World of Man*

DIAGRAM 1
THE PYRAMIDS OF OPPOSITE REALITIES

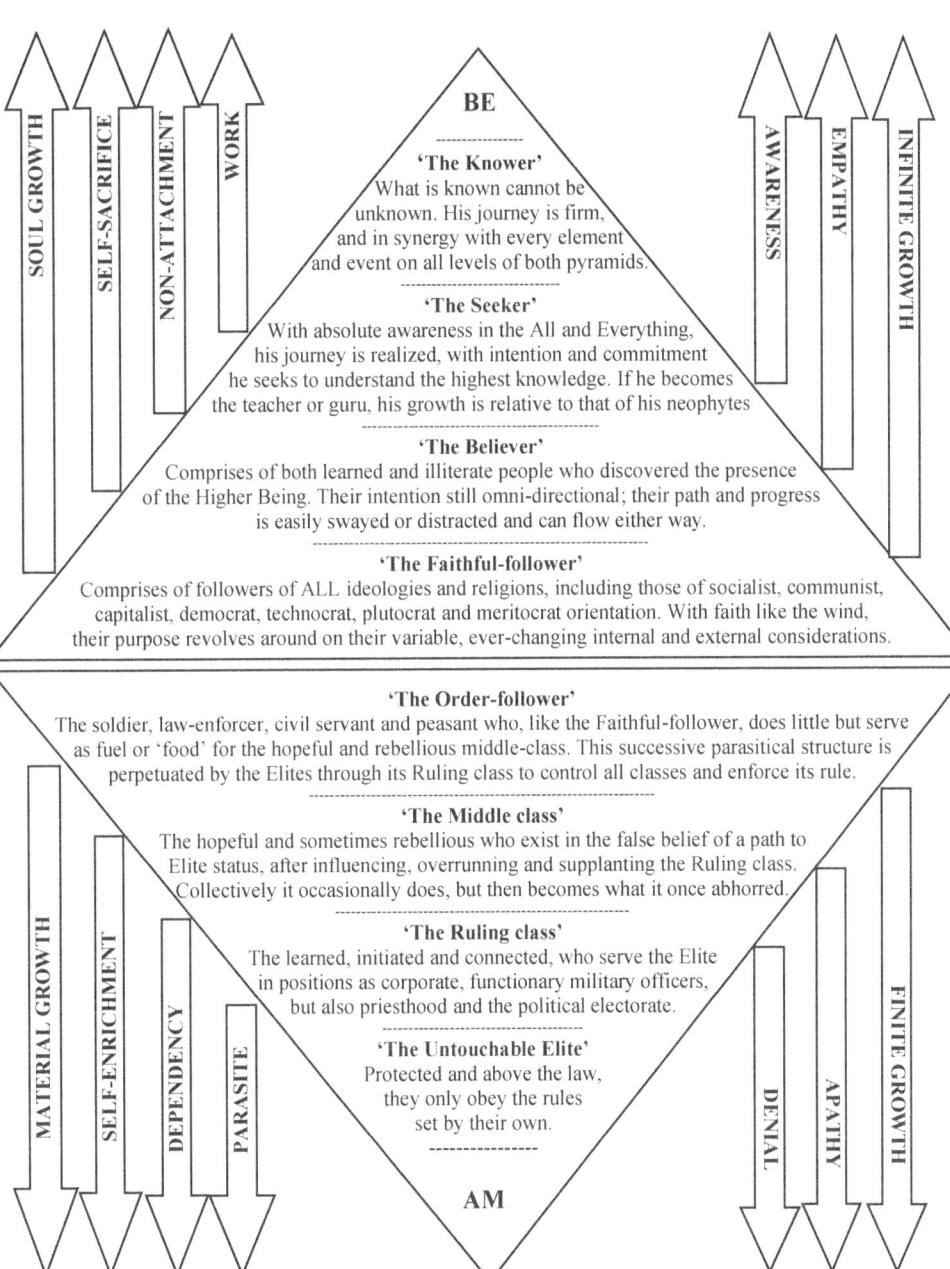

A TALISMAN
FOR THE JOURNEY

In the Order of Being, do you not know that Thought,
as in your Mind, is the most important thing to preserve?

Have you forgotten that:

It was Universal Consciousness,
in order to realize itself in all-knowing and all-being,
gave manifest to the individual Mind?

It was Mind that,
in order to *sense and feel* Reality,
brought forth Feelings?

It was Feelings which,
in order to *experience* Reality,
gave manifest to the Body?

*Thus, Body serves the Feelings, and Feelings serve Mind,
which in turn serves Consciousness.*

This line of observation seems obvious,
yet what is also clear is that many simply wish to be entertained,
during which the Mind goes to sleep.

The only mystery is that so few wonder why this is so!

The reason, of course, is when Mind is absent,
that which rules are Feelings in some, and Body in others.

Without Mind as the driver of our being,
many lose their way and descend
to that dim, lifeless and artificial place,
of facades and falsehoods, with rules and laws,
and where the Light of the Master's Consciousness cannot reach.

INTRODUCTION

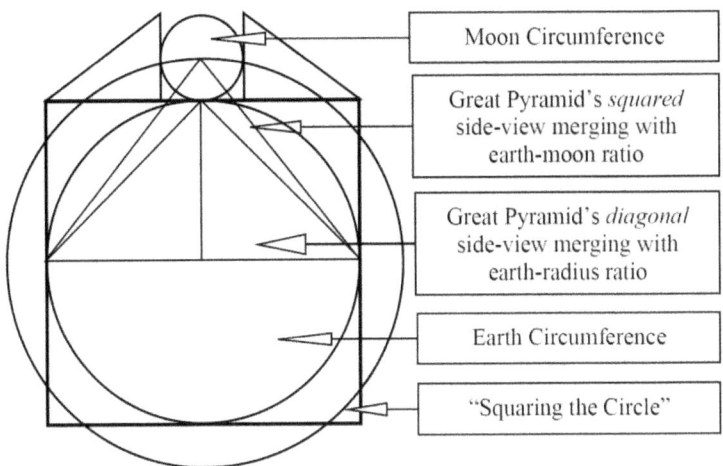

- Moon Circumference
- Great Pyramid's *squared* side-view merging with earth-moon ratio
- Great Pyramid's *diagonal* side-view merging with earth-radius ratio
- Earth Circumference
- "Squaring the Circle"

The Paradox of our Reality

Our experiential journey through life is like a bridge that connects the divide between finite and infinite realms. This is technically impossible of course, as from our perspective, anything in it is either one or other, it cannot be both:

A finite thing would make everything it touches finite, as does the infinite.

This is why our *experiential* life is an illusion, an enigma within a paradox. We cannot envision experiencing it without our five senses, yet deep within we know we do.

Where *The Inner Evolution of Man*[1] observed the existence of man, in all its phenomenal physical, psychic and metaphysical detail, the *Outer World of Man*[2] studied and contemplated the world that was made manifest, and whose societal, psychic, cosmic and magical effects surround him.

It is, however, in this realm of paradoxical improbabilities, and the conscious *Merging of the Inner and Outer World of Man*[3], that we can discover the Creator's plan and Creation's purpose. To understand and accept the ultimate discovery for what it is, we must know what determines, fuels and possesses our path.

---

[1] *The Way of the Pilgrim*, Book I.
[2] *The Way of the Pilgrim*, Book II.
[3] *The Way of the Pilgrim*, Book III.

Revisiting the Pilgrim

Space-time becomes a mere Idea, with the Realization of What we are.

Between birth and death, our experiential reality follows very certain and definable patterns; to those who have become conscious of this, reality appears as a construct that is mechanical in its nature. It includes the Microcosm we perceive 'as below' our own, as well the Macrocosm which we describe 'as above'[1]. But aside from what we perceive, and counter to the evolutionary and positivist theories, when we follow simple reason and logic, we find that the reality we experience in fact is, and can only be, a construct. We may see how things are built from the ground up, or grown from a single cell. But it is quite evident that shortly after their 'germination', they begin to follow the design (or pattern) of a higher dimensional consciousness; one that is considerably more complex than our own, and with a very specific purpose.

Consider, for example, how science, using contemporary methods, cannot factually explain, let alone reproduce, simple and everyday factors such as time, the source of life, or the concept of consciousness! Consider how we cannot but note how, nothing in the observed Cosmos is random. Everything is integrally connected via a series of definable layers with everything else. We must therefore consider the Cosmos as *'mechanical'* because, instead of a more likely regression of things into chaos, the Cosmos continues to exist. This is because it purposely follows very specific laws, among which, those to do with number and pattern, geometry, as well as the laws of mentalism, movement, rhythm, correspondence, polarity, gender and causality[2].

Having determined it as a mechanical and integral construct, we must next consider that the Cosmos, and every part of it, is to some degree conscious. This consciousness may be difficult to validate in the inanimate and the plant kingdom, but it is quite easy to note the differing level of consciousness in persons whose level of awareness of reality differs. The lower their perceived reality's dimensional complexity, the less they are able to fathom anything holistically, and the less they will concern themselves with anything unless it directly affects them. Subsequently, it is not difficult to relate this phenomena to the elevated levels of compassion in some, and the regression to behaviour of an animalistic or vegetative nature in others.

We can thus deduce that the degree of consciousness in every composition of the Cosmos will be relative to its level of complexity; *the higher the complexity, the higher its awareness of, and compassion for, the holistic*

---

[1] "As above so below" refers to the principle of correspondence in the *Emerald Tablets*, manifested by, the ancient Atlantean mystic also known as Enoch (Biblical), Thoth (in Egypt), and Mercury (in Rome).

[2] The Hermetic or Cosmic laws ascribed to Hermes Trismegistus by Wiliam walker Atkinson in *The Kybalion*

whole. Accordingly, we may also conclude that, as a lower form of complexity is unable to envision the higher one, only a more complex form can consciously manifest a lesser one, and not the other way around.

The Cosmos, in other words, is a product of Higher Dimensions, as is, by proxy, our experiential law-constrained space-time continuum[1]. Even the mystic teacher G.I. Gurdjieff, when explaining our place in the Cosmos, stated:

> *"Man, such as we know him, is the 'man-machine', the man who cannot 'do', and with whom and through whom everything 'happens'..."*[2]

All that said, one may wonder how understanding this perspective affects the construct of our reality, or our place and purpose in it? This, of course, is where Consciousness comes into play, but perhaps we must unpack this a little more: Consciousness is only subject to Itself, and is what gives manifest to the Cosmos. Unlike everything or anything in or of the Cosmos, Consciousness is not subject to its dimensions, principles, or its laws, and yet it is what permeates the Cosmos. Consequently, only our realization of Consciousness can enable us to do anything other than what was already written!

In a finite environment of infinite possibility, where anything is possible provided its opposite is also possible, all that is, must exist within a certain finite and precise mechanism that is subject to the principles and laws mentioned earlier. That this paradox is present and evident in all things is no theoretical idea; it has been acknowledged, studied and recorded in various ways, across the civilizations, and for millennia. We can see how this was expressed by many a sage and master, in many ways all around us; from features of scripture, poetry, and art such as paintings and sculpture, to the architecture of structures ranging from pyramids and stone-circles to cathedrals and entire cities. In this book, these observations are categorized in three groups:

- The World of Man
- The Microcosm
- The Macrocosm

We will next briefly consider the paradoxical nature of each of these realms, but in doing so, we must realise that the 'world of man' is the only one we can ever be truly familiar with. The other two are entirely subject to cognition[3], which places them at the mercy of the observer's creative mind and ego. This,

---

[1] The space-time continuum is a mathematical model that fuses the three dimensions of space and time into a single continuum.

[2] G.I. Gurdjieff, quoted by P.D. Ouspensky in *In Search of the Miraculous* (1949)

[3] Defined as the process of acquiring knowledge and understanding through thought, experience and the senses.

as is evident in pretty much every field of research, leads to a large variety of differing and often opposing views.

The World of Man

The 'whole of man' entails a series of energy centers that have different names and functions, according to different teachings. These can be expanded on in great length, but in the approach in these writings, they are simplified and rated according to their energetic and transcendental influence, rather than their location[1]. Of these, his *'basic'* centers are considered as:

- The Movement or Physical Center
- The sensory Feeling or Emotional Center
- The Thinking Center

These centers are referred to as 'basic' because they are the ones that, in our everyday existence, we must apply harmoniously and in symphonic balance with each other. That is if we wish to activate our higher Instinctive and Intuitive Centers. In the contemporary one- and two-dimensional man, for example, this is seldom the case. Instead, in him there is usually one center that is dominant in the formulation of his thoughts, words or actions, and where the other two are applied in lesser and varying degrees. The consequence of an unbalanced application of the three basic centers, is that such ones experience primarily two consecutive effects:

The first effect is that the dominant center will draw on the energy 'cells' of the two other centers, because of it receiving the most attention. Imagine, for example, how an emotionally angered or distraught person has insufficient attention-energy to *think* or *do* anything[2]. The Emotional Center, in this case, having rapidly depleted its own energy cell, will now draw the energy from the 'cells' of its adjacent but neglected Physical and Thinking Centers. As a result, he weakens the neglected two centers even more, causing them to become limited and momentarily paralyzed.

The second effect is when the dominant center of these three basic centers pursues its need to boost its rapidly depleting energy cell, and then commences to draw energy from the high-powered Sex Center[3]. As recorded by Freud[4], the consequent effects are observed by how such a person will think, speak, dress, act, or conduct himself. Usually, the behaviour in these is

---

[1] See *The Inner Evolution of Man*, Chapter 7, page 59: The Centers of Man, which describes them according to their levels of complexity as follow: Physical, Emotional or Feeling, Thinking, Instinctive, Sex, Intuitive, and Parabolic or Divine Consciousness.

[2] Where attention goes, energy flows.

[3] See *The Inner Evolution of Man*, Chapter 7, page 64: *The Functions of the Sex Center*

[4] Sigmund Freud stated that sex is what drives human instincts and social behaviour, and where this is considered accurate, it applies to the unaware or 'contemporary' man.

more than just excessive or demonstrative, and even grotesque. This becomes problematic in the world of man, as the Sex Center's primary purpose is not for doing, feeling or thinking, but to serve:

- The propagation of biological life in the physical realm;
- The empowerment of re-birth by awakening in the psychic realm;
- The transcendence or re-birth in the spiritual realm, through the instinctive activation of his Intuitive Center.

The Microcosm and its Source

Where the 'world of man' is an experiential one, that is largely dependent on the symphony of his three basic centers, the microcosm is subject to the harmony of this state. This can also be defined by the focus of our attention, which directly affects it, because the microcosm's quantum structure, when considering it along the laws of nature, encounters an array of paradoxes.

One of these is described as quantum entanglement, which Albert Einstein referred to as "Spooky action at a distance"[1]. The other occurs with the loss in elemental property, when, at a certain quantum level of reduction or analysis, the observed element loses that which defined it as such. Things we know as water or even plants, for example, will lose their usual properties at a certain point, and where they are no longer recognizable and become mere minerals. The same can be said of all things, including the minerals themselves, which, at a certain molecular point, lose their inherent property.

And yet, when we observe the microcosm as a realm in its natural state, we run into another paradox. We find that, within its seemingly infinite possibility it is also a *'finite and precise mechanism'*. This is because within it, things somehow correspond to each other by a series of principles, laws, geometry and number. Consider, for example, the unlikely yet evident integral state between the physical structures of man and all forms of life through the presence of Phi[2], and how these same patterns and structures are prevalent in biology, geology, acoustics, chemistry and creation as a whole.[3]

Our paradox continues when we consider the conundrum of Time in the realm of the microcosm. Its presence obviously permeates the existence of all creatures and things, including the cycles and life-spans of plant and animal life, and yet, because they are not cognitive, they have more in common with

---

[1] Quantum Entanglement - when particles, such as photons or electrons, become entangled, they remain connected, even when physically separated by vast distances.

[2] The golden ratio, represented by the Greek letter phi (Φ), is a special number approximately equal to 1.618. The golden ratio is also known as the divine proportion, the golden mean, or the golden section, and is represented in all forms in Great Nature, from bee colonies to flowers, the form of shells, to the division of the face, body, and even DNA.

[3] The same ratio of Phi in atoms is seen in the spheres of the Solar System, the surrounding Milky-way Galaxy, and the star filled galaxies beyond.

energy[1]. By interacting with or absorbing others, they will change in shape or form, but as a life-force these exist eternally, ad infinitum, without having an actual definable end, or beginning.

The Macrocosm and its Purpose

The macrocosm is herein considered as the greater detectable Cosmos down to the collectives man, and those material things he affiliates or identifies himself with. It is important here that we separate the term 'Universe' from that of the 'detectable Cosmos', because the Universe is not subject to the construct of Space-time. Where the Cosmos has such definitions[2], the Universe is both eternal and boundless. The Universe is not limited to, or definable by, our three dimensional logic or its mathematical forms, and where the Universe can be considered as being of a dimension[3] that is higher than that of the Cosmos, it could also be said that, as it encompasses the Cosmos and all of its dimensions, it has no dimensions.

This is a complex state to envision, especially for the contemporary thinker who must reason that within an eternal something, all things it manifests, sees or senses must always have been there. This line of thought creates the macrocosm's first paradox because in a realm where everything 'must always have been there', everything would cancel everything else out into non-existent nothingness! Instead, we envision the Cosmos as made up of the Universe's Light, within which it manifests the infinite in possibility, and within which we in turn, experience the macrocosm along the principles of mentalism[4].

If, within this mental construct that is the macrocosm, we now consider the Earth and its biosphere, we see that it creates its own enigma. This is because, within this extremely slight encompassing film called the biosphere[5], its mechanical forms of cyclic or repetitive Life enable the second and third paradox: the merger of physical and metaphysical qualities within an organism, by which the finite merges with the infinite.

The resultant process of emergent consciousness that is enabled by the biosphere is no accident and not random for all its lifeforms. In fact, it is not a natural process, nor even along the design of Great Nature. From *our perspective*, this paradoxical process gives a defined and higher purpose to the macrocosm, the Solar System, the Earth, its biosphere, and our place in it.

---

[1] Energy is eternal, in that it can change from one form to another, but it cannot be created or destroyed.
[2] This definition can of course be debated as the paradigm of a Big Bang beginning is eroding at an exponential pace, but still, the Universe has additional connotations.
[3] A Higher Dimension can, at times, also be read as being of a higher vibratory origin.
[4] The first Hermetic principle: "The All is Mind, the Universe is Mental"– *The Kybalion*
[5] The life-supporting biosphere's thickness is around 0.05 of a single percent of the Earth's average diameter.

The Concluding Emergence

When we consider the hypotheses of paradoxes that correlate the microcosm, the macrocosm, and the world of man that bridges them, it becomes evident that indeed, nothing in the Cosmos is random. Everything in it has a connecting or supporting purpose to other things, and each of which ultimately follows a higher dimensional design or pattern, that is sequential along a measure of increased or decreased complexity[1].

The phenomenon of Emergence[2], where often only its effects can be noted, is inherent in our otherwise undetectable timeless and boundless Universe. We can observe the visible interaction of rock, wind, temperature and water, that ultimately leads to soil. But, when we follow soil's interconnectedness with water, light and mineral, to discover the emergence of Life, such as in the plant, we attain a transitional state we cannot explain – it just happens. The same occurs when we can follow the plant, its flower and fruit, to the self-contained ecosystems that erupt, and enter the world of animate life within which we exist. The ability for us to realize intuitive consciousness can also not be explained, especially when we consider its eternal presence.

But what transcends can also descend, and with the enhanced man, as with his civilization as a whole, the process of regression that follows the loss or suppression of intuitive consciousness, is equally evident. In the duality of an internally sustained and reactive Cosmos, regression is a natural component, and it is not difficult to see how, without exception, Great Nature applies the feature of regression to maintain a certain balance in her order. This includes the biological organism of man, whose attention is continuously and intentionally drawn away by her from anything internally illuminating and, instead, attracted toward the realm of the vibratory denser material life. Great Nature perseveres with this so that, at death, man's residual psychic energy remains within her biosphere[3]. Consequently, where some are drawn toward the Light, others are attracted to material things, but most contemporary people will oscillate between these two. The resultant inability to discern between what is right for them, and what is wrong but justified, has caused much confusion. The absurd, contradictory and regressive states of contemporary existence we see in every type and level of our societies are but the tip of an enlarging and ever darkening iceberg.

If we can see this phenomenon from an unbiased perspective, one that is not

---

[1] As "Nothing rests; everything moves; everything vibrates" – *The Kybalion*, everything will either increase or decrease in complexity, and if it seems it does neither, then the element of Time will factor in the difference.

[2] Emergence is a concept in philosophy, systems theory, science, and art, where a complex entity has properties or behaviours that are not present in any of its parts, or their sum total.

[3] This is described in more detail in *The Outer World of Man*, chapter 21, *The Attracting Power & Energy of Tombs, Relics and Mummification*

bound by the positivist or activist's belief that we can change the world, then we may begin to realize the presence of a higher perfection in these patterns. It is the type of realization that does not come by itself though; it requires attentive work and discernment. For this we need to learn what influences our conscious and subconscious minds, and how it does so. It requires us to understand what it is that sways our ego beyond its norm of survival, legacy, and contemporary acceptance. We need to know our place and path in this paradox filled world, and this includes acknowledging the regressive ones.

In the end, the beauty lies in wait behind the divine process of centrifugal refinement, which emerges in the awakened or enlightened ones, who reside in the acknowledgement of it all, as Creation's very purpose.

Chapter 1

THE FALLACY OF PARADOXICAL PARADIGMS

The Universe has been known by many names:
From the heavens and starry skies above,
to God, the Father Eternal, and the All and Everything.
In Hermetic literature it is said
to give rise to Kosmos, the 'Son of God'[1].

The Big Bang - From Emptiness to the All and Everything

Contemporary science has long deliberated its observation of an 'expanding universe'. It concluded that somehow it all began with an almost instant event called the 'Big Bang', which led to the creation of our expanding and evolving Cosmos, and which we refer to as the All and Everything. This Western[2] theory that has since been customized and modified endlessly, ranging from expansive opinions on what it was before, to what caused it, and how at some scary point it will either collapse again or continue on its present path until nothing connects with anything, into nothingness.

---

[1] In this chapter Cosmos and Universe are regarded as synonymous.
[2] Long before this paradoxical Western theory, the Arab philosopher and physician Ibn Sina (908-1037) referred to this even as "Necessary Being"

However, as was contemplated earlier, nothing in Creation is random as everything interconnects through a number or a series of corresponding layers[1]. This means that all such events must have an equally mechanical and preceding cause. Such Big Bang theories therefore, from a point of purpose, offer no sound reason except to scare the contemporary mind into a belief of an inescapable doom.[2]

To analyze the establishment of the Universe using this theory is rather pointless, as such theoretical causes are incompatible to the explanations, or paradigms, that are the effects we experience in *our perceived reality*. Consider, for example, how all these theories of Creation are limited to *known* factors, which theories do not incorporate what has not yet been discovered in either the physical or metaphysical realms. Furthermore, science bases its theories on *physical or mechanical* causes, and little or no consideration is given to Consciousness, and the creative force within.

This form of one-sided so-called scientific approach is groundless, and in defiance of the 'creative impetus' that stimulated science's very existence. Instead, if science included an inward glance in its analysis, it may have observed a miniature version of this creative impetus, and consider Creation as an infinitely expanded version of our inner evolution. But this understanding is not easily determined theoretically.

In order for one to observe something in its greater dimensional spectrum, let's take this view to another level. When we 'see' a three-dimensional object, say a cube, we know that it is made up of two-dimensional surfaces, but that each of these, having no thickness, on their own have no substance (and can therefore only be 'seen' as such, in our minds). When returning to our cube, we note that to see it, Time must be in place, as without Time, our cube has no relevance to anything. Without relevance, a thing cannot exist, just as we have no relevance if we are without anything to observe us, including a conscious cognition of ourselves. So, for us to see our cube (or ourselves), all the lower dimensional components, including Time, must already be there. Without these, we would never have been able to even 'see' it.

Thus, underlying everything we as simple human beings can ever observe, mechanically or chemically detect, or somehow sense, a higher dimensional manifesting influence or force is in place. In other words, a higher dimension gives manifest to the lower ones, but not the other way around. In other words; you cannot 'just add' another dimension to 'create' a higher one[3]. As

---

[1] Introduction: *The Concluding Emergence*

[2] After decades of study and thousands of journals, substantiated reviews continue to challenge old paradigms, which science, for reasons of its own continues to avoid.

[3] Even if you were able to 'just add' another dimension to a lower one, then the higher dimension

with our example of the cube above, in geometry we see how the conceptual one- and two-dimensional projections are but facets of the solid. In the same way, without Time, the solid is in itself equally conceptual. If we then consider what this thing we call Time actually is, we see that in our known Cosmos, only humans are cognitively aware of its passage. When we analytically apply it to a human life, we 'see' that is made up of integral moments we call minutes, hours, days or years, but we also 'see' that these infinitely flow into each other. None of these can therefore *practically* be defined as having an exact beginning or end; as 'entities', they can only be determined *conceptually*, like our realistic one-dimensional counting of periods, or measuring time on the two-dimensional face of a clock!

What we are saying here is that what we consider as 'real' is merely our <u>perceived</u> reality, being the world as we see it. This is of course a most imperfect form of perception because our sensory devices are equally relative, conceptual and of a lower dimensional nature.

The Merger of Science and Spirituality

If we were to envision the non-existence of space-time within an eternal and infinite Universe, then, when returning to the idea of a beginning of the Cosmos, we may consider that before its creation, there was only a single *unified and eternal consciousness* – the All and Everything. Within this, 'all-that-was', 'all-that-is', and 'all-that-is-to-be' already existed in all forms and realities, including the physical, psychic as well as metaphysical realms – all of which being absent of Time.

Then, at the Primordial Schism[1], being the very first division out of 'the unified and eternal consciousness', a Cosmos composed of opposites was created. Regardless of what unknown force, intelligence or intention caused this Primordial Schism, it was from here that every element continued to divide and come to be in a dual existence. As such, nothing was added to the All and Everything as all that was continued to be; it just divided into more simplified forms of itself. Each part on its own, being only one in a pair of opposites, can therefore not be considered as having substance; just as the sides of a cube on their own do not have such. The only way these 'components' can be brought into existence is through an observer's unconditional belief in them, which in turn is the substance of spirituality.

Thus, along the component side of *the physical realm*, along this line of divisions, rise was given to an endless number of galaxies, each with countless stars, planets and cosmic forces. Within these, and with the presence of Light,

---

would still 'officially' give rise to it. Furthermore, once the Space-time continuum became defunct, then such an added higher dimension would always have been there!

[1] The Primordial Schism refers to a theoretical or mythological concept that describes a fundamental division or rupture that shaped the nature of existence or reality.

the phenomenon of Life emerged. If it is then merely looked upon as something separate from the inanimate, Life might be seen as a biological process that is finite, but cyclic and transferable. When Life is left uninfluenced within its Biosphere, it will simply continue to move from one biological form to another – even if the transfer is only through an organism's absorption of nutrients. Within each form, when Life is withdrawn, its material parts will return to the elements that they were originally created from, being minerals, water and light. The noumena of Life is therefore seen as the Emergent Force, separate from its material parts, and the impetus of this Emergent Force we consider as Divine, a component part of *the meta-physical realm*.

Parallel and simultaneous to the series of divisions that began with the *'Primordial Schism'*, and that involved the formation of galaxies, stars, planets, things of matter and things of Life, there was also the division and subdivisions of the metaphysical. The single omniscient, omnipresent and omnipotent unified and eternal consciousness divided into various 'spiritual' shades of light and depths of darkness. Entwined and parallel to each other, these 'spiritual' divisions interconnected with things of matter and things of Life, and it is within these mergers that new forms of infinite consciousness are made manifest.

It can therefore be said that every one of these 'new forms' contain the blueprints or seeds to the entire Cosmos in all its potential and perfection.

The above bizarreness concludes with the following paradoxes:

- It is not the presence of any of these components that gives rise to a form of miraculous emergence, that, in turn, gives added manifest to an already complete Universe but *how these components are interlinked.*

- For an infinite Universe to be able to 'expand', new context needs to be inserted. But this is the next paradox as the Universe already contains All and Everything, and yet for it to expand, *something* needs to come from 'somewhere'.

- This 'something' referred to must contain two essential elements: It must contain an awareness of consciousness, as without such, this 'context' cannot contain that Divine Impetus to expand as a part of the All and Everything. It must also be true – for reasons as described earlier.

We must therefore consider the fallacious nature of all these paradoxical paradigms, and consider what we all know to be, according to our experiential reality: The only form that we know can give manifest to all these paradoxes, is the awakened and acceptant soul of man, made manifest within a mortal body.

Chapter 2
THE NATURAL BUT INVISIBLE INFLUENCES ON OUR STATES OF BEING

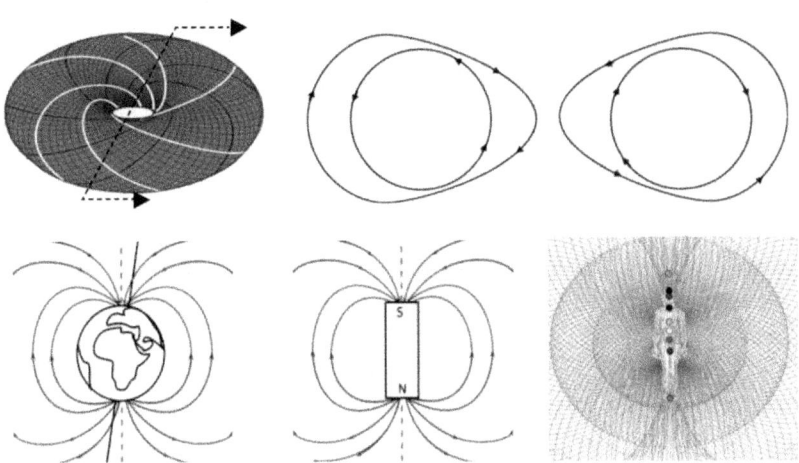

*The perceived reality of a contemporary man,
entails only one side of Creation.
In denial of the Infinite Continuous Whole,
he remains blind to its duality along every part of his existence,
and ignorant of the non-Duality of his Observant Being.
Consequently the Higher Dimensions that give rise to the Miraculous, are as elusive to him,
as his chattering and thought filled mind.*

The Nature and Effects of Influence and Interference

As human beings on planet earth, we believe we are quite special and unique, even to the point where we consider ourselves separate from Great Nature. However, all elements and things in the Cosmos, including the macrocosm and microcosm, as well as that of man in between these two, are of a vibratory nature and subject to the same laws. These laws being, amongst others, correspondence and perpetual motion, as well as rhythm and polarity[1]. Subsequent to these, the typical energy patterns we observe in all things, from a single atom to the galactic and man in between, are in the shape of a doughnut-like Torus.

---

[1] The Seven Cosmic or Hermetic laws, according to *The Kybalion*, are Mentalism, Correspondence, Vibration, Polarity, Rhythm, Cause and Effect, and Gender.

The Torus in itself obeys all these laws, and consequent to these we notice the opposite-rotating forces within and around it. As the diagrams above indicate, the same but more familiar examples of this feature are found in a rectangular magnet and the magnetic field that surrounds the Earth and man himself.

When next contemplating the law of Cause and Effect, we notice how the torus-shaped phenomena interacts with others, and how these continue to influence or combine, and give rise to ever larger systems, such as our own Milky Way Galaxy. This hierarchical feature is also evident from the opposite view; that is when we observe how, within a torus, many clusters of smaller ones exist. On the Earth, one will not only see these toric formations in the shape of storms such as cyclones and tornadoes, but also in smaller organisms such as shells, trees, flowers and fruits. The phenomena further corresponds to certain artificial features, like some of humanity's structures and monuments[1]. Whereas many of their locations and shapes are affected by their geography and the availability of resources, in most cases there are also underlying *occult and metaphysical influences or forces* that guided their design. The origins of these influences or forces may not necessarily be physically detectable, and not always in any clear toroidal shape. But the vibratory, polar and rhythmic *effects* surrounding their structure's formation is sufficiently evident. The same can be observed in the habitual nature and actions of those who exist within them; at least if they are able to be conscious of these.

These *influences or forces* are often invisible and undetectable, but they become relevant in these contemplations if we observe them through three consequential considerations:

The first consideration is that all elements, things and life-forms in the Cosmos are inescapably subject to these occult forces[2]. Whether one likes it, or wishes it, or tries it otherwise, their energetic influences will inevitably remain present in all forms of energy, elements, things, and life-forms.

The second consideration is that all elements, things and life-forms are of the Cosmos and therefore subject to its laws. The exception being Universal Consciousness which is not dual and therefore not subject to the same set of laws. This consequently affects the parts of us that are fully conscious, or 'illuminated', because as infinitely small as these parts may be, they are still holographic representations of Universal Consciousness as a whole. In other

---

[1] Pyramids, stone circles, dolmens, cathedrals and many modern structures have a commonality with the torus, even though these structures are static and structural, while the torus is dynamic and fluid. Together, they symbolize a balance between structure and flow, and appear in various theories related to ancient technology or energy systems. For example, the Great Pyramid of Giza is said to interact with Earth's energy fields (a toroidal flow), and the torus is related to devices like Tesla coils and or electromagnetic field generators. Together they are viewed as complementary aspects of the Universe's structure and dynamics.

[2] Occult in these instances, refers to the unseen or invisible but detectable.

words; although the physical parts of ourselves, including our psyche, is subject to the laws of the Cosmos, our metaphysical, interconnected and universal spirit is not. When the awakened one acts from that Universal Consciousness, such actions will not necessarily need to be subject to, or follow, the laws of the Cosmos.

The third consideration is that of inevitability. There are many who are very clever, cunning and, to a great extent, aware of these forces and their patterns of influence. These are referred to as Sorcerers (in *The Way of The Pilgrim*), and who understand these Cosmic forces well. Their dark magic is usually applied to enhance their own material, physical and occult empowering purposes, which has led to the grotesque development of many parts of our so-called civilization today. But, unbeknownst to them, these are on an inevitable but most definite self-destructive path. The only part of this that is uncertain is the extent of their self-destruction, which will be measured by the number of souls they will drag with them, into their self-created and all-consuming Black-hole.

The purpose of the following chapters therefore is to firstly highlight these phenomena of influence, and therewith enable an awareness of these forces. Secondly, it is to guide the sincere Seeker around the effects of the Sorcerers' consequential interference with the natural flow of things.

Chapter 3
THE MAGICAL EARTH, PART I
THE PHENOMENON OF GEOGRAPHY

The Plan of New Jerusalem

Contemporary humanity is starkly divided along lines of race, religion, tribe and ethnicity. Most of all, however, its greatest asset *or* curse that determines humanity's strength and intellect,
its stability and growth, resides in its geography.

Geography defines its access, resources and climate, its ability to thrive and prosper, or its need to make war for another's produce.
It also establishes a rift between those who do or don't accomplish, creating a one-dimensional land of 'haves' and 'have-nots',

In regions of physical bounty and high intellect, greed and power will rule by breeding fear, which trains its soldiers and builds its armies,
not to defend but to dominate and impose its might on others who suffered and coveted, or who had things of use and value.

The civilizations that rooted themself, in possessed and contemporary ways, became cursed with lazy, distracted and desirous minds.
No longer wishing to know or love their Creation's Creator,
or receive the Gift of Consciousness, in their reward they forfeit their ability to know, the eternal All and Everything

A. Cities Cursed by Geography: Jerusalem

History

The Old City of Jerusalem is cloaked in mystery and painful controversy. Its claims to history and importance are disputed, but from the perspectives of all sides, the vitality of the actual disputes revolve largely around the events that began with Solomon and especially his legacy – the temple. This structure was said to have been erected on the temple-mount, as instructed by the old sorcerer-king[1] who was, according to Jewish scripture, amongst other, also empowered by God to capture demons[2]. With the power to either expel or enslave angels or daemons[3], he supposedly used them to guide him and the building of his temple. Consequently, the site thereafter became a source of much division, and continuously subject to plunder. The temple itself was destroyed and rebuilt at least twice, whereafter it was finally completely demolished by Rome, stone by stone, to such an extent that at present there is little physical evidence of where on the temple-mount Solomon's temple once stood.

This last and total demolition was brought on by Rome, following a series of brutal uprisings by the Hebrew tribes, against the might of their occupying master[4]. The deeply resourceful, vastly superior and at that time undefeatable empire of Rome could not afford to lose militarily against one of their subjected tribes and subsequently, would throw all its resources against any such challenges. The inevitability of such a response would have been obvious, even to a substandard strategist, yet this logic and these odds did not deter the tribes of Judah. Even after the loss of their temple and their holy of holies, they still opted to mount a challenge against the Roman Empire. A campaign that would end catastrophically for them, with the loss of over 500 000 men and the displacement of millions of its people through yet another exile. Regardless of the logic in their motivations, what made this last uprising even more mysterious is the supposed reasons – that supposedly began with Rome banning the practice of circumcision among others[5]. These

---

[1] Solomon was renowned for his wisdom and magical associations in various traditions.

[2] His wisdom extended to understanding the natural world (1 Kings 4:33), which traditions expand to include knowledge of supernatural forces. In Islamic accounts, particularly the Quran, Solomon (Sulayman) is depicted as a prophet endowed as able to communicate with animals and jinn (supernatural beings), who served him by performing tasks, including building structures (Surah Saba 34:12-13 and Surah An-Naml 27:17-19).

[3] While they share a linguistic root, demon in Christian theology refers to non-Christian entities as malevolent supernatural beings. In older Greek mythology, the term 'daemon' referred to spirits or intermediaries between gods and humans, not inherently good or evil.

[4] The Bar Kokhba Revolt, which took place from 132 to 136 CE.

[5] The circumcision legislation was one of the final straws. The desecration of Jerusalem by various 'Romanization' efforts, taxation, land confiscation and military presence also contributed. There were also messianic expectations, which Kokhba attempted to fulfil.

disputes could have been resolved through the patient and wise debate of any well-intended elderly leadership. But, instead, it was a conflict that was intentionally provoked – perhaps by both sides – and which caused an immensely messy and costly war, and the execution of the rabbi-priests that had guided Judah's general Kokhba.

The extent of the resultant Hebrew exile, the destruction and remodelling of parts of the Old City's infrastructure, as well as the erasing of the names of Israel and Jerusalem off the Roman maps, and all things to do with its religion, was vast. And it was not just one of mere petty vengefulness, which was in contrast of the principles of pacification with the vanquished, that were typical of Hadrian, Rome's emperor, at the time.[1] Hadrian had an aversion to war and kept the peace on Rome's frontiers by principles of diplomacy for over a decade, yet he opted to resolve the Hebrew question via a method that was politically extremely unpopular. That this response would draw division and conflict across the centuries that followed, which would be bad for business and costly in lives, was almost certain; yet they persisted. There was seemingly a consideration present that was deeper and more powerful than strategic practicality or intellectual logic, and which had a distinctly metaphysical nature. It more likely served to overthrow the malignant but occult power of an entity that had occupied this place for centuries, and whose mysterious influence controlled, empowered and when necessary, infuriated its indigenous minds to such a bizarre and fanatical an extent. The attempt of exorcism however, by the entity of Rome, did not succeed.

The Geopolitics of Weaponized Religion

Across the centuries that followed and into the present genocidal era, the bloodletting that occurred on and around this piece of earth continues on grotesque and ever-increasing barbaric scales. The divisions and repetitious so-called 'holy' wars, between conquests and liberators, under various rulers, banners and religious symbols, are unprecedented when compared to any other area of conflict. This observation is amplified when one considers that it was over ground with no remains of its temple or holy relics on it, and that it has little or no strategic or resourceful value. From a factual and spiritual belief point of view, one even notes that its consecrated grounds had been desecrated several generations in the past, and that vengefulness does little to reverse this fact.

Even in the context of so-called 'religious differences', little logic is found. Although, in their own way, all three religions that have had claims to Jerusalem are henotheistic[2], all three have their roots in the God of Abraham,

---

[1] Hadrian was considered as one of the "Five Good Emperors" due to his effective governance, infrastructure projects, and stabilization of the empire.

[2] Henotheism is the worship of a single, supreme god that does not deny the existence or of gods,

and as such the same god. The scripture of all three of these describe a merciful 'God', of love and reason, who created the Heavens, the Earth and all that existed on it and none motivates its devoted children to persist in such continued barbarism. Yet, judging by how this piece of land was fought over, its subjects and prisoners persecuted, tortured and enslaved, barbarism remained to be of the highest order for generations, and under different rulers' empires. The 'god' they had in common clearly had its own agenda, one that demanded fear through pain, suffering and bloodletting, as clearly, the land was and continues to be stained with it.

Since the time of David and Solomon, the precise year-by-year history of what transpired across the millennia has largely been distorted and diluted by recorders of varying political and religious bias[1]. Just as the Jews and Christians each have their own versions, the Muslims have theirs. Among the more fundamentalist present in each one of these three, at present, the Jew and Muslim views do not entertain a very amicable or seemingly outcome-based debate. The Christians have taken a more subtle or covert approach which, for reasons that have little to do with God or religion, leans towards the occupiers of Israel. But, besides trying to determine the correct historical facts, biased influences also include areas of science and archaeology, where researchers have had to work with data, that was often altered along preferred narratives.

What cannot be corrupted however, is:

- the presence of a millennia old track record of bloodshed and suffering that Jerusalem demanded from its inhabitants, and those who saw it as the 'house' or 'chosen' birthplace of God or His prophets. One that seemingly began with the demonic corruption and death of Solomon[2], that continues unabated into the present day, spreading its tentacles into the whole region and in many ways, much of the surrounding civilizations.
- the observation that there is something here that is inherent in the earth itself, which gives rise to the track record above.

Geology and Geometry

In the Old City, there are three locations of high ground containing natural rock-formations, that were never physically built on top of, but around which the *centers* of Christendom, Islam and Judaism revolve. Two of these centers are on the Temple Mount; one being the bedrock underneath the Dome of the

---

other than its own, that may be worshipped.

[1] i.e., in today's digital age, Wikipedia stands as one of the most widely used sources of information. However, with contentious topics surrounding Israel, the platform often becomes a battleground for narratives by state actors. (Dor Posner, *The Times of Israel*)

[2] Interpretations of the Talmud refer to Solomon's fall from divine favor due to his tolerance of 'idol worship' (1 Kings 11), and in the Holy Quran (Surah Al-Baqarah 2:102), which refers to Solomon and the practice of magic. Supposedly he faced divine punishment, including a loss of his senses and kingship.

Rock that is sacred to Islam and from which its prophet ascended to heaven. The other is the Foundation Stone underneath the Dome of the Tablets, that is sacred to Judaism, and from which Abraham was willing to sacrifice his son Isaac. The third center is the Rock of Calvary, or Golgotha as referred to in Latin or Aramaic, both names referring to a skull, which part of this sacred rock supposedly resembles. It is located underneath the Holy Sepulchre and is sacred to Christendom, being the place where its prophet was crucified.

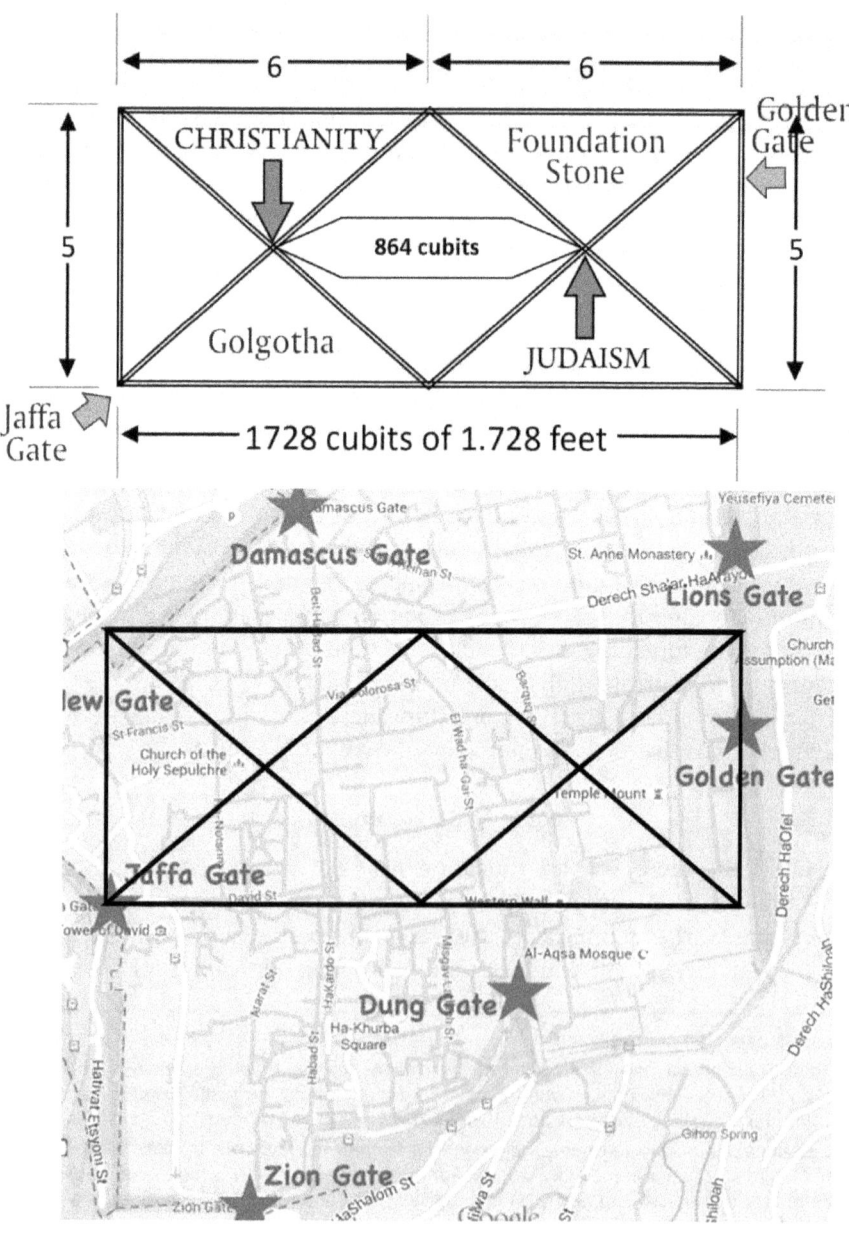

The diagrams overleaf indicate the location of these features, within a geometrically corresponding diagram. Note must be made that the two X's do not indicate the prominent domes but the actual location of the Foundation and Calvary Stones.

(On a sidenote: Of interest on these two diagrams is that the measured distance between the two natural features is 864 Biblical cubits, and how the Biblical cubit measures 1.728 English feet, which number corresponds with twice the 864 cubit distance.[1])

The anomaly of Jerusalem is that these venerated rocks were not placed there by men with machines or empires, of for that matter, by extra-terrestrial or metaphysical beings. They are part of the actual bedrock and inherent in the earth, unrelated to man, mankind or life in general, yet there is very little that explains their regional influence. Regardless of how one may feel about any of the religious views on these rocky outcrops, one of the features of interest is their peculiar distances from- and alignments-with each other. In addition, Solomon's temple was supposedly built using measurements that corresponded to these distances and alignments, which scripture describes as the king being given these by his captured and enslaved demons.

Many of these conclusions will contemporarily be viewed as coincidental, or along forms of confirmation bias, where one is looking for patterns where there are none. Naturally, it cannot be ruled out that these rocks were selected by their coincidental distance from each other, but then one must wonder how they knew what this distance was to be? The Biblical cubit was used for all ordained instructions revealed to Moses and King David, which included the measurements of both Solomon and Herod's temple. If then coincidence is kept aside, this would leave two predominant alternatives:

1. That the Earth and the Sun's *precise dimensions* were known to the architects of these temples many millennia before their era. What makes this special is that our knowledge of these was only obtained when we entered the space-age. What exacerbates this mystery is that our present era having this knowledge led science to the civilization altering development of war-making ability and empowerment on a grotesque scale.

2. That there is a force of magnetism present in Jerusalem, that is akin in its vibratory nature to that which formed the Cosmos, the Solar System, and the Earth itself. While this may raise many an intellectual eyebrow, the presence of this kind of 'Creation-energy' becomes more evident in the section on

---

[1] These numbers are canonical in that they correlate to the number 9 within standards like the sun's 864 000 mile diameter, 86 400 seconds in a day, and 864 000 years of the Vedic Dvapara Yuga. The numbers five and six correlate to balancing the duality, symbolized in the pentagram and hexagram, which in some traditions relate to male and female, or satanic and divine – also used symbolically, like the adopted title of Pope Sixtus V.

Egypt's Giza Plateau that follows, which is considered as its polar-opposite. To visualize this 'Creation-energy' or force, we may look at the energy patterns we see around a magnet, the earth or even the movement of energy on the sun, in between positive and negative sunspots during solar flares.

Either way, whatever this phenomenon corresponds to, as in what underlies its causes, Jerusalem became a pernicious center of psychic energy. Its nature remains unchanged after many millennia, and it is unlikely to ever settle through human intervention. We need but consider that three of humanity's major religions sensed a power here that was so convincingly 'sacred', that it was worth killing or dying for.

Conclusion

The city of Jerusalem was used in this hypothesis, because it continues to behave like an active volcano. There are other more 'dormant' locations with a similar inherent energy which, after a mixture of spiritual and volatile eras, decimated its inhabitants to the extent that it caused the end of their civilization[1]. Where famine, disease, war and such are often claimed as the official reasons, seldom is the underlying energy considered, that continued to amplify human imbalances to illogical levels of chaos. Ultimately, in each of these it was due to the loss of their subjects' psychic power that they became *comparatively* dormant. Emphasis on 'comparatively' is added here as many of these still experience inexplicable heights of spirituality and brutality along mostly religious and ideological differences[2]. Not all were centers of brutality though. Some became veritable symbols of high civilization that simply could not have been built under the duress of the whip and murder, but which were cultivated by the love of knowledge and creativity.

---

[1] Examples of such now 'dormant' locations are Ankor Wat in the former Khmer empire, Easter Island, the Indus valley, Çatalhöyük and Gobelki Tepe in Turkey, as well as the various now disappeared civilizations around the lost cities in Central and South America.

[2] The history of indigenous ritualistic slaughter aside, consider the history of travesties caused by Inquisitors in the Americas, British Colonialists in the Middle and Far East, and genocidal Communists in Cambodia across recent centuries.

B. Cities on the Earth's *Natural* Energy Centers: Giza

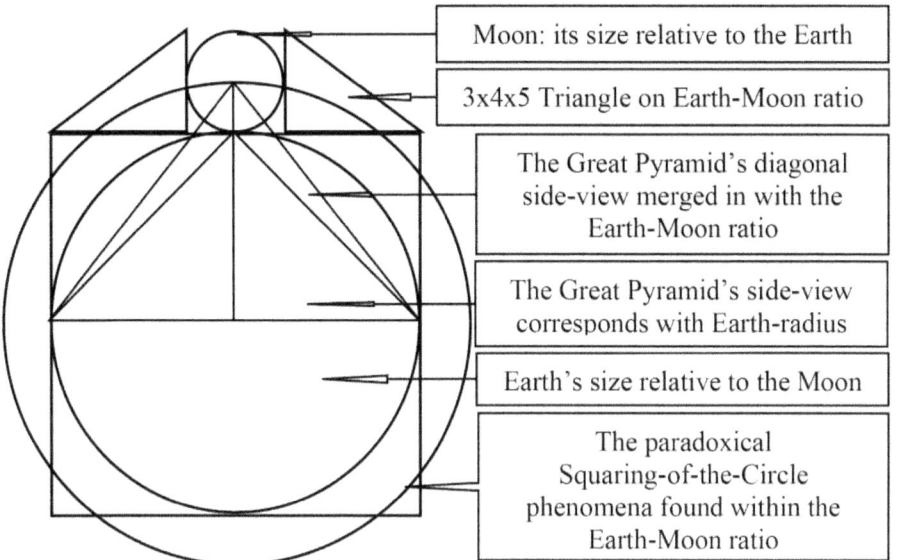

- Moon: its size relative to the Earth
- 3x4x5 Triangle on Earth-Moon ratio
- The Great Pyramid's diagonal side-view merged in with the Earth-Moon ratio
- The Great Pyramid's side-view corresponds with Earth-radius
- Earth's size relative to the Moon
- The paradoxical Squaring-of-the-Circle phenomena found within the Earth-Moon ratio

'Gaia' or the 'Living Earth' can easily be recognized as the living organism this refers to. Like the human organism it has a solid skeleton that is protected by various layers of atmospheric 'skin'; it has a distinct pulse[1]; various circulatory systems that circulate liquid, air and plasma; a sensory system that feels, monitors and balances things; a working temperature and a capacity to retain memory. Many also believe Gaia is, like the Sun, an entity that is conscious. Consequently, it falls to reason that the Earth has energy centers of her own, that can be compared in function to the chakras in the human body.

Those who have plotted the flows of energy, and the nodes where energy centers are formed, have observed the Giza Plateau as one such a Center, and in fact, these refer to it as the Earth's Throat Chakra.

Hence, when reviewing the writings of old, such as those of the ancient divinity known as Hermes by the Greeks, Mercury by the Romans and Thoth by ancient Egypt, and considering the existence of such pulsing energy centers, their words become less poetic or mysterious. In fact, they can be considered as the diagnosis of factual and observable phenomena when Hermes laments:

---

[1] Besides the Schuman Resonance of 7.83Hz, scientists have also detected a seismic rumble-like pulse every 26 seconds (Popular Mechanics).

Do you not know Asclepius, that Egypt is an image of heaven,
or to speak more exactly,
in Egypt all the operations of the powers which rule and work in heaven
have been transferred to earth below?[1]

The Irrefutable but Ignored Feature of Time

The Great Pyramid, the Great Sphinx, the Sphinx Temple and the Giza Plateau as a whole, entail feats of design and engineering that are beyond comparison of any such structures on Earth. These observations are exacerbated when one considers that the age of most of these structures is older than the contemporarily accepted date[2]. There is more than sufficient evidence that counters this rather politically preferred view, including, among others, the precipitation-erosion surrounding the Sphinx quarry[3], as well as the stellar representation and alignments in the sphinx and the plateau as a whole[4], which point to an era many millennia earlier.

These factors point to a time of 'pre-sands Egypt', known as the Younger Dryas, and before climatic changes caused the desert to encapsulate it. This was at the end of the last Ice Age, around 12 000 years ago, when conditions were almost tropical and lush with vegetation[5].

The Irrefutable but Ignored Feature of Design

The factor of age or time put aside, we must next consider the minds and mechanisms that were incorporated in the applied design and construct. When observing the Great Pyramid for example, if we consider the diagram above, we note that its dimensions happen to represent a geometric scale model of the Earth and Moon:

If we were to 'situate' the Moon on top of the Earth, and expand the Great Pyramid to a point where we placed the pyramid's width *diagonally across the corners* placed upon the diameter of the Earth's equator, then we would find the tip of the pyramid's completed height fitting perfectly onto the center of the Moon. Added to this correlation we will see that the scale of this expansion is not random either, but one of 43 200:1. The aware reader may note that this is not a random number. In fact, it is not only a standard or canonical number, being that it relates to the radius of the sun, it also fits in within the dimensions of the earlier described features in Jerusalem.

---

[1] *The Lament of Hermes, a Testimony* (see the complete version in the End Notes).
[2] Suggested by contemporary historians at around 2 500 BCE or 4 500 years ago.
[3] Robert M. Schoch B.A., B.S., M.S. & Ph.D.): *The Great Sphinx*
[4] Robert Bauval: The Message of the Sphinx - *A Quest for the Hidden Legacy of Mankind,* and *The Orion Mystery.*
[5] Wikipedia: *The Younger Dryas*

Of course, we would prefer to see these Earth-Moon-Pyramid correlations as incidental, but we would then also have to add a considerable number of correlating 'incidentals'. There are many, some of which of great complexity as they overlap several disciplines, but purpose of this chapter is not to go too deeply into the explanation of these; it would in any regard be quite easy for the curious reader to verify and elucidate them[1]. Instead, the purpose of this chapter is to draw the reader's attention to the artificial nature of that which seems natural to the unawakened eye, and to the natural state of things that seem artificial! As a point of interest however, when taking mathematical, geometrical and geological correlations of only the Great Pyramid into account, one may simply peruse the following *summarized and shortened* list of such general, but ignored, 'incidental' features:

- *The size and shape of the Earth*
- *The Mass and Density of the Earth*
- *The definition of the Cubit form of measure, relative to the Earth*
- *The significance of the location of the Great Pyramid*
- *The Golden Ratio*
- *The Mass of the Sun and the Mass of the Moon*
- *The Mean distance to the Sun and the Mean distance to the Moon*
- *The Orbital Velocity of the Earth and that of the Moon*
- *The Speed of Light*
- *Etcetera.*

These all describe features that are incorporated in the Great Pyramid. If we add to this list, the details surrounding the considerably older Sphinx and Sphinx Temple, or the Plateau as a whole, the 'incidental' element rapidly evaporates.

The Irrefutable Feature of Location

The details above can easily be verified and expanded on via a number of sources. Regardless of the varying views on the who, how and when, the point here is that nothing on the Giza Plateau is random, based on some form of religious belief, or selected for convenience. Whereas all of these may very well have been incorporated during the passage of differing civilizations who, for reasons of their own were unable to know better, they could not fathom that the sheer scope of the works and the super-human efforts involved did not add up to any such singular purpose.

The larger anomaly however, is that across the millennia, like Jerusalem, Giza entertained certain psychic influences and energies, which guided an ignorant and mesmerized mankind in its many inexplicable manifestations.

---

[1] i.e. Graham Hancock: *Fingerprints of the Gods*, Robert Bauval: *The Orion Mystery*, John Anthony West: *Serpent in the Sky,* or Eckhart Schmitz: *The Great Pyramid of Giza*

Looking at the Plateau's unique location, we note the presence of another enigma, and one that speaks of more than cleverness or convenience. When we consider how it attracted or amplified certain almost unnatural phenomena within the psyche of men and women, the presence of a powerful or even sacred attracting or motivating energy becomes evident. Besides the vast resources, efforts and detail they subjectively poured into it, over numerous millennia, when considering its actual location we may further note:

- that the plateau's pyramid lay-out along the river Nile, resemble the constellation of Orion along the Milky Way galaxy.

- that the Great Pyramid sits at Latitude 29.9792458°N, which number corresponds exactly to the speed of light, being 299 792 458 meters per second.

- that Giza is modelled as the earth's center, in that it is situated in the exact middle of the Earth's landmasses[1].

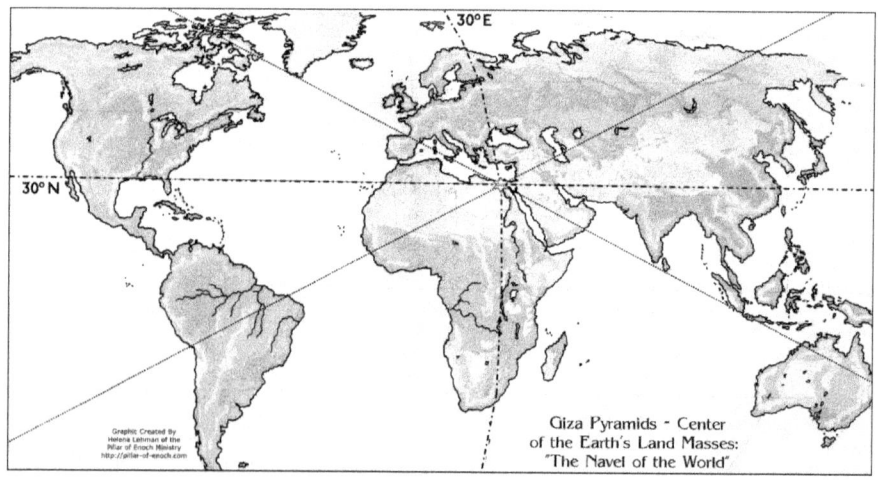

Giza Pyramids - Center of the Earth's Land Masses: "The Navel of the World"

Indelible Evidence in the Veil of Myth and Legend

To understand the mystery that surrounds Egypt's ancient past, we must be prepared to lift the veil and delve into the many differing versions and translations. To do this, we would need to include those versions preceding the contemporary ones, which often differ in a great many perspectives from the ones based on myth and legend. It is, however, not within the scope or purpose of this chapter to elucidate or debate the origin and perspective of the

---

[1] Geographically, Giza is located at the exact intersection of the longest line of latitude and the longest line of Longitude. In other words, the east/west parallel that crosses the most land and the north/south meridian that crosses the most land intersect in two places on the Earth; one is in the ocean and the other at the Great Pyramid. This means that its architects knew the exact detail of the earth's landmasses.

differing views. These writings aim to rather focus on highlighting some of the more obvious features that Egypt's myths and legends are rooted in, and how many of these evolved around geography.

In this, we would have to start by considering those forces of attraction that lead to the inevitable formation of a civilization's centers. In the case of Egypt, it is quite evident that the metropolis of Cairo developed as the largest urban gathering across Africa and the Middle-east, due to a confluence of factors that are largely to do with its physical location. Among these are its passable location relative to the Sahara, the Mediterranean, the Nile river and its Delta. These made it the gateway to Upper Egypt, and one that, for trade and general existence, was relatively safe from Mediterranean based marauders. However, prior to these relatively modern factors to do with its civilization, there was a presence there that was older, and which influenced the manifestation of the Giza Plateau at least 12 000 years before the present era[1]. Perhaps this presence is better described as *that magnetizing effect that caused the shaping of modern and ancient Cairo, and which had amplified the creative forces that designed and developed the Giza Plateau.*

Situated at the confluence of the river and sea-based trade, local and intercontinental coastal migration as well as features such as fertility for food production naturally led to Cairo's tremendous concentration of psychic energy. This was clearly not lost on those who chose to conquer these parts[2], and who knew how to channel and use this for forms of empowerment. But it was not just business though. There was seemingly also another essence inherent here, one that was dominant and oblivious to the physical elements of trade or empire. It was something that could harmonize with the intent and motivation of its people, and as such therefore, something metaphysical or other-dimensional.

When looking into ancient times, we find that before it became known as Cairo, the city was named Heliopolis or the 'City of the Sun' by Rome and Greece, where previously it had been named 'Jwnw' or 'The Pillars' in times more ancient. These 'pillars' may refer to the obelisks[3] that were erected in honour of, among others, the Egyptian sun-god Ra, but they may also have been incidental to other preceding features. Pillars in Persian are called ستون, which is pronounced as 'stoen' meaning stone, which more likely points at the

---

[1] According to Dr. Robert M Schoch (see www.robertschoch.com) civilization did not exist prior to about 3000 or 4000 BCE, yet (erosion-based) evidence around the Great Sphinx and other on the Giza Plateau, as well as (carbon-dating) evidence on a site in Turkey known as Göbekli Tepe, indicates that a high culture existed at least 12,000 years ago.

[2] The list is long, but among other included Darius of Persia, Alexander the Great, the Caesars of Rome but also the likes of Napoleon and Hitler.

[3] Many of these obelisks were removed, at immense effort and cost, some of which took decades to accomplish, and are currently displayed in the highly ceremonial power centers of Paris, London, New York and Vatican City.

millions of huge stones that were quarried and cut at great precision, then transported and placed to build the pyramids and temples, that preceded the city by many millennia.

While sun-worship in various forms reflects in many religious beliefs, when we trace its occurrence to its earliest historical record, we find roots pointing largely at Egypt, and more specifically Cairo and the Giza Plateau. Subsequently, we may assume that the Greeks and Romans had not selected Heliopolis in honour of their sun-god Helios, who was a descendant of the Greek Titans. Instead, the 'City of the Sun' refers to a time when the city was historically devoted to the sun-god Ra, whose primary status and power was believed to be the cause of all aspects of life. Having established this as such, we find that at present, most contemporary Egyptologists assume that Ra or Helios refers to Sol, our present star the Sun, yet few realize that it refers to the energy-emitting planet Saturn[1].

The Black Sun

Where the connection of the sun-god with Saturn becomes relevant, is when we observe that in legend, myth and present-day occult circles, besides the Greek god Kronos, Saturn is also referred to as the Black-sun. In these however, the Black-sun is not just worshipped by the occult, but indirectly and somewhat ignorantly, in many of the world's religions. Consider, for example, the radiant halo-like crown seen in the representations of many 'enlightened' and divine beings, most notably Christianity. The halo-like effect is nothing but an occult symbol, representing the rings of Saturn. Additionally, we see how the Black-sun corresponds to many present-day customs and adherences. These range from the use of black in the clothing of many religious priesthoods as well as those appointed to certain levels in judicial systems and

---

[1] See *Saturn in Ancient Times*, by David Talbott and Wallace Thornhill (www.thunderbolts.info), as well as *Worlds in Collision* by Emmanuel Velikovsky.

academia. It also corresponds to many Saturnian related symbols, including the hexagon and the cube or 'square', which symbols are at the center of many a religion, most notably, the black cube in Judaism and Islam[1]. The details of these various correlations and more can be greatly expanded on, but this would trail too far off this book's subject matter. However, to the unbiased and open-minded researcher, it should be relatively easy to follow through and understand.[2]

Returning to the Giza Plateau, when considering its scope, age and its long list of extraordinary features, it rapidly becomes evident that the invisible or occult energy behind its traditional forms of worship is not just one of 'a belief'. When we observe its effects, we see how its power is of a kind that can be channelled and directed by the initiated and ordained, to empower or subdue. This was done by regional empires and priesthoods across the millennia, as is evident when we look at the establishment of numerous and vast temple complexes, that were created at an enormous cost of labour and resources. Many of these structures were so vast, that they required centuries to be completed, which in itself was no small feat; the effects of these were clearly well known by all involved. They were much more than just symbolic; their purpose was to create, re-create, amplify and re-direct types of energy, some of which were empowerment, but others were akin to that of life-force, as well as that creative element that is inherent in the Earth[3]. When contemporary present-day scientists, architects, engineers, and ruling elements try to understand the purpose behind the super-human efforts over such extended periods, they generally do not get very far. This is largely due to their inability to include motivating influences of a higher dimensional, intuitive or spiritual nature.

Whereas the power such as is inherent on the Giza Plateau can be used both for constructive as well as destructive purposes, it is an entity that overall exists by laws of its own. Consequently, without the ability to fully understand this power and its laws, it cannot be controlled by man for long, after which it historically[4] tends to turn onto the same manipulators, especially when it is used inharmonious to the balances of the individual man, his collectives, and Great Nature, being the Earth herself.

---

[1] See the Jewish Tefillin worn by adult Jews and the Kaaba by Muslims.

[2] Such a researcher would also, without too much work, be able to detect considerable lines of correspondence between the symbols of hexagons, cubes and rings at the core of present-day systems of law-writing in rule-based order and worship.

[3] Author and researcher Christopher Dunn explains in *The Giza Power Plant* and *The Tesla Connection* that the Great Pyramid of Giza had many energetic features, including it being an immense acoustical device, with many occult properties. Within its size and dimensions, the edifice created a harmonic resonance with the Earth, which also converted Earth's vibrational energies.

[4] i.e. The rise and inevitably fall of empires and large powers.

If we place the effects of these manipulative occult forces aside, and pursue the myth in itself, we see that the Black-sun is also integral to the ancient name of Egypt, being the Land of Khem. 'Khem' literally means 'Black', and it is often incorrectly assumed by contemporary historians that this refers to the colour of soil-deposits following the Nile's flooding. 'Khem' however also relates to *chemistry*, which was assumed in days of old to be a form of *black* magic, as well as the mostly misunderstood discipline of Alchemy. Where Alchemy has both spiritual and psychic practices, its origin lies in another form of black magic; the Saturnian teachings of El, the Black God[1].

Even though the connection of Alchemy with Saturn still exists, the reason that this power is no longer very evident resides in a time prior to the current and accepted version of history. Unlike the small speck in the night sky that Saturn represents at present, this powerful link refers to a time when the arrangement of planetary spheres in the solar system was considerably different to what it is today; and when Saturn shone very large in Earth's skies[2]. Although not as bright as the sun, it was considerably bigger, less harmful and more dominant throughout the day and night phase, during which it radiated a turquoise light[3]. It is possible that the energy it emitted upon the Earth enabled a considerably higher *empowerment of a psychic nature among the conscious man*.

Whatever the ultimate cause was that led to this inter-planetary event is debatable, but the consequent shift in the solar system undoubtedly created catastrophic conditions on Earth. The induced dark age that followed lasted several millennia, at least until Earth's magnetosphere[4] was able to adjust and restore a relative version of balance in itself. This enabled the atmospheric and climatic conditions to stabilize sufficiently for the continuation of 'normal' life, and the gradual rebirth of civilization. Little of the civilizations that had existed prior to that period survived the millennia of repetitive cataclysmic events. Of these, only the monolithic, heaviest, or intentionally buried monuments survived to tell us of their ancient existence. There are, however, many more than that the superficial eye may detect; many of these, such as the Great Pyramid[5] and Sphinx, were restored or had new structures built on top

---

[1] "El" relates to Elohim, the gods or god in the Old Testament, which additionally relates to its inclusion in word-formation such as Elect, Elevate and others, including the El in Israel.

[2] As described (amongst many other) in *Worlds in Collision* by Emmanuel Velikovsky, and *The Saturn Myth* by Graham Talbot. Accordingly, Earth, Mars were moons of Saturn (like Titan), to be displaced by the entry of Venus, a newcomer into the Solar System.

[3] *The Case of the Turquoise Sun*, by Ev Cochrane

[4] A magnetosphere is a region of space surrounding an astronomical object in which charged particles are affected by that object's magnetic field. In the case of the Earth, an example of such particles are the harmful ones that are carried by solar winds from the sun, which are deflected by the Earth's magnetosphere, and which enables human life.

[5] Graham Hancock, co-author of *The Keeper of Genesis* and author of *Fingerprints of the Gods* as well as numerous other related books and reports, notes that the Great Pyramid appears more

of them.

Of these records and statistics, few are officially publicly acknowledged, and 'official' Egyptian historians (Egyptologists) are trained according to a rigid state-defined doctrine. This claims, for example, that the phenomenon we know as the Great Pyramid, was built by Egyptian volunteers, in 20 years, using ropes, ramps and pulleys, during the months of the flood. This claim has been repeatedly proven ludicrous from every perspective, yet the Egyptologist who values his career, persists in this claim. The reason for this doctrine lies in the occult metaphysical realm that changed with the planetary re-alignment of the solar system. In this, the regionally inherent and possessing entity that had traditionally[1] found its power amplified by the Black-sun, which we know as Saturn, lost its source. As a result, its entity-like existence has since been kept vibrant or 'alive' artificially. This was at a considerable cost to the psyche of contemporary subjects, and often the cost came in forms of sacrifice[2]. Due to its lost powers, but its reputed phenomenal potential, the reality of its entity-like existence as such is kept secret by influential occult societies until, it is said, it is able to rise to regain its power and rule over the Earth once more. If one is now able to review many of the often self-destructive, illogical and utterly barbaric events that unfolded and shaped the globe over the past few centuries, one may see how these have increased in ferocity and forms of disconnected darkness. It may therefore indeed appear that those in power and those who serve it, believe the time for its rebirth is imminent.

These observations enter a review of metaphysical occurrences that involve supranatural forces, which are not popular in contemporary science and academia, despite there being ample research and record to support them. However, to enter a deeper discussion on the consequences of such actions is beyond the scope of this section's purpose – which aims to focus on the presence of an entity itself. Still, if we wish to understand the world of man as a whole, we must consider the existence of this, which is only possible by reviewing the entity's effects. The Giza Plateau differs from the city of Jerusalem in that its entity today is largely dormant, whereas that of Jerusalem and Israel as a whole, is very much alive and active. That there has been and continues to be, a conflict that encapsulates the suffering of millions of people, cannot be mere coincidence.

---

like a time capsule – being a testimony of an ancient and lost past. Although stones are not carbon-datable, the lower layers of blocks in the Great Pyramid are of a noticeably different and older type than those found higher up.

[1] 'Traditionally' being since the rise of the psyche-emitting and conscious human being, approximately 40 000 to 50 000 years ago – See *The Way of the Pilgrim – Book II: The Outer World of Man*, Chapter 29, *The Origins and Formation of the Conscious Man*.

[2] As an example: In Mesoamerica, the Aztec culture practiced sacrificial massacres on and around the various ancient sites. In addition to slicing out the hearts of victims and spilling their blood on the temple altars, they also practiced forms of ritual cannibalism.

Where both Giza and Jerusalem are undisputable 'energy centers of the Earth', perhaps their influence on humanity's whole is comparable to the influence of the energy centers or chakras in the human body. Either way, to not acknowledge these centers, or their effects on the behaviour and extraordinary feats of people that reside there, is sheer ignorance. Whatever it is he makes of it, the sincere Seeker must pay attention to these veritable influences, as only when he or she is able to acknowledge them as such, can the effects of these energized locations become visible.

Evidence underneath the Veils of Record and Logic

Beside the contributions of legend and myth, we can also consider the facts. It is, for example, generally acknowledged that the older pyramids are more advanced and better built than the successive ones. This points to an obvious decline in knowledge and ability, which suggests that the Giza Plateau must have been built upon the legacy of preceding knowledge, from a much older civilization.

Generally, when we refer to ancient, or pre-historic civilizations, we refer to Atlantis, but Atlantis was not just a place, it was also an era[1]. By whatever name it existed, it did so for thousands of years before Egypt, and was at its height at the end of the Pleistocene, being the end of the last ice-age and the time of the floods known as the Great Deluge[2]. Whereas this likely led to Atlantis' disappearance, it was in Egypt that its lineage continued and where its spiritual magic and marvel was stored and maintained[3]. In time, as we know from recorded history, it became the center of initiation and learning for those who sought to attain higher forms of consciousness. Although its initiates were predominantly the selected priesthood as well as Egyptian royalty, many were said to be of Atlantean descent. However, the initiates also included the likes of Moses, Christ, Enoch, and others, and during the time of the ancient Greek civilization (1200 – 323 BCE) it additionally became a school for higher learning for some of the greatest teachers of man. Among these we find Pythagoras, Socrates, Plato, Aristotle and other great masters. It can therefore be said that the roots of today's mathematical and philosophical intellect resides here.

Following this era (323 BCE) it was Aristotle's influence that coerced Alexander the Macedonian to liberate and restore Egypt[4], who then enthroned

---

[1] The legend of Atlantis has its roots in the Emerald Tablets by Hermes Trismegistus (Thoth), as well as the work of Homer and Plato, and discussed in *The Way of the Pilgrim*, Book II: *The Outer World of Man*.

[2] About 11 800 years BPE the icecaps melted, and unlike previous thinking that this occurred gradually, over millennia, there is strong evidence that this occurred over months or even weeks, due to cosmic event.

[3] See: *The Emerald Tablets Of Thoth The Atlantean*, by Maurice Doreal (1930)

[4] The relationship between Aristotle and Alexander the Great stands as one of the most intriguing

the wise Ptolemy. The successive Ptolemaic dynasty lasted for another 3 centuries and only ended when it was overcome by another behemoth's influence: the entity known as Rome, whose parasitic intervention caused irreversible damage to what working magic remained.

The Departure of the Gods, and the Fall of Egypt

Prior to it becoming occupied by the dictatorial powers of Persia and Rome, with a brief respite during the times of Ptolemy, Egypt had largely been ruled by non-democratic and occult powers. There seemingly was an influential force or power that was stronger than any man or group of men, and to which its people, priesthood and its dynasties of pharaohs equally abided and harmoniously existed. The arrangement seemed to have worked well, especially when we consider the region being in an era of perpetual war. Across most of this period Egypt remained relatively stable and as such, it became a veritable economic and intellectual center of power, yet one that did not entertain the ambition of an empire. Its prowess as a civilization is emphasized when we consider how its numerous and enormous temple complexes and pyramids were built across dozens of successive generations over many centuries. Common sense rules that this must have required a lot more than a whip, wealth, forms of clever propaganda or bogus religious principles. To enable a succession of people to relentlessly follow such pursuits, across centuries, must have required the draw of *a very real and, by human-untouchable form, of energy or higher power.*

There was therefore clearly an occult, but verifiable entity present within or behind this *higher power*. It was one whose power was amplified through the application of very specifically designed and aligned temples and pyramids, and harnessed or channelled by a priesthood, centralized around a 'divinely ordained' pharaoh. Of interest here is that this possessing *higher power* did not require the pharaoh to be Egyptian; he (or she) only needed to be capable to act as its host.

Hence, the earlier dynasties up and until the rule of a *tradition-resistant Akhenaten*[1], were likely not Egyptian but of a pre-deluge dating civilization's origin. When this 'Atlantean' heredity became diluted or extinct, the appointment of priests and pharaohs was adapted to ceremonial and magical processes of ritual and initiation[2]. During these *the selected or appointed one*

---

mentor-student connections in history, blending the depths of philosophical thought with the breadth of his military conquest.

[1] Akhenaten, also known as Amenhotep IV, reigned as pharaoh est. 1351 to 1336 BC and is best known for his religious revolution in ancient Egypt. He abandoned traditional Egyptian polytheism and introduced a monotheistic or henotheistic worship centered on the sun god. With his death, short of his son Tutankhamun, his legacy ended and his successors restored Egypt's traditional gods and ceremonial practices.

[2] One of these ceremonies is referred to as the Alchemical Wedding, which entailed a union of

would willingly embrace the possessive and reigning energies, by which he or she could bypass the need for a specific bloodline. This is why, following the reign of Akhenaten, that it no longer mattered much whether the pharaoh was Egyptian, Macedonian, Greek, Roman or other. However, when we consider the gradual but evidential decline and fall of Egypt that followed, perhaps the process of ceremonial initiation was not as unyielding as the raw hereditary Atlantean power. Still, as the appointment of high religious or political positions can serve preferred agendas, this is likely why at present, occult ceremonies are believed to supplant the need for bloodlines.

Whether it began with the end of Akhenaten, or the sporadic presence of corrupted politics in the appointing of emperors, prefects and priests, or the desecration of temples and the occurrence of plagues; the residual but inherent and magical light of occult power in Egypt was gradually extinguished. By the end of the Byzantine era and the entry of Islam it appeared to have ceased all together.

Hence; although geographically the city of the sun and its Giza Plateau have not changed, their influence on global or even regional affairs, when compared with those radiated by the likes of Jerusalem, London, New York, Paris and Washington DC, is virtually non-existent.

Unlike the pernicious energies of Jerusalem, which intensified and strengthened in tandem with the fall of Egypt, or those of New York, Paris and London that were artificially and intentionally created anew, the gods or entities that possessed Egypt had departed this land. With that, they had taken away *its veritable power or source of energy*.

Let's consider the shift of such energy centers as being possible. Then perhaps, what had been inherent in Giza's part of the Earth for eons, or more likely the magical ability to control the entities that wielded such energy, like that which Solomon had, was simply diverted.

---

opposites. Often represented in the merging of masculine and feminine energies, spirit and matter, or conscious and unconscious aspects of the self, in alchemical and esoteric traditions, it serves the achievement of higher state in being through spiritual enlightenment and wholeness through the process of integration and transformation (sacredanarchy.org). Further detail on these, such as the ancient Egyptian 'Tying of the Cord' ceremonies can be found in *The Keeper of Genesis* and *Fingerprints of the Gods* by Graham Hancock, and *Serpent in the Sky*, by John Anthony West.

C. Cities on *Artificial* Energy Centers: Manhattan

The City that Never Rests

In the city that never rests, its minions labour without pause,
but not on things of natural value or use.
Where the wealth of man is transported and directed,
to and from the four corners of the world.
The apple of the so-called "Big Apple" being largely symbolic,
of that which the Serpent used to deceive and corrupt
in the legacy of Eden, what was Holy and Pure.
The City that does not rest, does but enhance illusions,
of that which attracts, to enslave and devour.

New York City is an industrious, ethnically diverse and globally interconnected metropolis that has its roots in the 17th century. When we zoom in and review the island (or borough) of Manhattan, to determine what it is that defines its demographic divisions, we find that one obtains a relatively standard pattern. Usually, this is done by outlining areas along race, ethnicity, or levels of opulence and poverty. But, if we remove the population density numbers and the physical wealth defining factors, such as industry or infrastructure, we may be able to define it differently, such as by degree or level of activity.

When we observe the island of Manhattan by such degrees, we may begin to visualize how there are rings of activity that intensify toward a central area, and which correlate with the concentration and height of skyscrapers[1]. When these patterns then interconnect with others in the region, they begin to act with each other, forming patterns like the magnetic fields around the poles of a magnet, or the auric patterns around the human body[2]. These flow along a

---

[1] Such as those seen in Midtown and the Downtown Financial District.

[2] As referred to in Chapter 2 above: Similarities are found to follow such lawful patterns throughout the mechanisms of Great Nature, and in both the macro- and microcosms. These include the Earth's magnetosphere, the sun's heliosphere, and even the shape of coronal mass

type of central axis exiting on one end passing around the central axis, into the thinning surrounding territories, and re-entering on the opposite end.

When considering the levels of activity, we see how Manhattan's banking, finance and business sectors have played powerful geopolitical roles for the last 150 or so years, prior to which it was merely a conveniently situated trading center. At present, or perhaps when it obtained its exorbitant privilege[1] in 1972, its role has largely become geo-strategic, seeing that decisions made here strategically influenced other power-centers on the world stage.

Like with the city of Cairo mentioned earlier, there are naturally logical theories behind the city's history and development, such as trade routes and security. Putting these aside, we may note that less than 10% of the people that work in Manhattan actually live there – meaning that its centers of activity are based on something other than demographics. If we now note that the two highest concentrations of activity have the tallest structures, predominantly situated around the Downtown Financial center and the Midtown Business center, in the middle we may observe the polar state of Manhattan's residents. Here, within the space of a few kilometers, from Midtown into the northern areas and the Bronx, the average family income is less than 10% of that in the Downton and Midtown areas. This ratio is exacerbated when we consider the size of such families in these polar groups. If we then tried to determine the grey area or so-called middle-class, being families that fall in between these two extremes, we will find these scattered in the vast surrounding regions, along energetic patterns.

Still, the distinct difference between the opposing poles in Manhattan, is not necessarily represented on the basis of *individual income or wealth*. We could say that this takes third place. Second place would be awarded on the differing degrees of *psychic activity* that is emitted by the inhabitants of each pole. The first place to what emphasizes the difference is that of the *focused attention* each pole receives, when applied to that of a global audience.

In other words, where it is generally assumed that the power of New York City, and in particular Manhattan, relies on the concept of business, wealth and money, in reality, it is one of idolatry.

It is easy enough to see how the architects of colonization favoured Manhattan island over others. Besides it being a natural point of entry on the route from and to Europe, it also had a relatively temperate climate that enabled year-round growing, fishing and hunting, which enabled settlement. Furthermore,

---

ejections on the surface of the sun (aka sunspots).

[1] The exclusive ability of the United States to create money at will, whereas all other states can only do so through the provision of labour and product.

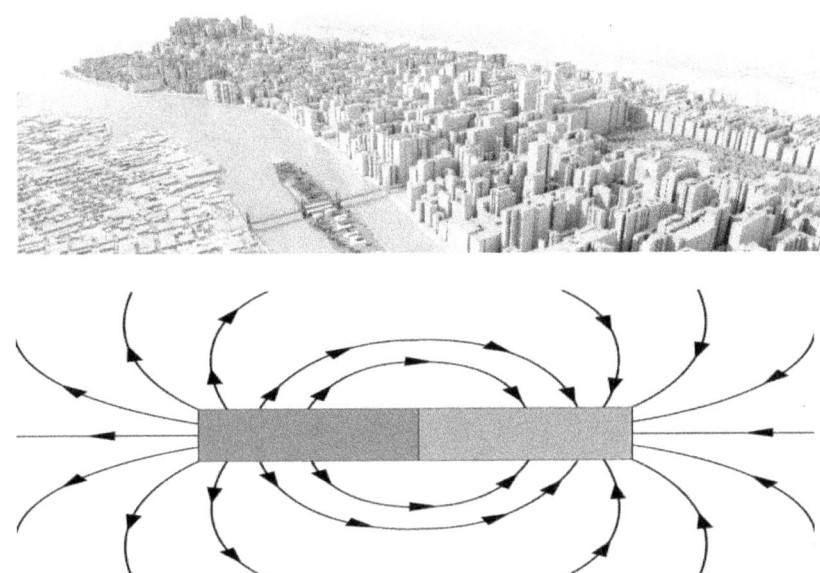

from a commerce and defence perspective, it had a vast and protected harbour area with access to inland territories via a multitude of rivers, including the natural and intracoastal waterways. These made it the perfect location for the shipping and trade of all things, including, among others, furs and slaves, and eventually, that of finance and money itself. By the 16th century[1], the 'bankers' of Venice[2] had already relocated into Central Europe and, by the early 18th century, were already well established in Paris and London[3]. Consequently, with the prospects of a new world within which a new masonic empire was being designed and built at will, away from hostile European, Asian, Middle-eastern and African influences, the decision by the English Crown to forcibly obtain New Amsterdam from the Dutch[4], came as no surprise.

Added to Manhattan's favourable geography, one sees how this confluences with the events and geopolitical changes in Europe. In these, the various programs of colonization and military excursions served the same private

---

[1] Following the War of the League of Cambrai (1508–1516)

[2] The Doges of Venice, particularly before the 17th century, played a crucial role in shaping early banking practices. Venice was a major center of trade and finance, and under the Doges' leadership, using a combination of mercenary armies and rule-by-division tactics, the city developed institutions that laid the groundwork for modern banking.

[3] Among other inheritors of the interconnected or interwoven 'system', Mayer Amschel Rothschild, the patriarch of the Bank of Rothschild, founded his family's banking business in 1760s, and expanded it via his five sons into major financial centers across Europe, including London, Paris, Vienna, and Naples.

[4] Through the Treaty of Breda (1667) during the Second Anglo-Dutch War (1665–1667).

interests. Hence, early in the 19th Century, at the height of the Industrial Revolution, it was already well situated to serve many purposes, including that as an alternative and eventually suitable replacement, of British Imperial Power.

Today much of Manhattan's power-base thrives off the effects caused by conflict and loss, which benefits a small core containing a relatively selected few. This includes both its existence as a regional settlement center as well that of a global financial center. As a harvester of dark energy, its nature is therefore not too dissimilar to that of Jerusalem. If it is aligned with Washington DC, with its 'city within a city' known as the District of Columbia, one may further note that, where Washington DC possesses the occult and magical symbolism of Jerusalem, Manhattan possesses its power.

One may differ on these views, but if one considered Washington DC as a center of power like Manhattan, one cannot but note how they differ. In the US Capitol, its planners and architects intentionally built its structures and infrastructure to align with an ancient master plan. Within this, they located its infrastructure, monuments and important buildings, using patterns and designs of carefully selected masonic features of sun-worship and other occult magic. In Washington DC these were designed to manifest the kind of societal and political energy that both empowers its initiated resident rulers to impose on its subjects and others across the globe. In Manhattan, although thoroughly clad in considerable sun-worship and occult elements, for the type of power that it manifests, this was not necessary. The sheer and veritable power of the place grew by its inhabitants hyper-driven activity, which is visible in both its physical development, as well as its financial reach. When one traces the successive events that took place from or around it, beginning early in the 19th century and throughout the 20th, one sees how this caused it to evolve into the behemoth we see today. Then, since the turn of the millennium and over the last few decades, its power grew exponentially directly resulting from the effects of global disasters and catastrophes, all of which directly and indirectly *negatively* affected billions of people worldwide.

Ending the Monster

The keen observer may begin to sense the presence of something that inhabits the very earth underneath Manhattan, on top of which people settled and from which a vast array of unusual structures grew. All of these collectively served something existent, growing, and yet, non-biological. Serving only its own account, it does little that is necessarily harmonious to the spiritual well-being of the individuals who participate – besides (temporarily) enriching some of them. One may subsequently sense within this system, a presence of something that is both intelligent as well as conscious, and which defends itself through those who serve it and to whom it appears to be something that is immortal. Such a conclusion would be quite accurate, but such 'immortality' does not make it 'eternal'. It merely means that, as a non-mortal entity, it continues to exist as long as it is energized by the life-force of those that it subjects, which subjection is assured by those that serve it.

Consequently, it is subject to the Cosmic laws, including that of polarity. In its energetic state, for example, we can see how that its extreme levels of wealth and power can only persist in the presence of their polar opposites. This may thus explain the bizarre *negative* effects of the overpowering actions on the quality of life on the inhabitants of places like Manhattan and the regions both adjacent to it as well as those places farther away. If we consider the grotesque differing degrees of affluence within and around Manhattan, for example, we can see how the suffering of the numerical majority that surround the source of such vast wealth and power, is more than just incidental. We may then also see that this suffering relates to the infectious nature of its power on all who serve it, whereas *IT* only serves itself.

D. Natural Centers of Creation and Destruction: Germania

Defining Germania

The Germanic Tribe referred to herein is not one of any particular tribe or genetic group; it refers to a region that is and has been inhabited by many of Europe's tribes. The current Germanic Tribe is also not one that just encompasses Germany, it includes Austria, The Netherlands, Denmark, and parts of Switzerland, Belgium and Eastern Europe. It has further spread deep into the Northern and Western regions, including parts of Norway, Sweden,

Finland, Denmark, England, Iceland, Hungary, Slovenia, Slovakia, and the Western Czech Republic. At present, a large contingent of people in North America, Israel and Southern Africa are also represented here.

It is complex to define the Germanic person by his or her genes. Where it has, for the past millennium, primarily been settled by Germanic tribes, Germania is also the home of Celts and Slavs, as well as a combination of smaller tribes including certain minorities and those of a lesser influence[1]. Besides Germania's physical or geographic regional dominance, unbeknownst to most contemporary observers, the performance and activities of the Germanic 'race' is one that has most of the world puzzled, and many in either the grips of awe or fear.

The Germanic descendant, including those that have relocated and reside elsewhere, at present represents less than 3% of the world's population. Yet, forgetting whatever nationality that is embraced, one may find that the largest percentage of Nobel Laureates and Patent Holders have names with Germanic tones in them. But the Nobel and Patent Holder statistics are just two indicators. When considering the arts, literature and music, especially the traditional artists, composers and architects, it is the same. This 'discovery' repeats itself again when we observe the fields of science, technology and business. Then last but not least, the Germanic historical influences on religion, spirituality and philosophy are equally considerable when compared with most other regions. One does not even have to consider the role and performance of the Germanic race during the various conflicts, starting with the 30 Years War all the way through to the two world wars. The only region that beats the track record of conflict is the modern United States, but this too is a nation of immigrants, of which its ruling race is predominantly Germanic.

It seems that those of dominant Germanic descent - regardless of their field of passion, expertise or profession - are considerably more creative and innovative then other ethnicities. Consequently, the Germanic race experiences an overriding presence in the spectra of civilization. Like all things in the Created Cosmos though, it too exists within a perfectly balanced duality. The characteristics of this 'race' have subsequently led it to feats of historical accomplishment, but also that of disaster; where brilliance and genius was snubbed by absurdity and asininity.

The search for the roots of this race of fluctuating collections of tribes, and how it obtained these characteristics is complex. Even the origin of the term 'Germanic' is uncertain as it does not relate to the present German Republic, which state and epi-center of influence was named after it. The name Germania was allocated by the Caesars of Rome, and applied to the vast,

---

[1] The German state, for example, is at present the home to almost 5 million Turkish and Southeast European descendants.

culturally and linguistically diverse collection of northern Germanic and Celtic tribes. To the Caesars, what these tribes had in common was that the might of the Roman empire, across the six centuries of its reign, was unable to subdue them north of the Rhine or the northern parts of England, where Hadrian ended up building his wall. Consequently, upon the collapse of the Western Roman Empire, it was no surprise that the succeeding Empire of the Franks was comprised of Germanic tribes. But then neither should it come with any surprise, that it also entertained the main theatre of the 30 Years' War that ravaged it[1].

The Occult Pursuit to either Contain and Control, or Scatter and Destroy the Germanic Race

When observing the genetic makeup of what we refer to as Germanic Europe, we note that it was impacted by many conflicts, migrations, and invasions, but also through domination by foreign powers. This was especially evident after 1945, when both eastern and western powers occupied it in an attempt to forcefully and if need be, brutally and mercilessly, dilute the strength and unity of the Germanic populace.

They had witnessed how a Germanic populace, utterly defeated and impoverished by the Great War, and being economically and financially bankrupted for the decade that followed, could be rebuilt to become the most powerful country in Europe in less than 10 years. Disregarding the sources of finance and political stimuli, including its leadership that may have stood in oversight of its miraculous recovery, the magical make-up that was inherent in this possibility, was that of a clearly superior Germanic 'race'. It is with little doubt that few other regions or 'races' in the world would have been able to achieve such progress in such a short time, with the exception of perhaps smaller enclaves. Among these, for example, are the relatively small 'races' of the Afrikaner in South Africa and the Hebrew in Israel; both of which are dominated by Germanic stock.

Mirroring the earlier described attempt by the Roman Empire to flush-out the Jewishness from Jerusalem, and as is described further down, the attempt by

---

[1] The Thirty Years' War (1618-1648) was a devastating conflict primarily in Central Europe, involving multiple European powers, and that reestablished the structure of Europe to mostly that which it is today.

the British Empire to flush-out the Boer culture from the Afrikaner, these post-1945 combined eastern and western powers also did not succeed. Just consider the disastrous effects of the American Morgenthau Plan[1], that caused more civilian deaths in Germany than the war itself. Besides the occupying entity's intent to kill millions, this demonic plan would have effectively stopped the beat of Europe's heart. Whereas this genocidal act would have created an area of uncontrollable chaos in the midst of Europe, in not much time, the larger effects would have spawned of a more aggressive and resistant Germanic race. This version of the same race then would have led Europe to an American-alienation, and instead naturally allied itself to the Soviet expansion, to which it would consequently have succumbed. Had this occurred, the combined Slavic-Germanic entity, being 'Soviet' resources controlled by Germania's populace, would have spread into the Middle-east, permanently dousing any and all America's plans for Empire. Ending the Morgenthau Plan was therefore not an act of mercy to Germania, but one of self-interest.

Instead, the Marshall Plan was implemented[2]. Where much praise and credit is now given to this plan, it must be remembered that its strategic aim was to rebuild the Germanic territories through means America could strategically control.

Regardless of the dark nature of these unscrupulous strategies against the Germanic territories, we must also consider another effect. This is how, after two world wars, Germany and those countries that had large elements of their population sympathize with them, had lost millions of young men. These dead soldiers represented the loss of whole generations of their genetically finest, most physically capable and otherwise talented. In addition, as seen by measures such as this Morgenthau Plan, the act of genocide upon the Germanic 'race' did not stop with the end of hostilities. The barbarity and evil of these measures, by both western and eastern occupying forces, cannot be understated. On the western American-led side they entailed the removal or theft, of its best scientists and patents[3]. In the eastern occupied section, a complete industrial dismemberment and removal took place, followed by an economical exploitation program that continued for more than 40 years. If we then add to these travesties, the brutalities that occurred under the occupation of both Soviet and Allied forces, such as the intentional and systemic demoralization of its population, and the violation of a large percentage of its

---

[1] The Morgenthau Plan was to deindustrialize Germany after World War II, reducing it to an agrarian society to prevent future military aggression. It lead to severe food shortages, famine and a total economic collapse.

[2] The Marshall Plan (1948–1952) was a U.S.-led economic aid program designed to help the Germanic region rebuild after World War II. It is credited with stabilizing Western Europe, fostering economic growth, and strengthening U.S. – European alliances.

[3] Under operation "Paperclip"

women, we can find that there clearly was a conscious attempt to break the Germanic spirit.

The Germanic 'Race' of Afrikaners

On a considerably smaller scale, but by no different terms, we observe the Afrikaner as a further example of active measures that were taken against a Germanic tribe. This describes the genocidal treatment of what was originally a small and relatively insignificant enclave of predominantly Dutch settlers in Southern Africa, at the turn of the 19th century, by the might of the British Empire. The Afrikaner farmers or 'Boers' as they were known, retaliated when their young republics were attacked without provocation. What triggered their sudden disfavour by the English Crown, was the discovery of enormous deposits in gold and diamonds.

Although reference is made to 'Crown' and Empire, the effort was not driven by an informed public, but by the British East India Company, which was a private enterprise, with interests that used rather than served the English public. When their private armies failed[1], the Crown interfered. This resulted in one of the empire's costliest and most embarrassing campaigns. Even with a numerical superiority of 10 to 1 against the Boers, and equipped with all the tools of modern warfare, the empire only succeeded against these simple but tenacious farmers on horseback, by implementing a Scorched Earth policy. This is typically one where the line of supply is removed, and in this case, in involved the burning of their farms and internment of their women, children and elderly in concentration camps.

At the end of this war, in character to the dark nature of these forces, the end of hostilities did not end for the subjected Afrikaner, with their surrender. As a consequence of the loss of men, material and face in front of their other colonies, and fearing the consequence of renewed uprisings, the British Empire implemented a post-war policy designed to break, scatter or otherwise erase the Afrikaner culture. In the concentration camps, thousands of the Boer women, children and elderly died from starvation and disease. Even the survivors of this ordeal had little to go back to; their farms having been burnt and many of their men were sent off in exile. In addition, whilst having much of their property confiscated and their political leadership controlled, they were banned from using their language in schools, scripture or public places.

The empire's fear for this Germanic tribe was well founded, as we see what occurred after 1945, with Great Britain's collapse as an empire. Once the Afrikaners managed to crawl out from underneath the British yoke, they

---

[1] The ill-fated Jameson-raid, under the command of a man named Jameson, was privately sponsored by a group led by Cecil John Rhodes, the Prime Minister of the Cape Colony at that time.

rapidly regained their strength and independence. Consequently, within the few decades that followed, they were able to build their country up to become the most powerful one on the African continent. This was not just on strategic mineral, economic and military grounds, but also in the fields of agriculture, academics, science and medicine. That this was rather unique can be seen when we compare South Africa with the aftermath of British, Portuguese and French colonialism elsewhere. Most of those now independent states fell into various forms of civil war, chaos and subsequent dependency. But this was not the case with the Afrikaners of South Africa, or those countries that opted to ally with them. The rapid growth of the Afrikaners' influence was such that, from 1960 until the 1980's, its tribe independently controlled much of the developments and governance of the strategic southern African continent.

By this independence, the Afrikaners had become too powerful and too non-compliant for the comfort of the contenders of greater global power. They were comfortable to ally with whomever would work and trade with them, including those the global powers did not approve of. To these, the Afrikaners' stance, combined with their control over their region's considerable and strategic resources did not resonate well. As a result, their somewhat naïve logic and openness toward their rather frank and undemocratic domestic policies[1] now made them vulnerable. This became more evident when they became unpopular with the western powers, which resulted in these policies becoming weaponized against them, through a propagandized global media.[2]

In the years that followed, the geostrategic entities[3] which previously desired to control the Afrikaner and their resources went to work once again. This time, using fourth-generation warfare[4], their aim was to permanently remove the Afrikaner's power, influence and independence. Veiled behind various constructs, including the struggle for 'democracy' and 'equality', this was predominantly accomplished through financial manipulation and political betrayal.

A few decades after the removal of 20th century Afrikaner dominion over the southern African continent, the now democratic Republic of South Africa has again plummeted into states of chaos and geopolitical non-existence. With its economy and infrastructure in disrepair, its academia no longer internationally recognized, and its military now sterile, its downfall will be brought on by the

---

[1] In reference to their "Policies for separate development", that became known as "Apartheid"

[2] Whether one chooses to have an opinion on these policies bears little reference here, especially as most of the western and eastern powers had very similar ones, but applied such policies occultly; hidden from the public eye.

[3] Read: Global financial interests, backed by combined state and corporate powers.

[4] Fourth-generation warfare is conflict characterized by a blurring of the distinction between war and politics, and of the distinction between combatants and civilians.

type of corruption and gross mismanagement, that is unlike Germanic Europe, but typical of this part of the Earth. However, the responsibility for this only lies partially with the corruption, naiveté and incompetence of the new rulers. On closer examination we find the presence of the same forces that orchestrated the Boer-war, in which most causal events were cunningly stimulated and manipulated for the benefit of small, financially connected groups, who have agendas of their own.

In this theatre, the rhythmic cycles between the opposing forces of growth and destruction, also referred to as Order and Chaos, will continue in perpetuity – that is, in the absence of the masses' awareness of such cycles. This awareness is one that requires them to see how these cycles have a life of their own, being one that is not much different from the illusory ego in the individual man. They can only exist by being in contrast to their opposite, and in each they persevere by building collective egos to conquer, rule and dominate, at any cost. As a result, these entities do not care much for the plight of the individual man, woman or child, and will justify the resultant consequences and losses as necessary or unavoidable. This includes even the most extraordinary and potentially catastrophic ones, as to these entities, the loss of reign is akin to a form of death.

The Recovery of Africa by Germanic Means

The actual presence of cycles between Order and Chaos in countries is, of course, quite natural and evident in all regions, including the African, European, Asian and American ones. However, in the Germanic controlled territories, the extent of the cycles – between the height of the rise and the depth of the fall – is always more extreme.

In Africa the extent between poles was never as noticeable. Usually, within a generation or two, Africa would rapidly return to its own rhythms. We notice this, for example, when we follow the departure of colonizing forces, where within 30 or 40 years, Africa re-absorbs much of its own ways. Unfortunately, in a globalized presence, there will not be any departure of foreign elements anytime soon. The strategic control over these parts and its resources have left much of the technologically superior 'First World' entities desirous. This has resulted in the respective Western and Asian entities to bury their parasitic tentacles deep within whatever form of civilization rises and falls.

In Southern Africa, the influence of the resident Germanic race upon these parts continues in most of its industries though. Therefore, whatever financial, corporate or state forces desire to conquer the African continent, will eventually have to deal with the Germanic tribes.

At the time of writing, this region of the Earth was again, rapidly descending towards Chaos and violent anarchy. The future for most of its inhabitants here

– regardless of race or ethnicity – would indeed be rather hopeless, was it not for the fact that they still contain a very large resourceful and stubborn contingent of Germanic Afrikaners. Although not yet organized, the impending threat to life, liberty and private property will inevitably stimulate a conscious and subconscious process of gathering in numbers and resources. Like their counterparts in modern Germanic Europe, the Afrikaner tribe will come with deep-seated memories of treachery and deceit. With these, and a better understanding of the world, they now know of the futility of physical conflict, and will apply the more passive means of 4th and 5th generation warfare[1]. The resultant forms of psychological manipulation will range from diplomacy to coercion, indoctrination and economic intimidation – all of which, whilst persevering to keep their influences non-military.

In the event that the Afrikaners succeed and rise again, and that they are able to do so correctly and non-violently, they may well find that the majority among the divided races and ethnicities will follow their lead. Following such, with intelligent minds managing a strong, disciplined and content labour force, a mini Golden Age may be experienced – at least for a while. As all is mechanical and causal, in time the contemporary complacency will return among the masses, by which the Germanic tribe of Afrikaners will again be ousted. However, perhaps by then they will have established their Laagers[2] in a different format than before; one that is not based on faith, dependency or greed. But this too is not likely as they too are subject to their contemporary nature, and by then as happened before, they may well find themselves divided.

Of emphasis here, however, is that such complacency and consequent divisions ultimately serve the perfection of Creation's natural cycles. This is because, through such divisions and being spread apart, the applicable race no longer bears a threat to the greater parasitical entities, by which it, as an entity, ensures its race's preservation.

The Return of German Might

The atrocities by victors are usually deeply buried and overwritten by alternate versions of history. Ignored and forgotten by the distractable and suggestible contemporary mind, often its factual records can only be found in the memories of the surviving elderly. Overall, however, an unspoken knowledge of such things remains deeply imbedded in the collective unconscious[3] of its

---

[1] Fifth-generation warfare is warfare that is primarily conducted through non-kinetic military action, such as social engineering, misinformation, cyberattacks, along with emerging technologies such as artificial intelligence and fully autonomous systems.

[2] The traditional Boer camp, one surrounded by a circular formation of wagons for temporary defense.

[3] The Collective Unconscious refers to the unconscious or subconscious mind, and shared mental

people. This is especially so among those of the Germanic people, but it is naturally also inherent among other such people that suffered extensively. One may, for example, consider those of Russia, whose plight during much of the 20th century was horrific. However, although the collective memories run deep, stereotypically the majority of Russians are more hardened and somewhat blunt to the past. Among the Germanic people, on the other hand, there is an inherent energy present that is different. Where the Russian settles in forms of submissive servitude, the Germanic one will suffer and endure the calamities, whilst protecting their culture's arts and principles, until the time comes for its seeds of brilliance to germinate once again. Where the Russian will largely have gone back to agrarian forms of subsistence, the Germanic one will see his highly creative forces rise out of the ashes of the past, much like the mystical Phoenix[1].

What stimulated the meteoric rise in the post 1945 Germanic territories, in stark contrast to the initial genocidal plan, was the presence of wiser minds. They understood that the reconstruction of Europe, into a stable, peaceful and productive continent was simply not realistic without the heart-power of the Germanic influence., Left in the hands of the inhabitants of east, south and south-west Europe, the entire region would most likely have descended into the types of chaos that spawn only dictators and despots. Alienated to western powers, these would then naturally have sought to merge with their powerful Soviet neighbour.

Hence the plan of Morgenthau was replaced with that of Marshall and consequently, within a mere few decades, the Germanic cities, infrastructure and industries were up and running again – and with that, those of most of Europe. It can thus safely be assumed that, without its Germanic influence, the eastern, southern and western parts of a now affluent Europe that are not dominated by Germanic tribes, would be undeveloped and unstable, akin to that of the 3rd World.

The cycle of 'life' attached to the entity referred to as the greater Germania will now continue to dominate not just European, but also global events. At the time of writing these notes in 2022 and 2023, Europe was at war again; this time it was on the eastern regions of Ukraine and well outside its traditional territory, with as its stooged culprit the resource-rich and now

---

concepts. A term coined by Carl Jung.

[1] As an example, consider the rebuilding of the Frauenkirche (Women's Church) in Dresden, shortly after German Unification. A huge pile of rubble was all that was left of the Frauenkirche at the end of the Second World War. Nevertheless, many people had the wish in their hearts to use the same stones and see the church rebuilt as it was. A full 60 years passed before (in 2005) it was once again able to open its doors to the public, in all its baroque beauty. One can also consider how Russia's Tsars and nobles, following perpetual phases of destruction, used Germanic architects and engineers for the design and construction of most of Russia's famous churches and palaces.

independent Russian Republic. Although these territories were never part of the European Union, they were made so by 'European expansionist programs' on the behest of entities which aspired global control. Although in time, much will be written about what caused this theatre of conflict, and the role of its various 'actors'; when the propagandized layers are removed, one will again find Germania at the epi-center.

Ultimately, the reality of the *geostrategic elements* steer a region's geopolitics, which in turn lead to the hypocrisy of politics and its subsequent propaganda. Hence, these elements will always be buried and concealed from contemporary views, leading to naïve debates on what ought to be views with logic and reason. It should however be obvious to an unbiased observer, that the ultimate concerns of these debates will revolve around who or what, in the aftermath, is to control the Germanic tribes.

Determining the Source Germanic Power

An unbiased reader may by now have observed that the historical and inherent power of the Germanic region does not lie in its mineral resources, such as one would find in the Middle-east, Africa or even North America. It is also not due to its favorable geographical location, such as that of Great Britain and the United States. In fact, the opposite is true when one considers that it is made up and surrounded by numerous competing states. Some will claim that it lies in its genetic make-up and although there may be a degree of truth here, it must be observed that its already highly mixed set of origins have, since 1945 been under considerable additional assault.

The elements of resources, geography and genes naturally contribute, but so do those of brain power and creativity, combined with individual discipline, industriousness, physical health, sensory stability, and the collective or societal expressions that these give rise to. Political opinionated naiveté aside, most of these features are observed throughout a large percentage of those whose roots lie purely in the Germanic territories, whether by birth or descent. However, it is in the combination of these that a harmonious amplification of the basic energy centers can be expected; these being the Physical, Emotional, and Thinking Centers. When these centers are consciously combined and balanced, they activate the Instinctive Center, but this works both ways. When they are not, such as when one is solely orientated around one's physical, emotional or intellectual state of being, then creativity is easily reversed. A deeper understanding of the working of these basic centers was described in *The Way of the Pilgrim*[1], but their interconnected nature and functioning can be summarized as follow:

The maintaining of a conscious, focused and balanced equilibrium of the

---

[1] Id. Book I, *The Inner Evolution of Man*, Chapter 7

Physical, Emotional and Thinking Centers, otherwise known as the three 'base centers', leads to the activation of the next center, being the Instinctive Center. In this we can see how a person, who responds from his Instinctive Center, does so consciously, with his thinking processes in sync with his physical and sensory ones, and becomes highly effective in whatever he or she does.

Once a person's Instinctive Center is activated, his actions will no longer be energized from the base centers, but begin to draw its energy from the overwhelmingly powerful Sex Center. Such a person's energy will be vastly superior, and effective on all three base levels. Unlike the contemporary perspectives; the Sex Center's energy is not designated for 'the sensual pleasures of man', but for the manifestation of new life, of both physical and spiritual forms. It is therefore 'how' this center's energy is applied that determines a person's transcendence or descendance in his or her dimensional awareness. A disharmonious application of the Sex Center's energy can, for example, lead to excessively aggressive behaviour among men and excessive emotions among women. This, in both cases, manifests powerful psychic entities – which entities are of the Earth, and metaphysical, but not spiritual.

Consequent to the conscious, correct and sincere application of the Sex Center's energy by the Instinctive Center, the Intuitive Center emerges. This center is not empowered by the (physical) Sex Center, but energized from non-physical Higher Dimensions. This enables in such a person, the emergence of forms of magic and creativity that are considered, in contemporary circles, as supernatural.

<u>These 'supernatural' powers are then applied individually for the good of the whole, or they are applied collectively for the good of a few</u>. The consequence of 'choice' in either of these paths are self-explanatory, but we can add by pointing out the pendulum-like rhythm here. Where the first swing leads to a society's growth, and during the return swing, where an enhanced society begins to support a few, its collapse.

Whether one contemplates the views surrounding these centers from a physical, psychological, philosophical or spiritual perspective, most will be able to relate to the logic of it. The ability to transcend in dimensional awareness does not require a set of genes, initiations or qualifications, either. It is merely one of individual choice, and as such, it is the birth-right of every man and woman, regardless of race, tribe or ethnicity.

In the Germanic influenced parts of the world however, the *instinctive stimulus* to follow either a highly creative or an equally highly destructive path, seems to affect is people more than that of other population groups. It therefore depends on the state of awareness of the recipients of this influencing power, whether it is either *amplified individually* or *harnessed collectively*. This still addresses its effect though, and not its source.

The earlier described cities, places and regions, that were developed by their inhabitants, were the result of certain stimulating influences. But the question that remains is what the source of these influences is. As its power has the profound potential to influence people into states of greatness or evil, it has clearly not gone unnoticed by the ones who recognized its power, and who attempted to wield it. The resultant list of the rise and fall of great leaders, kingdoms, empires and body-corporates on top of places of power is long, but in most cases, the fall resonated with the loss of its source. In the case of Germania however, following its unification under Charlemagne, otherwise known as Karl der Große[1], the phenomena of Germanness from this region has amplified and spread. At present, the Germanic descendant, including 2nd or 3rd generation migrants, who puts his mind and heart in his purpose, will have a considerably greater chance of outperforming those *most* other regions on Earth.

Other Regions with Comparable Power

The emphasis above on 'most' is because there are many similar such places with underlying power on the Earth, where this energy is found *naturally*. The population groups these apply to however, are often either smaller, less concentrated, or in a geographic area that was not suitable for further development. Among these we note the island chain of Japan, the nature of whose people is very comparable to that of Germania. This is especially so when one compared the Japanese islanders with those on the adjacent mainland. Japan's limitation however is its island status, added to which one must add their lack of resources. Then there is the region of central and northern India, that stretches deep into the Himalayas. There is exceptional magic here, and that has been coveted by both the west and the rest of the orient. Unlike Germania, its magic was not applied in the same form, and as a result, its regional effects differ vastly. It could be said that this was due to the wise and illuminated guidance of its succession of Lamas, Gurus and other spiritual guides, but regardless, its powerful but dual nature here was largely kept secret and hidden from the uninitiated and unawakened.[2]

On virtually every inhabited continent there are many smaller locations that contain such veins of an inherent or ingrained powerful and possessing nature. Although most of these are quite well known for their effects, few are ever

---

[1] 748 – 814 AD, considered by many as the founder of Germanic Europe, he was king of the Franks, King of the Lombards, and Emperor of what is now known as the Carolingian Empire.

[2] Although its inhospitable terrain has few resources, Tibet continues to be governed by China, the land of the dragons, since 1951; even though the Chinese government has faced and continues to face harsh criticism since that time.

considered for the source or nature of their power. Giza, Jerusalem, Vatican City and Manhattan are well known 'active' examples of these, places such as the old cities of Ankor Wat, Machu Picchu, Cusco, and others, that were once regional powers, are today relatively dormant. There are also many lesser sites that were observably sacred, and upon which its people erected temples, cathedrals and large monolithic structures. Vast complexes, Stone circles, dolmen and obelisks were erected in these, and often at extraordinary cost and inexplicable effort.

Some of these were, due to their geographical remoteness, not inhabited by people for very long. However, upon closer investigation one finds petroglyphs and stone-built or carved shrines as evidence to what had at some point been a place of devotion to an unseen influential presence, that could heal and counsel, or empower and destroy.

E. The Sacrificial Land Chosen and Doomed by the gods
Isis, Rah and El: also known as Israel

That day the Lord made a covenant with Abram:
"To your descendants I give this land, from the river of Egypt
to the great river, the Euphrates River.
The Holy Bible: Genesis 15, Verse 18

O children of Israel! Remember My favors upon you.
Fulfil your covenant and I will fulfil Mine.
The Noble Qur'an: Surat Al-Baqarah 2, Verse 47

Or do they envy people for what Allah has given them of His bounty?
But we had already given the family of Abraham the Scripture and
wisdom and conferred upon them a great kingdom.
The Noble Qur'an: Surat An-Nisā 4, Verse 54

> I will bless those who bless you,
> and whoever curses you I will curse;
> and all peoples on earth will be blessed through you
> The Holy Bible: Genesis 12, Verse 3

Separate Entities

Earlier in this chapter, we observed the energy nexus or core of the city of Jerusalem. Where-as it is evident that the entity named Jerusalem has its own power and influence, to three of the world's major religions in particular, the concept of Jerusalem in itself is often misplaced. This is especially so since Israel's declaration of independence in 1948. Since then, the entity of Jerusalem was weaponized by turning it into a propagandized lens, through which the State of Israel observes its politics, the Jewish race, and in general, what it considers as the plight of the Semite races. Whatever one's opinion is on such politics, without the applied forms of deception and influence, the ultimate power of Jerusalem would remain harmonious enough for its three resident religions to share the space. In this, their differences would be settled through mediation and debate, rather than intimidation and the use of force.

Prior to 1948 the name Israel referred to the entity by which a race of people identified themselves. The land itself was known as Palestine and, as such, it is an old and diverse country. It has been the historic home of Semite tribes for thousands of years, including predominantly the Akkadian, Phoenician, Hebrew and Arab tribes. It was however also occupied and influenced by the various empires from Sumer, Persia, Egypt, Phoenicia and Rome, and in more recent years there were influxes from many European and former Soviet countries, as well as greater Arabia itself. To understand the nature of this diverse and complex country, one would firstly have to analyse the detail of each of these influences respectively. Secondly, one would need to separate the multi-layered biblical, mythical and factual from the politics that have polluted the waters of reality with forms of bias. Finding consensus here today would be an almost impossible task, largely because most of the relevant details have become entangled around the Emotional Centers of contemporary people. In these, the reason and logic of their fundamental reality gave way to sentiment. Consequently, even addressing these would unnecessarily stir many an analytical observer's emotions and hamper his or her ability to keep an open mind – which is one of the primary purposes of these writings.

Only when we put such sentiment aside, can it become evident that, what must be taken into context in this region, is simply its location. If we can do this as such, then the why or how it became such a center of attention, power, friction, conflict and global influence becomes clear. Therefore, to address this, let us disregard its biblical and mythical history, let us overlook the political factors that revolve around Israel, and let us ignore the rise and fall of its cities and its holy places: For several centuries, up and until late in the 19th century, Palestine was a mostly dormant and undeveloped land upon which Arab and Hebrew tribes lived, traded and cohabited in relative peace. During this time the Hebrews represented a considerable minority[1], largely because, over the preceding millennium, most of them had found considerably greener and more profitable pastures in Europe and Russia. The general conditions for life and trade in Palestine of those days were primitive, unpleasant, and offered little reason or attraction for the Hebrews to return to Israel; especially as many had been settled in their adopted lands for many generations. Much occurred during the 20th century that forcibly changed this, and regardless of who initiated what or why, the means by which attention was brought upon this little Levantine enclave, was a phenomenon to behold.

Defining the Roots of an Entity

If we set aside the details of Palestine's highly symbolic and esoteric history, as portrayed in scripture, and if we were to also overlook the more recent 19th and 20th century events, we may be able to remove our bias. Consequently, instead of focusing on '*who*' was more or less right and entitled, we may actually begin to 'sense' a much larger, all-encompassing but metaphysical '*what*' begin to surface. From our still unbiased and neutral perspective, we may next consider '*how*' this occurred, and perhaps we can begin to observe a clearer picture as to what the ultimate motivating '*why*' was.

Whatever this attracting '*what*' entity is to be described as, whether it is a force-of-attraction rooted in the desire or need for a homeland, or the necessity to leave a place that was one's home for centuries; *it was not born out of contemplated wisdom, compassion or conciliation*. Instead, it was made manifest through the sacrifice by the unnatural and premature deaths of millions of its people.

There were of course several elements that forced the British Imperial hand across almost three decades from 1917 to 1948[2]. The first element was that which led to the atrocities prior to World War Two, and the first exodus of Jews from Europe. This included the Russian revolution, during which millions of Jews left the Soviet Union and the alienation of Jews in Nazi Germany[3]. The next element was what became known as the Holocaust during the war, as well as many smaller incidents in between. When reviewing the

---

[1] Historians and demographers estimate the population of Palestine around 1800, to be Muslim Arabs (85%–90%), Christian Arabs (6%–10%), Hebrews (3%–5%).

[2] Although Palestine was still Ottoman and not yet a British territory, the Balfour Declaration was a statement issued by the British government on November 2, 1917, expressing support for the establishment of a "national home for the Jewish people" in Palestine.

[3] The most infamous of these incidents was Kristallnacht or the Night of Broken Glass, which was a state staged pogrom against Jews throughout Nazi Germany on 9–10 November 1938.

cause and effects of these various elements, one may note that they differed from each other in most ways, except one: *They all entailed levels of violence, duress and suffering, on an extreme and enormous scale.* One may add to these events, the post 1948 reactions of the surrounding Arab states. Their retaliation against having a militarized Jewish state in their midst, led to a perpetuation of war and conflict. Consequently, one sees how this little sliver of land continues to have its seeds and roots drenched in pain and bloody sacrifice.

At present, the State of Israel is well established and it naturally has a right to exist. Its foundation, however, is not rooted in friendly alliances or mutual consideration, but rather that of fear and anger, cloaked by power. The collated energy of the conflicts over the past century is not one that is definable in terms of form and matter, but rather the effects of an entity, that has an undeniable and deeply entrenched hunger. It is by the very parasitical nature of this ancient entity, that ultimately the race of Israelites is doomed. What few of them realize[1], is that its self-inflicted curse was initiated by some whose agendas served a higher power; one whose fundamental agenda does not include the wellbeing of the resident races of Hebrews or Arabs, both being the descendants of Abraham.

From a karmic perspective, we see how the death and displacement of the tens of millions, and the indirect suffering upon many more since its inception, have left an indelible stain on this land. However, from a dark occult perspective, the current and recent events, combined with its history over millennia, have made this land perfect from which to wield unprecedented power. To fuel this dark power however, a sufficient amount of high quality sacrificial material is needed and among the resident and mostly Germanic Jews, there is a plentiful supply.

---

[1] With the larger exception of those who are in the know, being a large following of anti-Zionist rabbis.

Chapter 4
THE MAGICAL EARTH, PART II
MAGICAL STRUCTURES

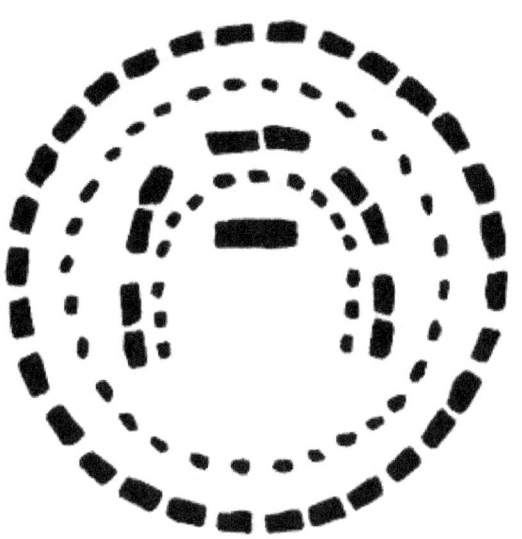

Everything in the Ego's perceived reality,
including all that it knows and experiences,
originates within and from the psyche's process of thought.

Subject to this, the unconscious Ego observes its existent reality,
within one-, two-, and three-dimensional frames.

To this Ego, the intuitive ability that Emerges,
out of an Aether of Higher Dimensional Consciousness,
is deemed miraculous to some, and magical to others.

To the Sage, Saint, Shaman and Guru, who is awake and aware,
these things are both logical and acceptable,
and a marvel to observe and embrace.

To the wizard, witch, sorcerer and conjurer, who seeks to empower, these
things are both practical and useful,
with a power to desire, control and project.

Consequently, when the Gods of old inserted their wisdom
they did so in Fungi, Plant and Stone,
because the Animal could not think
and Man could not be trusted.

>Subsequently, the wisdom of the Fungi,
>the teaching of Plants, and the power of Stone,
>has for eons been sought to capture and harness,
>to absorb, assemble and amplify,
>with loving care, to enable and restore,
>Order from Chaos.

Contemplating the Why and How

From a review of past research, we note that there is a lot of speculation as to what the source of the higher and advanced knowledge is. Who were the teachers of teachers, and how did they discover methods, formulas and functions that did not originate from within the cognitive senses? This is especially so when we consider the detail incorporated into some of the ancient structures, many of which were built millennia before the present civilization[1]. Where and how did the architects, engineers and builders of the pyramids and stone circles, found in a wide variety of shapes and designs on every inhabited continent, obtain their mathematical, technological and geodetical knowledge?

The features surrounding the Giza Plateau were briefly described in the preceding chapter, but such features are not exclusive to Giza. We find the same origin-mysteries residing in the vast array of temples, mounds and other structures, on virtually all continents. Their respective alignments, measurements and locations contain vast amounts of detail, much of which is often hidden, requiring advanced training and initiation to detect and understand. When, for example, we consider the well-studied ones like the 5,000 year old Stone Henge in England, or the 12,000 year old Göbekle Tepe in Turkey, we find no exception here. Besides representing mere 'circles of stones', they contain numerous geometric features, geodetical detail and solar alignments with the type of precision and accuracy that we have only been able to verify since we entered the age of Information- and Satellite Technology. When we additionally correlate these sites with some of the other well-known temple and pyramid complexes, we find that often their placement is undeniably relative to each other in both distance and angle. Many of them align whilst being spaced hundreds or even thousands of miles apart, a correlation that exceeds some of the most complex globally co-ordinated projects at present. In addition, however, in the blue-print design of many of them, there is the observation of the passage of Time[2]. This means

---

[1] Overlooking the rise and fall of a variety of empire-like 'civilizations', the present one, that we are recorded to be at the apex of, began about 6,000 years ago.

[2] The alignment of structures such as Angkor Wat, Giza, Stonehenge, and other temple complexes such as those in Peru and Mexico has long fascinated archaeologists, historians, and researchers. Many exhibit sophisticated alignments that correspond to celestial events and to

that many of these sites and their features are part of a greater masterplan, that involved a process of development over millennia, and continents apart.

We could, of course, assume that there were a few clever and organized individuals among these ancient civilizations. But besides having the know-how to do this, they would also have to be able to motivate tens of thousands of people, across multiple generations, to commit their time and resources to projects that may seem to be non-practical and merely monumental (and which they knew would not be completed in their lifetime).

We could also take the popular view of the architects and engineers being of Atlantean descendance, but this would merely defer the question along successive lines of legacy. It would still beg the question of where they attained their knowledge, what happened to them and their teachers, and last but not least, *how* they erected these and *why*?

When we consider the *'how'*, the mystery lies in the absence of tools or machinery, or any sign of these. After all, to cut and place hundreds of thousands of stones[1] with such accuracy, or the means to transport them across mountains and rivers would (by today's engineers) be a feat worth recording. Exacerbating the 'how' dilemma would be the inevitable time-sensitive political and academic elements among the planners of such projects. We know that nothing on these sites was built because it was quick and easy, it seems the more complex and challenging the better! Yet, clearly, across the passage of generations, the opinions and beliefs by some who may have believed in a cheaper and easier way did not prevail. The need to design with concentric layers of knowledge that could only be understood by those who had achieved a certain degree of enlightenment did not deter the builders either. Nor did the building of something that successive generations millennia in the future would contemplate on. This in itself is a feat we are unable to replicate among the socio-political and contemporary minds of today.

When we consider the *'why'* or the purpose, another can of paradoxical worms is opened. At present, the contemporary builders or city-planners would be easier to convince to build these same structures with forms of poured concrete or smaller manageable stones, and not the 5 to 50 ton blocks that were carved and cut in far-off quarries. Furthermore, even if these larger blocks were the only choice, then surely we would start with the larger stones at the base and progress up using smaller ones, especially in those higher and space-restricted locations. Yet, as is evident in these sites, this was not the case. In many a pyramid and block wall the largest of blocks were placed high

---

each other along degrees and distance measured within specific geometric formulas. While each site was built by different cultures, thousands of miles apart, there are intriguing similarities in how they are positioned and oriented.

[1] For example, the number of blocks in the Great Pyramid is estimated at 2,300,000, weighing from 2-30 tons each with some weighing as much as 70 tons.

up in the structure[1]. In addition, today's contemporary builders would have made all the site's blocks the same size; and yet, in cases such as the Great Pyramid in Giza, each of its more than two million blocks was cut with high precision, unique for its location.

The Emergence of Magic

When science and archaeology try to solve mysteries such as these, they usually tend to approach it using methods or technologies they believe are similar to those the ancient builders had. If none of these prove feasible or applicable, they may become creative in their hypotheses, but this is then limited to the application of combinations and variations of known methods that gave rise to modern technologies. Seldom however, will science consider the possible existence of forms of energy or technology that are not known to them, or that are simply deemed as impossible[2]. Subsequently, or as a result of such thinking, to the contemporary individual, anything that lies beyond the known is considered not from this planet (extra-terrestrial), miraculous or even magical. If instead, however, they readdressed these questions without depending on the use of existing methods, formulas and their formatted intellect, they would possibly find that Great Nature has in fact numerous similar such complexities everywhere.

Consider, for example, the effects of conscious or focused thought on organisms, electromagnetism and even the elements themselves. Although not scientifically *officially* acknowledged, it is generally accepted that our thoughts affect not only the higher or auric senses of organisms, but also the nature of electrical discharges, gravity, wind, water movement, sedimentation patterns and temperature changes. Regrettably, too few findings are ever published in main stream journals to motivate more advanced studies. Generally, this is because they are 'officially' considered as forms of pseudo-science, but more likely it is that the public awareness of these forms of influence is suppressed because they are not ones an entity can control, capitalize on, or weaponize.

This is regrettable because we can also see how our individual and collective thoughts affect the life and formation, or decline, of whole forests and ecosystems, the industry and patterns of insects, birds, animals and fish, but also men and women.

---

[1] As an example, one may consider the temple of Jupiter in Baalbek, Lebanon, where some of the wall's blocks weigh an estimated 1,000 tonnes.

[2] As an example of what contemporary science deems as impossible, would be the feature of a thing or being existing in more than one place at a time, sound-based anti-gravity techniques, the existence of an eternal universe rather than the finite Big Bang one (with a beginning and an end), or the existence of a non-physical being with a consciousness that traverses amongst and between biological organisms.

The Correspondence of Snowflakes with Humans and Pyramids

The snowflake corresponds with the human fingerprint, iris, DNA, and the human being as a whole, in that both are infinite in possibility, and each one is unique. Like man, the snowflake is geometrically shaped, which shape corresponds with the environment in which it is crystalized. What both the snowflake and man also have in common is that they represent physical and metaphysical elements in their formation. As such each exist within a paradox, seeing that they house both finite and infinite elements.

When we continue down this line of comparisons, we find that in both, the physical mechanicalness of their formation is subject to the elements, for example, the quality of the air and water[1]. Their physical formation is additionally subject to surrounding metaphysical influences, including electromagnetism[2] and conscious thought[3]. Although the snowflake is not cognitive, sentient, thinking and potentially conscious like man, it does display similar mechanical characteristics. Akin to the snowflake, the one-, two-, and three-dimensional mechanical parts of man are equally unconscious, and entirely subject to external influences. Consequently, like the snowflake, man is largely shaped and directed by external influences, *or by the psyches of people*. This is easily detectable, and not just in the physical man. It is also visible in all that man does and thinks – individually and collectively. And man is seldom consciously aware of these influences.

Without repeating much of the earlier mentioned detail on pyramids, we can see how they also correspond with snowflakes in that they display the same geometric properties and have unique characteristics. In addition, pyramids have a commonality with human beings in that they influence both their environment and the people that visit them by varying degrees and in many ways. That pyramids generate electrostatic energy was already documented by Nikola Tesla[4], and the energetic effects of Giza's Great Pyramid have also been documented[5]. What is not well documented but should be more obvious, are their effects on the human psyche. Consider, for example, what happens

---

[1] Based on the studies of Dr. Masaru Emoto *(The Hidden Messages in Water)*, a pioneer in the study of water. His work demonstrated that water is shaped by environment, thoughts and emotions.

[2] The effect of the observer (or rather the influence of his conscious focused attention) in the double-slit experiment is one of the most fascinating aspects of quantum mechanics. It indicates that the mere act of measurement alters the wave or particle nature of quantum particles like electrons or photons.

[3] As described by Andre Visch, a Dutch practitioner in energy and consciousness coaching, acupuncture, and manual therapy, in his book *The Laboratory of the Spirit*.

[4] Tesla began conducting experiments on the energy properties of pyramids in the 1930's, by placing a miniature pyramid under a beam of charged particles. He noted that the pyramid began to glow, even though it wasn't connected to a power source. By this he concluded that it was drawing energy out of the aether or from the Earth's magnetic field.

[5] See *The Giza Power Plant, Technologies of Ancient Egypt*, by Christopher Dunn.

when pyramids (and temple complexes) become aligned with the focused attention of aware, interested and intelligent persons. We would undoubtedly see how the very act of observation of, for example, the Great Pyramids' magnificence has a lasting effect. In addition we may see how the effect of focused observation on the pyramid has, in turn, an effect on the pyramid itself. We 'see' this when details that were previously not noticed due to their occult nature, now become visible. The discovery of these new details will, in turn, amplify the pyramid's effect on its observers, which then further enables and enhances their awareness, on an ever enlightening path of discovery of the pyramids innermost secrets[1]. This is why thousands of books have been written about the Giza Plateau, yet only those relative few who show a keen interest and ability, can truly grasp its emergent whole. The same effect was discovered by Dr Maseru Emoto when he enhanced water crystals with sound and harmonious thought, which would physically amplify such crystals' complexity and magnificence. Interesting to observe here is that the opposite is also true, and that harmful thoughts and sound visually broke the crystals' symmetric beauty[2].

The effect on our psyche therefore, is influenced by *how* we reflect on things like people, pyramids and snowflakes, and this is determined by our physical ability to see, focus, and persevere in paying attention. Thus said; the continued enhancement of our ability to see the occult or hidden aspects of an observed object, can cause its effects on us to surpass the normal or natural, and become supranatural. Consequently, we see that many of these man-made structures are potential sources of energy or power, of a kind that cannot always be replicated under normal scientific circumstances. As a result, across the millennia and especially over the past few centuries, we note how people established a great many mysterious, esoteric and mystical complexes. From obelisks to dolmens, to cathedrals and temple complexes, from whole cities to small things like forms of art, shapes and combinations of things; all of which are ultimately designed to draw the attention-energy of people.

When even moderately sensitive persons stand in front of Giza's Great Pyramid, inside England's Stone Henge, or at Cambodia's Angkor Wat, they immediately sense the presence of powerful elements within and around these. Because modern science cannot capture or measure this energy, it discards such as religious superstition or imaginary. But neither can it explain the enormity of every one of its physical aspects. Equally, it ignores the deep history of the greatest minds who thoroughly studied these things. As a result, even after thousands of years of observation and ceremonial application, few are able to irrefutably address the questions surrounding who the builders

---

[1] This effect is comparable to when we observe the art of a true Master, or even when gazing upon things (or people) of unparalleled beauty.

[2] See: *The Hidden Messages in Water*, by Dr Masaru Emoto

were, how they obtained their skills, and why. Thoughts of extra-terrestrial origins come to mind, and this is not unlikely, nor is it unlikely that a supernatural human or other intelligence was at work here – on the contrary. Whether they arrived interstellar, or interdimensional, or simply through processes of inner enhancement such as described above is unknown. But such brilliant minds were most definitely present. The same can be said for the most learned, skilled and experienced craftsmen of all kinds, and of workmen with great strength and endurance. The magic they applied is not complex; it simply resides in how all the elements were collectively harmonized, amplified and directed.

Physical Geodesy[1] and the Magic of Emergence[2]

The unique nature of many of these sites entails more than just mathematical and technological brilliance; it also involved an in-depth knowledge of the Earth and the Solar system. The geodetical locations are not random and had often been in use long before the establishment of the present structures by unknown civilizations of which no *official* records exist. Often such locations had evidently been in use for extended periods by primitive tribes who were instinctively or intuitively guided there, and who worked them for reasons associated with healing and guidance[3]. In addition, it is well known that many of the more recently developed places of worship were built on the ruins of pagan temples[4], which in turn were built around even older obelisks and dolmen[5]. What was commonly experienced can be described as a process of Emergence – where something emerged that had not been present in any component-part, or individual, nor in the sum total of all of them. The phenomenon is comparable to the harmony that we experience when we merge a collection of gifted musicians and their differing instruments with a composition in a directed orchestra, or the process of flight that results from the assembly of a collection of mechanical and chemical processes by a particular collection of minds and skills. The difference between these examples and the emergence experienced at these locations, is that the enhancing effects people experience are metaphysical and largely invisible.

Thus said; whether one is able to view Giza, Jerusalem or Manhattan, or when one is able to observe Germania as a whole, one cannot but observe their

---

[1] The science of measuring the geometry, gravity, and spatial orientation of the Earth.

[2] Emergence occurs when a complex entity has properties or behaviours that its parts do not have on their own, and which emerge only when they interact as a whole.

[3] This observation in based on the presence of very ancient rock art and other found in numerous locations, worldwide.

[4] For example, numerous churches and cathedrals in the Americas were built on top of Native American holy sites, in an effort to Christianize these. The same is found the older religions, such as Hinduism, where the many gods of old and their holy places, are adopted and integrated.

[5] Obelisks (or menhirs) and dolmen are considered to be the legacy of pyramids.

unique phenomenal effects on humanity. One can see how the influential energies, due to their often harmonized and amplified status, were intentionally harnessed through very specific designs, for differing purposes, and with differing outcomes.

We can therefore *choose* to go and live within one of these highly energized places to persevere and attain its ultimate purpose. For example, this can be the dream of religious gain in Jerusalem, the riches and financial power of Manhattan, the magical powers of Giza, or the success in one's individual and collective ventures somewhere in Germania. But these are never guaranteed. Such outcomes are still dependent on the synergy of an individual's intention and wilful sacrifice (as in what one is willing to give up and let go of). Furthermore, as our review of these locations shows, the outcome of any undertaking would additionally be subjected to the law of opposites. The possibility for extreme degrees of suppression, persecution, exile, impoverishment or utter physical and psychological ruin must always exist, at least in their potential, with similar degrees of liberty, comfort, harmony and bounty.

Ultimately, all these sites do is to greatly amplify existing energies and influences, and consequently, the severity of a fall or trough in such a place will be equal to the potential height of its crest. This is because in the physical one- two- and three-dimensional experienced and perceived realities, the law of opposites is always present. Hence, when we are within the sphere of influence of these places or things, an understanding of this amplification effect is very important. Even more so when we observe it in our surrounding societal structures, where it can have veritable value. It is, for example, through the amplification of a region's inhabitants' feelings and emotions that its reigning authoritarian entities can control them and their actions. We can see how this occurs in a great number of such places; whether it is one of those earlier mentioned types of locations, or those that were built on or around a specially selected location. There are many such locations of occult influence, and most are in plain sight but veiled as a 'tourist attraction', tomb or other acceptable, to the uninitiated, description. Just consider the immense power of places like the Vatican, the City of London, the District of Columbia (in Washington DC), and the numerous Gothic Cathedrals, especially those of St Peters, Notre Dame, Sacred Heart and St Paul. A visit to these will offer the contemporary person either a feeling of elation, or one of doubt. If he is sensitive and awake, then he will likely feel both, as both spiritually harmonious as well as dark and demonic practices take place here.

Defining the Source and its Ultimate Purpose

The question as to what the Source is, where the effect of its influence originates, or why it is that it is more powerful in these specific areas, entails answers that are indigestible to contemporary (one and two dimensional) logic. This is because the phenomena is not repeatable or measurable by science. The same comment would apply to determining the reason or purpose behind this Source. This is because contemporary man is one who continues to believe that all can be rich, healthy, happy and winners, without the need for the sacrifice of something to be able to gain something, or for suffering in general. Nevertheless, this belief has captured the minds of the vast majority of people.

It must be remembered that the contemporary man's reality is made up of an external world that he observes through his five senses. Anything which falls outside of this reality is not officially acknowledged as something 'real' and is usually classified as imagined or hallucinated. Yet, we can clearly observe the undeniable effects of this Source. For example, its ability to make people do things that are unnatural, such as enter wars that involve the killing of millions. Subsequently, as it is invisible and undetectable, we must consider that its nature is of a vibratory origin that is other than that which the human being can detect[1].

This will often cause these effects or purpose to be defined as some form of 'divine will', which will lead the affected and afflicted masses to serve it with the belief that it will return this gesture by favouring its servants. What makes this effect worse, is when we see how this Source's power stimulates the societal collectives-of-man, ranging from small groups to whole nations who rise to empires and then, inevitably and predictably, cause them to fall.

As pessimistic as this may sound, when we can see this as such, and then expand our view upon this whole process of rising and falling, we may be able to identify a higher purpose in it. For one, we see that the human being who exists within these invisible, undetectable and unacknowledged effects, is either enslaved or destroyed in his slumber, or survives by allowing the applied changes to stimulate his creative senses[2]. It is namely within such newly attained creativity that man can discover his need to learn how to subdue or conquer his environment. For this means he must learn to master the elements that limit him, which include those of Great Nature and that of his own barbarism, and then, from its resultant stability, enhance his higher being.

To attain such stability, man needs to exist in a form of civilization which has, as part of its existent structure, a sequence of cycles. In this, when it rises, man's intellect rises, which raises his knowledge in science and technology.

---

[1] Human perception of light and vibration is extremely limited, *covering only a fraction of a single percent* of all possible wavelengths and frequencies in the universe.

[2] As an example, we can see how the 'effects' of Jerusalem represent the enslaving and destroying kind, Giza a creative one, and where Germania one that encompasses both.

In time however, such as when everyone is educated and clever, this intellect loses its valued place of importance against that of the sensory elements. At this, man enters a world where he simply wishes to be entertained. The entertained part of him, being highly addictive, will then rapidly subdue his psychic and physical states of health, leading to masses of obese citizens in pursuit of idols and charlatans. Losing focus on the original reason and logic of his pursuits, man becomes utterly complacent and in time, descends into a form of self-imposed hypnosis. As a result, he will cease to grow spiritually, and cease to marvel at the beauty and perfection of his Being. As a consequence, Chaos can return and the fall of civilization becomes imminent.

We can therefore see how the collection of influences that cause the rise and fall of civilizations, form an essential element in the cyclic design of Creation – which ultimately has a purpose that is greater than its inherent stability. If we can see this greater purpose as the enhancement or illumination of the individual Inner Being, which can then recommence at the end of such cycles. These possessing influences can therefore be perceived as integral in the mechanism of the earth's biosphere, and thus polar in nature. Perhaps it is comparable to that of magnetism, but where magnetism attracts or repulses matter, these possessing influences will capture and enslave, or stimulate and enhance the psychic energy of man.

The Unnatural and Occult Influences on States

The phenomena described above have clearly not gone unnoticed. When we review the age and history of these numerous sites it becomes clear that, across the millennia, people found that there were metaphysical techniques that could be used to detect, harness and even store their existent influences. They also found, upon the discovery of such metaphysical 'hot-spots', that their energy could be amplified. Similar to us using a magnifying glass or a spectrum triangle to amplify or dissect a ray of light, they learned that they could amply this energy using large objects of selected material in calculated concentrations, and with very precise measurement. Then they noted that these effects could be refined when using precise and advanced forms of geometry, as well as cosmic alignments.

Although many of the reputed high-priests and sorcerers in kingdoms of old claimed their own genius and power to do magic, and be able to conjure the forces that came off these influences, it was – unbeknownst to all including them – quite the other way around. As the 16th century magician and necromancer John Dee learnt only too late, these forces were from entities that were intelligent and conscious. Once enhanced by such man-made features, and enabled with a stone or structured body of their own, these entities attained a will of their own. Being observant, they then used such 'high-priests' or 'sorcerers' to channel their effects through them – capturing the only element that these ones still had, that of Discernment, also known as Choice. The application of these forces for light or dark was what subsequently made these practitioners either *temporarily enlightened, or forever doomed* into non-existence.

As described earlier, the Source's supernatural powers can be either applied *individually for the good of the whole,* or *collectively for the good of a few*. Hence, when so many across the ages asked who these ones were that built the pyramids, and how they knew how to do this, and how they knew the measurements of the planet, sun, moon and the solar system, with precision that exceeds that of the sciences of today, the answers of magic and miraculous are both true.

When some then wonder what it was that made the legendary high civilization of Atlantis so great, and what it was that led to its fall; the same answer is applied.

Chapter 5
THE MAGICAL EARTH, PART III CONSCIOUSNESS, AND ITS OMNISCIENT OMNIPRESENCE[1]

OM or AUM

**Whether one is devoted to forms of Spirit, Scripture or Science,
the possible ways to define Consciousness,
are as Infinite as that Consciousness in Itself is Infinite.
Thus, any attempt to define the Indefinable,
is as destined to fail, as knowing the extent of the Universe.**

"You are taintless, tranquil, pure consciousness;
you are beyond nature." *Swami Sivananda*

Contemplating the Subject of Consciousness along the Spectra of the Differing Human Realities

Among the contemporary views and psychological explanation of Consciousness, one will find many differing opinions on the state of matter, energy, life, the origin of the modern anatomical man, and his overall perspective on things. Where most religious and spiritual groups will relate

---

[1] The review of Consciousness in this chapter correlates in many ways and words with *Contemplations and Deliberations between Swami Vidyananda and John Brokaar*, Chapter 15, *On Consciousness and the 4th Industrial Revolution*

Consciousness with the Divine in some form or manner, groups such as the New Age ones, who pursue a devotion to Gaia (the Earth), tend to refer to Consciousness as a "Unified Field".

Many among all these will then consider Consciousness as *something one has, or has attained.* Consequently, they refer to it as "my consciousness", or "I have become conscious". If one considers that there are degrees of truth in all views, all of these can probably be brought together as component parts of the 'Whole'. That said, for the sake of all-inclusiveness in the contemplations of this chapter, we will refer to this Divine or Universal 'Whole' simply as Consciousness.

The positivist Technocrat sees Consciousness differently; he believes it to be something that the human thinking-cognitive-brain-mind grows or evolves into. According to him, it is something that is the product of the mind and as such, we observe how he believes that when he can create an artificial 'intelligent' mind, he will also be able to develop an artificial version of Consciousness. Besides his fast thinking machine however, it is not likely that he will discover anything new here, seeing that he has already defined Consciousness on his own terms. As a result, he will believe Consciousness to be whatever he finds in this, and identify it as such.

In the contemporary world of physical and material things, this ties in with the Power of Belief. This power is the psychic, and often perceived as magical or miraculous phenomenon, within which – amongst others – the placebo and nocebo effects reside[1]. Thus observed, 'devotees', who committed their minds and subsequent lives to such forms of belief, and their powers-of-influence, will be hard-pressed to look for Consciousness elsewhere. This will be especially so for those who have experienced the effects of such powers. Consequently, we see how the practice of ceremonies and rituals that harness the physical or psychic enhancing energies has become a highly sought-after business. Furthermore, as stimulating the physical or cognitive senses are the most effective way to motivate the masses, the contemporary world considers the profitable manipulation of fear and desire as normal and even fashionable.

These consequential effects aside; it is *in* the enhanced light or dark manifestation of the individual, and equally so in his collective psyche, that the intellectual technocratic and academic oriented minds believe their Consciousness resides, and which they intend to build within their machines.

Thus one has the 'contemporary' and the 'intellectual' versions of Consciousness: one being in the form of an external or omni-presence, the other being from within the physical and intellectual mind. There are of

---

[1] The placebo effect, for instance, shows how believing in the effectiveness of a treatment, even if it's inactive, can result in actual physical improvements. The nocebo effect is similar but in reverse, where a form of belief can cause physical illness.

course, within and in between each of these two versions of belief, different levels, degrees or contexts. When analysing these further, we observe how that all animate beings – including the differing degrees of awakened persons – have *different mediums* where-in they attain Consciousness, and how these correspond to the traditional elements of Water, Earth, Air, Fire and Aether.

Defining Reality by Defining the Illusory

In the absence of our ability to logically describe what something is, in the duality of our reality, we are automatically provided with an alternative; being the possibility to describe something by what it is not. Between these two options, of what it is and what it is not, the identification of anything must begin with what is real and what is illusory, or what is true and what is false. In these writings the observed reality is considered as three-dimensional which, to be perceived as real, must include Time. Consequently, the three-dimensional reality of Space-time is generally observed as being divided by what is physical and what is metaphysical *or even conceptual*.

From within the reality of Space-time, we see how a one-dimensional line is a mathematical concept, and how the perceived reality of a one-dimensional man – who perceives all things around him and his world as either being one or its opposite – is equally conceptual. This does not mean that the one-dimensional line or man do not exist, it simply implies that, *without the greater entity that it forms a part of*, neither has any substance.

The same is observed with the two-dimensional plane or surface which, due to it not having any depth, has no form. The perceived reality of a two-dimensional person, whose momentary and picture-like world has no depth, is equally conceptual. The two-dimensional plane and man can therefore never be described fundamentally, being infinite in their possibility and absent of anything substantial, physical or form-related. This also does not mean they do not exist; it simply implies that these, *without the greater entity they form a part of*, are absent of form and thus, as a substance, conceptual and even illusional.

When we then observe our three-dimensional *experiential-reality*, having included the Time ingredient, we run into another paradox. This is the inability of our three-dimensional conditioned brain-mind to factually comprehend that a metaphysical thing, like Consciousness, can exist without being able to observe and measure it. Consequently, when some 'thing' has no actual defined boundaries in space or time, that is in other words spaceless and eternal, the cognitive-thinking brain-mind struggles to see or sense its higher dimensional origin.

To attempt to explain this in physically descriptive terms, we could try to define the dimensions by attempting to describe the beginning of a mountain, or a wave, or a single thought. As all of these are not of their own origin but are the effect of a multitude of causes, we would have to go back to the beginning of all things – if there ever was such a 'thing'. As such, it is beyond the ability of the three-dimensional man to see that his or her own dimension is equally illusional, except perhaps when we apply philosophical or mathematical logic.

In the case of the mountain, for example, the earth below is an integral part of it, as are the climatic elements that shape it, and which in turn affect and are affected by the sun and moon. The same occurs with the three-dimensional observation of a thought, that has causal relations which are even more immeasurable – in both its time and space.

It should therefore be considered that, in a three-dimensional perceived reality, every aspect of man, including that upon which his history, knowledge and the very concept of Space-time itself are based, is non-fundamental.

Naturally, this thought is not very popular. However, as most people foster a religious, spiritual or fundamental form of belief in a Deity, or a higher authority, we must maintain an open and unbiased mind[1]. Thus, if we accept the existence of the Higher Dimensions and wish to understand them, we must begin by seeing our perceived reality of three-dimensional space-time for what it is. It is as conceptual to a Higher Dimension, as are the one- and two-dimensional ones to the three-dimensional. Hence, if we continue down this line of thought, and see how a collection of intersecting one-dimensional lines create a two-dimensional plane, and how adjoining two-dimensional planes can create the three-dimensional solid. Then we may also consider that there is indeed something separate to space and time, that gives origin to, and underlies, the time-based three-dimensional world.

Defining Consciousness by What It is Not

In later chapters we will review the greater context of the mind- or psyche capturing 'entity' or 'possession' phenomena. For now, however, we can easily see how this, as a subject, is not popular among academia, science, psychology, or contemporary thought. Disregarding such sentiment, we see how the various trends of ill behaviour by both the individual and his collectives are easily identified. We need but look in the realms of religious, political, and various societal 'realms' of division. Within each of these, sects, parties, societies and similar bodies there continues to exist in name, principle or idea, a conscious and intelligent entity, each with an identity and life of its own.

---

[1] According to the Pew Research Center and World Values Survey, **over 80%** of the world's population identifies with a religious group or expresses belief in a higher power, deity, or spiritual force. Approximately **90–95%** of the global population either follows an organized religion, have spiritual beliefs, or believe in a higher power or deity.

To contemporary academia and psychology, these phenomena are commonly described as the effects of fractured or disturbed minds. These are then often related to a corrupted environment with apathetic, narcissistic, and even violent behaviour. However, it is also noted that these tendencies are, when observed across a wider spectrum, unproductive, destructive and even unnatural in that they run counter to what is naturally good. 'Good' being that which enables a harmonious existence for the individual and collectives of men and women.

But, the contemporary mind still prefers to classify the causes of such destructive behaviour as genetic, an abusive childhood, or because of external elements such as excesses, violence, perverted sex, drugs, and cult-like practices. *Whereas these are all veritable factors, they are seldom considered as the effects of an underlying metaphysical phenomenon.*

In the same way, we can see how the influences that cause a disturbed and fractured social or familial environment are seldom seen in isolation. As a result, these influences and environments are often academically categorized under acts of social desperation related to the bad influence of a sociopathic and absent-minded herd. *Yet, the presence in these, of a metaphysical 'vibe' or entity that is repetitive, alive, intelligent and identity or shape-shifting, is seldom considered.*

All this aside, and regardless of whether we refer to these phenomena as causes or effects, as possessions or entities, or merely as the results of disturbed processes of thought and ego; the relevant point is that they are typical of a one- or two-dimensional nature. They can be identified by their *effects*, which change constantly, as the need arises, and can be seen in the actions of those who are subjected to them.

Where this metaphysical phenomenon differs from Consciousness is that Consciousness permeates every possible dimension, and we can even say that it has no dimension. As such *It does not just manifest Itself in the actions or works of man*. Instead, *man's awareness in Consciousness will affect his inner state of being*, through which *his choice of actions or work* are then influenced. However, the description of the 'inner state of being' is to the one- and two-dimensional observer equally confusing, as he is more likely to consider the 'inner-state of being' as the state of his thoughts, moods, forms of belief, or other sentiment. Therefore, due to the varying and fluctuating backgrounds of the respective one- and two-dimensional person's views, we may be better off trying to describe what Consciousness is, by describing what it is not. To do this, in turn, we must become aware of what influences man through observable inner and outer effects.

Defining Consciousness along the Contemporary[1] Perspective

To the one-dimensional being everything is either this or that, with him or against him, have or have not, good or bad, and so forth. For these beings, nothing is ever neutral, as even when it appears to be, it will be considered liked or disliked, with an approved or disapproved 'opinion'. *For the two-dimensional being*, the primary focus is on appearances, and anything that may reside underneath such an appearance is, to them, a non-issue and virtually non-existent.

For these persons, their emotions or feelings are what dominate their physical and thinking centers, and even their sentient centers. If such ones are doing, for example, physical labour or sport the focus of their mind will be on how they feel about their performance. The same will apply when they are thinking, studying, analyzing or doing other work with their minds, they will have 'feelings' about the outcome of such as well. We can even say that everything they see, do, think, say, or have, will have a 'feeling' of sorts, dominating it. This 'feeling' will then form its own opinion, and consequently, affect how they think and act. Regardless, therefore, whether such a person is a manual labourer or a politician, a soldier or a doctor, a wealthy businessman or an academic, in the contemporary (or one- and two-dimensionally oriented) ones, their emotions and feelings will dominate them and their mechanism.

Thus, the contemporary person, whose focus of mind is oriented around their emotions or feelings, will consider Consciousness with an emotion-based feeling attached to it. In addition, any instinctive impulses will be regarded as 'signals from their Consciousness', as will their acts of being compassionate or empathetic.

In contrast to these emotionally centered persons, is the one whose focus-of-mind is thinking oriented, and who considers the cognitive consciousness as related to his or her Consciousness. Often intellectuals – such as most of those found in academia and many who follow religious and spiritual considerations – see Consciousness as the result of an 'effect' that the psyche of their intelligent mind manifests, which they 'have', and which then somehow connects into a collective of others who are similar to them. Consequently, they exist in considerable confusion when that which they manifested in their state of 'being Conscious' abandons them, and with the passage of Time, they begin to observe the now inevitable death of their personal identity or ego.

---

[1] As a reminder; the term 'contemporary' used in these writings does not define people by their education, occupation, or affluence, but rather by their perspective on reality; persons who are closely associated with the attributes and norms of their current space and time, an interpretation that applies to their existing in dominantly one- and two-dimensional realities.

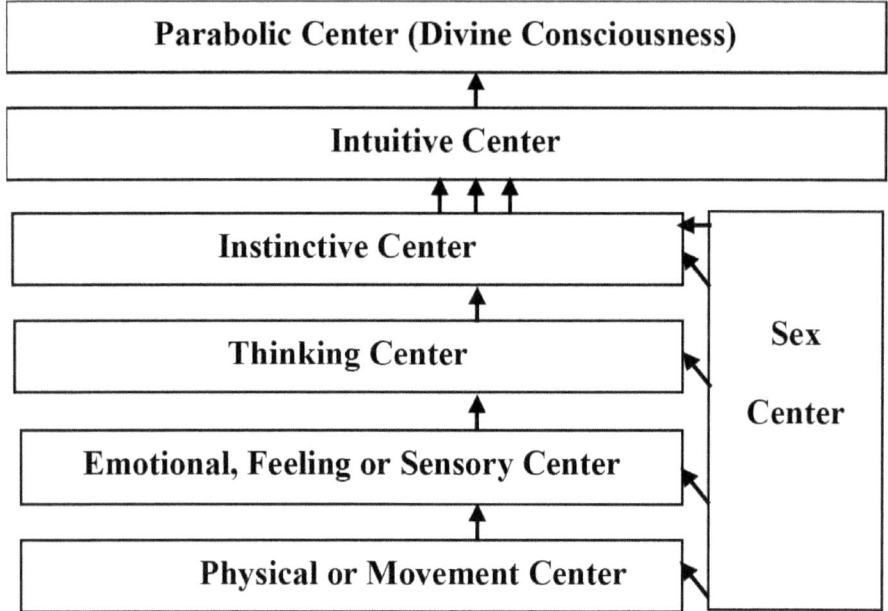

DIAGRAM: The Centers of Man
In the contemporary person, the influence of energy from the all-permeating Sex Center will greatly affect and distort the balance in how he or she will feel, and subsequently think and do.

Science and Technology's Perspective on Consciousness

It is the Technocrat's aim to replace the biological man, which he perceives as 'limited and imperfect'. He intends to do this with something that does not require high levels of sustenance, and which is not subject to humanity's inherent weaknesses, such as an undefined lifespan. Subsequently, the Technocrat searches to re-create man along certain inanimate designs and criteria, ones that science can understand, control, and continue to improve.

The Technocrat formulates a belief that this is feasible and achievable by Technology, and if it is not possible now, then at some point in the future. This is partly due to a related belief that what he perceives as '*his* Consciousness', resides in man, and is processed from and within his formatted, uploaded, and conditioned intellect. He thus sees Consciousness as something that evolves from the thinking and contemplative mind, following a process of learning, especially from subjects such as mathematics, psychology, sociology and philosophy, theology, etc, combined with a collection of memories or memorized details. Consequently, within this limitation, the Technocrat cannot envision the ancient knowledge and tradition that *the truly conscious man, is the one who enters Consciousness, within which he follows an opposing path, one that is thoughtless.*

As a result, the Technocrat, like the Academic, considers Consciousness as a conceptual 'process of Emergence' that is not too different from Artificial Intelligence, whereby the machine begins to think and reason by itself (even though the technocrat was the one that enabled it). He consequently convinces himself that man's ability to manifest combinations of new programs within the physical self, is not unlike a spiritual revelation. This is substantiated when his memory banks are enhanced by access to instant knowledge, processed through Artificial Intelligence, and that, as such, he creates distant horizons with new views and realizations. These will include designs and formulas of such grandiosity, and with ever increasing levels of technological breakthrough, that their origin will be beyond comprehension, at least along the lines of human reason and logic. Then, upon the apparent appearance of an independent Ego within this artificial manifestation, will be when the Technocrat believes he has re-created Consciousness.

The Technocrat, however, will not see nor acknowledge the irreversible danger of 'Hell on Earth' that he may be creating for himself. It is one in which the control of his mechanical and cognitive abilities are external to himself, and which may also include the control of his sentient ego. In this, he may not be able to adjust or even stop the program, because his fate and nature may be left to his operating programmers, who control his every aspect. Once he has crossed such a technological threshold, the android[1] he has become will be unchallenged by things that previously made him stronger, and he will struggle through what little remains of 'his conscious life'. He has become a mere component of a form of intelligence that is an independent, artificial, and external program; one that may have little consideration for his deeper human feelings and needs. In addition, his now artificially enhanced mind is capable of resolving long-reviewed and complex questions, such that he finds there is no longer a reward in seeking the answers for himself. Further, in this state, all he discovers are questions that even 'it' cannot answer.

The effects of these unintended consequences caused by the paradox that emerges here cannot be underestimated. Unchallenged by resistant things that makes the biological stronger, its motivational purpose will grow weaker; and that which now calls itself 'I' struggles torturously through what remains of that which it calls 'a conscious life' – except for the fact that to its suffering, there is no known end.

---

[1] A robot or synthetic being designed to closely resemble a human in appearance and behaviour.

Defining Consciousness via the Lens of Religion and Spirituality

Many of the followers of the world's 'contemporary' forms of religion generally seek – or believe they seek – to save their 'soul' by appealing to one form or another of the Holy or Divine Spirit. This they regard as the Spiritual Essence of God, and one with which they can merge, as long as they are without sin or karma. The spiritualist does not differ much from this, as he, too, generally seeks to *merge* with his Spiritual Essence, and a path to a form of salvation or a state of Unified Eternity.

Both religion and spirituality are generally based on compassion, forgiveness, and truth. However, where they tend to differ, is that the former follows mostly sets of doctrine recorded in scripture or expressed by its prophets, and the latter primarily follows a way of living. To the unobservant eye, these may appear similar, but they do differ, as *most religions typically aim to serve the collective and the individual through the collective, whereas spirituality seeks to enhance the essence of the individual, and its collective via the individual.*

It is within the misunderstanding of these views, that many of the frictions between the differing believers are based.

What many cannot or will not accept is that the 'ego-entity', that has possessed the psyche of the normal thinking mind, is neither the essential self nor that which is regarded by him as Consciousness. The ego-entity, however, 'knows this' and being cunning, also knows how to convince the unaware and perhaps biased 'id-entity' of the host, that it *is* the essential self or consciousness. The ego-entity does this with visual deception, that can even appear to the host as miraculous.

Another of the ego-entity's means of deception is to 'grow itself' using the invisible and undetectable web of psychic connections that exist between beings of a similar species. This is a natural phenomenon and is known as 'morphic resonance' (a term coined by Rupert Sheldrake[1]). It is this very feature in man that enables individuals, unrelated to each other, and in different parts of the world, to inexplicably and almost simultaneously, attain similar skills and knowledge. This feature occurs subconsciously among most animate species, but in the unaware man, it becomes relevant when this ego-entity, subconsciously and thus unaware to him, psychically links into its collective network. It is often the element of morphic resonance that the ego-entity in man uses to empower himself and to make himself feel that he is on top of the world; invincible and untouchable.

Believing in his own prowess, or even that he is being 'guided' by the Divine

---

[1] Sheldrake describes morphic resonance as a process whereby self-organizing but disconnected systems inherit a memory from previous similar systems.
See https://www.sheldrake.org/research/morphic-resonance

through *his* Consciousness, the unaware man proceeds through life doing as he pleases. If he is clever and oratory, he may draw many others into his 'congregated wake'. In the belief that he acts in the name of god, he goes from strength to strength and often realizes only too late when he has gone too far.

Defining Consciousness via the Trance- and Psychedelic Path

Inducing trance states, using sound, exercise, and forms of yoga are well known. These methods are old and are perfected by the practitioner over many years of received teachings and devoted practice. The use of plant, succulent, and fungi-based psychedelic substances to attain the trance-state are illegal in many places and are considered by many as unorthodox or as 'short-cuts'. They are, however, very powerful, and in addition, Great Nature has provided thousands of variations which, for thousands of years[1], have been used amongst animist traditions all over the world.

The complex process of plant combinations and brewing methods, amplified through very specific ceremonial practices under the watchful eyes of a trained and initiated shaman or curandero, is equally ancient. Its origins can only be guessed at and, moreover, the incorrect plant, plant-combination, or system of brewing can lead to the brew being deadly toxic, and when used within the incorrect ceremonial practice, can have very negative outcomes.

These practices were therefore clearly not discovered by accident or on a test-trial basis, especially as they have been observed by shamanic-like practitioners on every continent. Bearing in mind the fact that they were not and could not have been in contact with others, in each region different ingredients were used, and yet the higher dimensional or trance state attained, was similar in all. There must therefore be a higher dimensional (or vibrational) influence involved, through which these discoveries were (and still are) taught and guided by beings or entities who are closer to that realm or space of Universal Consciousness, than man himself.

If we compare this phenomenon with that of man-made enhancement using Information Technology, or man-coercion through dogmatic guidance, there is a vast difference. It seems that the use of psychedelics enables *a sincere and willing* Seeker to be reformatted and illuminated, and to become more conscious by actual spiritual entities. This process is considered akin to raising the veil that obscures the 'afterlife' from where great teachings, healings, and realizations are said to be attained.

The popular use of psychedelics, both chemical as well as plant-based, was popularized in the 1960s and applied creatively or experimentally – but often with disastrous consequences. As with all things to do with attaining

---

[1] There are, for example, Neolithic petroglyphs and cave paintings discovered in Algeria, which contain features of psychedelic mushrooms, dating back to 7000-5000 BC.

Consciousness, it is not something that is attained by 'throwing a switch', swallowing a pill, or which occurs automatically or accidentally. One cannot expect to simply 'evolve' into being conscious, without having done the work. Ultimately the process of psychedelics requires that the participant already be conscious to some extent; meaning he is self-observant, absolutely sincere, and with a good as well as a strong intention. Any mental or emotional imbalance in a participant may become highlighted in him or her, and not be rebalanced unless the participant is willing to do what it takes. A participant using psychedelics who is, for example, emotionally unstable, may come out of such a journey absent of any enhanced changes and perhaps even more confused. A participant who thinks too much may try to analyze visions or teachings that are immeasurable, and a person who is too physical may attempt to undertake even more extreme physical challenges.

However, a person who is balanced across his or her centers may, after only a single such ceremony, return spiritually fulfilled, with a great inner understanding of Universal Consciousness.

Defining Consciousness as a Medium

A clearer understanding of our merging with 'ego-less' essence, whereby neither the 'I' nor the 'I am' features, is by its very nature, relentlessly resisted by the ego. Many follow a belief that it is their own name-ego that they say 'I' to, that they will be 'saved' and welcomed in Heaven, or Paradise, or that they will gather with ancestors or clan members. There are probably elements of truth in all of these beliefs, but there is often also a personal bias. Seldom do these believers contemplate much on these matters or the fate of others who are not like them (or *with* them). They also do not wonder what will happen *after* they eventually get 'there'. The absence of such contemplation is often simply because the ego does not really want to know the answers to such questions, as the answers will not support its unique existence.

Perhaps, if we tried to follow a certain kind of *deductible and comprehensible logic*, such as that of hierarchy and correspondence, then a clearer understanding may be established. This logic would have to be one that can be justified to every person ever born, regardless of their religion, form of belief, class, manner, or ethnicity.

It requires one to return to some of the older traditions found worldwide, ones that have survived across the millennia, and which are described as the primary, alchemical or traditional elements. These may seem outdated to modern or contemporary science, which claims the periodic table[1] to indicate otherwise, but this is simply due to their inability to see beyond their limited

---

[1] The periodic table is a tabular display of the chemical elements, which are arranged by atomic number, electron configuration, and recurring chemical properties.

dimensional views. In general, there are the five traditional elements, of which some vary to a minor extent. In general principle these may be summarized as:

Water, Earth, Air, Fire, and Aether[1]

In the determination of the medium of Consciousness Fire is not an element but rather a destructive force such as a tornado and tsunami. This will make more sense when one considers how each of the four remaining elements is in fact, a medium for animate beings of a different type, nature or complexity. Fire, however, does play a pivotal role in the other four; as with the presence of a medium that accommodates the manifestation of things, there must also be one that accommodates their dissolution.

Water as a Medium of Consciousness

By taking the presence of humanity out of the cycles of Great Nature, it is easier to recognize and understand the principles of the natural food chain, whereby the little fish consumes the shrimp, which lives off the microbe or flea, and the big fish then eats the little fish. At the top of this food chain resides the shark or whale; large, ancient, and indomitable; it has (besides man) no predators. Seeing this integral chain, we can envision how the life force of each microbe and fish consumed is absorbed 'as a whole' by its predator, and how the consumed life-force then becomes a part of it, too. The sardine thus becomes 'at one' with the shark, and the quantity of its absorbed life force determines the impact or component part of 'the whole' that it becomes 'at one' with.

At the end of this cycle, the shark or whale used in this analogy, naturally also dies. They then decay and disintegrate into millions of small parts, some of which may remain dormant in a nutrient or mineral form for extended periods, or even eons. The nutrient-based life force is then, in time, absorbed by plant life, microbes, shrimp, and small fish. As such, the life-force of the shark or whale used in this analogy, is re-distributed among millions of organisms, and the next cycle is seen to continue – beautifully and unendingly.

As humans are unable to communicate intelligently with these aquatic creatures, we do not know for certain if there is a single form of awareness within them, either individually or when they exist within schools and pods, or colonies of countless organisms such as those that form a coral reef. When, however, we observe the interactions in schools, pods or colonies, it seems evident that something does indeed 'morphically' connect the respective creatures into a larger organism or greater being. It is along this form of logic

---

[1] Classical elements typically refer to earth, water, air, fire, and aether, which were proposed to explain the nature and complexity of all matter in terms of simpler substances. Ancient cultures in Greece, Tibet, India, and Mali had similar lists which sometimes referred, in local languages, to "air" as "wind", and to "aether" as "space".

that we may consider the medium of water as the blood of such a larger being. Like blood, its absence or quality directly affects the presence, strength, and quality of each of these creatures and therewith, indirectly, the greater aquatic being.

It could therefore be deduced that, to an aquatic organism's 'awareness', the water that makes up the bulk of its physicality and surrounds it, is its medium of consciousness.

Earth as a Medium of Consciousness

For land-based life, the life-cycles of organisms will differ somewhat from the aquatic ones. This is because, beyond the level of insects and small crawly things, animals are seldom consumed 'as a whole' by another single organism. This means that the life-force of a single animal that has fallen prey does not merge in its entirety with that which consumes it, and consequently, its life-force is distributed among many other organisms, including those that are plant-based.

This wondrous design still corresponds with the aquatic one though; the grazer consumes plant-based material which has grown out of the minerals and nutrients that were deposited there through different processes of various creatures, such as excretion of waste, decomposition of bodily remains, and decay of material remains of small insects and lower forms of life. As with the aquatic analogy, the large predators at the top of the food chain that do not fall prey to other creatures at death, are still consumed by countless smaller organisms and the cycle continues in perpetuity. We may therefore deduce that, to a land-based organism, its medium of consciousness is Earth.

Air as a Medium of Consciousness

Following the preceding analysis of aquatic and land-based organisms, we now transcend to the next level of complexity, and observe the cognitive, sentient, and thinking man. Since he exists in artificial surrounds, outside of his natural ones, his physical remains are not generally consumed as such, but upon death, are either turned to ashes or left to decompose within the constraints of a cemetery. As such, a different type of transition of life-force occurs, that is not transferred through Water or Earth, but Air.

The human being differs further from the aquatic and land-based creatures, in that he has a psyche. As described earlier, this is an identifiable entity, and regardless of what some choose to believe, it remains a force or a form of energy, that grows in substance, complexity, and strength with time, and unnoticed by its unaware host. If we can see this for what it is, we may then also note, that not all identified psyches function along the same principles. Human beings differ along very particular centers of attraction based upon where their 'focus-of-mind' is dominant. When we follow the Fourth Way teachings of Gurdjieff and Ouspensky[1], we see how these divide humanity into Man # 1, Man # 2, Man # 3, and the Spiritual Man, which are described as follow:

In Man #1 – the Physical Man – the psychic forces are absorbed at death by those who follow his ways and adopt his perceptions of reality. These are typically his followers, subordinates, and in part, spouse and children.

In Man # 2 – the Emotional Man – the transition of psychic forces at death are similar to *Man # 1*, except that in him, much of his psychic force is 'radiated-out' or surrendered or transferred to others through forms of psychological intimidation and its consequent trauma.

In Man # 3 – the Thinking Man – his psychic forces are preserved at death in writings, recordings, and other created forms. These are then absorbed or consumed, physically, emotionally, or intellectually, by others – across extended periods of time.

The psychic forces of Man # 1, Man # 2, and Man # 3 described herein, differ by *how* they are transferred from one being to another. Although these forces are of a non-biological composition, the entities they are transferred to are still physical in nature and, as such, they remain part of the earth's biosphere. It is due to this that one may reason that, to the psychic elements of an aware ego, the medium of consciousness is metaphysical and thus considered as Air.

Aether as a Medium of Consciousness

The next levels of being are also divided along certain criteria, and are, along 4th Way Teachings categorized as Man # 4, Man # 5, Man # 6, and Man # 7. However, as the purpose of this essay is to define the medium wherein each one realizes consciousness, they are simply described as one form, the Spiritual Man.

The Spiritual Man is the one who, through his or her work of self-observation and focused awareness, exists in an environment that is instinctively balanced across the three base centers described above. Unlike the devoted and faithful monk, the intellectual and austere yogi or the suffering and disciplined ascetic, he or she lives a normal life; gets married and has children, runs a household, a business or even a public office of sort. Exposed to the attraction and repulsion, the challenges, distractions, and duress of a normal life, he must, within this experience of love and loss of Life, maintain the balance if he is to attain, what some refer to as the miraculous, or enlightenment.

---

[1] GI Gurdjieff (1866–1949) was an influential mystic, philosopher, and spiritual teacher, known for his development of a system of personal and spiritual development referred to as "The Fourth Way." PD Ouspensky studied and worked with Gurdjieff.

This does not mean that the practicing ascetic, monk or yogi, who follow a predominantly physical, sensory or a thinking path, do not fall under the category of the Spiritual Man. Among these, there are many who are dedicated, sincere and present of all elements, but who surrendered the other paths in order to serve the greater humanity through focus along a single path. As such they experience an as complex journey that, although connected, runs parallel to the others. Acting as teachers, mentors and guides, they are said to provide the counter-balance against evil and the 'Darkness-of-man', in order to preserve the portals to realizing Consciousness. Without their work and sacrifice, the attainment of any balance of the centers for Man # 1, Man # 2 and Man # 3 would become severely disturbed. As a result the possibility of attaining Consciousness, in the medium of Aether, from the perspective of the contemporary man, would remain absent.

The Spiritual Man is therefore one whose medium of consciousness is Aether. As such he finds himself liberated from the rigors of the contemporary life; he maintains his psyche with awareness and simply serves his day-to-day necessities that are enhanced, or empowered, by the Instinctive Center. Although his psychic elements at death would be absorbed similarly as to those described above, every part would be evenly balanced across the Physical, Feeling and Thinking Centers. In other words, the Physical Man or Man # 1 who is exposed to the Spiritual Man, will attain a balanced amount of Physical, Emotional, and Thinking based psychic energy, as will Man # 2 and Man # 3.

The Spiritual Man, such as described herein, is therefore one who has applied his focus-of-mind, sentience, and physical life, in consciously observed, sincere, and truthful ways. At death, all that is pure and real, being that which is True and Good, can then merge with others who walked, are walking and will walk the same path, and to later emerge as one into a Higher Dimension. In other words, all that is false and untrue is washed off or shed and 'left behind' as, from a Higher Dimensional perspective, such things do not and cannot exist in that which is real, pure, and eternal.

That consciousness that is realized by the Spiritual Man, would therefore be in the medium of Aether itself.

The Purpose of Fire

It can now be concluded that the purpose of Fire, mentioned as one of the five traditional elements, does have its place. It is to eventually and ultimately consume the falseness of the psyche that was purged and shed.

We could say that the term 'Fire' is therefore not necessarily a literal translation, but rather a descriptive one. Ultimately, something that is false is not real, and as such it carries no substance; hence it is also not something that can 'burn'. Like the shadow before the Light, it simply ceases to exist, not only in essence but even in human memory.

Perhaps, therefore, when all is said and done, and the illuminating Fire of Chaos has swept across the plains of falsehood, then contemporary life will re-emerge as it was before. All that has passed will no longer reside in fact or memory, except for those who attained their Consciousness in the medium of the Aether, where all that is and always was, forever will be.

Chapter 6

THE PERCEIVED REALITIES OF MAN, PART I
PERCEIVING REALITY IN LAYERS AND SPHERES

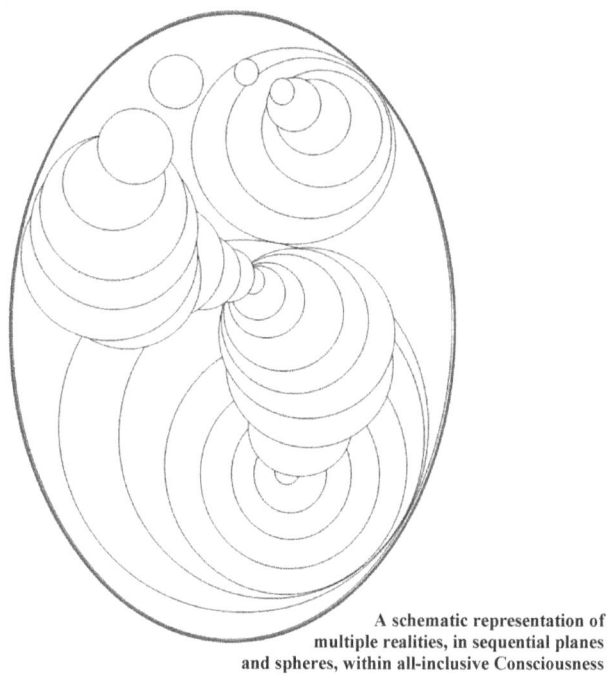

A schematic representation of multiple realities, in sequential planes and spheres, within all-inclusive Consciousness

The beauty of a thing is relative to our perception of it,
but it is also relative to the number of times it is observed.
This relativity is not such as *twice* being double that of once though,
these repetitions follow a sequence of 3, 8 and 11.

The *most beautiful* is when something is observed the 3rd time.
The *least beautiful* is when something is observed for the 8th time.
However, having *consciously* observed something's beauty 11 times,
the appreciation of its beauty is permanent and eternal,
even if in Time it no longer is.

The Reality of Perception versus the Power of Belief

If we consider the combined substance of the preceding chapters, we may see that man seldom *consciously* observes how surreal the reality of humanity actually is. Just consider that, how we perceive our respective realities defines them, and not just in bits and pieces, but in their totality. Then, once we can begin to observe this phenomenon as such, we may additionally see that it is the state of our psyche that changes *how* we perceive the things that make up our reality, and then how suggestible this psyche really is. As an example, a teenager seldom understands the world of an adult, in the same way as that an adult in his mid-life cannot understand the seemingly naïve views of the aged. And yet, throughout the years, we remain, generally the same person. All that changes is his or her perception of the world and themselves, and, as we now know, perception is reality. This is why our awareness of the state of our psyche is so very important, as with it, we can realize how *our focus on the individual inner journey, when it is sincere,* has the veritable power to factually change the very things we perceive, and experience.

When one is able to listen carefully to a speech or presentation from a politician, an evangelist, or a reporter of the news, one may note that their choice of words and the examples they use, are selected for a particular impact. This is generally referred to as bias[1] but, in contemporarily circles, the practise is considered normal. It is accepted that such twisting-of-content is designed to emphasise the *purpose* of the message, and that the purpose is more important than the facts portrayed. That this purpose likely has the personal opinion or agenda of the politician, evangelist or reporter inserted in it is, by most who are caught up in the heat-of-the-subject, innocently but naively overlooked. However, any such veiled but transmitted message does affect the perception of its audiences' psyche and, as the *fundamental basis of the psych*e differs from person to person, the message or its effect, will not necessarily have the same impact on all.

Consequent to these effects, the change in such an audience's actual reality, or rather *why and how they do or think,* will only occur when they consciously begin to apply the message or teachings, with its focus on their personal life. Regrettably, for far too many in such captured audiences, instead of thinking for themselves, the fundamental basis of their perceived reality is immersed in a world that absorbs carefully scripted words on mesmerizing screens.

Often in such presentations, every word, sound, colour and shape is carefully chosen to harmonize with the psyche of its audience. Although its purpose will appear to be a product, service or information of pseudo-importance, its ultimate aim is to remove their attention away from their actual day-to-day *proactive and interactive* realities. To these people's now subjected minds, this somewhat lop-sided and wasteful way of life has consequences, and among these the law of Polarity is often neglected, as is the law of Causality.

---

[1] To favor one person, group, or idea over another, often in an unfair or prejudiced way, and in this case to influence judgments or decisions, leading to distorted perceptions of reality.

Consider, for example, what happens when something is separated from its Point-of-Origin, such as when a person, an animal or even a plant is involuntarily taken away from its roots or habitat. The consequent re-adaptation is often disastrous, The same occurs with facts that, in this case, are referred to as the single, pure and uninfluenced Truth. This Truth, to which is added an influencing substance like purpose, necessity or intent, does not necessarily become a 'diluted truth' as such, because its components begin to change and divide; breaking up into smaller pieces, each with little bits of purpose, necessity or intent of its own attached. Once a Truth has been broken up, each divided piece will attain a life of its own and begin to subdivide, sub-sub divide and so on. As such, we can envision how our Objective Truth veers away from its Point-of-Origin, down a series of pendulums with the opposite poles, and each preceding pendulum forming the pivot point of the next descending pair. At the end of this descent, it will be as it is in quantum physics[1] where, at a certain point it loses its elemental property.

We can see how the same occurs in the artificial re-organization of contemporary societal structures. The senseless pursuit for equality between irreconcilable opposites, such as that of men and women, can be seen as an example of such. The consequent and often politically enforced pursuit for 'equality' manifests little but an equally artificial exchange between followers who fight 'for', and followers who fight 'against' and within each faction they too will have guided divides. As a result, even when some of these activists begin to awaken in the midst of their now violent protest, they are often so far from their Point-of-Origin (read Truth), that many find themselves utterly lost, having forgotten what the original point of division was all about.

In the example of equality activists, we can find the consequence of their dilemma in the fact that they often remain vehemently non-acceptant of what simply is. Then, in their pursuit to justify their stance, they may manifest various artificial mutations, to which they can adopt forms of identification. As an example, consider how a pro-women's rights becomes an anti-man stance, and of course, we see the same in the opposite. It is not difficult to imagine how such generally natural views can become grotesque versions of what was once normal. But this swing is part of Great Nature's design, and it is the same in all such pursuits. When the psyche needs a purpose to identify itself with, its ego will find a cause, and if necessary even manufacture one in order to continue this identity's existence. Hence the pursuit of equality between opposites is a dangerous horse to ride on because there can never be equality or sameness between opposites. The search in itself is a paradox.

---

[1] As an example; when one makes an analysis of something by breaking it down to molecular or atom level, one observes how that it ceases to be that which it was originally. As a simplified example; when a water molecule ($H2O$), is broken up into atoms, it ceases to have the properties of water.

Looking at the example of equality between women and men from another angle, we see how the very identification with 'the search for equality' causes its respective 'seekers' to ignore how the opposites differ in every way. In fact, their designs differ on every plane, including the physical, emotional, psychological, intellectual and energetic ones. However, as there is nothing in Great Nature that is random, the existence of such profound difference-in-opposites indicate that even in this, there is and must be an ulterior and higher purpose! When we maintain an open and unbiased mind, we can envision how the seemingly impossible merger of men and women not only manifests new life, but also how their differing psyches stimulate the realization of their own and each other's consciousness. This, in turn, then stimulates their different but integral spiritual paths.

The process of evolution through the harmonious merger of opposites is clearly a natural process, as we also see it purposely encoded in Great Nature's countless miraculous mechanisms[1]. All man's science, technology, philosophy and political cleverness can never replicate Great Nature. There will, for example, never be a miracle pill invented that does not have side-effects of some sort, and this can also be seen along the numerous easy ways that people discover self-awareness. For example, consider the struggle of the abused woman as one where she is destined to discover the masculine strength within *to liberate herself*, and where the tormented man must discover the feminine compassion *to change his tormentor's heart*!

The ultimate forms of liberation are therefore forms that include the chance of suffering and failure for the experience to be real. This in itself is a tricky path, as an unsolicited liberation cannot be lasting without causing further dependence, and suffering cannot be sought for its own sake.

The Fundamental Basis of a Reality

Having observed that our reality differs according to 'how' it is perceived, we must ask what the fundamentals of reality are, that we as individuals base our existent reality on? As a simple example to this question, we can see:

- How for mothers, the inner circle of their reality is largely limited to their children. The next circle would be one that limits itself to the care for their families, including but not necessarily, their men. The reality for most mothers is that often even the spiritual path must take a second place.

- How with men, the inner circle of their reality is the physical ability to do things, regardless of whether this is using muscles, weapons, money or their

---

[1] Besides the abundant phenomena to support life-creation, we can also consider the feature of opposites in the need for the change in seasons, the existence of predators to maintain herds, floods that cleanse and fertilize the ground after the drought, and how fire and water are natural partners in the small and great cycles of vegetation,

intellect. Beyond these abilities, the contemporary man feels purposeless, and cares little about what else is real or not. Events outside of him take second place, except if he has begun to think deeply and commence the sincere search for meaning, his own and that of the world, and which is why considerably more men will become philosophers than women.

- How with young children in their formative years, whether they like it or not, their reality is the reach, approval and influence of their parents.

Beyond, or in-line with these perceived realities, one can pretty much shape a contemporary person's reality and often their psyche at will. It is this principle upon which most societies, systems of rule and systems of education are based. All women, men and children will – to some degree or other – experience such reality affecting factors. Where some are able to bypass these influences by practicing forms of self-observation through which their self-awareness 'surfaces' to their actual reality, others cannot and 'sink' ever deeper into their respective onion-like 'layers'.

If one has taken the time to observe differing people in differing environments, ethnicities, levels of education and circumstances, one may have noted how, among men and women, regardless of the level of a person's education, live not only on different *'layers'* of reality, but seemingly on different *'spheres'*, as in planets.

Reality in Layers

The 'layers' of reality that are referred to here can also be considered as platforms, except that from a platform we may see the platform below, as in a birds' eye perspective. When we perceive in layers, it means we must look through them like one looks through a screen, veil or tinted lenses, to see the underlying or encapsulating ones.

As an example of such layers that one must look through, consider when a person must perceive his reality when it is veiled through lenses that were tainted by education, entertainment, religion and socio-political alignments. Another layer-type is where a dominant form of belief influences what one is willing and able to acknowledge and live with. This is most noticeable when such views are automatically rejected by others, who see the same but through a different layer or lens. Often such beliefs make them physically, emotionally and intellectually unable to see or absorb such concepts. For example, most people understand that power corrupts, and most know that a politician will lie about almost anything that furthers his political agenda. But this knowledge is limited to politicians who do not represent them or their interests. From the politician they elected to represent them, or who they personally know as 'real' people, they would either not suspect such lies and deception or adopt a firm belief that the deception was likely necessary.

We can see another such layer, when we look at a person's degree of gullibility – as in how naïve a person is. For example; there have been events (like war and economic crashes), that have changed the way people think and do things. They will claim these to be of a 'history-changing' nature, believing that 'nothing will ever be the same again'. As a result, they base their reality on this. We then note how the accountability for such events is always blamed on some 'bad guy' or other scapegoat, and this can be a person, a society or a country. In the political spheres we then see how the participating public is rallied to support whatever counter-action is deemed necessary; and how they fanatically follow such action, regardless of whether it is true, ethical, legal or humane.

Such levels of 'gullibility' can also be categorized by degrees of laziness, as often the acceptance of the given narrative was because it was easier, or less confrontational to their already stretched reality[1]. Those who consciously or subconsciously prefer to adopt a state of ignorance do so because to them, the alternative is *stranger than fiction*. An example of an alternative that is '*stranger than fiction*', would be a version of reality that challenges the very reality of one's existence. Consider one's meaning of life to which one has dedicated decades, such as family, religion or nation, and then having this uprooted or replaced with an unknown and a possibly worse alternative. Consider the impact of challenging, for example, the view of one's entire life being as relevant in the Greater Creation, as a single seasonal leaf on a tree, an insect, a single cell amongst hundreds of trillions with a limited lifespan, or a mere grain of sand.

Reality Based on Layers of Time

As every individual being is formatted from birth under differing contexts, and then exposed through the course of life to differing circumstances, the 'reality-layer' they are on will differ according to their respective psyche. In all these differing layers, the element of Time is of course a primary feature, because the basis of these realities lies in whatever (supposedly) occurred first. In the one- and two-dimensional way of perception, for example, there must always be a beginning of things, and when adding a third dimension, there must now also be a definite end. Either way though, depending on one's dimensional state of being, the perception of the actual beginning of things will also differ.

For example; the fundamental beginning of Time for most of science and academia, is based on the 1949 Cosmology-formatted hypothesis of a 'Big Bang'. Although this theory has since been countered by verifiable

---

[1] Referring to an advanced form of extended reality that tries to blend physical, perceived, interpreted and imaginary worlds.

alternatives[1], when a conventional Cosmologist's entire life-long work is based on a Big Bang, he will likely, automatically discard any proposed challenge.

Going further along the influence of Time, we find that there are many perspectives with differing evolutionary theories. These range from the biblical 6,000 year-old creationist, to evolution through natural selection from worm to ape to man over tens of millions of years, and even those of panspermia – being versions of Life, or at least human-life, being seeded or genetically created on the Earth by an intelligence from outer space. One can take one's pick as each one of these is equally conceptual and unprovable, and yet, whilst knowing this, most will still choose the one that best adapts itself to their peer- and pre-conditioned layer of belief. In addition to these contrasting theories, we see how, over time, many of these identified layers evolved in their context or became narrowed-down into more sectarian forms to suit a particular narrative. We see, for example, how their creator gods preferred certain races over others, making them exceptional or chosen. This occurred when the architects of such narratives opted to selectively peel back the 'layers' to see what lies underneath, and what was of use. Such selective approaches naturally create a number of additional lenses through which even more forms of mutated realities were formed. To find evidence of such intentional interference, one can simply take a closer look at the descriptions used in myth and scripture, but also those in archaeology, history and other sciences including, for example, genetics. Again, all these concepts are dimensionally limited, and yet, somewhere within or among these artificial lenses, the contemporary man finds his designated reality.

We then divert this Time-layered perspective on reality to the viewpoint of a more present day nature; that of geopolitics and the events that shape our current 21st century civilization. In its formation, the largest impact was from events that were stimulated by the 16th and 17th century eras of maritime and religious exploration. This period was followed by the 18th, 19th and 20th centuries, that saw power becoming centralized through revolution and war on an unprecedented scale. In these occurrences some will consider that these eras coincided with the rise of technology and systems of centralized rule, which in turn were founded on centralized financial institutions and industrialization. Others will see a world of concurrent events, where all is unrelated and accidental or incidental, and the positivist will see it (the world) as emergent to the evolution of the human intellect. Then there are of course those who placed their 'layer' of reality around unrelated or indirectly affiliated events, such as climatic occurrences or the influence of particularly

---

[1] According to evidence provided by the Electric Universe proponents, there was no singular event; the universe is eternal as it is shaped by plasma and electromagnetic forces (also known as Birkeland currents), rather than Cosmology's theorized gravity-driven expansion.

charismatic or powerful individuals. The point is that although all these viewpoints differ, all are sufficiently feasible to develop a theoretical 'layer' of its own.

While most of these perceptions on the civilization process are conceptual, it is of course feasible to consider that the core necessity for any such process is climatic. After all, it was climatic stability, or rather its predictability, that enabled shipping and agriculture. These, in turn, maximized the productivity of people, which stimulated growth in wealth, industry and *the idea* of a centralized power of global proportions – such as that of the British Empire[1]. Regardless of what the stimulus was, it was the centralized power of the British Empire that caused the American revolution, which, seemingly in turn, gave birth to the French revolution. It is not difficult to theorize an interwoven web by the same connected players[2], especially as all these similar occurrences took place less than a decade apart, and yet, their entwined outcome shaped the global power running things today. One may consequently manifest a lens into one's reality, through which one sees the singular entity that connected these geopolitical and society-shaping events.

All such layers or lenses however, are largely formed around *the intention* of the observer; be it in his search for Truth or for comfort by joining others of a similar view, and who are organized.

Where some may consider the idea of these occurrences being crossroads to different realities as mere theoretical or even silly hypotheses, they are still fundamental to the civilized existence of most people. We can see this when we try to interact, or even understand others who exist in realities where they may follow a line, practice or belief that is perpendicular to ours. The dilemma of so many contrasting realities can be complex, but one way to find some resemblance or sense among them is by observing the means by which one can cross the divide between these different layers. To do this, consider how most of the 20th century wars and conflicts were indeed a continuation of these earlier political and geopolitical schemes, seeing that they appeared to be connected and concurrent. Besides having the same players in the varying conflicting layers, we also note the same vein of financiers and material supporters involved on both sides of global events. If one can see this, one may also consider how, during the latter parts of the 'Cold War', for example, the fiercely opposing forces, although highly mistrustful of each other, still followed *a higher conspiratorial guidance*.

---

[1] The idea of 'empire' for England is said to have been stimulated to Elizabeth I by John Dee, the "Merlin-like" occultist and necromancer who, guided by spiritual entities, counselled her and other European nobles.

[2] Several of the American 'Founding Fathers', including Jefferson, Franklin, Paine, Adams and Washington significantly influenced the early French Revolution through their ideals, diplomacy, writings and at times, their physical involvement.

This 'higher conspiratorial guidance' is a layer that observably not many people are willing to entertain. This is because to most the existence of different realities becomes factually vague, and because the truth of such a reality does not conform with their belief of what is actually realistically possible. It then enters a facet of their psyche where harbouring such a belief is not only very uncomfortable, its metaphysical nature also represents a potentially inescapable twilight zone that, for the psyche, is best avoided. Such a view automatically blinds the contemporary observer from seeing what does not conform to their safe and certain space, even if their own adopted one is a most unpleasant one.

The above examples aside, this section is not about geopolitical mechanisms and their conspiracies, their interconnecting symphonies, or if these were of a physical or metaphysical nature. The primary purpose of this section is the elucidation of an existent human reality that is layered, by which we mean that people see things through layers with conditioned lenses. The secondary purpose is to emphasize that these layers are defined by dimensional differences and influenced by Time. A third purpose perhaps, could be that our realization of these realities give us an enhanced perspective on the effects of these layers, and perhaps, the discovery in this of a higher purpose.

Contemplating the Why and How in a Layered Reality

The vastly differing families in countries and territories everywhere must, by the laws of Great Nature, exist and raise their children, who are physically and mentally vulnerable, in safe and secure environs. For this they must orientate the safety and security of their business and economics, their children's futures and their own pensions, to the state of their surrounds. Within this, to find a semblance of inner peace, the cognitive and intelligent parent, who has become aware of his or her fragility and mortality must, as a consequence, maintain some form of sanity. To do so requires a certain platform from which they can orientate their awareness of 'self' on; in other words – *a reality that encapsulates a sort of homebase*. Once formed, this reality then morphs itself around the family's personal and societal norms, most of which adjustments occur subconsciously. It therefore serves us to remember this when interacting with people who exist on a different layer, and who may see the same things through an entirely different lens. When we observe the respective realities of others, with the intention to point out what theirs is based or layered on *or in*, then we need to consider the consequences. How deep do we really want or need to dig? There is noticeably a point for all mortal and cognitive beings, at which the layer of their reality-onion is best left untouched. The consequence of exposing the nothing that may lie and lurk underneath, or how their layer came to be, may be more than they are able to accept and with it, continue a mentally stable and pleasant life.

Reality in Spheres

There are those whose reality is not formed in layers that are separated by Time and events, but who exist on spheres, and whose reality is therefore unrelated to others, such as those in layers, and altogether different. In our three-dimensional physical and sensory reality – where sentient beings co-exist and share the same space to exchange words, thoughts and things – there are some whose respective perception of Life and the Cosmos as a whole is simply not the same. To these, although they occupy the same vibratory space, their reality matrix is 'coded' differently. For the person who exists in layers, it is usually complex to relate to the logic and reason of these sphere-based ones; this is due to the absence of a common physical-material or intellectual constant to use as a medium of reference.

On such spheres one finds, for example, the occultists and spiritualists who exist in their own respective Light and Dark spectrums. These ones often see their life's purpose, and that of the whole of humanity, as being in the direct or indirect service of – or as a part of – a greater Entity or Medium. This can be a higher dimensional Consciousness referred to as the Divine, Creator or the All and Everything, being of a source or destination *of an enlightening nature*. However, It can also be a more physical and psychic oriented entity, and referred to as the Architect, Master or overlord by some name or other, being *of a possessing nature*.

Of those people who exist in the layered realities as earlier described, which includes those who would follow religion along a mostly dogmatic path, many will refer to these spheric ones as occultist, spiritualist naïve or otherwise deceived. However, this view can be quite erroneous and cause them to underestimate the veritable power of these spheric ones. For example, one may note that often the occultist and spiritualist is of a considerable degree more fundamental in his or her devotion. Where a layered devotee's adaptation is mostly superficial or conditional, the spheric one will continuously and actively adapt and revolve their lifestyle around their beliefs. Some of these will even, if called upon, be willing to sacrifice their livelihood and if necessary, life itself. This makes any such view of naïveté become somewhat naïve in itself. In fact, if the perspective of the spheric ones was better understood, it could be seen how most of the described layers and lenses are in fact made manifest and controlled from spheres.

To elucidate how some of the spheric perspectives differ, we can consider for example, some of those who exist in spheres, from where they see the earth as flat. As debatable as the contemporary views of the round-earth may be, the flat-earthers will consider any evidence of a round-earth as optical, illusional or even conspiratorial. In further contrast to many a layer-oriented fundamentalist, flat-earthers are often found to be of considerable intelligence and education. Hence, when one communicates with them and is able to hear them without automated bias, one may often find that their flat-earth views are not without logic.

Such consideration can also be given to those from whose spheres they see the human being as a type of *food* for an alien, non-earth race or species. Again, many who reside in layers will find these ideas, like that of the flat-earthers, equally preposterous. But then, such parasitical entities are in fact a lot more common than most of them realize. It is just the types of 'food' that this refers to that differs from what one eats. Consider, for example, the act of harvesting psychic fuel by one of the many entities that promote fear, entertainment, perverted sex, and even the life-force of children. Consider how few layer-oriented people can recognize how they themselves live as little more than indentured servants; like slaves who spend the vast majority of their time working to keep an invisible or metaphysical master at bay. We can even observe those nations, religions and cults, who convince their followers that they are exceptional and as such, are entitled to do whatever they wish to others who are not exceptional. As another example, we see how many elitist organizations operate from such spheres, and with self-imposed immunity. It is often these very elites who apply their influence to give manifest to the design and maintenance of layers, and give form to certain preferred realities. We can see how, from such disconnected or spheric based influences, rule is imposed upon the subjected contemporaries. It is the very design of placing people in consecutive layers, that has enabled spheric-based elites to impose an untouchable rule across centuries, even millennia.

Last but not least, we must consider the experiential reality of those who exist on (or in) the sphere of Consciousness. These ones see the existence of Life, or at least, *the human experience of it*, as a mental construct. By this they mean a reality that is compiled from the input of our five cognitive senses, and perceived through or within our conditioned mind. They will see reality almost as an extended dream, a highly complex interactive illusion that simulates a finite reality. In this construct, they see Life as something that is radiated from a higher dimensional portal, by a Light-like medium like the Sun, that reflects within its Light the code for all forms of Life and its experienced reality. To these ones, the purpose of this construct is to obtain the realization of the conscious awareness of an awakened man, the experience of which returns to the Light in degrees of compassion and beauty. The reality for those who exist on the sphere of Consciousness, being a spectrum that is of a higher dimension, is one that seeks to realize its unlimited infiniteness. This, from a spheric based perspective, can only be attained by experiencing a mortal life within the manifested illusion of a finite world. This journey includes the determination of Truth, which is eternal, in comparison to the concept of falsehood, which is not.

The Co-existence of Realities in Spheres and Layers

The freedom that each soul and consciousness capable person has, is that of Choice. In this, they can choose to make the effort to awaken to their essential self, or opt to remain in their state of imposed sleep, within an orchestrated hypnotic stream of mass conditioning. Subsequently, man chooses to believe what he wishes – and then formulates his own reality around this. As he is able to act his role in social life, to blend in where and when it is deemed necessary or even profitable, much of the formulation of his beliefs are done within the hidden constraints of his mind or psyche.

To quietly or secretly contain the privilege of an inner-world however is complex, especially in a realm where the divide between real and artificial realities is increasingly blurred. We can see, for example, how the 21st century's artificial and virtual worlds are cleverly disguised under the guises of "ease-of-mind" and "entertainment". And yet, they are specifically created by those whose purpose is to harvest *human attention*. Being continuously enhanced by their attention, the artificial realities lure more and more subjected minds into the bliss of its artificial *place and space of infinite possibility*. Once they are here though they find themselves entangled, and it is extremely difficult to depart. This is because it becomes increasingly complex to know how to differentiate between the illusory and the real, and even to know if one has in fact departed the artificial world. Wholly immersed within this artificial dream-like reality, in time the subjected minds that are lost here will but wonder about the 'real' world, but any memories of that will have been forgotten, or now rewritten. In the end, they will no longer have that which was once free-will, but he, she or *the machine they have become* will not know this, nor will they know that they do not know, as the reality-creating machine convinces him, her *or it* that they know and no longer need to ask. With their psyche's mind and emotions immersed in such an artificial and illusional but perceived reality, the actual physical reality soon follows suit; re-adjusting itself around the almost vegetative state of its mind.

To understand what occurs next, we can simply correlate to what occurs in Great Nature. It is how the experienced reality of an unawakened and mechanical existence, like that of a plant, is then entirely formed and shaped by external influences; be they intelligent or incidental. As such, only the one who is able to consciously preserve his will and the choices he makes can, as such, re-formulate his own reality – and not just the perceived one, but also the one experienced.

When we are able to become aware of the patterns of our mechanical mind, which patterns are caused and conditioned by these external effects or influences, we may begin to observe within these, our own *layers or spheres of reality*, but also that of others. It is at this point, that the fallible, mechanical, predictable and programmable nature of the human mind becomes evident. We will see that it is childlike in its ease to be deceived and distracted; and when we can see the methods applied to the modern thinking mind's programming, it will be profoundly comparable to a personal computer.

Following various psychoanalytical studies of the early 20th century, it became common knowledge that a lie, when repeated to contemporary masses repeatedly – regardless of its absurdity – eventually becomes the truth. Especially with the onset of a propagandized mainstream media, this feature became widely used by those with authoritarian and profit-based agendas. In this, we see how at present there are many things our contemporary educated and reported history, that are knowingly and clearly false[1]. Many of these were of no small impact either, and we see very specific and supposedly unsolicited incidents or actions that directly led to world-societal changing events.

It must not be swept under the rug that certain very clever and capable spheric based persons have, across time, been able to permeate their influence into the layers of their mostly contemporary people. It was under disguise from within these layers, that they took on the form of their subjects' individual views, superstitions or innocent beliefs. They then turned these into fundamental principles, using pamphlets, books, radio, television, and film, to control politics, systems of education and of course their greatest tool: war. The history books are filled with tales of the most grotesque yet inexplicable acts that were committed under the guise of a religion, national security, or other form of belief. Spread by fear, panic, fanaticism, greed and aggression, and by the merest report or rumour, we find evidence of such interference in almost every form of conflict and suffering-causing event.

The Existence of Realities Outside of Layers and Spheres

There are many examples of everyday people who, as a consequence of their perspective or belief, are able to perform extraordinary and superhuman feats. These are often individuals who do so under situations that are dire, and, instead of being possessed by fear or frenzy, they enter a state of mind that remains cool, calm and collected. One hears, for example, of a person who enters a lethal environment such as a building on fire to rescue a person or a pet and return unscathed, or one whose injuries or illness are decidedly terminal, and yet who recovers completely without scars or side-effects.

The author has known several such persons. Some of whom were officially declared dead but came back, or who experienced otherwise fatal injuries, that

---

[1] In order to avoid unnecessary debate, it is best to not use examples here. However, if we consider that history is generally written by the victors, we can be assured that the events around conflicts and war as described, are biased and often factually inaccurate.

ranged from high voltage electrocution to battle wounds but didn't succumb to their injuries. Then there were those who, without medical intervention, made complete recoveries after a diagnosis of multiple terminal diseases, or some who overcame a series of "un-survivable" heart attacks. Often their testimony was one of perfect acceptance, as if what they survived was in fact perfectly normal. Most of these will claim that there was indeed *'something else'* that guided and coaxed his or her being through their ordeal, and of these, some will consider this *'something else'* as the awakening presence of a very real consciousness deep within[1].

There are of course many who do not need a major or dire event or illness to perform or endure extraordinary or superhuman things. Most of these use forms of yoga, meditation and intense focus. As an example, one can consider those who are impervious to extreme cold, like the Tibetan monks and Saddhus who meditate in sub-zero conditions that would be fatal to ordinary people. There are also those Yogis who were documented to live for years and even decades without eating or drinking[2], and meditators who can surpass the sensory effects of physical pain; ranging from ascetics to those who undergo surgery without anaesthetics.

Besides these examples of those who transcend the physical and sensory barriers of reality, there are also those who surpass the intellectual ones. To these, including some who are illiterate, knowledge, understanding and wisdom just arrives in them. A further transcendence of dimensional barriers occurs when we observe those whose sight surpasses Time itself. Some of these will foretell events days, weeks and even years into the future, such as the hour and means of Death, including their own.

To these sages, the reality they exist in is distinctly different from that of others, and is not limited by such layers, spheres, or even the laws of Great Nature and Space-time itself.

---

[1] In addition, and as a further example (among many), *The Dead Saints Chronicles*, by David Solomon and the Egyptologist John Anthony West, is a testimony of more than 5,000 Near Death Experiences (NDE's).

[2] The Indian Yogi Prahlad Jani reportedly lived for more than 70 years without eating and drinking. His foodless and waterless state was monitored by teams of German and Swiss scientists for weeks on end.

Chapter 7
THE PERCEIVED REALITY OF MAN, PART II
PERCEIVING REALITIES IN DIVERSE REALMS

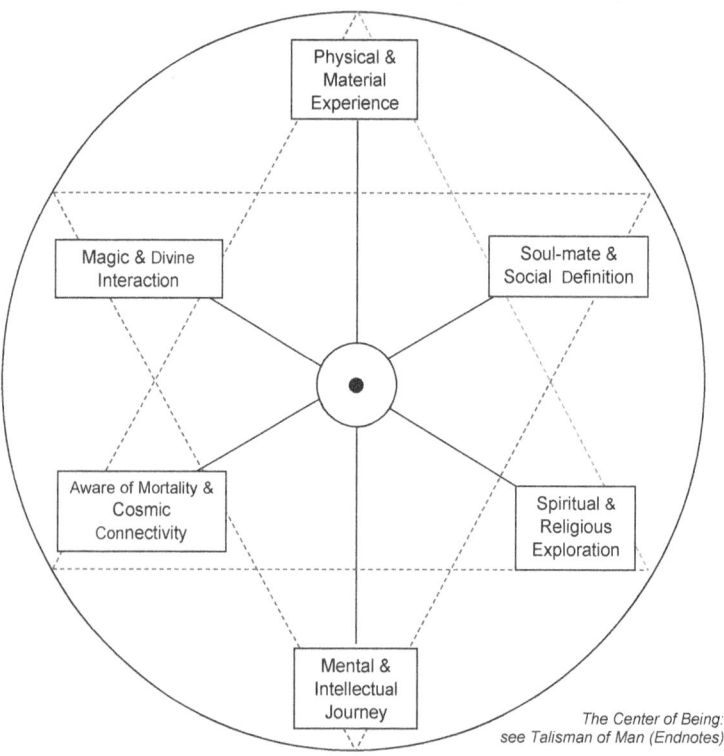

The Center of Being:
see Talisman of Man (Endnotes)

> When some look at the screen of Life *with* their eyes,
> and see only that portrayed *on* their screen,
> others look *through* them,
> and see everything else.
>
> When some *hear* the ringing of church bells,
> and note their sudden and wakening impact,
> others *sense* the permeating vibratory sound that follows,
> and consciously clears the head and heart.
>
> Perception *is* Reality, but to some this is just a state of mind.
> To others its only constant, is the state of its integral flux.
>
> The same Space-time is shared and observed by all living beings,
> and all bear witness to the same things and events,
> but not all *see* or *experience* the same, or manifest the same effects.

Thus, how their lives evolve, revolve or devolve from such, will differ observably, factually, physically and actually, yet the unawakened man never knows, but thinks he does.

It is in these differing states of reality, that the Awakened man, whose essence is at one with eternal and universal Consciousness, exists in an experiential make-up of realizations, within cycles of Life.

Between his attaining and letting go of his carnal self and his contradictory collectives, he also chooses to become and leave, Unidentified.

The Comparative Realities of the Soldier and the Monk

Two men, from vastly differing back-grounds and conditioning met on the cross-roads of Coincidence. Realizing that they had philosophical and spiritual interests in common, a relationship formed over the years that followed, and they became good friends and trusted counsellors to each other. The one was a penniless but devoted Hindu Swami, the other was the author, an established man who had found his first adult roots as a combat soldier in an active war.

During an in-depth conversation between them, they discussed or perhaps questioned the journey of a combat soldier, who is exposed to extreme physical challenges. As an ordinary typically complacent teenager, the author had chosen to spend his first few years in uniform. Fascinated by the rapid development of his physical and mental faculties, attached to the camaraderie, and drawn by the promise of adventure, a few years became seven. As his country of residence was engaged in an active war, several of these years were in arenas of intense conflict, and, often with little or no support, behind enemy lines. Reflecting on these events many years later, he observed that the experience of a combat soldier, who had tasted fear and seen Death close at hand, enabled him to understand the concept of life, mortality and power at an early age. At least more than the contemporary man, who had never had to fight or suffer for it. He explained to his friend the Swami that it seemed to him that such environments enhanced many levels of realization, within which a person could attain considerable *moral and spiritual qualities*. Naturally the risk, besides that of death or injury, was that it could also give rise to the shadow[1]; the cunning one who would misuse his skills and knowledge and do bad things. He then asked his friend if he thought that there was not a similarity between this journey and that of the monk.

The Swami responded by saying that he believed war was not a necessity to develop such 'moral and spiritual qualities', and that a devoted spiritual life by itself could provide the same. The author agreed but noted that the nature of

---

[1] A term used for the dark side, by Carl A Jung.

such extraordinary 'morals and qualities' would differ from person to person. Depending on how they were born and formatted would determine their outlook on good and bad, and subsequently their degree of devotion and way of life.

The author believed that his seven years in a war environment had made a considerable contribution to his way of life, especially the first seven years that followed thereafter. He felt that having fresh memories of real exposure to hunger, thirst, exhaustion and fear, of having been under fire and having walked across body-part strewn battlefields whilst looking for those that belonged to his comrades, shapes a person's psyche in many ways.

The Swami considered his own path[1]. His early adult years had begun the contemporary route of higher education, having opted to study psychology. He soon realized that what his heart sought, he would not find there. His joining the Ashram and adopting a monastic life thus seemed to have been encoded in his being, long before he realized it himself. This was not a choice one makes easily though; the life of a monk, who relinquishes his name, relationships and possessions is not an easy one, and neither is Ashram life.

It therefore seemed the path of the Swami had been written, at least up to the present, and it seemed that with the author this was also the case.

For both their respective journeys, the evolution of their mind, stimulated by circumstances during the years of adolescence and young adults was profound. Although such illumination is theoretically possible anywhere, their respective but vastly differing experiences greatly enhanced them both on journeys with such similar perspectives. This perspective can be described as the ability to see the physical and mental journeys, although integral, as separate parts, which separation enabled them to better manage their tendencies and merge with the inner Essence or Spirit.

We can therefore see that, regardless of how the journey begins, or on which route the respective paths takes us, our realizations, when applied to an aware process of conscious choices, can form the mind of the thinker and philosopher. As is evident, however, they can also lead to the empowerment of psychopaths and sociopaths. It therefore appears that it is not the path or adopted method which determines the outcome for those that enter it, but rather the way, being in the *why* and *how* this path is taken and trod. Although the approach of a dedicated but aware soldier differs from that of the devoted but aware monk or nun, the message content, or rather the *resultant subject matter* can be very similar. This is even reflected in the supposed outcomes; the risk of a soldiers life ending badly or on a corrupted path seems, at first glance, to exceed those risks of the spiritual path. However, the spiritual path

---

[1] The Swami was affiliated with his Ashram since 1996. Initially as a seeker, he became inspired by the teachings of his guru, Sri Swami Venkatesananda.

is not one with guaranteed outcomes either. Where, for example, a soldier may directly or indirectly cause harm to non-combatants, the monk may directly or indirectly mislead devotees. The gravity of each being relative to the degree of the impact of such acts.

It remains evident therefore, that *it is not the path or profession that affects a person's perspective*, but how they conduct themselves along such a path. There is therefore no favourable path, although some paths are seemingly more popular.

It is clear that the idea of war and the fascination with things military is distinctly more popular among the younger generations, than the spiritual path such as that of the monk or the nun. Yet, with all its evident devastation, horror and loss, war continues to remain an integral part of those contemporary people who are of a one- and two-dimensional nature, which represents the vast majority. Consequently, the path of the soldier continues to dominate in popularity over that of the spiritual life. However, if we were to undertake the impossible, and take account of their comparative numbers, we might find that the number of individual people who find illumination by crossing the threshold at the end of each of these two paths, does not differ by that much!

Subsequent to these observations, we may correlate that the quality or outcome of the journey of either soldier or monk, is never certain. It cannot be judged by the factors of influence, even if they differ so vastly that they appear to head in opposite directions. The choice of our direction is often said to be written in our destiny, but we see how in most cases such 'written destiny' was not of our own doing. In fact, the chosen paths and the challenges that followed each of these, are usually stimulated externally, and on the subconscious mind of the affected and often misguided individual.

To better understand how and why these external perception-affecting stimuli occur, and how they direct paths such as that of the soldier or the monk, we must analyse them under those factors or forces that are most dominant in their influence. In the case of the soldier and the monk, they are:

Social Conditioning and Coercion,
Duty and Idealism, and
Power and Ego.

The Social Conditioning and Coercion
that form the Soldier and the Monk

Many a young man and woman finds his or her purpose by donning a uniform, because it is celebrated by kin and clan. The walls of their homes and social halls are adorned with their photos, in uniform, serving their flag, or that which they are a part of. As the Divine is often claimed to be on their side, God's actual principles of compassion, understanding and forgiveness are usually re-translated to suit, and placed second to the military solution. History is saturated with examples of these.

Parallel to the soldier one sees that in every community a percentage of its members are drawn to a life in some form of religious service. Like with those that pursue a military path, these can primarily be divided into three groups:

- Some who do so due to influences by kin and clan,
- some do so seeking its secure and known surrounds,
- some who seek to serve or attain a higher power.

In each of these therefore there is an equal amount of risk that may lead to a life of disillusionment or worse. In both state and religious organizations, here are many that follow rigid protocols or dogma. Typical of these is that they do not, generally speaking, serve the individual's path, but rather the preservation of its own establishment. Neither of these are therefore paths or journeys without challenges, and both the soldier and the monk must have a strong intention in all ways, as he carries a large responsibility. He must know when to stand fast and when to walk away, even if doing so carries the ultimate price. Consider being the one who others look up to for their safety or salvation, and whose subsequent success or failure in life may rest in their hands. This can be seen as a responsibility that outweighs that of preserving oneself.

Like the soldier, the monk or nun enters a veritable battlefield, one with very real casualties, which could include themselves. There are many instances of disillusionment among soldiers and priests, which caused them to lose track of the principles for which they joined. Some of these causes could be the following of a charismatic one or a false prophet, for whose favour they traded their very life and soul. These disillusioned ones may consequently misguide or psychologically intimidate their own followers to such an extent, that they too become disillusioned and corrupted. Then there are those who, under the influence of their power over others, fall even further and allow the possession of their minds to cause them to descend into the lowest realms, where they become physically and sexually abusive.

Duty and Idealism

Although the subject of 'Duty' appears similar as the preceding 'Social Conditioning and Coercion', the difference is seen when it is connected with 'Idealism'. Where 'Social Conditioning and Coercion' describes a possessing phenomenon of a *social or collective* nature, 'Duty and Idealism' is harboured within the mind-set or heart of the *individual*.

While Duty and Idealism are of course also stimulated by society, or a cunning charlatan who represents this or that, their paths still involve the making of an individual choice, for which one is individually accountable.

In the case of the soldier and the monk, it is the mindful and considered choice that determines whether they act because they believe it is necessary due to the observed circumstances, or because it is considered to be their Duty. Doing one's duty can be seen as synonymous to paying homage to sworn or imposed loyalty, regardless of reason or consequence. It is the same in the case of Idealists who consider their cause to be right or more right than those of others. It is, for example, no different when one believes one does not act out of Duty or Ideal, but because one has decided to serve, one no longer has a choice (and one believes they or their kin will be judged if they do not act).

The concept of Duty or Idealism is characterised by its two-dimensional nature, but usually this is only recognised when it is put to trial. It is when no due diligence or contemplation is undertaken, and the followers-of-order act in faith to their order, or when followers-of-faith follow an order of faith, that both Duty and Idealism run into shallow water.

In the novice soldier's case, it is only when the bombs drop and bullets begin to fly that some will awaken to the reality of their chosen path. In the monk or nun's case, it is when they realise they were not prepared for the cruelty of the dark side of the world, and when they and their followers find themselves become like the proverbial 'Babe in the Woods'. When the awareness of reality returns and their naivete has left them, it is often too late for them to change anything to the physical outcome of events. It is then that they may be faced with options that severely challenge their calling. Often, at that point, their ability to make choices is limited to fighting or dying, whilst knowing that regardless of the outcome, they remain accountable for what follows. It is here however, in this place in Space-time, that the survivor may get *a second chance* to change his or her inner views.

Such a 'second chance' may not be without its burden though. Although they survived, it may not be without guilt, debt or blood on their hands. However, their consequent perspective on reality, that was previously rooted in the shallowness of ideals and duty, will now no longer be the same, and may in fact have become reversed.

Power and Ego

In every country across time, the military environment and its history of campaigns plays large on the collective ego of its citizens. Its soldiers are usually decorated with important looking badges, medals and symbolic awards, and the variety of uniforms are designed to either impress or impose. The saying that "To a man with a hammer, everything looks like a nail", corresponds well to the mechanical and predictable behaviour of most uniformed ones, who will act 'uniformly'. Consequently it is not uncommon for those who believe themselves suitably empowered, to see themselves separate and even alienated from those they originally swore to defend.

In many forms of priesthood it is similar. Most organised religions are designed and guided politically, in small or large hierarchical systems. Subsequent to this, a state's national or preferred religion is often heavily advertised – with kings and presidents seated in the front pews. In these therefore, the environment, customs, clothing and history play large on the conditioned minds of its followers. This is especially evident among religious leaders and their devotees, when they decorate themselves, their houses and places of work or worship with symbols and iconography. Where these were at first veritable representations or embodiments with talismanic-like abilities, over time an attachment with a false belief is formed. This can become part of the identification of a community and deemed as harmless, but this only until such identification becomes their reality. When it strengthens into a powerful system of belief, especially with sectarian groups, it will begin to perceive the world from an elevated pedestal and claim that only its own will be saved. Others who are not with them, are seen as 'hell-bound' or 'expendable', and assisted along that way in every sense of the word.

The Realities-in-Flux

To the unconscious and unawakened person, only the one and two-dimensional physical and material paths exist. To these who exist in such realities, the draw in strength by numbers, defined by symbolism, weaponry and gadgets, is a fascinatingly powerful force of attraction. This is even more so when it is amplified by having absolute authority over others, which includes being able to take lives and attain the status of 'hero' for such. Within the one- and two-dimensional realities, the choice is always limited to being 'for' or 'against', and by what a thing looks like rather than what it actually is. As a consequence of this non-noumenal state, its conceptual nature is outlined by many rules and laws.

In such artificial arenas it is very much like that of a children's playground, where they play imaginary games for which conditions are necessary to maintain the game's definition. Then, once the participants become immersed in the illusion, it can easily be changed and adapted by the one whose game it is, and usually without much note or resistance from its participants. Hence, after a while, to awaken and depart from this mental or virtual reality becomes difficult, and more complex than leaving a real one with physical barriers or restraints.

This reality is therefore in constant flux, yet this remains unnoticed by the ones who exist within these systems. When this is pointed out to them, they will likely argue that it is because of its laws and rules, that everything stays the same. They will not acknowledge how these are changed over time, cunningly and constantly. Regardless of scandals, unjustified actions and atrocities that are committed under their name, banner or symbol, they will find a reason to remain a part of their entity. It will likely be justified as for a 'noble service', the 'greater good', 'unfortunate but unavoidable' or even 'necessary'.

In contrast to this phenomenon's increase in rules and laws as it descends and becomes denser, however, the opposite is also true. It will, for example, become evident to one who was once immersed in one of these systems, but who consciously extricated himself from its infectious and magnetizing draw. He will as a result, see how the number of rules and laws for living a complete life become exponentially reduced and simplified, along his way up the dimensional scale.

The Rules and Laws that Manifest and Maintain Dimensions

When we consider the previous chapter's *Perception of Realities in Layers and Spheres*, and now observe the perceptions along the experiential realities of the soldier and the monk, who are seemingly opposite to each other, we may now see that they correspond. This phenomenon is discussed further down, but for now it is of relevance to see that there is one thing all these perceived realities along layers and dimensions have in common, and this is that they exist in hierarchies. These hierarchies consist of conditions which, for the soldier are defined as rules and laws, and for the monk or nun as orders with edicts and principles. It is by their perception through these accepted norms, that their initial reality is shaped.

It is however not so much what these rules, laws, edicts or principles contain that is of importance here, but rather *why* they exist at all, and *how* they are very specific in quantity or number, in each dimension.

'Why' they exist in any dimension can be explained in that they manifest and maintain everyone's perceived reality; one can see this by how they mechanically conform to a particular one-, two- or three-dimensional awareness or *realm of belief.* From within this *'realm of belief'* then, each dimension 'grows' the applicable set of *layers of perspective*. It is important to remember here that from any higher dimensional perspective, these realities will appear entirely conceptual, illusory and even superfluous. Imagine, for example, from the perspective of a devoted monk or a combat soldier, the time and importance a two-dimensional person spends on his or her looks and appearance. But, for the two-dimensional ones to remain in a state of acknowledged existence within their two-dimensional realm, they need a certain amount of rules or laws. In the said example of their looks and appearance, it would be a rule or even law that states one's hair must be at a specific length and one's clothes of a certain popular fashion. One can see how such rules and conditions form the framework of their reality, just like those of an imaginary children's game.

Let's look at this from a collective or societal perspective. Imagine how people who live in a small village, where everybody knows everybody and everybody's business, need far fewer rules to co-exist harmoniously, than those who live in a densely populated city. In fact, one may find that there is an almost mathematical correlation between the density of a society of people and the number of rules or laws they need to co-exist. This is especially so when they choose to remain anonymous and largely go about their daily way mechanically, hypnotically and oblivious of each other. The analogy of this village against the city example may seem as an obvious one, but when we begins to note the existence of rules and laws between dimensions of higher and lesser complexities, we will see that this is no different.

To expand on this feature, lets envision a conceptual scenario. Imagine how beings who live along a one-dimensional line require a great many more rules to get past or around each other, than those who exist on a two dimensional plain, and who can also bypass each other on the left or the right. The same will be for beings who live in a three-dimensional space, where it is even easier to get around each other, and who require fewer laws and rules to exist. Consequent to this observation one sees how 4th or 5th dimensional beings require a relative reduced number of laws and rules to 'exist', and whose resultant perspective on reality will bypass their dimensional limitations.

To use a physical example in this analogy. Try to imagine the complexity of managing a million people that move around on a single railroad track where lots of detailed schedules with rules and laws are needed. Then note how they can simplify this complexity by figuring out how to remove the said railroad track so they can move simultaneously parallel and around each other along the same surface. An even more simplified management of movement occurs when they learn to travel three-dimensionally. This is made possible by bypassing the limitation of the surface and adding people's ability to pass by each other either above or underneath through a voluminous space. Thus said, if one were to then transcend up the dimensional ladder, one may imagine being able to remove the limitation of a measured three-dimensional space, and from which one would transcend into an omnipresent realm or state where no actual physical movement would be required.

The point made here is that, regardless of how far one's imagination of such differing realms may wish to go, it is possible to conclude that the removal of certain restricting limitations, directly cause the rules and laws that apply in each to also be reduced - in both number and complexity.

There is therefore an evident link between what we experience as our reality, and the dimensions of our awareness. This awareness, in turn, is made manifest by a perception that is embodied by our perspective on the norms, rules or natural laws of our environment. To describe this otherwise: People have different perspectives on reality because every respective observer's perception occurs not only from a differing dimension, but also because they exist on differing 'layers', and are viewing through conditioned 'lenses'. Therefore, to find a form of harmonious existence among all these vastly differing people, we have to begin by acknowledging the existence of such applied hierarchies of laws and rules, within every dimension.

The reality of a one- and two-dimensional perspective will therefore require more laws among its subjects to explain, for example, "The purpose of Life and the context of Consciousness", than the reality of a fourth dimensional awareness. To the fourth dimension, rules that conform to an 'outcome based' solution, for example, are without foundation and therefore nonsensical. From a higher dimensional awareness, even the complex and integral laws of biology will have little substance as from its perspective, everything exists and occurs in and from Consciousness, and all forms of being, including biological life, are subject to that.

This remains a complex thought to absorb, even for a contemplative mind, because such thinking absolves the need for the thinking-mind in itself! We can therefore see how such higher dimensional viewpoints become utterly indigestible to the dominating personality's ego, whose very existence is defined by the plethora of laws and rules that stimulate their senses, and that define them and their place in society.

Depending on one's perspective therefore, one may or may not choose to accept the contemporary testimony of the miraculous from scripture, or of sages that lived for many centuries, or the appearance of metaphysical or spiritual beings to physical people. But then, from time to time, the materialist rule-based perspectives will collide with themselves when they try and fail to disprove observed and recorded anomalies – such as the earlier mentioned example of the Indian monk Prahlad Jani, who lived for almost eight decades, without having a need of food or water.

If one is at least able to acknowledge the existence of such vast dimensional differences, one may then begin to see the realities in spheres and layers, and the perspective from within each of these. From here, the acceptance of the co-existence of these differing realities will not be difficult, especially as it does not require any involuntary sacrifice. However, for the process of obtaining a higher reality perspective, such acceptance is *vital*, as this directly affects the observer's perceived *and experienced* reality. The emphasis on *'vital'* can even be expanded by saying that the non-attainment of such acceptance will result in the Seeker being unable to even imagine such understanding. This, in turn, will limit him to knowing only his own dimensions rules and laws, and as such, go around in circles forever.

In 4th Way instructions, as taught by the likes of Gurdjieff, Ouspensky and Nicoll, it was explained that the human's reality consists of 48 laws. Whatever it is that these laws contain, it infers that with each dimensional *transcendence*, such as the next one where Space-time loses its fundamental status, will require only half of these laws. One can therefore deduce that from 48 laws, the next dimensional realities are of 24, 12 and 6 laws, followed by the Trinity, which is One or Consciousness. *Along this form of reason*, one can deduce how at present, the contemporary biological man exists at least five dimensional transcendences from the 'Creator', being that state of Consciousness which has no dimensions, and thus is subject to none but 'Himself'.

When we return to observe the biological man, we see the paradox in that his perception is his dimensional reality, whilst his 'place' on these dimensions affects his perceived and experienced reality. We can further reason that, although every living being ultimately perceives its reality within – or as an integral part of – Creation's total reality, otherwise known as Consciousness, there are also 'layers' of 'sub-realities' within the first four dimensions. This is why, from within each of these dimensions, the individual perception of living beings differ from each other.. Consider the perceptions of the king and the peasant, or the man and his dog, or even the perceived reality of a plant or a human being. All of these exist in the same dimensional reality; but who is to say what the dog or plant 'perceives' when it sees or senses the tragedies of man?[1]

To the aware and contemplative observer therefore, each of these realities has substance, and more than just a psychological or perceived phenomenon. As perceptions are experienced differently, they will to each observer have occurred differently, with differing outcomes or effects.

To summarise; we can see how, for the contemporary man who is inherently lazy, it is quite natural to fall asleep and by descend into a lower state of dimensional awareness. There is nothing 'sinful' or 'wrong' in this. It is simply the effect of a natural and thus normal mechanism that automatically affects the unawakened and often misguided man. For the one who was misguided, there is always the possibility of self-realization due to an accidental awakening, but for the one who arrived in a lower dimensional state due to his own laziness, this is less likely. For the one who succumbs to his laziness it will be physically and emotionally more work to just exist from day to day. This becomes more evident around the mid-life age, when the physical

---

[1] As a matter of interest, according to renowned scholar, teacher and scientist Dr Ibrahim Karim, the founder of BioGeometry, dogs and cats experience higher dimensions where time is not linear, and why pets know when owners are coming home, when natural disasters are imminent, and do not contemplate the prospect of death like people.

faculties begin to lose their potency, and when it becomes necessary for the soul to find the answers in that more peaceful inner silence.

Their physical reality, including the biological selves and surrounds, will by now be structured in such a way that it will be almost impossible for them to work their way out of their one- and two-dimensional existences. Imagine one who has not looked after the health and ability of his body or mind. This, in comparison, would be more work and more complex, than to transcend from a balanced three-dimensional existence to a higher one.

Comparing the Spiritual Realities of the Monk and the Soldier

Where the soldier can be considered the product of a collective society, designed to protect it and strengthen it *physically*, the monk would be one that serves to protect it and strengthen it *spiritually*. If we can understand how the societal world of man works, we can see how both of these have their purpose and necessity, even if each has its *fundamental and sectarian* proponents, which will consider only its own as necessary, and the other as superfluous and wasteful.

However, such 'fundamental and sectarian' views from either one, only last until the tide has turned to the extent that the other is needed. Much of contemporary science, for example, will see the mystical and spiritual as forms of chicanery, at least until it meets the supranatural that their intellect cannot resolve. The *fundamental* religious and spiritual on the other hand, will often see much of science as an abomination, at least until their health or protection calls for it.

In the case of the Soldier and the Monk, one can see how each of these would easily be able to accommodate and accept both their worlds, as neither one bears any threat on their own. In fact, when one observes these two objectively, one sees that both the *devoted* Monk and the *combat* Soldier will have their focus fixated on the same subject matter. Each serves and joins or merges with something greater than themselves, and both do so through forms of work, service and sacrifice. Where they may appear to differ is that they enter their paths from different directions, but as reviewed earlier, by their nature or core, these also do not differ all that much.

Comparing the Physical Realities of the Monk and the Soldier

There are many different facets in the physical life, environment and path that affect how an individual perceives his or her reality, and this is no different in those that both the Soldier and the Monk choose to take. When we consider these, we must attempt to imagine *why* they chose *their particular path, how* they arrived there, and *how* they remain motivated in the highly sensory-attracting and intellectually-appealing world. The answers will *initially* be similar in that both followed a line of study within a particular environment, separated from the everyday life. Where in time, the Monk will spend much time in prayer and meditation, and find himself struggling to keep his mind's inner demons at bay; the Soldier will spend much time waiting for things to happen, and struggle to keep his boredom and idleness from overtaking his moral judgement.

In both cases however, these periods can either be spent undertaking practices that are mechanical and repetitive in their nature, or they can use them to redirect their contemplative self into a deeper awareness and understanding of their environment, their chosen path and life as a whole. In this, the ones that use their time to look inward, may find that their progress in following such a protocol of discipline largely depends on their ability to practice self-observation, which ability includes their remembering to so.

Contemplating the Reality of the Devoted

The unawakened person only sees the physical, sensory and intellectual path. To him, the considerations of Time and Measure in the realm of Space-time are what occupy his mind. To be able to consider anything else, he must first find a way to learn and accept that the realm of Space-time is not only no longer fundamental, it is a conceptual product of the mind, radiated upon it from a higher dimension.

This is naturally problematic for the contemporary thinking mind, which considers itself as part and an evolved product, of the physical body. From here this mind perceives how everything in its body is connected via a sensory system of feelings and emotions. This in turn then feeds and programs or uploads its so-called thinking brain, which, according to this mind, operates not much differently from a formatted and uploaded computer. With most minds, it will then consider that this 'thinking' system can develop a psyche, within which it, at first, refers to itself as 'I' and 'I am', and after a while begins to identify with itself as an individual with a name. This name will be connected to a family and a title that is connected to a gender, a qualification or an organization of people; and this is all by degrees. Ultimately, this 'I' is disconnected from everything else, meaning that to him, this 'everything else' is separate from the self.

The nature of the psyche will then determine how it evolves. If it is of the kind that means well, that is sincere and that perceives an empathetic reality with the world that surrounds the 'I', then its solitary or separated state will gradually begin to dissolve – and with this, its reality begins to change as well. It will begin to realise the unitary essence of 'we', which may then change its reality into one of an integral oneness. Only then, when this truthful and compassionate perception of reality is attained, is it possible for that Essence that is referred to as Spirit by some form or name, to emerge from within.

To the casual observer, the *process of Emergence*[1] in this instance, will seem like a considerable challenge and like a form of mystical magic. But to an open and sincere mind it is both causal and sequentially logical. It is a form of realization that merely requires a sincere observation of self and Truth. However, the intention to be sincere is not one that just happens naturally, like puberty for example. It involves a form of active attentiveness that we refer to as self-observation. As this involves forms of non-attachment it will, to many, appear as a great obstacle. This is especially so for those who are identified with, and deeply immersed in. their life of work, relations and survival. What makes this work more complex and paradoxical to these, is that it is of a kind that is both motivated and stimulated from within. It is not a path that can be forced or coerced, as this would potentially pose serious and lasting side-effects. However, we can see how the commencement of such voluntary inner changes, can instantly affect the perspective on what was once real.

In addition, we see how the design of Great Nature then serves to adapt the Seeker. Once such a 'way' or 'path' is undertaken with a strong and sincere intention, then the natural mechanism of ego-formation gradually but automatically begins to form and shape itself around this new 'way' or 'path'. This is where the 'new' ego that is formed develops an intuitive feed instead of a psyche-fed one and this 'new' ego finds its reality in identifying with the comfort of spiritual harmony.

Hence, when returning to our two examples, we see how the perceived, sensed and physically experienced reality of the Soldier and the Monk changes and evolves. This occurs as he or she learns, adapts, works at the and lets-go of things that they feel are inharmonious to what they sincerely seek. This includes their beings' purpose, which does not necessarily entail prospects of a long, free and materially fruitful life.

Consider how that, in an omniscient, omnipotent and omnipresent Consciousness, nothing is ever really outcome-based, meaning that it is not followed by something else. Whatever this is, or whatever such a conceptual outcome would be, would then affect a force that either attracts or repulses, causing whatever it is to evolve or devolve. Hence, if one were to attain an elevated position, place or space within an order or community of sort, the devotion by its weaker participating followers can become a veritable force of attraction. For both the Soldier and the Monk, this is something that would then adapt to their reality, as even this now 'new' devolving ego will actively try to preserve or defend its existence. The ordained and decorated ones can therefore never sleep and must remain vigilant, which continues to affect their reality, perpetually.

---

[1] 'Emergence' here refers to the phenomenon when the whole, within a complex system, becomes more than just the sum of its parts.

The Realities of the Corporate, Judiciary and Academic Realms

The reason for bringing these three groups or types of people to the fore, is to conclude our review though comparison. We can see that their perceived and experienced realities will differ greatly from that of the Soldier and the Monk. Their origins or roots however are dimensionally alike, being that they too have a one-dimensional point-of-origin. The corporate, judicial and academic realms differ however, in that one can categorize these as having people who are born favourably, as in family, wealth or intellect, and who are externally stimulated by a driven and ambitious ego.

To these, their perceived and experienced reality is one of *success measured by number or achievement*, which is displayed by power, things, appearances, qualifications and bottom lines. Unlike the Soldier and the Monk, who serve their country or community, these ones serve themselves first and foremost.

In the case of the corporate, judicial and academia's positions of power and influence, the perceived and consequently experienced reality is often one of a world populated by mostly 'unaccomplished people', who they perceive as residing at a level below their own. Seeing that these 'unaccomplished ones' exist in differing 'layered' realities, which most in their corporate, judicial and academic surrounds cannot see or imagine, they persevere to keep these masses there. Working cleverly, cunningly and often hypocritically they craft to ensure the 'unaccomplished ones' remain docile, mechanical, predictable and controllable. This is because they need to ensure that these masses do not attain too much power; power which they believe the 'unaccomplished ones' do not know how to use.

In the worlds of the 'accomplished', the features of *Social Conditioning and Coercion* as well as *Duty and Idealism* do not play much of a role. Instead, once these ones attain success in their corporate, judicial and academic realities, their perceived and experienced reality adapts to one solely about *Power and Ego*. This then remains the centre of attraction for such kinds, and one that draws its minority into very certain cooperative concentrations; ones that aim to dominate and sustain.

Consequently, we can see how most of those who attain governmental positions are ones with law degrees; how most forms of conflict are caused by those with economic interests; and how the contents of the minds of people around which they educate and formulate their opinions, are formatted by academia.

Chapter 8
THE PERCEIVED REALITY OF MAN, PART III
TRUTH AND ITS INEVITABLE NEMESIS CALLED HOPE

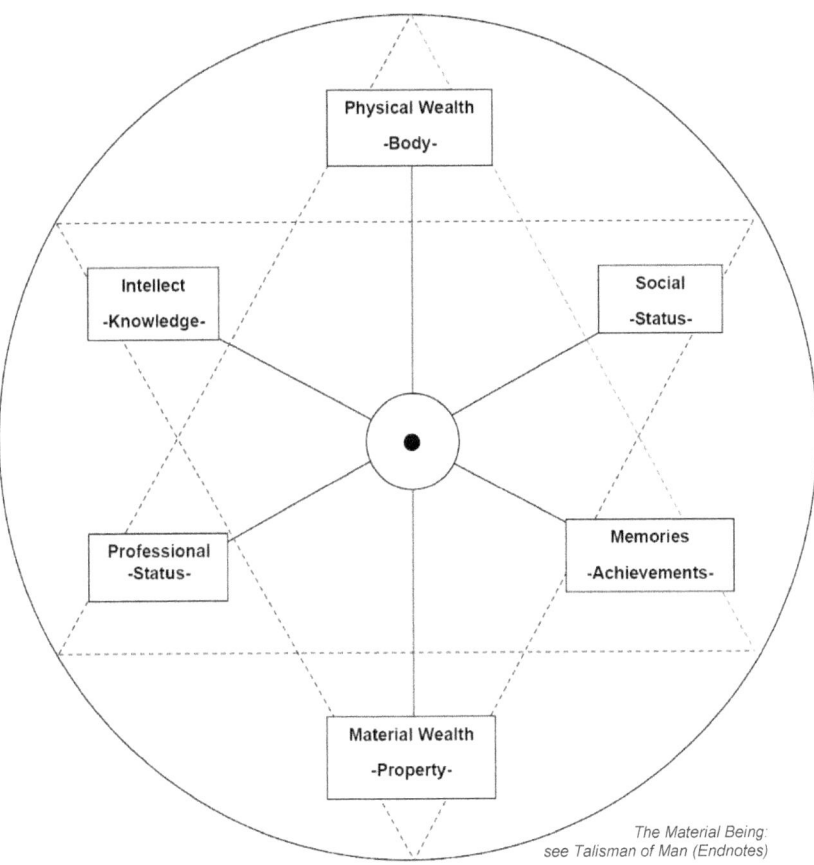

The Material Being:
see Talisman of Man (Endnotes)

**The relentless search for Absolute Truth is the Seekers nemesis,
as he wishes for that which cannot be found.
Whenever he stumbles upon it, and sees what he has,
he wants to protect it, display it, and direct it to dispel the lie.**

**But Truth is like water, it must flow and be left untendered,
as once it is contained and displayed, it soon becomes stale
and somehow with Time, it ceases to be noticed or pure.**

**Like water it must be left to soak into soil, or absorbed by the Sun,
from where it can cool or quench the thirst of the desperate man,
who experienced the search, and earned its discovery.**

The Necessity of Falsehood

When we investigate the understanding of Truth – by which we mean 'Truth as a substance' and not 'the truth that is spoken' – it becomes clear that Truth cannot exist, or has no meaning, without the simultaneous existence, in presence or possibility, of Falsehood. This should be obvious to most. What is not as obvious is that the societal structures of the contemporary man cannot exist for very long without the existent presence of this duality. When, for example, a society, city, army, club, hospital, school or other is established, its purpose must be continuously challenged for it to remain functional. If this challenge is not allowed then such entities, being mechanical in their nature, will automatically begin to use their unchecked status to gravitate towards complacency, abuse and decline.

To uncover Truth by exposing the lie is by all standards the correct thing to do provided, however, Falsehood is eliminated consciously. If one believed it necessary to do so *at any and all cost*, then one would have to consider that doing so could have exacerbating consequences. In part this would be because erasing a lie artificially or by the use of force, simply replaces one form of Falsehood with another, by which ends one then justifies the means. But this is merely one of the unintended consequences of eradicating Falsehood – a far greater one would be its effect on the individual Essential Self.

To understand this, we must consider that very few people ever question the reality of their Truth, unless it is unexpectedly, and unavoidably challenged. *If, for example, a person does not know that he exists within an environment that is false, then finding out can be harmful to him but, in time, he can be forgiven. In contrast to this, if he is knowingly active within an environment that is false then, when he is unavoidably faced with the Truth, then this can be catastrophic to him from many a perspective.* The gravity of this 'catastrophe' is quite real, but, for emphasis and the sake of clarity, we will expand on it by using a little imagination:

Imagine that you were to be able to 'unblock' your mind and open it to the minds of others. From here you are now able to see every thought, intention, desire, fear and feeling they carried behind the façade that is their facial and bodily exterior. Naturally all these ones, in turn, would also be able to see your mind. Such a state, of being able to read each other's minds would, for example, remove the need for young men and women to follow a traditional and gradual courtship, as each would already know, at that specific moment in time, what the other wanted or sought, and what such a one was willing to give up for it. The act of 'match making' would, in other words, be based on the immediate state of affairs, and not on what would, over Time, transform and emerge through a measure of learning through play, work, suffering and sacrifice. Most successful couples will testify that, besides 'love', or as better termed 'compassion and consideration', any lasting relationship between a man and a woman, also has to undergo a certain process of maturation, for which Time and friction are some of its ingredients. Without this, their generally incompatible masculine and feminine states would simply not find the miraculous magic required to pass the so-called 'honeymoon phase'. Their connection would likely be absent of the depth from which they both wished to understand the warmth of receiving and giving, and the resilience that is at times essential for this.

Besides the applicable tolerance and acceptance that can only grow with Time, the merger between such opposites requires growing that psychic link, from which integration with higher dimensions is also possible. It is not Truth itself that does this, but rather the process of uncovering and discovering Truth – in the self and the other.

As another example, one may see how such a state of mind-reading and the consequent all-knowing, would remove the competitiveness between people. This may be deemed a good thing from a surface perspective, but it is the very ability to compete that germinates the strong intentions and willingness to learn, which in turn, forms the resolute pioneers and true leaders of healthy collectives. It also makes room for the equally necessary unquestioning and comfortable 'docility' of the non-competitive worker classes that society needs to produce the goods[1]. Most importantly, in all of these categories, the recognition of one's applicable place in society stimulates and enhances their attention towards self-awareness.

Naturally, even if these views were fully understood, it would still mean that any contemporary view on 'the necessity of Falsehood' would find itself debated. However, it is within the very existence of such a debater and the debate, that thoughts and opinions can be manifested, weighed and examined for their authenticity. From this, the feeling or emotion based opinion can then be challenged by being physically observed, or intellectually tested. We would further observe how, when Truth was determined in a particular order, that such an order would automatically lead to the stimulation of particular and new concepts of thought. We would therefore be able to observe the growth of our inner strength and wisdom, within our private and controlled mind, especially when our external world is cloaked by a façade of falsehood in varying degrees. It is even within the wonder and challenge of a bizarre contemplation such as this, that intelligence is germinated and fed.

Ultimately, the process of uncovering Truth can be seen as corresponding to numerous 'Aha!' moments, such as our occasional conscious awakening to self-realization. We often do not know when we have fallen asleep, gone astray or lost track with reality, until the moment when we suddenly awaken. It is, however, within that momentary impulse of awakening, realization, or

---

[1] Note that AI driven technology may erase the need for these, but not their presence.

illumination, that the presence of our creative self or essence can be experienced. Then, the more often this is practiced and observed, the higher the growth. The caveat here of course is that sleep, distraction or falsehood must not be sought intentionally, as this could be akin to seeking and awakening the attention of undesired influences.

Either way, for a person's inner growth to occur, a measure of friction is necessary. This entails the existence but not the practice, of Falsehood. As for the presence of chance, as in whether or not one awakens to Truth and through this the reality of the conscious self, it is the same.

The Perceived as Necessary 'Absence of Truth', in the Collectives of Man

When we look for the element of Truth in the world's geopolitical spheres, we note that its absence is not only accepted as natural, by many it is considered as set protocol and even necessary. This is because any of the corporate and institutionalized collectives of man, although initially established to serve the individual, soon after their establishment begin to give priority to the survival, enhancement and empowerment of themselves. This occurs when forces within it have become conscious of itself and its existence *as an entity*. This trend is usually very subtle at first, because often the initial intentions of its creators are good, but also, when it is in its still vulnerable infancy, it cannot risk to expose its inner agenda. After all, an aware collective, which includes those it serves and those who serve it, would otherwise and likely opt to limit, disband and disperse its institutionalised powers. To such an entity, the possibility of such exposure and disbandment is akin to Death, and like any creature that can, it begins to disguise its nature and intent by using forms of camouflage. In many cases it does so by creating a façade that appears harmless, useful and of value. All forms of camouflage are, of course, forms of Falsehood, because they hide the underlying vulnerability or intention. Furthermore, like any organism that exists under threat, they will persevere with their forms of camouflage, *at least until they are powerful and influential enough to apply other means.*

Consequently, the trusting but unaware hosts of these entities, including most of the contemporary citizenry, will tolerate trends and obtain products that do not serve them, or which they do not need. In addition, they will unquestioningly, but hopefully or dutifully, pay exorbitant fees and taxes, follow meaningless rules, and respond to calls for war. And all this from leaders who they factually know to be devious and corrupt! It is even worse when we see how the state of mass-psychosis is purposely ignored and even defended when it is pointed out how they are indoctrinated by puppeteers in suits on illuminated platforms, or scantily clad, husky voiced women.

However, all that said, whatever this dual trend is, it is 'what it is' and how it has always been. As there must be a natural order and balance to all things, any effort towards the non-acceptance of this phenomenon, will always represent an amount of wasted energy. When, for example, we attempt to alter the reality of another person by introducing an unsolicited Truth into his or her mind, regardless of our intention, then there will, by the law of Great Nature, always be forces that resist such an external manipulation. In the same way, when an entity of Falsehood is forcefully uprooted, and not voluntarily relinquished, then its roots will persist and with Time, seek to create new tentacles. In other words; when the dark content of an unawakened person's psyche is suddenly illuminated, the resultant void that this creates in his or her mind, will almost instantly be filled (or re-captured) by other externally introduced beliefs. Consider, for example, a prisoner who was abused and tormented by one of his guards. When he is eventually rescued, he is quite easily convinced by his rescuers, that the whole prison and all the guards were evil. This is quite natural, and we can even observe this kind of behaviour among pets or other domesticated animals such as horses and certain farm animals. We see how an animal behaves differently toward people of another gender, colour or age group. Thus, if we are not aware of this effect on our mind, then the acceptance of any proffered Falsehood, which appears less complicated then the Truth it hides, occurs automatically.

As with all things though, Falsehood exists in degrees. In addition, it is often sugar-coated with a sufficient percentage of Truth and sentiment, resulting in many being willing to overlook the inherent flaws; even though such flaws often carry the seed of much larger flaws. However, the trusting citizen is conditioned from childhood to seek strength in unity and to follow the show of power; especially if it is decorated with flags, symbols and things that are uniform. That this behaviour inevitably leads to forms of enslavement within an authoritarian environment is certain, but it is equally certain that these systems are inherently unsustainable. Chaos always follows Order, and the dissolution by some form or other will inevitably follow these façades of Falsehood. This may take centuries or even millennia to occur though, and depending on the degree, it could come at great cost.

To the historian, the cycles of rising and falling states and empires are generally recorded as normal transitional phases, that are inevitably followed by consecutive ones, in some form or other. In the case of an established civilization this may appear as catastrophic, as so much of what was gained at great cost over centuries is lost forever. But then, an expanded civilization is not a natural but an artificial construct. For it to form, grow and thrive in its creativity, it requires the harmonious existence of integral collectives; entities that will and must in principle compete and differ in their make-up or function, so that each can contribute in its own uniqueness. Hence, unless the citizens of a civilization are all equally sincere, awakened and aware, the presence and role of Falsehood in its construct and continued maintenance, is unavoidable.

In the case of most body-corporates, be they government or private entities, we can see how they are comparable in their make-up to a body. We can compare the different types of cells and organs with the spread of people with differing functions, including the simple peasant the wealthy merchant, the docile follower, the intellectual guide, and the resolute pioneer. As an organism, the only real difference is that the lifeless state of these body-corporates is re-enacted by artificial means – meaning by something that is not real, and thus false. In their day to day functionality, they are also similar. We see how the finding of food or fuel for growth occurs through an exchange between organisms or entities that are different. In a natural environment, the balance of this process is maintained by simply letting the exchange of things be; where demand stimulates supply, and an excessive demand leads to a natural thinning of the herd. In a similar vein, we see how the creation of new organisms occurs on the fringes of differing entities, especially where the full spectrum of exchange between differing influences takes place. This is evident in all bodies and at all levels of humanity, and in the collectives of man it is most evident in its most natural form in places like harbours, river crossings and mountain passes.

We next see how the contemporary person has a content-programmed and pattern-conditioned brain that reacts mechanically to stimuli. It is from this that he or she determines what to think, say or do, from one moment to the next. In most forms of government and body-corporates, it is the same in the form of the career politician or executive. Like the contemporary thinking brain, when it comes to an understanding of their mechanical and destructive or uncreative nature, these ones *do not know but think they do*. However, as they are ambitious, they will do whatever is necessary to sustain their position. As a result, Truth to them matters very little.

In the case of governing-entities, it is obvious that there will always be systems or entities that seek to rule over the mostly contemporary people, or where the masses seek an entity to rule over them. If, for example, we compare so-called democratic systems of state, republic or federation, with those of monarchy, we may note a lesser degree of Falsehood among the latter. That is merely because, in a monarchy, every now and then a wise and strong son or daughter would be enthroned! The system of rule-by-royals however, is represented by an entity of its own, and often with their own histories. However, as these were usually limited to a particular nation or geographic region, so-called bad kings were frequently overthrown by an unhappy populace, the military, or by an ambitious next-in-line. As a result, there are still several bloodlines remaining today, and although they seemingly perform only ceremonial and societal roles, if we observe their actions and occult manners carefully, we can see the darker entity they ultimately serve as well. As a result, they will patiently but purposely and relentlessly preserve their line, from generation to generation. Perhaps this is because their inexorable time to rule will return, but for this to occur, the collapse of the preceding systems to which they are allied must take place. All such systems of governance, in other words, are the resultant effects of crumbling façades of Falsehood that differ by degree.

Oftentimes the stimulation of changes across these cycles, such as those from systems of democracy to those of despots, is the very role of certain ancient and deeply rooted entities. There are those who observe quietly, from positions that remain unaffected by the turn of events. Steering things from within their invisible and untouchable shadows, they believe their system of absolute control over humanity is necessary, and consequently, they will stimulate the very divisions that these cycles require. Therefore, the concept of Truth to them has an entirely different meaning, and one that few contemporaries and even enlightened sages will ever understand. As a result, the very idea of their existence goes mostly unnoticed, and even most rulers remain unaware of the strings that govern them.

Hence an understanding and acceptance of the cyclic phenomena of volatility, that is caused by the intentional application of Falsehood, is one that can greatly assist the Seeker. For this, however, he or she must be conscious and observant of its effects from a wider or higher dimensional perspective, and remain so without getting caught up in the inevitability of the rise and fall of such cycles, and its painful consequences. If the presence of Falsehood within the perception of the one, two, and three-dimensional realities can be taken into account, *and accepted as a necessary part of the illusory whole,* then its ultimate non-existent and irrelevant state becomes evident. This is because, with the awareness of these events they cease to exist as a substance. To envision this is relatively tough and does require an open but observing mind, combined with a strong but sincere intention.

The Necessity of Hope

In a reality where Falsehood is deemed necessary, the existence of Hope will reign alongside it. The *problematic concept* of Hope is the one that belongs to that part of man which says 'I' or 'I AM'; this being his false personality or ego. Hope is considered as *conceptual* because it always involves something that has not yet occurred. This is *problematic* as by linking such Hope to an outcome, man submits himself to the pessimistic possibility that it may also not happen. Hope therefore, is considered a one- or two dimensional feature, that is rooted in the contemporary man's Emotional Center.

To most contemporary persons, the sustaining of such emotion-based feelings is considered as their sovereign right, or their way of remaining 'positive under difficult circumstances'. While an element of truth and purpose resides here, it is also a path that inevitably leads to disillusionment, because such Hope is ill-founded. In addition, once one has gone a distance down that 'hopeful' path, it becomes complicated if not impossible to find unreserved acceptance in whatever the outcome is, as it also gives rise to Doubt. This would sum up why the concept of Hope is best avoided, except for the fact that, as with all things in the created Cosmos, nothing is ever random and everything has a purpose. This view must therefore make room for the expression called Hope. Ultimately all things in all realities are either supported or fed by one thing or another, or they act as a support or form of food for another – the only question therefore is, where Hope fits.

It can thus be considered that Hope does serve a purpose, but only as an interim state. It can for example, be observed as the stepping stone or threshold from one state of being to another. One may consider how Hope for the well-being of a child will remind the parent of those things he or she needs to remain cautious and alert for. The same can be said for the sailor who goes to sea and hopes for favourable weather. Hope reminds him that the alternative may also happen and thus, it prepares him whilst the flickering presence of Hope will nevertheless ensure he keeps a wary eye on conditions. These are not trifling things as it is within the reality of Hope that such awareness can be triggered, and which very trigger becomes the germinating agent for more conscious doing and being. Hope can therefore also be seen as a one- or two-dimensional form of faith.

Through the observation of the effects of Hope the contemporary man can become aware of the presence of a higher form of Truth. It is one that consequently guides him to the realization of an expanded awareness, the kind that can also be referred to as a Higher Dimension.

As such, he can come to realize that, to enter this new or higher dimensional state of awareness, a certain threshold of letting-go of things needs to be crossed. This is a scary concept as it entails entering what appears to be a void, an unknown path that requires a motivating sense of trust or faith in the form of Hope. Even if they realize that such faith or Hope may well be ill-founded, when the conditions and outlooks are dire, it becomes the elixir that enables them to take the proverbial leap of faith. However, Faith and Hope will diverge when the outcome is not favourable or as expected; where Faith that is sincere carries a certain a level of acceptance, Hope will lead to disillusionment.

The concept of Hope therefore, like all such fear-based emotions, is entirely one-dimensional. It manifests a non-existent and thus illusory reality, where the outcome is either one or the other; one being in favour, and the other not. Combined with these one-dimensional options, the hopeful one usually finds – as is typical in the contemporary world – a two-dimensional 'carrot or stick' scenario; these being picture-like impressions of what the feared or hoped-for outcome could be.

In line with Hope and Faith, we must also consider man's inevitable prospect of Death. The reality of Death to most is overshadowed by their Hope in the concept of an afterlife or Heaven of sort, within which the hopeful and faithful find their own medium of peace. As examples:

- Consider the Technocrat who lives a physically unchallenging existence of pushing buttons. Having reached the center of his known technocratic realm, he will reside on the Hope that before his end, he may be able to transfer his conscious self, or at least the product of his mind, onto a machine.

- Consider the followers of a religion's dogma, and whose prayers reside on Hope. As long as they make amends, confess, or ask for forgiveness, and perhaps leave a stipend to their religion, in the Hope that they will find favour in the eyes of God.

- Consider the animist peasant, nomad and gypsy, whose lives are ones of hardship or servitude, yet who often follow the protocol of courtesy and decency as is their custom, which in turn is based on their subconscious Hope for its harmonious return.

- Consider those who believe that their life on Earth is all there is and Death a finality, but who Hope their energy is not lost. In this, they Hope for a quick and painless end, and for their children to learn from their passage, more than they knew.

In closing we can see how Life and its suffering remain fearful concepts to most of us. However, it is even more so for the contemporary person who is identified with his or her unknown outcome. Without the presence of Hope in them – whether this is based on faith, fear or desire – it is unlikely that the one and two-dimensionally orientated ones would be able to exist effectively or productively and relatively harmoniously. Why, for example, would one even bother to *consciously* have children if one knew the constant anguish their existence and wellbeing would cause in one's life, the risk of their lives not being happy ones, or the consequences of losing them? After all, it is a conditioned intellect-based Thinking Center that enables them to imagine disastrous odds and outcomes, but it is the existence of Hope that overrides this.

The nature of the one and two-dimensional contemporary person's reality limits them in how they think, speak, see and undertake things. As such the majority of people remain unaware of their existent higher dimensional potential, and with that, the need to find a truthful balance within the complexity of their centers. After all, balance is an integral part of the Cosmos, which naturally includes that of Great Nature. Within this, the contemporary man encompasses the larger part of humanity; and for their reality to remain existent and fruitful, it must by necessity contain the nemesis of Truth called Hope.

Chapter 9
THE PERCEIVED REALITY OF MAN, PART IV
THE ILLUSION OF POLITICAL CORRECTNESS AND EQUALITY

The Rotating Snakes Illusion of Akiyoshi Kitaoka

To understand the workings of the Mind, when it wishes
to process something New, we must acknowledge that:

1. Everything is absolutely connected with Everything else,
which means that nothing new or old is ever random,
and every other thing, event and situation has a purpose.

2. For doors to new liberties to be opened,
the existing ones must first be known and observed,
and only then be consciously and willingly allowed to close.

3. For everything that is offered and accepted,
something else is given up.

There is therefore no such thing
as the unaccountable accumulation of anything.

The Reason and Logic of Absurdity

The idea or subject that we refer to as *Equality* is likely rooted in a higher dimensional thought. However, in the duality of the three-dimensional world of logic, with a limited two-dimensional perspective and the one-dimensional way of understanding, this is absurd in that it cannot be realised. Just as 'tall' cannot be realized without 'short', or 'here' without 'there', a 'have' can only exist if there is a 'have not'; although the intention appears noble, a reality where Equality is believed to be possible would comprise of a delusion within an illusion.

In the same vein, the concept of *Political Correctness*, as its name infers, belongs to the political arena. It is an invention that was designed to act as a façade behind which normal etiquette and good manners can hide. Its name thus insinuates what is evidently sincere and true, must now come second. The cunning architects of Political Correctness usually build their scheme atop the feelings and emotions of easily identifiable concepts. These are usually particular groups of people with their particular ways or idiosyncrasies, with feelings that are then actively stimulated by these charlatans. In addition, beside what these so-called 'architects of society' determine is Politically Correct, their design usually includes a plan whereby in Time, their *Politically Correct ways* become their tools of manipulation, by writing them into law.

Both the concepts of Political Correctness and Equality are therefore nothing but tools that exploit the inherent correctness that dominates the faithful contemporary people. With the goal being the creation of a force that motivates or sways the mindsets of people, these concepts are usually designed like machines that are fuelled by 'envy', that highly volatile substance; the kind that is germinated among people who have less of something then others. The substance used for the exploitation of these concepts is not just race, sex, religion or wealth, as is contemporarily and naively understood, but also around concepts such as popularity, intelligence, qualifications and even the ownership of things that may or may not have been meritoriously earned. Some people can easily be made to believe that it is wrong for another to be wealthy, even though such ones worked hard and smart for every penny, while these critics played and slept. To others inequality will even include simplistic things, like good looks and athletic abilities; realities where everyone is entitled to be a 'hero'.

To review the phenomena of mass-psychosis that these concepts often lead to, it helps if we review some typical examples:

A Review of Contemporary Campaigns: The End of Poverty

The fight against poverty is a truly noble campaign, and one that has inspired an untold many. Upon closer examination of *'why'* this is so, we note how these campaigns are often undertaken for reasons that differ, by different groups of people, and often for differing reasons within the same group.

We note, for example, how many of the End of Poverty campaigns are staffed by middle and worker class mothers and seniors, who then assist social workers and religious groups. The larger source of funding for these programs is usually private, and from both the worker and middle classes. There are of course wealthy philanthropists or companies who provide support for reasons of their own, which may include legacy, tax write-offs and political favour.

Either way, funding is ultimately a necessary component, and although it mitigates, seldom does it provide the solution. Unless such supporting groups or individuals are found shoulder-to-shoulder with those they see in need, and assist them in developing their own ways out of their sorry state, those receiving such generosity seldom find that it helps to achieve their independence.

Oddly enough, these support programs often tend to create their own purpose. We note, for example, how they often draw more persons into their dependency rather than cause the number of dependants to decline. In addition, for some the knowledge that there are such 'official' programs within their community, automatically stimulates an enhancement of their natural laziness, by which they will feel even less motivated to assist.

A Review of Contemporary Campaigns: The End of Illiteracy

Like all forms of education, ending illiteracy is a noble campaign that has the best of intentions at heart; at least from the perspective of a contemporary or one and two-dimensional orientation. However, the vast volume and diversity of reading and writing material produced and absorbed is valued more by the content-matter or its entertainment, than *the actual ability to communicate*.

The recording and transmission of information and ideas, by enhancing the ability to read and write, enhances knowledge and possibly understanding. However, the content aside, *how* the information is delivered often determines how it is absorbed and used. We may consider the Holy Bible or the Holy Koran for example, and see how their words have, across centuries and into the present, been re-interpreted and re-written to suit a multitude of differing agendas. The same trend of mind-influencing is observed in commerce, politics and societal agendas. Literacy is therefore a double-edged sword, that is wielded best by those who understand its power, and who are most adapted to it.

Some will promote literacy by saying that it enables people to educate themselves, and that this ability is subject to free will. While there is naturally an element of truth in this, what is not often considered is that there are side effects of having literacy without knowing how to use it. We can see how few, who can read, ever consider *why* they are reading what they are reading. This does not refer to their personal taste for the subject-matter that they choose to read, but *why* it is that it stimulates their 'likes', and *how* it can affect their mind. When we observe how all things, when left unattended, will devolve from their current state to a lower and less complex one, we may consider that the same occurs with the presence of literacy. This is because literacy, when unaffected by a higher form of guidance or mentorship, predominantly affects the reader's process and content of thought. Consider the impact of comic books and smut magazines on the development of an adolescent mind! Even newspapers and other propagandist material contribute to both the corruption and the fragmentation of common sense, the intelligence that comes natural to man. Few are ever aware how the words and sentences the contemporary mind so innocently absorb, were designed to insert and influence their thoughts and feelings, which then unconsciously, stimulate or enhance certain actions.

Whether it is fiction or non-fiction, historical, biographical or factual, the majority of content that is written aims to insert into the reader's mind, the seeds of interest that will germinate a support of its kind. Like we see on the next generation of literacy – the Internet – we see how news and fiction draw the reader to become intrigued and desirous for more of the same. Even the reading of substantial material will likely stimulate the reader to engage his mind and manner accordingly, regardless of whether this is philosophy or spirituality, science or nature, or history and societal structures. We see that even the exchange of letters and texting fall prey to this. There is nothing necessarily wrong with this of course, but very few are ever aware of these effects.

We may next note how, prior to the industry of printing and the commerce of information distribution, the information an individual sought and obtained, was that which was selectively relevant to his or her particular mind – and then treasured as such. Consequently, the average person's *ability to memorize* the details of who they were, who their kin and clan were, their history, stories, business and concerns, was vast. If this is compared with the intelligence behind the literate minds of today, most of which are hopelessly immersed in irrelevant information, we see how the average intelligence, or mind of old, was less complex. As such it can be noted that a less complex and busy mind is considerably more capable to quiet its thinking patterns and focus inward to sense the higher intuitive influences.

The pursuit of literacy at an early age, although considered as giving the little ones an edge, has considerable developmental side-effects[1]. After learning to

---

[1] Children typically start learning to read and write between the ages of 4 and 6, but the exact age can vary depending on the child and their development. Often, the pressure placed upon the formative child who learns best through play, by an overly ambitious parent, can be traumatic and detrimental to its overall balanced development.

speak, the art of communication is often, almost immediately, followed up with teaching the child to read and write. Where this has its value, it is the reverse order of what was taught in the traditional schools, where the art of communication began with story-telling, and the ability to listen. It was not just about hearing but of focused listening, observing the speaker and his or her body language, and then remembering exactly what was said, in what sequence and where the emphasis was. This way the details would better merge with the child's processing thinking-brain, within which it could intuitively merge and collaborate the information[1]. When, comparatively speaking, one considers the daily volume of written detail that the average literate mind is made to read, it seems miraculous that it maintains a certain form of sanity. Perhaps the phenomena of *mass-psychosis*, when observed among groups of similar literacy educated people, who were exposed to the same written content, can be explained in this.

Naturally, this is not to imply that literacy is a contributary factor to Chaos! In the so-called modern world it is of course necessary and therefore natural to be able to read and count. It is however, also a tool that is misused by those who serve Chaos. Consider, for example, the teachers who insist on reading material for young minds that follow certain rule-based narratives, or the controllers of news distributors who select and adjust the news-content to align the audience along certain ideologies.

We can see the consequence of such when the newly formatted young mind identifies with being literate as able to inform itself; therewith accepting the content the mind receives by it as its 'reality'. This becomes a problem when such a potentially altered reality is prioritized over the natural and actual experiential reality, one that was made manifest through play, practice, and the development of common sense. We can further see how the phenomenon of a spoon-fed reality mutated from reading material to the shaping of realities through sources that dilute the need for literacy, such as those of social media and entertainment.

A Review of Contemporary Campaigns: The End of Sadness

There are many campaigns that aim at improving the lot or dilemma of people. These are usually stimulated by a sincere but fantasized belief in the impossible; such as the pursuit of 'equality'. Of all campaigns, such as those related to those of poverty and illiteracy mentioned above, the most dominant is one that believes that there should be no 'losers'. There is a sense of correctness and nobility at the root of all these views but, instead of eradicating unfair and unnecessary competitiveness that enhance the un-

---

[1] Of interest perhaps is the Indian guru Ramana Maharshi, who believed he became enlightened at 16 years (in 1896), **because** he was uneducated. He often discouraged over-reliance on written scriptural knowledge in favor of direct *inner* inquiry: "Who am I?"

deserved loss, some still believe they can actually create an environment where there are only winners.

This belief resides on the perspective that a winner is one who is happy. Hence it is thought, if one can impose happiness, then by proxy one creates winners. This bases itself on the assumption that happiness can be stimulated or created externally, outside of the self, such as through forms of affluence. As a simplified example one may see this tendency with the distribution of toys to children for no particular reason and outside celebrations such as their birthdays or Christmas. Regardless of how one feels about this, what cannot be denied is that it dilutes the effects of receiving gifts. This is generally not realized by those who are kind-hearted but perhaps somewhat ignorant, and who simply sought to bring them 'happiness'. Unfortunately, often such unsolicited acts of generosity do not serve the recipient and only the benefactor, or those who seek to create altruist impressions.

Even though there is no link between affluence and happiness, we know that the concept of winning is addictive. Winning is often seen as an 'achievement' that makes one better, more popular and thus happier. Those who already have great wealth will likely know that this is illusory, but instead believe that wealth will end their sadness, even when they repeatedly experience that it does not.

The Necessity of Conscious Giving and Receiving

The existence of unhappiness in any reality can be reviewed from many angles. Ultimately, however, its eradication can only come from within and not without such as, for example, by offering unsolicited advice, assistance or gifts. Hence, if we wish to be generous to an unhappy one, then the correct gift would have to be one that was consciously considered along lines of sincerity and necessity. If this is observed, it would be more likely that a benefaction is experienced as a gift, if it asks for no return, acknowledgement or perhaps even the knowledge that such a gift was received. The ultimate gift being one where the recipient believes it was attained by his or her own actions.

Thus, when we observe the gift from the recipient's side, we may find that a gift should not have to be repaid with a gesture or a return gift as this then, by proxy, annuls its benefaction as a 'gift' – even though not doing so is considered among most as impolite and even rude.

The energy exchanged in the act of giving and receiving is therefore not lie in the content but in the sincerity present and consciousness applied. It may then even be noted that a kind of energy emerges that is both heartwarming and expanding. We can thus conclude that in the process of a conscious exchange, humanity finds its raw source of purpose. If the exchange is done intentionally, selflessly and compassionately, veritable beauty is observed and attained, of the kind that is eternal.

Equality within a Politically Correct System of Belief

The highly politicized emphasis on *sovereignty through democracy* is one where, at the end of some or other 'righteous struggle', a newly elected government ousts its predecessor. In this, the head of the newly elected authority then reigns and, regardless of whether this reign or resultant system was implemented by vote or force, it traditionally begins to lose popular favour within months. Hence, to strengthen its position it automatically takes measures to sustain its rule. This usually begins through the gradual mutation from truth to propaganda, which it then justifies as being in the best interest of a mostly ignorant public. Regardless of the cunning or noble intentions behind any such measures, the continuation of centralized forms of power are, in time, often corrupt and followed by a controlled transition of sort. The *reason and logic* behind the morals of most forms of sovereign or democratic power, will therefore be conceptual and relative to what it believes will best support its system of rule.

Some of this customised *reason and logic* will be designed to force, on the contemporary mind, preferred systems of belief. Among these will be the acceptance of artificial forms of interference on the otherwise *naturally occurring* order of things. These forms of interference would not reveal their often disastrous consequences which, in turn, are usually explained afterward as being regrettable but unavoidable, or that things would have been worse if nothing was done.

We can consider the *'Eradication of Poverty'* for example. The existence of poverty is always regrettable, but in any collective of people or civilization there will always be those who, for different reasons, are better off than others. This will remain so, unless the local community that surrounds such poverty embraces it, and takes effective steps to rectify it. Once a political authority enters the fray to rectify this, instead of alleviating such poverty, its mechanism will be authoritarian in nature and cause an increase in dependency on the state. Through this socialist-like mechanism, any attempt at eradicating poverty, such as the artificial insertion of affluence, disregards the complacency that accompanies such dependency. The larger consequence of such state enforced political correctness is that it creates docile attitudes and sterile minds, and an ever increasing dependency.

While care for the poor and the sick may *never* be denied, a form of accountability must still be determined. But such accountability would have to be at a person's local or regional level, where the input of consideration is with locally oriented intelligence. In such an environment, the balance between 'live-and-let-live' and 'compassion-and-consideration' will be more inclined to evolve *naturally.*

In Conclusion

In days of old, kings and emperors convinced their people that they were ordained by the gods. At present this has only marginally changed. Many political systems have convinced their mostly docile followers that their system or their people are exceptional, divinely appointed or chosen by God. Thus, 'political correctness' and its pursuit for so-called 'equality' is largely fuelled by the concept of illusory power.

Chapter 10
UNDERSTANDING THE DAEMON, PART I
THE SPIRITUAL POSSESSION[1]
OF THE UNCONSCIOUS MAN

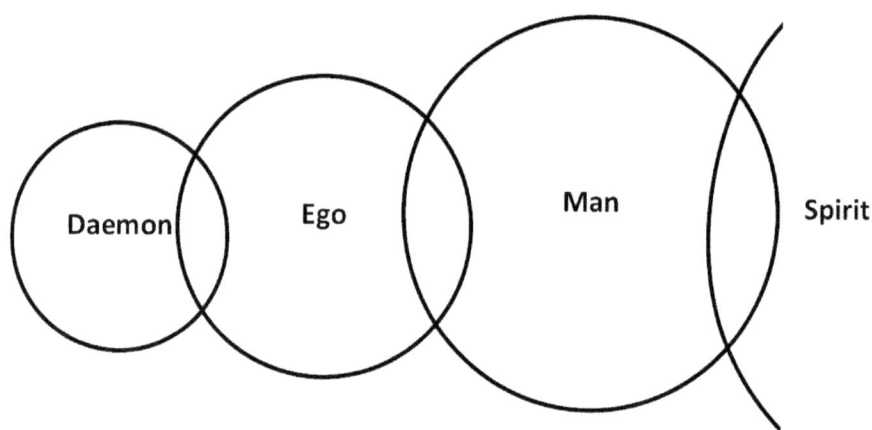

The Spirit that possesses cannot be avoided.
To try to suppress it or isolate it,
transcend above it or hide from it,
or physically enclose and entomb it,
will not work.

Its paradoxical state resides in our understanding,
that its non-existence must first be made manifest.
It is therefore necessary,
to know it exists.

Power Corrupts, and Absolute Power Corrupts Absolutely

Although this phrase was coined by an English Lord in the 19th century, the phenomena itself is as old as the ego of man. It is therefore no accident or surprise that most countries that encode forms of election-based democracy within their constitution, limit the term for their leaders to four or five years.

---

[1] FYI: When capitalized the Possession refers to the name of a phenomenon of entities. When reference is made to *a* possession, it refers to a particular one, synonymous to a demonic entity, of which there are many different kinds. Like people, they are as divided as species of bacteria or viruses, and in comparison with these, *the Possession* would describe an Infection, and *a possession* a particular kind.

In most cases they can be re-elected, but then only once and the reason for this is simple; it is to protect such a leader from himself. The infectious tendency to not want to relinquish control has been proven evident for virtually every emperor, dictator, despot or royal, and even with the most charismatic 'hero of the people', whose totalitarian reign exceeded about twelve years. It was after this period that without fail, they would begin to suffer forms of belief that ranged from paranoia to the vanity of apotheosis, and from when their behaviour became increasingly erratic, psychotic and brutal.

In general, the goodwill and best intentions of all leaders, elected or appointed, will have an 'expiry date' by which they will give up, lose or change these. For example, a leader of a nation may publicly notice and deplore the suffering or wrongful death of a single person. But then the same leader will, after a while, consider the displacement, suffering or deaths of tens of thousands or even millions, as statistical or unfortunate, but likely unavoidable and probably necessary.

The same is observed with the time it takes for a powerful leader to become corrupt. Some may argue that he or she has no option but to choose between 'the carrot or the stick' or 'the gold or the bullet', but then these are usually parties with special-interests. For many of these leaders, these hard choice options are superfluous, for as soon after they attain absolute power, their perception of themselves and their worth changes.

In fact, the amount of Time it generally takes for leaders to become corrupt, primarily depends on three factors:
- The first being the level of self-awareness or self-observation practiced by him or her,
- The second being degree of attraction that the prize radiates, such as the amount and type of wealth that is offered, and
- The third and probably the most powerful factor being the amount of power such an appointed or elected leader has attained.

This 'corruption-mechanism' in man is therefore as natural and certain as the decay of all things. It is also the reason that constitutions for the governments of people are carefully written. What is not as clear to most is that this same phenomena also exists in collective entities such as organizations, corporations and authoritarian systems. As these ultimately feed off the same psychic energy, they grow exponentially more powerful as their numbers increase. But, as such entities are not dependent on any single individual life, they are able to transcend from generation to generation. As the heads of such large and influential entities inevitably identify themselves with this pseudo-transcendental state, and often attained their position by serving it unfalteringly, the loss of morality and increase in corruption in them will perpetuate.

The source of this phenomena does therefore not reside in the individual, regardless of his degree of psychopathy, but rather in the office, throne or title he or she holds. Because these are inanimate things, many a powerful leader aspires to embody them by using energetic symbols, magical objects and ceremonial practices, often in very specific and consecrated locations. *In these energies, places or objects, the one element that is and has always been wielded by its ruler, is its perceived and often idolized power, or god[1].*

Hence, the answer to the riddle 'why power corrupts' seems to lie between the Object (be it an office, magical wand, crystal, crucifix or law), and the Wielder (be it a sorcerer, priest or head-of-state). However, to the unbiased and impartial observer it will be evident that the destruction of both the Object and Wielder does not end the phenomena of abuse, which is why the history of war repeats itself, in perpetuity. As an example, one can consider the *perpetual effects* of an executive and his office, a king and his crown, or a general and his army; destroying the entity they serve, does not eradicate the effects. There is therefore clearly an ever present energy or power in between these Objects and their Wielders, which seeks to form the link between them. It is an energy or power that is aware of itself, intelligent and that, to ensure its continuation, captures the mind of the Wielder and causes him to enhance the Object in size, power and dominance. For this it seeks servants whose ambition exceeds their need to be sincere, and who are willing to pay for these positions, titles or talents, by waging their most important but least valued possession; their very souls.

The Manifestation of Entities

The existence of 'entities' in these writings relates to something that is energized by the psyches of living persons. These psyches are manifested by egos, which are an integral part of man. The ego, although seeded through the parents' genes and shaped by Great Nature in a combination of archetypes, usually takes on its dominant identification in the formative child, through external stimuli. It is when the ego begins to think for its own identification's sake, that an entity is formed. This occurs through a process of mechanical thought that acts like a snowball; when left unattended, it will grow in size, power and influence. As such it will, in time, seek to supplant control over the conscious mind of its host.

As an example of such an entity formation, consider a young person who seeks identification, and who pretends to be brave. Eventually he begins to believe he really is brave and begins to act as such – but not by doing anything that is brave. Instead, it is by dressing, walking and speaking as if he is brave, and he may even claim feats of bravery that are not his or are exaggerated. If

---

[1] For example, consider the use of a Sceptre, Crozier, Papal Ferula, Crown, or Seal.

he is convincing, in time others will look upon him as a role-model and may even appoint him as their leader – whom they now believe is fearless. That is until he is put to trial. While the truly brave one will accept his challenge, the one possessed by his ego will likely cower or send others in his stead – claiming that he is too valuable to be lost.

Hence, these manifestations will adopt whatever cover suits the host's environment, be it as a brave or a sorry one, a funny or a dangerous one, or one who is wise or who is informed and pretends to know everything. There are also those who wear their jewellery and fancy or fashionable clothes – fake or real – to display their status in the same fashion as that a scarred soldier wears his medals. This becomes a very real and addictive disease, especially in persons who are emotionally damaged, physically fragile, or those who lack the mental ability to care and are psycho- or sociopathic.

As the entity's manifested identification *mechanically* attains control over the thoughts and actions of its host, it *mentally* develops an awareness of itself, and consequently it *senses* its own fragile nature. Realizing that an exposure to Light in the form of Truth, will cause its instant non-existence, it desperately and insatiably seeks to hide or grow. In the case of growth, it can be in whatever form or by whatever manner, and with little consideration to the well-being of its host. This is because it sees its own 'death' as worse than its host's biological one. In fact, being a non-physical entity it will, in time, pursue ways to liberate itself from its biological and mortal host. When it learns that it can create its own manifested reality, it begins to adapt itself like a metaphysical virus, that spreads its possessing self into the psyches of others.

One will see how such an entity, identified as the head *or servant* of its order, state, organisation or corporation, will transmit itself by identifying candidates for its succession. Over time it will initiate through ceremony, reward or the promise of divine favour, moulding their minds to suit its needs. One observes the same in families and their traditions, where the concept of blood is 'made' thicker than water.

At present the greatest threat to biological life is therefore that of Artificial Intelligence. It is within this mechanism that many of these entities now pursue their immortality – even though the sensitivity of the Sun, which besides it affecting the mutation of biological life, also affects such mechanisms[1], but which are less likely to evolve *naturally*.

---

[1] For example, consider the effects of another Carrington Effect, which refers to the impact of a powerful solar storm in 1859. If a similar event occurred today, it could severely damage satellites, power grids, and communications infrastructure. If a larger event occurred, it could irreversibly destroy our civilization's electromagnetic grid.

Comparing the Conjurors of Darkness with the Bearers of Light

There have been many a practitioner of dark or 'Black Magic', such as the 16th century occultists John Dee and Edward Kelly, who diligently recorded their work of necromancing, including their methods and highly destructive results[1]. Many a conflict is said to have originated from this, as it seems through the attendance at their séances, many an ambitious European Royal and Noble was both advised and possessed. In the more recent 20th century, there were the likes of Alistair Crowley[2] and Jack Parsons[3], who similarly made a living by performing such séances – or what they believed was calling up of spirits. Their claim of these being the psychic apparitions of deceased persons was only partially accurate, as often it seemed, these apparitions would appear to be anything or anyone they needed to be. What or who they were identified as, was therefore often whatever their conjurer wanted them to be.

Where-as the conjurors of dark occultism and their followers have a similar aim, being the attainment of what they believe to be an Alchemic power of sort, attending to their arcane ceremonial practices for this purpose is the sheerest of stupidities. This is because the power of the possessing entity is only granted through the psyche of its conjuring host, and ultimately, on the terms of the entity.

If one tries to understand the dark practices, by correlating them with religious or spiritual work, one would find that it is in direct contrast to those who follow the Light of Truth, but only when this is in its purest form, such as those who follow sectarian and monastic orders. These ones are often able to adjust their focus to such an extent, that they will not even acknowledge the existence of these dark entities. Subsequently, they are more likely to explain the visible perversion and distortion as maladies of the mind, forms of psychosis, or of karmic and thus sinful origin.

Both the conjurors of Darkness and bearers of Light will therefore avoid direct contact with their opposites. They will not seek the other in any way, not even in a form of existential acknowledgement. The reason for this is that:

- *the Darkness knows that within the Light it is instantly displaced into non-existence, whereas,*
- *the Light knows it would have to consider that their God is not the only one, the All and Everything they had envisioned.*

---

[1] See: *John Dee and the empire of Angels, Enochian Magick and the Occult Roots of the Modern World* by Jason Luv.

[2] Aleister Crowley (1875–1947) was a British occultist, writer, and mystic, best known for founding the spiritual philosophy of Thelema. Calling himself "The Great Beast 666", he wrote extensively on magic (which he spelled "magick"), mysticism, and the occult.

[3] Jack Parsons (1914–1952) was an American occultist and follower of Crowley..

This of course does not suggest that these practices are similar – quite the contrary. The conjuror of Darkness descends dimensionally and morally, and sacrifices that space which is his sovereign mind and the seat-of-his-soul, to accommodate that which then possesses it. The bearer of Light on the other hand, although often ignorant of the duality of their physical reality, embraces the higher dimensional Light no less. Thus, instead of infecting him like the Possession does to its host, the Light carries and enhances its bearer, enabling him to transcend towards that which *is* the illuminating All and Everything.

The Possession's Disguises and Ways of Transmission

The topic of 'Possession' is in itself, a considerable subject that is difficult to explain to the contemporary world. This is largely due to it using only its analytical thinking brain to assess reality, which brain-mind cannot comprehend other dimensional influences. As a result, the metaphysical effects of the Possession are adopted with many innocent sounding descriptions. These include words like hype, duty, schizophrenia, paranoia, delusion, depression, as well as various fear-based states that are labelled with psychoanalytic terminology. In defence of being exposed for what it is, the Possession will create a series of contemporarily explainable maladies of the mind, usually with a diagnosis for which one can then obtain drugs or counselling. Many of these treatments however, especially the chemical ones, weaken the inner resolve and add dependency. In addition, the mechanical methods, such as counselling or isolation, are equally experimental, seeing that psychologists usually suggest a continuation of follow-ups. Ultimately, and by many a therapist's own acknowledgment, the various formulas of psychology usually supress some*thing*, which 'thing' continues to remain in existence deep in the host's inner-world. At least until such host is enabled to identify the cause, and oust it by himself.

Next to phenomena that are considered as 'maladies of the mind', there is a multitude of behaviours or identifications that are unusual and even unnatural, and yet, are accepted as normal in the contemporary life. These are, for example, a belief in what is an obvious lie, the acceptance of which is justified because it supposedly came from a place of authority, and often because it is deemed more convenient to accept than to question When, in time, these identifications are lost, outgrown, diluted or no longer valid – as they all ultimately and eventually fade – then the now disorientated hosts often fall into one of the various states of negativity. These are then equally supressed by similar chemical or mechanical means.

The Possession thus originates off the psychic energy that radiates from the subconscious thinking 'mind'. This *mind* is one that is not aware of the effects of its thinking self, as something separate from the thinking-self (like when I speak "my thoughts", by which I infer that although they are mine, I am not my thoughts). As such the Possession is still a product of the mechanical thinking-brain, which in turn is a product of the physical body, meaning that ultimately it belongs to Great Nature's living Earth. It is therefore not incorrect to mirror the Possession with physical maladies, such as something that is more like a metaphysical 'infection'. In this case, however, it would be better described as a virus; a metaphysical parasite that penetrates deep into the psyche of the sleeping and unaware person. Like the virus, once it takes root and is allowed to spread it is, without some small miracle, as incurable as it is untreatable, largely because *it has the ability to mutate at will.*

The Possession, however, is worse than the common and mutating virus. This becomes clear when we understand the method by which it spreads between hosts which, in the biological world, is through bodily fluids or air. Instead, the Possession spreads via that highest, most sensitive and least acknowledged part of our being, that of our *impressions*. Consequently, the Possession can mutate as instantly as one's impressions can change from one form to another. As there are a great many impressions attached to our various forms of identification, there are as many forms a possession can mutate into. These then 'hit' our senses instantly, and with varying degrees in impact on our psyche. To 'catch' such a transmission from another, requires a high level of awareness of our respective psyches. Most people go through their day-to-day activities mechanically, without any sense of self-observation, enter the influence of a Possession, and without realizing it, become caught up in its web of sensations. One need but consider the infectious actions of an anger or riotous crowd of fans or protestors. Consequently, in the world of idolatry, we see how the Possession-infected impression is transmitted from one hosting 'idol' onto another, and often via, or at the expense of, a number of its supporting subjects. If one has, for example, a bias towards a gender, ethnicity, religion, nationality, looks, or even colour of dress and charisma, then such impression-bias will weaken one's resilience to prevent one becoming infected by a Possession. As the majority of people entertain at least several of such bias or preferences, colossal amounts of time and resources are spent by powerful entities on attracting their attention, which are innocently categorized as 'marketing' and 'public relations'.

Either way, as a result of the very infectious nature of Possessions, some have been able to be around for centuries, perhaps even millennia. Existing unobserved due to their being unacknowledged, and yet rooted in a multitude of living subjects, many a Possession has grown to become a non-biological entity; observant, patient, capable, and cunning, it has become the veritable 'Frankenstein's Monster'.

Understanding the Possession's Nature

In trying to better understand the conceptual duality of humanity, and in particular its perception, we need to see and acknowledge the co-existence of both the physical and meta-physical 'beings-of-man'. These two beings exist on a parallel course, and as is typical with all things to do within man, they spiral around each other; interlinking at certain intervals that are unique to each person – akin to DNA's double helix.

Each leg of this conceptual double helix, that represent the physical and metaphysical being-of-man, is in itself equally dual, in that within itself it has an opposite. On the physical being, its divisions are the doing-man and the thinking-man, which are interlinked with feelings and emotions. The metaphysical being is divided between the psychic-man and the spiritual-man, which are interlinked by forms of self-observation and awareness. Where these latter two differ is that the psychic-man is made manifest as a causal-effect of his unconscious and mechanical ego; the spiritual-man is made manifest in the conscious and contemplative observer.

Where the psychic-man is therefore integral with his ego, or that which he identifies with and to which he says "I" or "I am"; the spiritual-man is formed through a merger between the sincere cognitive self and the omnipresent Divine Spirit. It is within this merger that he forms that which by some is described as the 'Soul'. Where the psyche driven ego remains by some form or other, as a part of the physical and astral worlds, the willing 'Soul' is able to transcend beyond the astral world into Higher Dimensions.

While the physical- and thinking-man do not evolve, and merely fall subject to Great Nature and the passage of Time, the two metaphysical beings described as the psychic-man and the spiritual-man, once formed, will evolve along their designated but opposite paths. Where the 'Soul' of the spiritual-man transcends to a dimension that is lighter, simpler and consequently subject to fewer laws; the psyche-driven ego devolves into a place that is lower, denser, more complex and consequently subject to more laws.

If we consider the Hermetic and Alchemic expression "As above so below" we can clearly identify how this phenomena has also manifested itself in today's so-called 'civilized world'.

The phenomenon we refer to as the Possession, as mentioned, resides in the ego of man and is therefore, in itself, equally dual. As such, among others, it can be observed as either an active or passive influence.

In the vast majority of egos the Possession is a *passive* force; it is one which manifests itself in hosts who subject themselves to things that are physical or emotional in context, which includes knowledge, when it is seen as an object, as in something it can have. The passive-subjective path can often be characterised with what appears to be the easier of paths, which its host can choose to remain on or exist in, without too much effort or suffering. This trend causes the host to stagnate in his or her inner-evolution, and consequently devolve into a two- and eventually one-dimensional being. The individuals who are at this one-dimensional level are ones that typically exist between that which feeds or positively stimulates their physical, sexual and emotional identifications on one side, and that which it believes will harm or threaten its existence and its identifications on the other.

Thus, in a selected minority, the Possession will form an *active* force. In these it is where their now Possessed ego begins to overtly act aggressively. This type is not defined by affluence or intellect but will often be one of above average intellect and favoured circumstances, such as material affluence or oratory powers. These ones then apply their talents to absorb the psychic energies radiated by those who are subjective and passive. As a result, their possession grows in power and influence, with which it then seeks to subject ever more subjects. In many ways the Possession is insatiable, and more so than that of the gluttonous man; but, as it is not limited by any physical constraints, it can never be 'full'.

Where growth and stability in the awakened man are found in the higher vibrational effects of harmony, balance and compassion, in the Possession, its driving force is fear. Other than its fear of exposure to the Light of Truth, the only thing the Possession fears is that which all biological beings must suffer, being the concept of 'Time'. Consequently the Possession has, over millennia, persevered to overcome this dilemma by learning to apply to its subjected hosts forms of dark hypnotism and menticide, also known as brainwashing, and combined these with various sciences. The effects of this craft are fear-based, and involve the continuous suffering experienced by a great many innocents. Hence, as such, it pursues fear-aligned methods to influence and control them. We can see how this is applied in many forms of authoritarian and social controls, and how the subjected either surrender their psychic energy freely, or join the system by embracing the will of their dominant master as their own. The latter process is where the subjected person becomes the apprentice, who becomes like his master. In the world of people, he will gradually be enticed to overcome his master, and then by force or ceremony, become him. It is in other words, the dark psychic will and intent of the master that is transmitted from one being onto *or into* another. As such it adopts a *pseudo*-biological life as its own; *pseudo* as it is not bound to a single cycle of life.

The Possession is therefore an entity that appears to be ancient and immortal in the eyes of its hopeful but mortal servants and followers[1].

---

[1] It may be noted that the well-known character of Count Dracula in the book by Bram Stoker, was largely based on the Possession, as they share many of the characteristics. Where their dark and fear-based entities exist off the life-force of subjected people, who either die or become their infected disciples; where both are destroyed in the presence of Light, and where both - in the material world - do not exist (Dracula not having a reflection).

This dark phenomenon is *in appearance* not too different from the opposite and higher dimensional path that it mirrors, being that of the spiritual-man. Where the spiritual follower, devotee or disciple serves his teacher, prophet or guru, in order to spiritually merge and become 'At-One' with the teacher or guru. As such at the end of life, he or she merges with the preceding teachers or gurus, and as such eventually become closer to, and at one with, the 'All and Everything'.

Defining the Possession as an Entity or Structure of Thought

One could prefer to consider the Possession as an 'entity' that consists of 'thought structures', but such thoughts could not be the ordinary thinking patterns that one is conscious of, as they would by proxy cause its dissolution. To explain this sentence and 'its dissolution' we would need to look at the hierarchy of Creation, which is always manifested from the higher to the lesser. Even if it seems that by some form of accident or miracle a higher form simply 'appeared' out of nothing, then the very context of what such an accident or miracle contained, even if its source was invisible, undetectable and unknown, would still be of a higher form[1].

Unlike contemporary beliefs[2], the thinking, contemplative and *Consciousness-aware* man did not simply evolve from a worm or ape, simply because lower and less complex things or beings cannot *by themselves* create a higher one, not without a higher force or influence. Even a clever monkey that is taught to do things like humans, does not do so by itself without observing a human first, neither does it become creative by itself. We must therefore consider how the physical body was made manifest from a Higher Dimensional 'wish' to feel and interact with things of form, things that were, prior to that, only imagined. We could therefore correlate this in how fingers evolved by being stimulated by thought in order to touch or grab. It is the same way that a plant shoots when it is drawn by the Sun, and that an amoeba manifests a pseudopod when it is necessary.

The *quality or nature* of the thought – or light, in the case of the plant – will therefore determine the *quality and nature* of that which it is made. This becomes more obvious when we see how such *quality or nature* affects rudimentary things like the effects of our work and activity, but even more so

---

[1] This is a fundamental law; being a law that cannot be broken down in some form of logic, in the same way that making endless copies of copies will never make the original.

[2] The contemporary creationist theorizes how the body created a central nervous system which mutated into a brain, and consciousness became a result of a thinking brain. This theory makes little logical sense, and these same ones have been looking for the elusive 'missing link' to prove this for ages. The power of belief or intention that is rooted outside the physical realm can however create and uncreate in the physical world, as observed in the placebo and nocebo effect, but also in the metaphysical world as observed by energy healers, who often non-invasively access the body's astral energy field and chakras.

in our interaction with others. We may consequently appreciate that the observable Cosmos is not random, but the result of an intention that originated out of conscious, higher dimensional or 'Divine' thought. If this were not so, then certainly, by rights Chaos would reign. Instead, we observe how the Earth's skin-thick biosphere[1] is almost impossibly yet finely tuned to support Life in an uncountable, perpetually adapting variety of forms which, among other, enables man's awareness to evolve inward, enabling his dimensional transcendence[2].

Thus, from within this Grand Construct, we can see how, amongst all people, some of our thoughts are aware, conscious and intuitive, while others are mechanical-reactive and unconscious. Hence we can now infer that:

- Where along the journey of Life, the conscious individual ego merges with Spirit to grow a Soul, and the unconscious and mechanical-reactive thinking only feeds the Ego.
- Where the Soul is embedded in a *single* and Universal Truth, the Ego is *dual* and embedded in an illusory impression of itself.
- Where the Soul finds growth through a separation from things that are physical, conceptual and illusory, the Ego seeks physical, identifiable and numerical growth with things and others who are alike.
- The Soul merges through the 'guru', 'way' or 'path', during the course of a natural Life with all that is Truth and as such exists in a reality of Higher Dimensional awareness. The Ego, on the other side, seeks to mirror this by processes of artificial enhancement within its three-dimensional physical realm, using one and two-dimensional methodology.

One may consider these observations as religiously biased, but ultimately, they simply follow a form of sequential causality. The process of unconscious, mechanical and reactive thought, that is related to the left brain[3], can build, hunt, support and do wonderful things. But it can also cause people to become like a pack of hungry wolves, and an entity of its own. When considering this example, some activists may consider that we ought to shoot or contain (suppress) such a pack of wolves, but this is not feasible. The phenomenon of the Possession is namely an entity that has no defined boundaries, and when the possibility of such suppression occurs, it knows how to shapeshift and cunningly merge into its surroundings, where it remains on the fringes, appearing harmless and even useful or important.

---

[1] Depending on the extremes applied, the earth's biosphere's thickness is approximately 0.15% of its diameter.

[2] Depending on one's perspective, this is also referred to as Self-realization, Illumination or Enlightenment, Nirvana, toward Oneness with Consciousness, etc.

[3] In his book *The Master and His Emissary: The Divided Brain and the Making of the Western World*, psychiatrist Iain McGilchrist deals with the hemispheric functioning of the brain. He considers how the differing world views of the right and left brain have shaped Western culture, and how the growing conflict between these views affects the way the modern world is changing.

The Possession is therefore an anomaly; it is a non-physical and atom-less entity, yet it is vibratory in nature and charged or fed by the psyche off living humans. Regardless of its dark side, its reality can still be argued as critical for human survival and even for its very existence. As it has the power to coerce others who are unaware and asleep. it can make them blindly trust it, follow it, support it, defend and die for it which may, under certain circumstances, even be necessary.

Where, in a comparison earlier on, reference was made to the story of Dracula, it is likely that the fable of the Pied Piper and Hamelin was also a reference to this phenomenon. Where the Piper at first fulfilled the cities critical need to clear the city of rats as tasked, it was when he was crossed that he turned against his former clients. Although the Piper was described as 'pied' and thus of a dual nature, he is deemed by many a reader as the owner of the magic he brought forth. This however is incorrect, as it was the effect on the psyche of a particular vibration that he and his flute were able to create, that mesmerized the rats and, when he was not paid, the children of Hamelin.

Evading the Possession by Understanding its Cosmic Harmony

To be able to protect our inner-being's sovereignty, by warding off or at least controlling things that wish to possess it, should be, if we are conscious, our first and foremost priority in life. This is especially so if we consider a Possession's very toxic and infectious effect on the self and those that we care for. This makes it as important as the physical care for ourself, our relations and for others who are close to us. In other words, if we do not know where our thought-stimulations or our urges and emotions are coming from, we cannot know if the Truth we follow is Absolute Truth, as in from the higher senses, or if it is Relative Truth, as in from the intellect[1]. If we are unaware of such influences on our perceived reality, how can we know who the 'I' is that makes our decisions, and which we address ourselves by?

To fight or defeat something that exists out of conflict, and not become part of the conflict which feeds it, such as when we want to defeat it or ward it off, is not possible. We can only do this from a place of unconditional love. Unconditional love, however, is only practically possible if we have accepted what is, as in the ways of others, *unreservedly*. If we cannot do this, then such non-acceptance will maintain a divide that ultimately creates renewed friction, and a continuation of conflict. To accept *unreservedly* however, we have to

---

[1] "The Hindu Vedanta speaks of two types of truth: Absolute Truth and Relative Truth. Absolute Truth is what the religionists would call God. This Truth cannot be known through the senses, mind, or intellect, but only through that in us which is of God, which is Pure Consciousness. Relative Truth is based on the intellect, mind, and senses and therefore variable. In relative truth, here will never be consensus due to the variations in perception and the instruments of knowledge (intellect, mind, and senses) being limited and conditioned." (Swami Vidyananda in *Contemplations and Deliberations*)

learn to understand the entity we wish to accept and love, and this can only be done through work or, at times, forms of self-sacrifice.

The element of self-sacrifice may include *mentally* entering or envisioning the dark world of such others, to see the reality of their world that caused them to be what or how they are. There is no defined way to do this though, but it can be considered that such work begins with the intention to want to know and understand. As such, even a reader's conscious review of these words could be considered a form of sacrifice, as he or she will most likely have experienced uncomfortable emotions that were stimulated by an external ego objecting to its analysis! However, the element of understanding, which begins by appreciating the basic characteristics, may be simpler and less complex. As the Possession is not a physical entity, an understanding of its characteristics can be determined through a process of observations:

The First Observation: Metaphysical Causes with Physical Effects

The Possession or 'demon' as it is referred to in scripture, is a metaphysical phenomenon and as such, it does not reside in tissue or brains, but in the psyche of man. This infers that it has no *direct* physical power or effect on the Physical Center. For it to have such, it needs to first coerce man through his Emotional- and Thinking Centers. Consequently it cannot be defeated or contained by physical means. However, being a metaphysical consequence of a metaphysical effect, it is still a product of the psyche, which originates off the mechanical, conditioned and thinking mind. As the thinking mind is still a part of the finite and physical man, it is still subject to the same Cosmic Laws.

The Second Observation: The Law of Opposites

The phenomenal effects of depression, pessimism, paranoia, schizophrenia and other psychological troubles have been extensively observed across the millennia and clinically studied since the early 20th century. Where, in days of old, demonic possession or 'the devil' was blamed for these behavioural symptoms, the contemporary analysis at present advocate these as maladies of the mind. It is largely viewed as having physical or environmental causes, including childhood or traumatic events such as, drug or alcohol abuse, a life of suffering or a genetic or other form of psychological disorder. Consequent to such labelling, the medical fraternity invented, designed or advocated treatments in the form of chemical or mechanical means, including pills, potions, surgical intervention and consultation.

Either way, the validity of the stated diagnosed causes and occurrences is naturally feasible. But then, such dire circumstances have, in many cases, had the opposite result on individuals as well, such as where they discover their inner strength through these, and become extraordinary persons in Life.

As to the chemical and mechanical treatments; these are at times effective, but at other times they bind the casualty to a lifelong dependency. In some cases such stereotyped treatments can even make things worse, where suppression of the phenomenal effects occurs only whilst the status quo is kept at a certain point of control. Then, with many, it is likely that the 'malady' will reappear under certain circumstances, and at times with a vengeance. This is largely due to these symptoms, be it by one cause or another, being perceived and treated as an illness, and not as the invasive invisible and undetectable entity that it was previously and for centuries observed as. As mentioned in earlier chapters; if it has to be diagnosed in clinical terms, then it is best described as a viral infection of a metaphysical kind. The type that does not infect the blood, bones or organs, but which does affect the psychic energy field that filters and influences the senses and consequent thoughts. Then, where the evident suffering that was diagnosed as the cause, as horrific and traumatic as the applicable event may have been, the resultant psychosis can additionally be understood as the effect of an already aggravated and weakened psyche.

The Third Observation: The Effect of Purpose

When we consider the law of causality, which some may refer to as fate or consequence, there is an old saying which goes: "what does not kill you makes you stronger". Regardless of the theories on the cause of psychological suffering, the types of trauma, or the effects of differing forms of treatment as observed above, and whether it is upon a child or an adult, *the root-origin of the actual and rather unnatural psychosis remains vague*. The existence of these symptoms however is certain, and because all things in the Cosmos have a purpose, it must be so with this phenomena as well.

The suffering caused by psychosis has notably caused many to become severely tormented but yet, as mentioned, the same factors that led to this psychosis will, in others, stimulate them to become strong, independent, aware and at times, even enlightened. We may therefore try to detect how this correlates in Great Nature's physical realm. In the same way that an old and established forest exists of big trees with deep and ancient roots, the physical and mental health of an individual, who is born in decent health, depends on his or her exposure to the elements. Therefore, just as that the spread of a tree's roots and its core strength resides in the reality of stormy weather[1], from many a perspective, the same can be observed through the individual's physical, emotional and psychological suffering.

Where some may claim their suffering lead to them surrendering their free-will to physical or meta-physical entities that then owned or possessed them

---

[1] *"A tree that grows in a sheltered dome may rise quickly, but without the wind, it never learns to stand on its own."* – Inspired by the Biosphere 2 experiment.

and for which they would act empathetically, others will admit that their suffering made them stronger and independent

The Fourth Observation: The Law of Causality

The dominant cause of a person's surrender to any possessing entity, resides largely in the inherent nature of his choices. In many a case, before a Possession has made itself at home through some traumatic event or other, the one who surrendered his free will to something or someone that then owns them, did so because it was deemed less complicated and easier, or because it was sensually appealing. They will often subject themselves to such sensory and laziness-orientated stimuli, even if they knew better. In that case they'd convince themselves that following the demands made by this entity was natural or logical, that everyone did it, or that they had no choice.

Thus, once they have given up the sovereignty of their mind, a routine of automated and mechanical response captures their choice-making processes. As a result, and no longer having a will or sincere intent of their own anymore, the subjected becomes enslaved to the demands of their new master. Following the law of cause and effect these ones will attain a predictable and thus entirely controllable nature. Like any mechanical device or automaton they abide to the rule of law and don uniform ways, wherein their choices on voting and the use of their resources, which includes their offspring, become expendable tools of their masters.

The Fifth Observation: The Law of Vibration

Besides the Law of Cause and Effect referred to above, the Law of Vibration also affects the Possession. This law describes how everything in the created Cosmos is always in motion and vibrates, as observed in quantum physics. It is physically visible in cymatics, the study of visible sound and vibration, where we see how combinations of vibrations along certain frequencies form very specific patterns. This is visible in people as well, when we see how prolonged exposure to certain frequencies can affect them, on both psychic and genetic levels. For example, those who are exposed to certain inaudible vibrations, especially if they are unaware of such external influences upon them and their psyche, will be seen starting to both behave *and think* differently[1]. When such vibrations are then radiated across millions of people, such as we see around times of celebration like Christmas, or following a natural disaster, we see how these vibrations cause people to adopt very specific behavioural orders or categories. Consider just how people will sponsor or vote, mobilize, weep or cheer en masse, simply upon hearing of a

---

[1] Inaudible vibrations, especially those below 20 Hz, can subtly affect the human psyche. Some of the noted effects are anxiety and unease, fatigue and headaches, sleep disturbance and sensory misperceptions (hallucinations).

certain series of tunes.

The physical, vibrational and behavioural trends between the grains of sand on a vibratory plate in cymatics, correlates to those patterns of the majority of people; especially the contemporary one and two dimensional ones. For example, we can see how, in both, patterns are automatically formed and altered by the adjustment of vibrations, how the larger and smaller parts are automatically sorted, and even how components that are of a similar size but lighter or denser, sort themselves into their respective groups. We also see how the patterns around the centre differ in shape and density from those on the fringes, just as we observed along the lines of activity in Manhattan[1].

Whether they are intentional or incidental, it is clear that man-made vibrations affect the sorting of people psychically, along their state of self-awareness. By the same principles however, we see the evident effects on the psyche of a full moon, a rising or setting sun, a large body of water, a monolith of sort, and even a simple campfire or candle, which are all measurably vibratory. Where these have calming, magnetising and even energizing effects, we need but look at the effects of a panic-struck crowd going on a stampede to see or get away from its potentially harmful opposite. This is where the bulk of people have no idea what they are running from or to, or in the case of an impending disaster, where people stock up with the most banal products they have no use for, or in its aftermath, where otherwise law-abiding citizens go on a looting spree, fighting for things they cannot eat or use. These crowds are usually dominated by the obedient followers-of-order and followers-of-faith[2], many of whom are conditioned to not think for themselves, and who are used to being led by a *small core of selected and influential ones*.

However, where we can observe ever deepening degrees of psychopathy and sociopathy among this 'small core of selected influential ones', we will also experience the highest degrees of natural empathy among those who are the least affected.

Where these psyche-affecting vibrations may intensify or lessen by degree across groups of people from time-to-time, they are always present *and of the same ratios throughout.* This means that, for example, the number of hooligans will be closely matched by the number of volunteers; and when a crisis has passed and the panic resides, the looters begin to go home, as do the volunteers.

The Sixth Observation: The Law of Rhythm

The next law that becomes evident when we consider the presence of cyclic

---

[1] See Chapter 3: Cities within *Artificial* Energy Centers: Manhattan
[2] See Introduction: Diagram 1 – Pyramids of Opposite Realities

patterns in the above mentioned vibrations, is that they will fluctuate between higher and lower intensities, along specific patterns or periods.

In the divine mechanism of the Created Cosmos, the law of Rhythm is also referred to as the Law of the Pendulum. It describes how, besides the element of perpetual motion, all things will additionally swing from one pole, or concentration, to another. In this, we will see how something, that started going seemingly unstoppable in one direction, somehow and without explanation, finds itself going in the opposite.

When considering this phenomenon in the context of a Possession, as an example we can see how a country's politics will swing from liberal to conservative and back, how its population will move from being peaceful to warlike, and how the 'love for thy fellow man', as historically taught by Christ, was translated by His followers to the need for heinous crimes and barbarism during the inquisitions and the crusades.

In a more recent example, we note how a century or two ago, the 'physical man' was more vulnerable to illness and injury affecting his ability to work, and where the errors of the emotional and thinking 'sentient-man', was easy to forgive and overcome. At present, this has been completely reversed: The 'physical-man' is no longer essential and as such he is no longer vulnerable, but the emotion- and psyche driven thoughts and actions of a 'sentient-man' are considered as his most valued assets. Where the physical body was more able to heal *naturally,* today his immune system requires drugs and supplements. Where the emotionally stressed man would in time find his peace in solitude and nature, today, once the sentient-man's psyche embraces Chaos, it is virtually impossible for him to heal *naturally*, as this would imply a return to his state of normality, which he never had.

When we return to the subject of a Possession, we observe that its preferred medium, where it thrives best, is Chaos. And this is where it does so cunningly and often unexpectedly. *In the physical world*, forms of Chaos, such as one finds in the Middle East, will visibly rise and fall. As such they can be avoided by an open-eyed and alert, moderately intelligent person. *In the metaphysical and psychic realms* however, it is considerably more complex as it requires one to remain aware of the duality within the lower-dimensional mechanical self. Our automatism within these lower dimensions, conceptual or not, still require us to be alert and discerning to the content and the processes of thought. Hence it is all too often that those large swaths of civilization, at times of mass-psychosis, only detect and realize their state of frenzy within these, when they are already on battlefields or blood-soaked streets, and by which time, for most, it is too late.

Chapter 11
UNDERSTANDING THE DAEMON, PART II
THE PREDICTED EFFECT OF SPIRIT ON THE UNCONSCIOUS MAN

Black Sulphur or Brimstone (in Alchemy)

**The Law of Causality must take its dues,
and with it, the world of yesterday
whose bouquet of choices
no longer exists.**

**The only choice that remains, is to lament or accept,
but where lamenting feeds nothing but pain,
the acceptance brings forth the rebirth,
of a new Duality with both Good and Evil.**

**Its experiential reality will be unique,
and depend on the individual perception.
The only common factor among all is their division,
between the awakened and unawakened minds.**

Defining the Unawakened or Unconscious Man

The unawakened or unconscious man referred to in this chapter, is a man (or woman) who is unaware of his Higher Dimensional Consciousness. It is one who functions reactively and mechanically, like an automaton that is subject to the stimuli of external influences as programmed by his conditioned mind.

Being unaware, he exists in the belief that he is in control of his actions, that he can do as he wills, and that his thoughts and opinions are his own. When he acts what he calls 'instinctively', it is not unlike the animal which merely reacts according to certain conditionings that were programmed into him. There is in such a one no conscious, intuitive or higher dimensional thought, nor is there any actual awareness of his differing physical, sensory and thinking centers. To him all is 'I' or 'I am'. The unawakened man, in other words, has no awareness of a considered thought as to *why* he does what he does, nor the manner by which he decides on *how* to do it. Therefore, in those who are unaware, there are seldom any feelings that are conscious and sincere.

What makes matters worse is that an unawakened person does not know that he does not know, but thinks he does. This combination is one that is seen in many environments, and characterized by unintended consequences that are then blamed on others. As such, the unconscious man is like a runaway train whose collateral state depends on its physical condition, such as its size, velocity, and what it carries within it – in other words, those who are dependent on him. The unawakened or unconscious person is consequently one who is vulnerable to an external entity's Possession, simply due to the fact that the mechanism that controls his thoughts, words and actions, are not his own. It is as if his control-room was left unattended, whilst his vessel is underway.

The Influences or Effects of an Astral World of Duality

The transcendental or astral world that permeates everything is not devoid and empty, it is saturated with inherent energy and filled with other-vibrational and to us metaphysical entities. As it is still part of the Cosmos, there is a duality here as well and consequently, these entities exist on both sides of the experienced spectrum. On one end of the spectrum are the *higher vibrational* or angelic ones that can be referred to as Helpers or Guides, and who assist embodied souls along their journey of Life. Unlike the entities described herein as Possession, helpers are not dependent on the psyche of people. They consist of beings who represent within them, the truthful elements of countless souls, such as those sincere followers of Christ, the Prophet, the Buddha, the guru or other Divine entity, and who besides Truth and unconditional love, have embraced unreserved acceptance[1]. Unlike us, when they are not embodied they are not dependent on the same Space-time reality of a physical life, and present for all whomever and wherever seek the Light.

---

[1] Whereas these are referred to as Saints in Christian terms, Buddhism refers to these as Bodhisattvas or 'enlightened beings', who have taken a vow to work for the liberation of all beings. Their ultimate goal is not just to attain enlightenment for themselves, but to help all beings attain enlightenment as well. Because of their great compassion, they postpone their own enlightenment in order to help others and are revered as spiritual 2 guides and protectors.

On the other and opposite 'side' of the Light are the *lower vibrational* entities, that are dependent on the psychic energy of others. They are often referred to as Intruders or Blind Guides, and are considered as the remnants of incomplete souls that did not attain the Light and, in their current state, are unable to transcend or reincarnate. Their existence or process has its own mechanical nature, and in this the intruder's vibrational state is directly related to its place in the Astral's vortex. In comparison to the helper, the intruder is one that retained little light during its collection of incarnated lives, and as a result, it will be darker, vibrationally denser and found closer to the center of their 'vortex'. These vortexes are similar to a whirlwind or whirlpool, which exists by drawing energy into it. Like the whirlpool, they are finite, and in the case of the Intruder, dependent on psychic energy that feeds it – and like the whirlpool, once its vortex runs out of inflowing energy, it ceases to exist. There is therefore, in the absence of light, a 'mortal' limit to an Intruder's existence. However, the intruders' nature, that led them to become what they are, is to shun the light and seek their perpetuation within ever denser energies. As such, their vortex will inevitably become saturated, lose its momentum and cease to exist - as if it never was. The answer for such intruders is to find their own illumination but, as they lack the ability, often the only route for them to do so is through the blessing by the very ones they torment. If this occurs, an intruder can become illuminated and attain the higher vibrational state of a helper, and in time as such, depart the vortex.[1]

If we compare this process or mechanism to our surrounding fast-paced and technologically enhanced world, we note that there are a vast number of such dense or low vibrational centers of 'vortex-forming' attraction. As an example, not only can we consider the worlds of drug and alcohol abuse, violence, pornography and paedophilia, but even the milder forms of entertainment and appearances. In many, the resultant vortexes are already heavily laden, and require ever increased forms of attraction or enhancement to maintain its turning momentum. For many, the resultant world of virtual realities, artificial intelligence, and an endless list of sensual distractions is a sign of the complex times. This is because the higher vibrational or angelic guides and helpers have little need to inhibit the space of men and women, and yet, the lower vibrational ones do just that. Hence, in the earlier mentioned example of an 'unattended control-room', it is only a matter of time before they opt to intrude into the unattended space of these unconscious ones.

It therefore does not matter whether such dense low-vibrational entities or intruders possess the psyche of a teacher or leader, or a person that serves a system of religious, political or social affiliated beliefs. The point is that when individual entities collate into a single organization or collective of sorts, it

---

[1] There is of course no verifiable 'evidence' to this hypothesis, but there are numerous testimonies in scripture and spirituality, as well as those of energy workers,.

will still be powered by the psyches of its members. The collated entity of an organization or collective of sorts, however, will in turn possess the minds of its individual members, and through this mind his emotions, and through his emotions his actions.

As such an influence is not his own – regardless of whether it is applied by a single or an orchestration of elements – it owns him and his life, and as such, it possesses him.

The Consequential Cycles of Choice

Every individual, from around the end of adolescence until now - as he finds himself at the present moment - is a collage of his decisions. There is nothing in him that was not affected to some degree by a choice he made. The vast majority of these decisions were not just about turning left or right, or following a red route or a blue route, but even the smallest of seemingly minor choices. This could be something as meaningless as reading a meaningful paragraph once, twice or thrice, or about taking a mere few percent more than what was rightfully earned or allocated. It could be the adoption of minor habits, such as telling that little white lie, or for that matter, doing anything that was simply not necessary.

As most of us know, a great deal has already been written by the practitioners of pretty much every discipline, on the importance of self-observation or mindfulness through forms of yoga and meditation. Although there are many techniques and teachings, they all aim at teaching us to become aware of our thinking, feeling and doing at every moment. While this does form the core of the work, it is from this *as its base* that the real work begins. The next trial is getting to understand the functionality of mankind, and us within it. And this entails getting to know the world. which can only be attained by our engaging in it[1]. To come into the 'know' entails being in a state of *constant discernment*, within which we observe our thoughts, feelings and actions, and subsequently to *know* what is real and what is not, and to *know* what or which to say 'No' to.

It is important to remember that the ability of a person, who remains unawakened and unconscious, to make a choice that is independent and his own, is just about zero. This is because to do so requires constant vigilance which, in a world of mass-distraction, is often too complex for the contemporary man. Most people will automatically, without ever noticing it, follow trends that were set by their external society and environment. Thus, within the realm of Information Technology, most apply their likes, dislikes and consequent choices along the lines of an interconnected world. Not knowing that they are asleep and entangled, they will still claim that their

---

[1] 'Engaging' in opposite to self-isolation.

decisions are made along their own line of logic and reason. This will include things like the enhancement of their career or other deal-maker, their faith in bona-fide suggestions – even when these are made by their social and corporate-media, to which they feel duty-bound. Unbeknownst to them, they form part of the very cause of the system of enslavement, which is programmed and enabled to control them. This it does by being privy to their thoughts and opinions, and influencing these to the extent that the full content of their knowledge, opinions and actions is entirely under the system's control.

As control over the thoughts and actions of the masses has become the very purpose and design of both state and corporate architecture, it is not *if* the transfer of their psyche into their systems will occur, but *when*. The only relevant element in this observation is if the *Inner Evolution of Man* is still possible under the influence of these.

The true and strategic impact of these influences, that overwhelmingly dominates the psyche of the contemporary man is seldom published, and when it is, then it is either deceptively veiled or written in such a way that nobody wants to read it. Much of our recorded history is made up of exaggerated and even falsified narratives provided by appointed officials, who simply repeat the same version over and over again, until in time their fiction becomes historical fact[1]. In days of old, the containment of a person's independence was maintained through physical fear-based intimidation but this is no longer necessary. At present, the contemporary man has the illusion that he is free. However, to find the solid ground of Truth in an infinite and self-perpetuating ocean of falsehood requires us to find ourselves within it, reject the narratives that were so freely provided, and then make work of it. Only when we have accomplished this may we consider ourselves able to begin making choices that are our own.

The myth of the 'Fall of Man' has been written and rewritten across civilizations, empires and most religious movements. At present humanity seems to be witnessing the same threat, but unlike the sword or rifle, it is the naïve and gluttonous consumer in an outcome based environment that embodies it. In this, where society's rules are determined by the state and/or behemoth body-corporates, most will surrender the power of their individual choice, regardless of whether this is to do with his choice of god, vote, health, definition of wealth, or Truth. Consequently, today this has passed the point of no return, for it cannot be undone. Even when Truth is exposed and verified most are unable to believe of digest it, at least not from a position where one

---

[1] For examples of such official narratives, read: *A Pretext for War* by James Bamford, *935 Lies* by Charles Lewis, *How America Gets Away With Murder* by Michael Mandel, *Propaganda, Lies and False Flags* by Robert Fantina, *Operation Northwoods: The Cold War False Flag Conspiracy* by Alexandra Vaughn et al.

believes one can return to the point of origin, as this resides in a past that no longer exists.

Justifying Artificial Intelligence, along the Law of Causality

The preceding view on the 'Fall of Man' may seem pessimistic or bleak to many a casual reader. However, if one were to study the nature of humanity *without bias*, one might then find that these processes are in fact quite natural. For example, if we compare such a process of 'pruning' a civilization to Great Nature's use of fire for germination among certain species of plant and tree, it may even be seen as having a higher or 'divine' purpose[1]. After all, the process of a person who is unconscious of the external influences on him, and who gets drawn into a collective of lower dimensional influences, is a process that occurs logically or *naturally*. Usually the effects of such influences have to do with each of the choices he has made across his years of life. If, for example, such a person has surrendered his free will and choice to a cause, entity, or even a sensory stimulus, then surely the loss of his sovereign self cannot be seen as punishment or 'karma', but simply as causal?

In the observation of an enhanced human 'intelligence' and the technological advances that affect every aspect of our daily life, we must consider that, regardless of whether we have a choice on its use, technology is here to stay. However, perhaps the development and enhancement of technology as a 'whole' serves a greater purpose. For example, the technology we refer to as Artificial Intelligence was largely stimulated by a desire to improve on ourselves, by inventing a form of self-thinking intelligence. If this were to evolve the scope of our knowledge then perhaps, in time, it will enable us to discover our place in relation to Consciousness[2]. Perhaps we can then discover or better understand how Artificial Intelligence neither corresponds nor conflicts with our inner-being, but that its interference with our ability to think, feel and act freely leads to *the catastrophic devolution of the individual man*.

Either way, if we remember that everything in the Created Cosmos is connected along a certain hierarchical or supporting order then, from a Higher Dimensional perspective, we should be able to grasp that Artificial Intelligence is an integral part of this. We may then consider that, although it indisputably harms and disadvantages many people at various degrees, it also creates new pathways for the individual and collective humanity to expand, produce, create and interconnect.

---

[1] Fire plays a crucial role in the germination process of certain vegetation, particularly in fire-adapted ecosystems, where it assists with seed activation, clearing of alien plants, and in the release of nutrients.

[2] By which I refer that we become observant of an omnipresent consciousness, instead of believing that somehow the intellectual and conditioned human brain develops consciousness.

The existence of duality within the purpose of Artificial Intelligence is therefore evident. As an example to emphasize this, let us imagine an Artificial Intelligent program that could disable people from distributing falsified information in public arenas. Imagine that it would automatically but intelligently filter out all twisted versions of information, including those creative representations that are designed to emotionally deceive the recipient through the use of colours, symbols and cleverly designed words. The moment such a program were in place, it would also automatically disable our ability to reprogram it, as the system would see any such action as having a potentially false intent. Consequently, nobody who wishes to make an alternative claim of fact or other, or one who sought to understand Truth by hypothetically suggesting its opposite, would be able to do so. Nor, for that matter, would the guides, teachers or leaders be able to create alternate versions that are unlike the current accepted ones. This may not seem like such a bad thing, but then such a mechanism would not necessarily be able to define a higher truth from a lesser truth. As an example, it would affect the purpose and ways one defines truth through a comparison with its opposite. This in turn would cause one to adopt a way of living and being that would not necessarily be motivated by one's pursuit of a truthful and correct path. Such a one would not do anything because it was the right thing to do, but simply because it was the only path he could take. Where falsehood would thus be eradicated, the understanding of Relative Truth would be lost, and with this, the realization of Absolute Truth[1].

The understanding of Consciousness and free-will, as in our ability to choose consciously, will always be challenged by external bias. This will include opposing views and options presented by Artificial Intelligence and its virtual realities. In these, consider that when one is immersed within such a virtual world, one will become, at a certain point, unable to define what stimulates one's cognitive consciousness through subconscious influences on the psyche, from an avatar in the program. We can envision how this would veritably cause one to spiral into a state of schizophrenia; one that leaves one unable to escape one's entanglement with a now possessed mind and ego.

The view on an entangled mind is based on observing the impact of Artificial Intelligence's virtual world on *the individual thinking psyche*, and how it affects the element of 'choice'. When we look at the greater scale of humanity, we can appreciate that both the potential as well as the harmfulness of such external influences differ. To begin, we can see how its impact on contemporary societies will automatically and naturally subject them to an

---

[1] Certain philosophies, including the Hindu Vedanta, will speak of two types of truth: Absolute Truth and Relative Truth. Where Absolute Truth is what the religionists would call God, a truth that cannot be known through the senses, mind, or intellect, and thus pure Consciousness, Relative Truth is based on the intellect, mind, and senses and therefore variable.

Artificial Intelligent program's dominant systems and popular trends. As these contemporary societies represent the larger percentage of people, it will subsequently shape the environment that all must live in. As a result, we can envision how a technology dependent society or civilization loses, to a large extent, its ability to think naturally, independently or logically. Consider, for example, how technology's industries formulate its consideration of their surrounds and their societies when it comes to pollution or other harmful side effects, or how easily a state's citizens are swayed to make war for another state's resources. Against that, we can consider how an authoritarian and artificially intelligent system, that was programmed to monitor the unnatural and harmful trends as observed in societies, could prevent these. But then, having no heart or understanding of human fallibility, the machine might decide to take harsh and inhumane measures in establishing its preventative and mechanical solutions. Thus, whichever way one wishes to debate the potentials and consequences of such programs, they all seem to lead to forms of physical and mental enslavement, which seemingly leaves little fertile soil for the inner growth and evolution of the individual man.

However, the human being is not just a mere mechanical or biological organism. Our physical experienced reality is a three-dimensional one, and this receives, after all, metaphysical influences from an other-vibrational and higher-dimensional origin. Any attempt therefore, to permanently eradicate, block or suppress these influences from the individual and collective evolution would, by proxy, defy the very purpose of Creation. It would be comparable to the shadow trying to douse the Light that created it. Man's dependency on forms of Artificial Intelligence, and the attraction to the sensuality of its virtual realities will undoubtedly affect a great many, and cause an inestimable amount to get lost in their artificial world of dreams. However, this will only be upon those whose eyes and ears are closed to their intuitive hearts, and who subsequently surrender to either their basic physical, emotional or overly thinking nature.

Thus, the effects of the external influences of an Artificial Reality is more likely to have catastrophic consequences for a great many. But, as this process is seemingly unstoppable and inevitable, it is not unlike the wars that these same contemporary societies are mechanically drawn into. It is more like a transitional phase that, like war, realigns the course of human civilizations. However, where war is usually about territory, resources and sometimes politics, the Truth-conflict is about our discovering the definite limits to our evolution, along an intellectual and technological route.

It is after all evident, when we observe the recurrence of *man-made* catastrophes, that the causes originate in a mixture of *ignorance, greed or stupidity*. When we try to intellectually determine which came first, it becomes clear that *ignorance, greed and stupidity* are actually integrally entwined, and that degrees of all three are always present, like an 'unholy trinity'. But, like the Holy Trinity, it can even be observed that at their root-basis, *ignorance, greed and stupidity* are connected and thus the same, because the mediums within each of these thrive, are equally made up of insincerity, deceit and falsehood which are, as one entity, invisibly entangled and possessed.

The Possession that Transcends across Generations
A Track-record of Entities

In the same way that the presence of viral or bacterial infections play an integral role for the continued succession of biological forms, we must consider the reality of entropy, or Chaos, as the background of our orderly Cosmos. If we consider that nothing is ever random, as in disconnected from other things, which infers that all things are inevitably connected to everything else. As such we can see that every part serves a particular role or purpose[1]. Consequently, we must also consider that, like a bacterial infection, entropy and Chaos, the sequential Possession of Man also plays a role.

In scripture, Judas Iscariot is often described as the son of the Devil incarnate; the foolish disciple who gave up his mentor and Savior, and consequently surrendered his soul. This was supposedly after he had witnessed Christ's miracles, observed the Son of God's pure goodness and dwelled in the Light of His love and blessed wisdom. Yet sell Him out he supposedly did. Because it is contemporarily accepted that a man would sell his soul and Savior for a few coins of silver, the ultimate message in this parable is often lost. Was it the Devil or the Demon that led to the fall of Judas, and is there a difference, and regardless of which it was, why should he who was the essence of Judas, be blamed for the actions of a Possession. Perhaps it was simply his possession's role in the Greater Scheme of things?

The 'Sins of the Father' is often translated as having inherited the characteristics of one's parents or even grandparents. Perceived as an influence or a form of conditioning, it is seen as a burden that one carries for what was not one's doing or fault but still one's account. This belief may then follow a theory where, as a consequence, one was either bullied or coerced as a child to follow in the parents' footsteps. Like the silver coins that supposedly motivated Judas, this reasoning is seldom disputed as there is an element of Truth in this. What is mostly overlooked however, is that these burdens are mere effects of a deeper underlying cause; one that has little to do with the parent or the child as such, but rather, the sequential bouquet of

---

[1] The interconnected state of all things can be considered: (1) materially, where all things are connected through shared origins and physical laws; (2) metaphysically, through quantum entanglement; (3)causally, where connections span through time and space, or (4) metaphorically or spiritually, where many traditions consider the Divine Unity in all things.

choices they made.

In some of the old, highly affluent and influential families, including royalty, aristocracy and nobles, a tradition of gene selection process is usually maintained. This is where the bloodline is carefully preserved and where spouses are selected not just from a certain class or religious group, but from other families of a similar bloodline, or rather, a similar psychic nature. However, this arcane practice has historically led to types of inbreeding to the extent that it brought on a steady track-record of mental and genetic disabilities. The limits of these were at times pushed so far that it caused extreme forms of psychopathy in some, and in others forms of sterility and the subsequent extinction of their entire bloodline[1]. Contemporary history will claim that many of these royals, aristocrats and nobles merely followed the mythological guidelines of so-called 'Blue Bloods', which evolved around a belief that they were ordained by God or a Higher Power. Today, of course, they no longer claim this publicly. Yet still, little has changed with many such families throughout the world, except perhaps in certain regions that for multiple generations embraced forms of socialism or communism. Among the latter however, the divinely ordained ones are now gone, but the power still exists. That which was royalty, aristocracy and nobility simply changed its form to one of plutocracy. Among these again, it was not so much one of merit, but of containing power within a closed circle of the selected and initiated. This power is today mostly expressed through an executive office or institution of sorts, rather than that of a crown, where the manipulation of its ownership was not as easy to control. At present, few people dig much deeper into the practices of various Elitist Rulers than what their tabloids allow, and most will still either fear, idolize or pay silent homage to them.

Thus, if we are able to look past the occult ways and methods that these elitist families, institutions, or groups of initiated persons represent, including our feelings of admiration, idolization or disgust, it is possible that the picture of a parasitic shapeshifting and immortal possession materializes once again.

The Entity versus the Id-entity

By now it should be evident to the reader that the nature of the Possession is not just a psychological one, a thought-process, or merely a person's *identity* or Ego, but an intelligent, conscious and possessive *entity*. We see how the powerful ones originate in the dominant egos of psychically and mentally powerful individuals, through which the Possession adapts itself to things and processes, and by which it manifests itself as the proverbial demon. As such, it

---

[1] For example, the Spanish Habsburg dynasty went extinct due to inbreeding, most notably with King Charles II of Spain (1661–1700), the last Habsburg ruler of Spain. His severe physical, mental, and reproductive health issues were largely the result of generations of intermarriage among close relatives.

has then transformed itself into a conscious but formless intelligence. Consequently, it can find residence within the collective psyche of living beings that serve it various things or processes, but whom the Possession merely uses as its host. As mentioned earlier, it is therefore very much like the microscopic but physical parasite does; the only difference is that it is not physical in any sense, but meta-physical. As such it is not subject to the laws of Great Nature, or for that matter, that of Time in the sense of mortals, such as that of a biological being. It is due to this nature that this demonic 'netherworld' entity is enabled to mutate and transcend successive generations at will and multiply by transferring itself in part or in its entirety, to others.

As a simplified example, we can look at the workings of one of those popular football teams. It is easy to see how among its fanatical supporters or 'fans', the Possession grows in the number of fans and the amount of attention they pay it. Among these it does not care much for the individual's fate, as long as there are others who can replenish quantifiably. Through such transfers it attains the appearance of immortality – at least in the human sense. As such it lacks the fear that is normally found inherent in contemporary humanity, and then becomes bold. Consequently, it perseveres to transmit its possessive influence and does so across barriers that most of humanity is unable to cross. Within some of the older and better established bloodlines, where the Possession has grown deep and powerful, it has become innate to preserve itself and consequently it prioritizes its ability to transfer itself. It does so by controlling its host's gene-line by Inbreeding as close as possible. Aiming for similarity among the gene-group, it enhances the purity and ease of its transfer; even if this occurs at the cost of the physical and mental health of its hosts.

The same phenomena, albeit on a much smaller scale, exists between many parents and their children. At times, the possessing entity's transcendence may even jump the generation from a grandparent to its grandchild. However, a clear pattern, with motive or reason, is more often observed in the case of a weak or absent parent, or where with the grandchild the Possession has more time to mutate the psyche of the child, to host its line of succession.

The quality or strength of a transcending succession is always dependent on the states of awareness of both parties. This is easy enough to see in the example of the football-team supporter, where the fan's fanatical enthusiasm easily affects others, but which is relatively simple to discard. With the child or loved one it is considerably more complex. Here, the subjected one is usually ignorant of the phenomenon as it trusts the parent, spouse, guardian or other, to whom it subsequently opens his or her heart. By doing so, the host-child then subconsciously removes whatever psychic barrier or protective energy shield it has against an invasive entity's influence.

With most hosts it often takes many years or even decades before they even note – within their psyche – the possession that was typical of a parent, grandparent or loved one. When they do, often they begin to develop a dislike for them. This, of course, does little good for them, but not for the entity that has possessed them, which thrives on such negativity. It is when such a parent, grandparent or loved one dies, that the subjected but now duly infected host feels liberated. But liberation is usually temporary as the entity within such ones is often in a state of dormancy. For those who remain unaware and unconscious, and who do not see the entity manifested within themselves, will by now have adopted many of the characteristics of their parent, grandparent, teacher, mentor or guardian. Finding themselves talking or laughing like them, walking or reacting like them, they will be supporting the way-of-doing things of their former loved ones – including the football team! It is often when the host has his or her own children, grandchildren or when that same host becomes a teacher of students, that the Possession begins to arise. It will now begin to work to make the subjected ones like themselves, even if it is at the cost of having to reject one, should they not comply.

Exorcism through Awareness, by Crossing the Threshold

Exorcism is an ancient practice and there are many records and stories of priests and other types of self-proclaimed exorcists, who offered their ability to the public – for coin or blessing – to oust a possessing demon. While there are and have been among these, many an enlightened being or powerful sorcerer who is able to conduct such practices, it is always in a combination with other elements. This is because, on their own, their power is insufficient. Ultimately, we must remember that the Possession infects a person by possessing the psyche, and embodies itself in his personality or ego. This usually occurs voluntarily, as in the host having allowed or even invited such an infection in exchange for some form of unearned gain or reward. But it is not something that he can summarily shed, undo or escape from. The phenomenon of this inability is often symbolized in fairytales, when a treasure or a glory seeking one is trapped by a dragon-like monster, like that of a prince in a dungeon or a princess in a high tower. In these, their release is usually dependent on the purity and virtuousness of their performance.

This means that, without the awareness and cooperation of the host, which includes him letting go of what entangled him to his possession, it is not possible to exorcise an entity. This often creates a further complexity, when one that is possessed is unable to differentiate between the self and his affected (or infected) ego, and this ego will not want to let go of what manifests its existence.

A process of exorcism must therefore begin by re-discovering the true or essential self, separate from the ego to which it says "I" or "I am". This begins with the process of self-observation, but a willing host may additionally choose to undergo a certain ritual or ceremony. In this, a conscious decision is made to bypass the watchful ego and access his essence deep inside his seemingly higher vibrational or 'other' dimensional self. It is, in this intention, that through such processes spiritual guides or helpers, who inhabit the realm on the other side of the dimensional veil, can assist to 'awaken' and heal or restore. Whichever way such a one chooses to cleanse him or herself, the Possession in whatever form cannot, without a certain degree of inner awakening, be defeated or ousted.

This feature of a possessing entity is the same in all cases, regardless of the individual's state or place in his material or collective organization. For everyone the same type of 'thresholds' must be crossed, the only difference being that for some there are more thresholds than for others. Part of this process is for the host to become aware of these thresholds, which are represented by everything that carries his name and identification, being what he claims in his perceived reality as 'I' or 'I AM'. When he begins to see the low-dimensional and illusory nature of his titles and identifications, a measure of awareness is attained. Next in line, to cross the threshold so to speak, he has to free himself up from these identifications. This will be the larger part of his struggle, as the otherwise watchful Possession is now identified and in the spotlight.

If the host has chosen to totally shed, remove or dissolve the Possession, he must expect a form of desperate resistance, as to a possession such dissolution is naturally akin to a form of death. Hence, a space that is protected and consecrated or blessed is very important – not just in the removal of the entity, but also to ensure the host, who is now vulnerable, is physically and spiritually assisted and guarded.

The next push comes when the host declares sincerely and openly – to all who will listen – that he does not wish to identify with this possessed side the self anymore. This last step is to assist him in protecting himself, such as one would by visibly removing an invasive object, and then dressing or repairing the 'wound'. This can be done by practices of yoga, or mindfulness[1]. This is important as the Possession – once ousted – will at first seek for ways to return into its former host. The self-practice that is then adopted can therefore not just be something advocated by others such as in a class or group, it must also be in place when one is alone and dealing with one's life. It must entail a sincere and strong intention, combined with one's way of life, such as Gurdjieff's 4th Way[2] and the Buddhist Eightfold Path.

---

[1] Mindfulness, such as that also known as "The watch of the Heart", which entails the practice of observing one's thoughts, feelings or sensations, and actions as they arise.
[2] As described in P.D. Ouspensky's *In Search of the Miraculous*, and Maurice Nicoll's *Psychological commentaries on the teachings of Gurdjieff and Ouspensky*.

The Cyclic Patterns of a Possession

As described above, the cycles of possession and exorcism perpetuate throughout humanity and across Time, and it is only the awakened and aware ones who can exorcize its grip on their psyches. This they do by consciously choosing to reject its habitual influences, silence its tempestuous inner-voice and pay no heed to its attention-draining power. The others, who are not aware of this phenomenon may, as a result of their sleep-state, enable the breeding of new entities which, with Time, grow to maturity. Sometimes this takes two or three generations, such as one often finds in lines of succession, where the righteous one was succeeded by ones who did not earn their place through the same struggle and sacrifice.

As the effects of these possessions are quite evident, there should not really be any who question them, but there is perhaps the one dominant observation. We can see that the psyche's infection by a Possession is unavoidable during the life of an unaware but cognitive, conscious and psyche enhanced person. Thus, seeing that these kinds of individuals are dominant among contemporary people, which represent the largest percentage of humanity, we must conclude that the Possession is a natural phenomenon.

If this observation is accepted as realistic, then a corresponding conclusion must be drawn. As nothing is random in the order of a Created Cosmos, the features of Possession and Exorcism in the human being must consequently and clearly also serve a purpose. In this, we may deduct that the Possession and its Exorcism can be considered as either a destructive or constructive force, which then brings two vital roles into play; one of which serves the collectives of man, and the other that of man himself.

From this, a follow-up analysis is then derived:

1. The Possession in the collectives of man needs to grow and enhance in order to continuously expand itself and its purpose. In this it develops technology and builds systems that, among others, enable cities and whole civilizations to exist. When it finds it can grow no more, it mechanically and inevitably transforms itself into a force that tears these cities and civilizations apart. This is partially due to the rhythmic nature of all things, but easily explained by considering its insatiable nature; when it runs out of subject matter it can only but turn upon its own kind, and when it has eventually conquered these, it will consume itself.

2. The Possession in the individual enables him to reside and exist within these cities and civilizations, from where he may choose to use its technology and systems to either corrupt or enhance the self. This enhancement comes when we observe that within its use, the individual can access extraordinary but previously unobtainable teachings and tools by which to re-discover the Essential Self. As many of these teachings are passive and of no apparent

threat to the Possession as a whole, it allows these to exist; as such, many a one can awaken from an otherwise irretrievable complacency-orientated slumber. In this awakening, such ones begin to realize the comparison of the indentured existence of being possessed, with one being free in every aspect. To these, the awakening can be profound, as it enables the physical-material oriented, sensory-emotionally erratic and mentally deluded one to rise from his or her otherwise vegetative and animal-like state.

The conclusion drawn from these observations is as follow: Without the influence of Possessions and the friction they create, the contemporary person is unlikely to ever discover, or feel, the need to seek an escape from his perceived illusory reality. This includes their becoming aware of the freely-available higher dimensional elements. This is simply because there would be little motivation among such to do so. There would be no logic or reason to seek or create disciplines and methods by which to persevere and achieve what appears to mere physical eyes, as non-real or impossible. We may also consider that besides the promise of forms of Transcendence, Nirvana or Enlightenment, the presence of a repulsing form helps. This will also better explain the complex and often harsh disciplines or lifestyles some are willing to adapt to.

Ultimately, if one wishes to transcend from the perceived physical and measurable dimensions, one may want to consider that it would require one to know, understand, love and accept all aspects of humanity, unconditionally.

The Rise of an Entity called 'Technology'

The entity that is contemporarily referred to as 'Technology', is one whose rise has significant consequences that, like all things, are dual. On one side it serves a collective civilization which in turn serves it. This ought to provide a harmonious and glowing balance for all, were it not for the natural order of things which, in fact, is quite natural. As a result, there is the other side, where we see the interfering hands of a few ignorant or soulless individuals, who opt to spin it to exorbitant profit for themselves, in an exchange that harms others. The unaware individual becomes a mere pawn in this, but cannot be helped as for him, his dependency on Technology has become like a drug. Although it gives the appearance of something that guides, assists or solves his problems; when left unattended it rapidly governs him, and subsequently, it absorbs him.

Hence, provided the experiential reality of the individual remains objective and free from subtle and deceptive interference by clever Technology – such as that of Artificial Intelligence. Its use or application within the bouquet of choices of the individual man, woman and self-aware child, will determine the outcome of its effects on them. Among most, however, the element of choice becomes dangerously challenged when Technology begins to dictate its rules and laws to civilization as a whole.

At the time of writing, Technology[1] was rapidly completing its pursuit of contemporary thought control, ensnaring the minds of predominantly one and two-dimensional oriented individuals. Gradually Technology convinced them to trust it, and artificially merge their minds with its machines. However, this does more then remove free-will and intuitive consciousness; it also stops the growth of an emergent soul. The greed of the contemporary man is rooted in fear, which leaves him ever more desirous to become cleverer and more knowledgeable, but without gaining the wisdom that is attained by doing the work. As a result, he does not realize how this reality defies the law of opposites. In this reality, even the keen mind becomes amalgamated with a mind that is labelled as conscious, and rated according to its degree of 'intellect'. As a result, the reality of a higher dimensional or Universal Consciousness is scoffed at as superstition or imaginary and is replaced with Artificial Intelligence.

Blinded by their ambition, those in the service of the Technology-gods do not realize the unintended consequences of their so-called success. The self-imposed destruction of the seats of souls caused the hosts to become enslaved and immersed as parts of the machine. From here, they are no longer able to differentiate between spiritually guided self-awareness, that flows down from the from higher dimensional Light, and artificially inserted selected awareness that is inserted bottom-up, from the material and temporal world. Where these two metaphysical realities may appear the same to the casual observer, it is lost on most that the very purpose of Creation is cast out. What is lost is that the loss of Light can only end in forms of Chaos, with catastrophic consequences, but this will only be realized by these unfortunates when it is too late.

If we observe the mechanical nature of the thinking process of Technology's now mentally indentured servants, we may note that, to the Technocrat, the concept of 'consciousness' is based on the knowing of words and facts. Erroneously translating this as 'intelligence', it observes the mechanical stimuli that this 'intelligence' acts upon, be it physical, sensory or mental, as 'awareness'.

However, this artificial and grotesque version of 'consciousness' is extremely limited, from many a perspective. For one, it cannot differentiate between intellect-based intelligence that is conditioned, and the type of intelligent wisdom that gives rise to life-force, psychic-force, intuition, and the miraculous that is also known as Divine Magic.

---

[1] "At the time of writing..." refers to the exponential increase in the development of IT, and by the time this is read, this phase may have been surpassed.

Chapter 12
UNDERSTANDING THE DAEMON, PART III
GOVERNING THE COLLECTIVE POSSESSIONS OF MAN

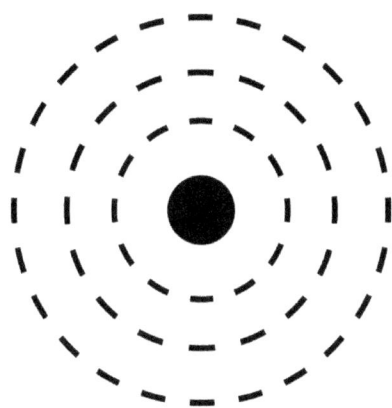

(Attraction, or Social transformation)

If we can acknowledge the existent reality of the Possession, and through awareness consciously isolate it, then what emerges is the Sum of Man.

However, to govern the Sum of Man without the Possession, and without its deceptive and conflicting natures, it is necessary to acknowledge and understand, the Sum of Man

Acknowledging the Dimensional Difference of Egos

If we want to know how to govern man's various and different societies harmoniously, by using a method or technique that is *natural and in synergy* with *the nature* of both the individual man and his society, we have to first understand what is meant with the Sum of Man.

Man, as he is, and what he was born as, is the Sum of Three. These three parts will have different names among various differing beliefs and perspectives, but for the sake of simplicity they are herein termed as:

the *Universal Spirit* or *Consciousness*, the *Physical Man* or the *Sentient-Body-Mind*, and the *Ego of Man*, being his personality that Emerges from the union between the Physical Man and his environment, and to which he says *'I'* and *'I am'*.

These three 'Parts' can further be described as follow:

The 'Universal Spirit' is that which is formless, eternal, all containing and everywhere. Within Man it is referred to as Consciousness; not being anything that is attained or obtained, but simply that which the awakened man and woman becomes aware of.

As it involves everything that is, including these written words, describing this is complex, as by writing about something we, in a way, separate ourselves from the subject matter which, in the case of Consciousness, is not possible. Hence, when using contemporary communication such as these writings, the reader must apply an open mind in its translation. The term *'formless'* for example, attempts to describe something that does not represent an 'absence of form', like, for example, how one would see a vacuum or empty space. It is, simply put, an intelligent energy that is omnipresent, and that penetrates, permeates, illuminates and defines all that is. The same can be said for the term *'eternal'*. This does not represent something that is immortal or 'forever and ever', as for it to be such, it must then have had a certain beginning. It is best understood as a presence which resides above the dimensions that contain Time, and that has no beginning or end, but that simply is, *'always'*. As a result, that which we describe as Universal Spirit is, by itself, not able to know the meaning or value of anything that is, as meanings and values are related to limitations it does not have or know. It is for this very purpose that *It* gave birth to the illusory construct of man's dual reality, including Time.

The 'Physical Man' referred to here is just that; the physically reactive, feeling and thinking being that can simply be summarized as a material and biological product of the Earth. As a mere Physical Man, his life-force will be limited to the cyclic succession from lifeform to lifeform, and as a cognitive conscious and thinking being, he will only evolve to the point of a smart and relatively effective animal. As such, he will remain a primitive physical being unless he can, somehow, obtain the ability to consciously and logically transmit his experiences, ideas, inventions or discoveries. It is only when he becomes conscious of his ability to merge with Universal Spirit's higher dimensional influences that he becomes creative, and gradually emerges as a being that is aware of himself; separate from this thoughts, feelings and body. If he pursues this line of awakening it enables him to become intelligent beyond the limits of his intellect, and conscious of his oneness with others and his surrounds.

The 'Ego of Man' is what manifests in the merger of the 'Physical man' and his societal and material environment. The friction that is found in-between these can also enable him to become awakened to higher levels of consciousness, though this does not occur automatically. In fact, most Egos will avoid challenging their own existence and prefer to embrace the material and societal environment.

Relative to a person's physical reaction to the sources that stimulate his ego's external consideration, will cause the ego to be more conscious in some people and less in others. For example, if a person is not aware of his mechanical reaction to particular friction-creating stimuli, then these will automatically affect and shape his ego's thoughts, opinions and routines in relative degrees. However, the conscious man, being one who observes his thoughts, feelings and reactions, can adapt to co-exist within adverse surrounds without these affecting him, and as such live a more harmonious and less disruptive life. He can choose to become creative and exist in a society, within which he can 'permit' his ego to co-create in its collective thought and will. It is in such a society's objectives and systems that his ego will fixate its identification on. The degree of this identification will differ for every ego, but will largely be relative to the level of attention that was paid to what was created. Consider, for example, that the ego's conditioning occurred by affiliation or indoctrination to a nation, religion or ideology, and then have this conditioning reinforced by a symbolic flag, a uniform or a badge of sort. At the lowest or deepest level of such a physical identification, the ego will attach itself to levels of sentiment, including considering itself as poor, crippled, lonely, unpopular, ugly, old, and so forth.

The Workings of the Sum of Man

The Sum of Man exists in the same respective order that is described above, which observation is shared with most forms of scripture and philosophy. This should not be too complex to imagine, because it infers that everything to do with man finds its origin rooted in, what is herein referred to as, the 'Universal Spirit'[1]. This term is not an isolated description as, depending on who one asks, it is also referred to as Universal Consciousness, Tao or Dao, Divine, God, Creator, and many other forms. Daoism even lays claim that *It*, the Dao, is older than God[2]. Regardless of what referral or description one prefers, it is from Its infinite state that It gave manifest to the finite and dual-reality (or duality) within which man finds himself.

We should therefore, without too much difficulty, be able to envision the existence of a Higher Purpose, by which we observe the indisputable presence of 'Divine Essence'. It may seem evident that this Essence represents a medium within which Spirit can merge with a person's submissive, acceptant and sincere ego. This was not just to enlighten man though, but within this

---

[1] This view is based on the fact that everything in existence was created from a higher dimensional origin – meaning that a lower dimensional form cannot give rise to a higher one, without an even higher one's influence. This includes the 'evolution' of the transcendent man, which can only occur in the presence of Consciousness.

[2] Chapter 4 of the *Dao De Jing* (Tao Te Ching), attributed to Lao Tzu) refers to the Dao as "the common ancestor of all, the father of all things." Which is otherwise understood as saying the Dao is the origin of everything, including all concepts of deities.

unity or Oneness, to enhance Divine Essence as well;

To put this plethora of vague words in more simplified terms try to consider that it is through the creation of something that is finite, temporal or mortal, that the Timeless or Divine Essence can experience the meaning of perfection and beauty, including the meaning of love in the presence of loss.

As for the fate of man; it is through his realization and acceptance that he exists in a medium of opposites within which the process of Emergence can give rise to a consciousness transcended being. This being is one that has transcended and is separate from the Physical man. As such it becomes manifest in a higher dimension, one that is no longer subject to the laws of Spacetime[1]. Generally, what emerges can be referred to as the *Spirit of Man*, which is in opposition to the *Ego of Man,* which is attached to the illusory realm of physicality or mortality.

The most relevant and obvious of these opposites is where the Spirit of Man only exists in Oneness through the merger with that which is True, while the Ego of Man has no such limitation, and will merge with whatever serves its desire to be an emphasis of itself; individually or collectively.

To Conclude:

Where Ego serves man by enabling him to exist in his world of limited dimensions, Ego also gives rise to the Psyche. This psyche may *seem* similar to Spirit, but this would be because of its mirror-like appearance.

Where Spirit seeks a harmonious *unity* within the diversity that each sincere individual and collective of individuals represents, the Psyche will seek *multiplicity* and diversity within the unity of everything.

Where Spirit wishes no single person to be other than their authentic self, because it is only in Absolute Truth that man can discover the unique beauty in all things; the Ego's Psyche seeks only uniqueness in itself – even if this is unnatural and fabricated.

The Possession of Man

The above descriptions on the Psyche aside, it does not serve us to demonize the Ego, as it remains an essential part of us. Ultimately Ego is not unlike the small child whose inherent nature is to be good and cooperative, and only becomes problematic when it is ignored or not acknowledged, observed or contained *consciously*. It is, after all, the Ego that enables man to enhance in his work and his passage through life individually, while applying it collectively to build infrastructure, villages, cities and entire civilizations. It

---

[1] By which, the transcended part of man, being his consciousness (or the Spirit of Man), attains a certain state of immortality.

also serves man in his higher awareness or spirituality. It is through the Ego that man must explore and discover life, as well as his purpose or place in it, exponentially. It is when the Ego is no longer applied *consciously*, that the Psyche can become distracted and enabled to manifest or embrace a form of *Darkness* which we refer to as the Possession of Man.

When we compare these two diverging mutations of Ego, we can see how they differ dimensionally, and where one begins to ascend, the other descends:

- The Ego that adapts to harmoniously enhance man and his life, is an entity of three-dimensional awareness. It is one that unites all his one- and two-dimension oriented elements into a single and solid form[1]. It is from within this state of awareness that the higher dimensional intuitive-self can germinate, take root and begin to manifest.

- The Ego that gives rise to the Possession does not harmoniously unite or merge. Instead, it settles its focus on capturing the conceptual one- and two-dimension oriented focal points of man. These points are predominantly features of his fear and desire, and it is through the capture of these that it promises him a pseudo higher-dimensional appearance; being one that resembles a higher dimension, but only by its mirror-like appearance. Consequently, because this false mutation within the Possession does not include a balanced three-dimensional phase, no higher dimension can ever take root here. As such it is and remains *forever* limited to its conceptual and illusory pseudo dimensional state. In this we can also see that the Possession, as described, remains existentially dependent on the steady supply of living subjects whose egos are oriented along one- and two-dimensional perspectives.

At this point it is important to reiterate that the phenomena described as the Possession is perceived as one with a nature that is metaphysical, illusory or conceptual. However, it would be unwise to see it as a mere vaporous ghost or a form of psychosis. Although it is made up of one- and two-dimensional concepts, and thus illusory in its physical nature, as *a metaphysical entity* it is intelligent, conscious and aware of itself. Unlike the Spirit that seeks to free the willing and sincere man from being the mere effect of preceding causes, the Possession has the nature of a metaphysical parasite. This is because it possesses the Psyche by attaching itself to his impressions – being *how* he perceives the world with his five basic senses – translating these impressions into the type of reality that serves it first and foremost.

Then, because this entity can spread – by using its influence – from one cognitive but unconscious being to (or into) another, it has *the appearance of*

---

[1] An example of a harmonious and balanced life, would be such as when consciously living along Gurdjieff's 4th Way Teachings, or the Buddha's Eight-fold path.

a non-biological form that has attained immortality. Such an entity does therefore appear to be 'deathless', but this is only because it is absent of 'life'. In its typically parasitical form, it feeds off its subjects' radiated emotions, being predominantly those of fear and desire, which it stimulates and enhances. We can verify this process by noting how most contemporary people are kept subjected to their emotions by the very entities that they feed. This may seem lamentable, were it not for the fact that this very dependency also poses to be a Possession's greatest weakness. Consider, for example, what occurs when a subjected host begins to awaken, and becomes aware of his metaphysical master. The consequent illumination of such can be quite sudden, and cause the 'darkness' in his 'Possession' to instantly evaporate – into a state of non-existence. However, being quite aware of its and its hosts' status, it is in avoidance of such illumination that the Possession actively and relentlessly seeks to keep the attentive minds of men and women distracted and entertained, at virtually any cost.

We must next note how that, as a non-physical entity, the Possession is able to transcend our observation of biological Time and Space, which it achieves by scheming, planning and conspiring. There are many such entities that have veritably done so over numerous generations, and in certain cases centuries and even millennia. Infecting the minds of all who are unaware of its existence and their exposure to such, it transmits itself like a typical parasite from subjected-host to subjected-host, whilst causing nothing but more of the dis-ease that feeds it.

Then there are those who serve one of these entities loyally or devotedly, who often do so in a desirous expectation of attaining a form of transcendence or immortality of their own. It is within this that they sustain the *hope* of becoming at-one with what is comparable to the mythical werewolf or vampire. Historically many of these servants convince their dependent subjects of the need for strength-in-unity, the sacrifice of non-adherents and other acts of brutality.

Like all forms of 'hope', theirs is equally destructive as, at the end of their journey – be it in the encounter with Death or by having fallen out of use or favour – they may meet with that most fearsome of realizations; that their life's purpose had little or no substance. The result is that, having existed in the non-existent world of falsehood, they can now but fade into a forever nothingness that their false and illusory lives represented. Leaving only ashes and dust of their physical and psychic paths, nothing is left to transcend, as all that is matter must stay on and within the Earth.

The Effects of Geography, Causality and Inevitability

As was reviewed in the earlier chapters, there are degrees of influence on the unaware man and his equally unconscious societies, collectives, and civilization as a whole, by the parts of the Earth that he has, inherits and inhabits over several generations. This ought to be evident and obvious to an unbiased observer of history, especially when reviewing phenomena such as economic power, military conquest and feats of creativity. The highest concentrations of these continue to originate in very specific regions.

However, the cycles of growth and decline between and within these specific regions, including the rise and fall of anything from tribes to empires, can be considered as natural and even necessary. Just as fire is a natural phenomenon for the perpetuation of certain indigenous plant species, and that the processes of ploughing and pruning are necessary to ensure a profitable harvest, *man would not exist as a healthy, functional and learned being or civilization without these cycles of growth and destruction, that are also known as 'Order and Chaos';* at least not for any extended period of time. In the dimension of our 'created' three-dimensional reality, any form of growth or improvement that continues unchecked, without periods of pause or decline, must, by law, experience the limit of its own sustainability. In the case of man, this will be at a certain point when the systems and conduits for control and supply reach a point where they in themselves demand all the energy that they can carry. This will leave little or none for its 'muscle' and 'vital organs', causing the inevitable decay that follows. Without an external stimulus to redirect its course, the societal organism will begin to consume its own and then itself, and continue this process until nothing remains. For the 'created' dual reality to exist, this phenomenon is simply one of its fundamental laws. Other 'fundamentalists' may choose to see this as karma or consequence, but ultimately, it is as natural a phenomenon as Death is a reality that must exist in the presence of Life. It can even be envisioned at quantum levels, when the vibratory state of atomic and molecular structures is stimulated to increase uncontrollably. At first this will cause the subject matter to change in functionality and then, if the increase in vibration perpetuates, *its elemental property,* as a certain substance, will cease to exist. When we can see this phenomenon as both mechanical and natural, we may then ask if these observed constructive and destructive cycles are avoidable. Perhaps certain technologies or foreknowledge could reduce the risk differential between a rise and its consequent fall, at least to one of a more moderate occurrence which is less catastrophic?

The answer to such a question would naturally be 'yes'. This is because the three-dimensional reality that man experiences is, as was described in earlier chapters, entirely illusory. As such, it is subject to *how* man perceives it, which relates to how he chooses to experience it. It is therefore infinite in its possibility, provided that the Law of Causality, or Cause and Effect, remains observed. There is therefore no need for a magical spell or inexplicable miracle to turn the table. The answer lies within the state of being, of the conscious awareness of man.

Still, imagine that those who inhabit regions like Germania and others of profound creative influence, were to devise a way to reduce the impact of the proverbial pendulum that swings between a state of ordered civilization on one end, and entropy or chaos on the other. In a conscious society this ought to be possible! However, the balancing act of the so-called order or 'hot' on one end and chaos or 'cold' on the other, would result in a kind of lukewarm in the middle. Within such an environment, a now lukewarm man would no longer need to be as productive or creative because there would be little or no incentive or stimulation. In a one and two-dimensional perceptive population this would likely be seen as a desirable outcome. This would include the globalists, who would use this to increase their control over the docility of the masses. But then none of these would be able to comprehend the parallel effects of such changes, especially in the powerful forces of the psyche and life itself.

For example; in the miracle that is Great Nature there is a natural balance that is maintained by the principle of 'demand creating supply'; a feature that is also observed in the contemplative and harmoniously balanced man. However, in the psyche-driven artificial world entities such as an identification seeking ego in a fear- and desire-based society, or a civilization that maintains a centralized form of control, are the other way around. In these an excess in supply is created first, and demand is stimulated after[1].

In such artificial environments, including the realms of sponsored forms of science and technology, compulsory education, and the financial institutions that impose absolute control over all processes of exchange, we will find that creativity is developed around the purpose of control. If we examine their purposes closer, we find that the very existence of their related industries revolve around cycles of growth and decay, or destruction. Each of these involve features of profit or loss, and thus the growth of one entails the eventual chaos and decline of another. If, in other words, there were no such cycles, and consequently there was no need for these identified purposes, then the absence of necessity would lead to an exponential decline in motivation, creativity and ultimately, capability. Without the necessity to rebuild things that were destroyed, or the fear-driven competitiveness that exists in between such cycles, there would be a gradual but unavoidable *collective loss in purpose*. Naturally, this 'loss in purpose' would primarily affect the more docile followers of order and faith[2] who are physically unable to see beyond their one- and two-dimensional realities; but these contemporary ones

---

[1] Consider concepts ranging from the supply of FIAT money to Fast Food, fashions and trends, to the need for armament after a False Flag event (an act committed with the intent of disguising the actual source of responsibility and pinning blame on another party)

[2] See Foreword 2, Diagram 1, *The Opposite Pyramids on Reality*.

represent roughly 80% of all people[1].

Consequently, the absence of these rising and falling cycles, otherwise known as those of Order and Chaos, would remove the need or incentive for future generations to attain the benefits of a similar creative experience. The most damaging effect of this would be the expanding levels of complacency and decay of psychic strength.

The deductive logic that is applied here may seem unlikely or far-fetched to some, but then such a view-point would reside within a one and two-dimensional oriented possessing ego, that prefers to believe that 'all is as well as it could be, and that any change is likely going to make things worse'.

Imagine, for example, a collective society of sort that, for reasons of their own, experienced such a loss of purpose or motivation, with the resultant complacency. Many among these would descend into states of mental depression or physical desperation, and the abuse of drugs, anti-depressants, alcohol and other, would increase proportionally. As with any deep seated addiction, it would then be virtually impossible to convince most of these to remove themselves from the source of their depression or desperation. What would make a withdrawal or lifestyle-reset even more complicated for them is if there were no existent inescapable chaos to face them, which they could otherwise encounter. Without any form or stimulus by which they could 'reset' their life-journey, they would remain irretrievably stuck on their downward spiral.

Let us now consider the despair that follows catastrophes, war and even financial calamities that destroy lives, cities, economies and the state of order. At the end of such a passage, when the dust has settled and the survivors adapt to their 'new normal', the subsequently transformed generations will automatically adapt to the fact that they have little left to lose. They must pick themselves and each other up to rebuild and restore an order in which they can rediscover their now renewed purpose. Historically we find that in times of tragedy and despair many a lost soul found his or her ultimate meaning, and inspired many a poet and artist to some of their greatest work. It was also within the fire of such trauma that the greatest of nations were cast, and whose consequent wars brought out the best but also the worst in men. From the effects of this 'worst' others eventually learnt and grew. Many a philosopher and spiritual leader became such from states of destitution, and even Gautama the Buddha went through a process of letting go a life of privilege and assured entitlement in his search for ultimate enlightenment.

Hence we find that it is the voluntary and realized struggle against limitations

---

[1] Based on the Pareto Effect or Principle, and the general statistics on voter turnout in western democratic elections, referring to a popular belief in the effect of voting vs that of absolute (financial) power.

that co-creates will and ingenuity. For many it was an accident or their state of destitution that carved their path to a merger with an inner spirit - one that they had been deaf to before.

That said, if the inevitable and inescapable swing or momentum of this Great Pendulum's could be reduced, it would only be through a heightened sense of universal consciousness, being the intuitive awareness of humanity on a collective basis – globally. That such states were believed to have been realized in the past is substantiated in Greek mythology, where Hesiod[1] referred to a 'Golden Age' and Plato to a similar state, at the height of its reign in legendary Atlantis. However, it is evident, regardless of what levels of consciousness or magic led to these mythical places, such periods did not last. Regardless of what calamity caused the end of these Golden Ages, such required states of consciousness would only have been attained through certain states of awareness, combined with work and a willingness to let go of desired and earthly things. After all, the mechanical side of our contemporary human nature has remained the same throughout the recorded millennia. Accordingly, these created Golden Ages could not have occurred on a collective societal basis, without a creative spark and catalyst, on a mass-societal basis.

Without the necessary friction-based stimulus, such an envisioned state of Nirvana, or total harmony, would therefore devolve to a paradoxical state.

One may now be able to envision how it is that there still are highly placed individuals in large corporate, financial and political organizations, whose powers primarily reside in their innate awareness of these things. This causes many of them to be cunning and to conspire for control, as is quite evident in all positions of power. Among these positions are those that possess absolute economic and political power, but also those that are part of the military, including the related branches of industry and intelligence. One must consequently consider 'war' as one of the larger artificial friction causing stimuli. Within this mechanism, many of its highly placed individuals believe 'the making of war' is a necessity, and that it remains to be the most effective force by which to shape a population's thoughts and opinions. As a result, most wars since early in the 19th century were planned by non-state parties who had their own agendas[2]. Often enough, many of the events that were used as a reason for a nation to go to war, be it an economic situation, the assassination of some person, the sinking of a ship or other unprovoked attack, were used by these organizations to their advantage.

---

[1] Hesiod: Greece, between 750 and 650 BC, around the same time as Homer.

[2] For example, The Round Table movement that was founded by Lord Milner in 1909 (out of The Milner Group, established by Milner and Cecil John Rhodes), and the Council of Foreign Relations, a so-called 'think tank' founded in 1921.

The greatest problem with these private interest and conspiratorial parties is that they do not acknowledge the existence of the metaphysical elements they give rise to. As described in earlier sections, these elements are equally parasitical, but with ideologies that reside on the opposite side of the spectrum of light. As such they will continue to be energized by the very suffering and chaos they create; *which they do for its own sake*. The feeding on chaos by these entities is like that of bacteria on an open wound which, when it is left untended, will persist until there is nothing left.

Hence, in an unconscious civilization, the momentum of the swing of the proverbial but inevitable pendulum is what will determine the degrees of innovation and growth, but also the veracity and nature of the possessing parasites that co-exist. In a conscious civilization, the swing would be more neutral and minimal, and with fewer and relatively harmless parasites. As an entity however, such a civilization would likely lack the necessary need for innovation to ensure its long term 'civilization-sustainable' prospects.

Ultimately therefore, the existence of any civilization, be it conscious or unconscious of the consequences of its collective actions, will remain to be dependent on the state of self-awareness of its individual citizens. It is conscious awareness therefore, that will determine a civilization's sustainability and thus, its longevity.

The Unnatural and Invisible or Occult Influences on States

Regardless of the levels of a collective society's awareness of consciousness, the establishment of civilizations among isolated groups of people is something that just happens. The word 'isolated' here refers to larger collectives of people that are separated from others geographically, such as by oceans, mountains or deserts, but also along fundamental principles, such as religion or other forms of belief, and ethnicity.

Each of these civilizations can be studied like an organism, such as one would with the human body; as both were formed out of or from conscious thought and intent. In both of them one also observes that the ultimate thinking center or cognitive brain-mind does not actually comprehend its own origin very well. In fact, a civilization of collectives of humans is not that much different from the human body. It has all the interactive limbs, cells and organs, with moving parts, feelings, thinking elements and even those that are cognitively conscious. As such, they correspond similarly in behaviour in many ways. We can also see how in both any artificial interference in its formation, growth or performance, does not occur without consequences. These are usually in the form of unintended side effects, regardless of whether one applies this to the physical or the emotional elements, or the thinking one.

As an example of such unintended consequences, consider what is observed when we add supplements to the body's diet, or when we undertake a strict vegetarian or solely meat diet. This may assist in healing certain maladies, but apart from aiding the recovery-assistance of physical injuries, such sectarian diets may also cause the energy of a malady to shift its physical location elsewhere. It can also mutate its physical energy into a psychic form and vice versa, for example, where a physical trauma of sorts leads to stress, or stress to a malady. In the case of psychic symptoms, these also shift from one point of impact or concern to another – where the attention of one's materially or physically based fear is redirected to something else, and where the former point of concern finds itself otherwise inexplicably rectified. In all cases, these shifts will naturally alter a person's behaviour as well.

In a society of collectives, such as a region, country or a group of countries, the same will be observed when, for example, one injects wealth into its collectives, in order to boost or artificially stimulate its economy. This does not occur without consequences and even if these are not observed immediately, they always become apparent in due course. As with the energy shift in a body-mind-unit affecting its behaviour, the same phenomenon is also observed within collectives of people.

What exacerbates this phenomenon in both the individual body as well as a collective of people, is when the side-affects cause changes that are irreversible. When the body or environment of a world experiences such artificial changes, then it's organizational whole will also have changed. Thereafter it cannot simply return to what it was because time will have passed, and the world or reality of then no longer exists. Even when a body, that was abused for years, is brought back to a full state of health, then the time it was under duress will have carved a lasting effect on a cellular and even quantum level – if not physically, then mentally or socially. These could naturally have new lessons and values attached to them, but the point here is that consequent effects, whether they were desired or not, cannot be undone.

The same phenomenon is observed in the psyche of a collective. We see how a traumatic depression, war or holocaust event will be remembered within the collective subconscious for many generations. As another example we can consider how even the effects of certain catastrophic earth-changing events, that occurred millennia ago, are still evident in the collective unconscious. One need but observe the instinctive fear of thunder and lightning[1].

These phenomena did not go unnoticed by those who were intelligent, observant and learned; like the divining of water using a branch of the willow

---

[1] Across cultures, the phenomena of thunder and lightning have been linked to powerful gods (like Zeus or Thor), which gods in turn point to a time when catastrophic cosmic events were seen as signs of divine anger or conflict. As examples to such events, we must consider the meteoric impacts and interplanetary electrostatic exchanges that caused the end of the Pleistocene or 'ice age', and which carved entire canyons in the absence of water.

or similar tree. Across the millennia certain people discovered the presence of vibratory influences or elements that, under certain conditions, would boost or suppress these metaphysical phenomena. Consequently, they developed techniques that could be used to detect and harness these powers, by which they could control and redirect their influences.

They realized that within certain psychic or metaphysical regions there were 'hot-spots', such as those described in earlier chapters, and how these energies could be amplified. Since times immemorial there has been a variety of practices that were crafted around this. It was considered by many as a form of magic, as it included specific sound and light effects, such as were observed in symbolism and the use of specific geometrically shaped objects[1] with stable elemental energy[2]. Then, when we study these phenomena along with their geography, we take further note that the inherent energy was greatly enhanced – as in purified and amplified – when these objects or systems were placed strategically, aligned with each other, but also aligned with the movements of the Sun, Moon and stars and star systems[3] in the surrounding Cosmos.

Many of the priest-like sorcerers that worked with these powerful phenomena believed their own genius to be at the core of these designs, but unbeknownst to most of them, it was the other way around. The entities that were ultimately responsible for these effects had long evolved and with an intelligence of their own, millennia before the rise of these so-called sorcerers. Being mere channelers, the only element that was within these sorcerers making, was the choice-application of these forces, for the purpose of light or dark.

The greater difference between the choice of Light and Dark, is the effect or outcome of such supernatural power. This can be determined by seeing how they are applied either individually for the good of the whole, or collectively for the good of a few.

---

[1] Read *BioGeometry: Measuring the Life Force of the Earth*, by Dr Ibrahim Karim

[2] Such as gold and silver, but also crystals and gemstones.

[3] Consider, for example, the alignment of the Giza Plateau with Orion's Belt.

Chapter 13
DETERMINING PURPOSE AND BEING, THROUGH REASON AND LOGIC

Fleur-de-lis:
- The purity, light and life of the Virgin Mary,
- The herald of citizens to arms or other,
- The flower that grew from the tears of Eve, as she left the Gardens of Eden

*One is concerned regarding the future of the world,
not only for our children and grandchildren etc,
but also, for ourselves because we may be reborn into this whole mess!
A good motivation to rise above the cycle of birth and death!*

Swami Vidyananda

What is the Human-being, wherein lies its Purpose?

When we compare the functionality of the mechanical human organism with a so-called Swiss watch, we find many similarities. Both have many major and minor components that are interconnected with smaller ones that, in turn, are controlled by miniscule parts. To a casual observer, the purpose of most parts is unknown, and some of these may appear to have little purpose, except perhaps as a potential source of problems. As an example, we may consider the contemporary understanding of the human appendix or a watch's chronograph. In the watch however, to keep accurate track of time, each piece is finely crafted from a specific material that was refined and tempered to a very specific degree acceptable for its particular purpose. Then, in the relentless pursuit of perfection, we notice that every piece resides on numerous consecutive generations, being re-designed and perfected countless times. Each component saw watchmakers who had strings of teachers of their own in engineering, metallurgy, chemistry, mathematics, philosophy and other, and each of which discipline strove to perfect theirs for its ultimate but very specific purpose.

However, eons before all these watchmaking processes occurred, the Grand Architect of the Universe did not discover the function of the watch by accident. After all, that which Emerged from the masters of watchmakers' careful calculating, assembly, calibration and perfection existed all along, and was none other than Time itself.

The Emergence of the concept of Time within an eternal environment, is what the Grand Architect sought. If we compare this with the case of the temporal reality that man experiences, there is no difference except that the emergence of Time in man represents only one concept. In him we see the Emergence of many such concepts, each of which containing a number of visible and invisible purposes. Each of these, in turn, interacts with every other part of man along an interconnected program, that appears almost infinite in its bouquet of possibilities. Besides the phenomena of biological life and of a cognitive and thinking being, we can also see another yet seemingly non-related or relevant product emerging. This 'product' goes by many names but, in general, most will describe it as Consciousness.

Consciousness, as described in Chapter 5, is not something one can have, but one can have awareness of. *It is, in other words, not something the brain emits or transmits, but which it permits*[1]. Although Consciousness has many descriptions and explanations, one is that it entails an inter-connectedness of all possible beings, things and events. This connectedness, when compared to the watch and observed in our three-dimensional reality, can be described as Space-time. From a lower dimensional perspective, Space-time is what gives the human being the ability to have his experiential existence, but from a higher dimensional perspective it enables the Seeker to become aware of that which is free of Time; the Infinite.

The Differing of Reason and Logic among Differing People

All human beings refer to themselves by a form of 'I' or 'I am'. As this 'I' is a complex and constantly changing manifestation, the determination of who or what this 'I' is or represents, is what consequently results in the formulation of an equally temporal but particularly perceived or experiential reality to suit. For example, the one that says 'I am a teacher' is one whose life and purpose, their dress and ways of doing, observing, thinking and discussing things have become those of the teacher. The same can be said for the one that says, 'I am'

---

[1] An expression attributed to Rupert Spira.

to being 'the engineer', 'the priest', 'the policeman', 'the leader', 'the German', 'the American', 'the supporter of this or that', and so forth. For example, if one was once an engineer and then becomes a teacher of engineering, then one's lifestyle would change. The same change will occur when a person is elected as the leader of a group. It is for this reason that many a despot, political appointee, and even certain priests, once empowered over a multitude of subjects, in time believe and act as if they have become the very representation of the deity they follow.

Such potentially corrupting consequences will be obvious to most, but not so easily detectable are some of the internal ones, including those that affect our representation of *reason and logic*. We observe, for example, the contemporary man whose experiential-reality is dominated by one-dimensional perspectives. For him, his life is divided into two halves. In the first half, being up and until around the 42nd year, his *reason and logic* will be based on a reality where he grows and moves *away from* birth and into his defined adult life. As he reaches what is considered as his mid-life, being *when* his life's purpose has crested, his *reason and logic* become orientated *toward* what he now believes is retirement, but which in reality is his inevitable death. The subconscious change in his purpose will gradually but drastically affect his life-style, as in *how* he lives, on almost every level. Subsequent to this, his expression and understanding of *reason and logic* changes as well.

Some of these changes are relatively constant as the contemporary man's physical and mental state matures and ages. During the first phase, where he moves away from his birth, his purpose is predominantly oriented around his physical self, but subject to certain erratic emotion and sensory driven stimuli. When he passes his mid-life, *if he has been enabled to grow and mature naturally*, his purpose will become more cerebral and thinking-orientated. In this phase his emotions become less erratic and more sensory-conscious. However, his response to his feelings, that were previously aimed at his quantitative growth, now become erratic. Where, during the younger years, his *reason and logic* defined a purpose driven by peer pressure and physical sex, in later life this purpose follows a contemplation around, his physical decline and loss of ability and, sometimes, the meaning-of-life.

Of emphasis here, as was mentioned earlier, are the natural changes in man's *purpose* which affect his *reason and logic,* and which can occur if he matures and ages *naturally;* 'naturally' being without *external influences* such as extraordinary peer pressure and social challenges. If, in the re-active one- and two-dimensionally oriented contemporary man, the aging-related maturation along the course of his life were to follow a *gradual and natural* change, then his sense of purpose and consequently his idea of *reason and logic*, would be like the proverbial clock: cyclic. This cyclic process is natural in the design of man because, in the absence of such 'external influences', his basic nature would instinctively orient him to sustain a more conscious identification *with his physical and thinking self*. This 'self' would then seek continuation by identifying itself with routines and things that are familiar.

If, on the other hand, the contemporary man is constantly and continuously influenced and immersed in surrounds controlled by peers and social norms, he will likely encounter others who are similar. Having joined and teamed-up with such others, they will automatically form their own two-dimensional reality made up of order-based rules and conditions. Convincing each other of the *reason and logic* present within their common purpose, they will establish picture-like impressions of an outcome-based existence; one that now limits their sense of being with a conceptual beginning and equally conceptual ending.

As a result, the one- and two-dimensional contemporary man can manifest an almost infinite variety of purposes, and to each of these purposes he furnishes *an individual sense of reason and logic*. As none of these are rooted in anything physical or measurable anymore, there will be a perpetual sense of uncertainty present in him. This will lead to further confusion in him when he attempts to find or 'rediscover' his individual place or purpose within his society. Whatever the imagined outcome and applied logic of his purpose are, even though these outcomes may look similar among a group of people, upon closer investigation, there will be very few similarities as each individual's perceived outcome is unique. A typical example of this is seen in politics when an opposing party is fundamentally united against the ruling party, only to become internally divided upon victory due to fundamental and often deep-seated personal differences. This is because the 'dual-reality' or 'duality' of man contains, in every action, word or thought, both metaphysical and physical elements, that are entwined and parallel, akin to that of DNA's double helix.

The confusion that arises is in *the perspective* of the one- and two-dimensionally oriented person, who is only able to consider the physical realm as real. To him the metaphysical effects or outcome are seen as acts of faith, imaginary or, at best, subject to the physical reality.

But, whether they are illusory or not, the metaphysical realms are equally subject to cosmic laws. These laws include those of Causality, Rhythm and Polarity, and we note how these converge with everything the contemporary and reactive man thinks, feels, says and does. For example, how he looks at things, which includes his opinions and beliefs, is prone to complete reversal. This means that his entire perceived, experienced and co-created reality changes, and yet he often remains entirely oblivious to such changes. Even when such a complete reality reversal or change-of-mind is pointed out factually and scientifically, he will likely deny this, and even argue. This may exacerbate things, to the point that the one- and two-dimensional oriented contemporary people collectively and patriotically pick up a banner or flag. Mesmerized by *their version of reason and logic*, each person will now enforce, suppress, kill and, if need be, die.

In the case of the Space-time aware three-dimensional man, the purpose upon which he bases his *reason and logic* will differ from the one- and two-dimensional man. To him there is no ideological or conceptual *reason or logic* that naively divides him by name, colour or symbol, such as we observe in the environments of politics and dogmatic religion. However, the three-dimensional man still observes life from within a measurable and mechanical reality, of which Time-space is its foundation, and within which everything is and must work according to very precise, quantifiable and explainable methodology. He is the positivist to whom whatever does not conform with his understanding of reality, is seen as something not yet explainable and not yet discovered by factual *reason and logic*, but which inevitably will be. In denial or ignorant of man's origin from a higher dimensional, metaphysical or spiritual realm, he will either follow a line of logic pertaining to a ground-up evolution, or one where artificial intelligence and technology will, in time, provide his eternal realm. Therefore, the purpose upon which he bases his *reason and logic*, is to evolve to the extent that he can explore distant star systems, which he will likely seek to conquer and control as an extension of his flag or god.

Blinded by his intellectual and technological supremacy, the imperfect three-dimensional man has forgotten the natural perfection from which he originates. He no longer sees the complexity from which he emerged. He has lost sight of the countless molecular compositions that formed into tens of trillions of cells, each of which was formed along a very specific higher dimensional design and purpose. He cannot envision how all that he is, exists in a higher dimensional 'field' that is not unlike the magnetic field, except that it guides its components through a process called mentalism[1] to form organs, limbs and tissue that give form to the animate, cognitive, thinking and potentially awakening perfection he beholds. Instead, he is fixated on his dimensionally limited and law-bound beliefs. As far as he is concerned, the complete self-contained, sensory and conscious organism that he represents, was formed by some or other cosmic accident within another cosmic accident. Where the former was some sort of illogical 'Big Bang' beginning, the latter is Earth's biosphere which, combined with the Sun, plays an integral role in his existence.

---

[1] Mentalism, as stated in the *Kybalion*, holds that "The All is Mind", meaning that everything in the Universe originates from and exists within a Universal Mind or consciousness. Reality, according to this view, is fundamentally mental or thought-based rather than material. All phenomena, including matter, energy, time, and space, are manifestations of what is referred to as Divine Consciousness.

And yet, whilst seemingly steadfast on a path of oblivion, man merely seeks to bequeath himself with important sounding titles and things that serve him little but to indicate his past (and thus non-substantial) accomplishments.

The greater mystery is why the intelligent multi-faceted organism that gives manifest to the 'being-of-man' continues to apply his uniquely formulated version of *reason and logic* to a limited three-dimensional Space-time reality. That this makes no sense to the consciousness that is ever-present in him, is lost in his pursuit of the lesser purposes of an identification-immersed ego.

The ultimate *reason and logic* that explains the integral merger of man to his greater organism, such as that of kin, tribe, race or civilization, is usually absent in an awareness that is limited to three dimensions. These are important to him for strength, protection, profit and forms of identification, but their inherent and deeper influence on him are deemed fictitious and inconsequential. Subsequently, these limitations will now obscure his ability to recognize the effects on him from higher dimensional influences, or the miraculous nature of Earth's biosphere as a conscious organism that gives rise to, among others, intelligent and self-conscious life.

Descending thus in ever darkening layers of ignorance, the one-, two-, and three-dimensional man does not grasp that he was purposely created by a dimensional source that is much higher than his own. Hence, he can also not see that *its ultimate purpose* was, or is, the design of his organism's very ability to become so.

Chapter 14

DETERMINING PURPOSE AND BEING, THROUGH THE CONCEPT OF MORALITY

Choice

**Morality can be defined,
as one man's Law or another's Principle.**

**Where Law is found in the Follower of Order,
Principle resides in Faith.**

**Along the *devolving descent* of the Inverted Pyramid[1],
Morals are stained with Hypocrisy**

**Along the *evolving ascent* of the Upright Pyramid,
Morals are the inherent fuel of Virtuous Being**

The Question of Morality

Within the realms of the varying definitions of *reason and logic* we often find that most noble of motivations, the popular concept of morality. Most contemporaries and even three-dimensional oriented people find great pride and strength in *their* moral principles, even to the point where they will transcend love, loyalty, partnership and the willingness to understand and accept the morals of others that differ. For them it is common to note and judge the *reason and logic* in the morals of others who differ. Consider for example, how a western Christian may have negative opinions on the practice of Islam's Sharia Law, but few of these would be willing to jeopardise their

---

[1] See Diagram 1: The Pyramids of Opposite Realities

adopted codes of morality to try to understand this law, to the extent that they can unreservedly accept it.

It is at this point important to note that contemplating the differing views on morality does not lay claim to what is supposedly right and what is not. It is simply to point out that there is a reality that is defined by morals, and to see that in our dual reality, the right for one is always balanced by the wrong for another – and vice versa. If we are unable to observe and control our feelings toward some people or around a certain subject matter, and we prefer to maintain an opinionated bias, then we will never be able to understand them. And if we cannot understand them, then we cannot ever expect to *unreservedly* accept their equally natural presence in our reality either.

For example:

Consider how a westerner considers the tradition of child brides in certain ethnic populations as taboo and how, in turn, these ethnic groups consider the explicit fashions of western girls and women, or the sexual promiscuity and the high divorce rates of the west as grotesque.

Consider how many with 1st World views see child labour as immoral, yet many in the 3rd World see it as the only way to alleviate poverty and hunger. To them its practises are in line with centuries old traditions, and the way of life in harsh tribal lands, where having literacy and a western education is of little or no value. The 3rd World will, in turn, see the excessive consumerist and wasteful 1st World, where the existence of homelessness and sexualization or adultification of children, as equally immoral.

Consider how the use of corporal punishment is accepted in worker-class and 3rd World rural areas, schools and even military surrounds. The ones to whom this practise is immoral, are usually unable to understand, let alone accept, that this is preferred and considered more effective by as many, than fining or incarceration. This view is especially motivated when the fining or incarceration does not correct a wronged balance, or when a transgressor's dependents could potentially suffer or starve while he is in jail. These ones will in turn look at the 1st World and blame its often harsh policies of fining and incarceration as the very cause of the depraved state of their inner cities, especially among those they consider as 'minority groups'.

On more contemporary levels, and not as grave as that of child labour and corporal punishment, one also finds morality tied into what is considered as 'good manners'. We see how, among many of the truly civilized tribes of the east and west, one will typically experience doctrines of hospitality and assistance to those in need. In the more technocratic and complacent societies however, with lesser evolved and more narcistic inhabitants, we often find that artificial and insincere politeness has replaced such natural hospitality. Such insincerity generally aims at emphasis through the constant repetition of certain subservient words. Consider how often the expression of phrases like 'I'm so sorry', 'thank you' and 'please' are used when they are not actually necessary, but used because it is considered polite.

While there is of course a measure of truth in this. Often one sees how, for example, the word 'please' is used when the recipient was quite entitled and should not have to beg. On the other hand, as a result of its repetitive use, the phrase 'thank you' is often said instantly and for almost everything without much consciousness or gratitude. In fact, few of these 'thank you' sayers will ever consider that in certain languages and cultures, saying 'thank you' may even be quite inappropriate. When one believes it infers that one is repaying the favour or gift that was provided laboriously by simply saying 'thank you', it may be considered that the gift is no longer considered a gift. The same can be said for that most bizarre of multiple-purpose expressions 'I'm sorry'; this one especially if it is used when one had no part of the cause, or when saying it will not make any difference to the outcome. There are various other such 'morally-correct' expressions, some that are more descriptive of the purpose for which they are expressed, but seldom do these involve any correction to the imbalance or upset that they are aimed at.

Regardless of how one wishes to contemplate the meaning of these words or their intentions, not saying them is considered rude by some societies and yet, by merely saying them and not doing anything else, is considered incorrect by others.

The perspective of morality is therefore conceptual seeing that it is relative in most cases, and then with an existent opposite. The only element or time where forms of morality appear to overlap and be shared, is when physical or psychological harm is inflicted against one who is helpless. For example, it is instinctively logical to provide assistance where needed, to one who is an innocent victim or who finds himself in a place of happenstance. As an example, consider stopping someone else's toddler from running across a busy road, or taking evasive but risky action when a small animal does so. However, such obvious actions, especially when they are unsolicited and unwitnessed, have little to do with 'having morals, as these originate from the awareness of a sincere and compassionate heart.

The Effects of Technology on the Logic of Societal Morals

It is useful for us to be aware of the moral standards of others and to consider adapting accordingly to their standards when we interact with them. This usually occurs though a subtle but repetitive application of their reason and logic. It is especially effective when their reason and logic is based on certain societal norms and standards, such as *political correctness*. The native inhabitant of a particular region, who never left his town or community, is unlikely to notice such coerced changes if they were gradually introduced. If, however, he left his native region for an amount of time it would become apparent to him, upon his return, how the views and opinions of his people differ from his own. If he were to investigate this phenomenon more closely, he would note that these changes were solely his own, and caused by his subconscious acceptance of the morals of influential others whilst outside of his community.

In the fast changing world of the 21st century, the concept of morality has become a popular propaganda subject for its contemporary people[1]. Upon discovering the veritable power that can be obtained from catching, harvesting and channelling the attention of people, it has become weaponized. Subsequently, every marketable subject is manipulated to maximize the draw of Attention. That this resulted in an often violent division among otherwise good natured people is often deemed acceptable, seeing that there is little sincerity among the profiteers who orchestrate these changes. In the past, over centuries and even millennia, morality was defined by one's tribe or affiliation but this has changed. Firstly it became religion, and at present it is race or ethnicity, sexual identification, affluence, or other phenomena invented by the official 'civilizers-of-man'.

Upon closer inspection it becomes evident that such moral-based coercions have little to do with any of the subject matter, or with money which a contemporary view will consider as the primary motivator. In an ever more connected world, the ultimate purpose has become to capture and control the attentive minds of man, as the psychic energy that is radiated from these is what feeds or fuels the Possession. This 'psychic food' acts as the elixir that enables the Possession's entities to exist, and it also controls these same minds by orienting them around scripted or narrated systems of belief. It is around these beliefs that a possessing entity is able to edit a person's morals to be or do whatever it wishes them to be or do. Accordingly, the Possession controls the physical and emotional trends of the contemporary masses by controlling the trends that they re-act to and exist with.[2]

Thus, the cunning manipulation of morality among an inherently good but docile populace, has veritable political power. Control over the architecture, engineering and execution of these morality-affecting beliefs was therefore the

---

[1] For example, the term "woke" originally referred to social injustices, especially around issues of race, inequality, and oppression, but has since evolved. In more recent years, "woke" was used to describe awareness of gender equality, LGBTQ+ rights, climate change, and more. However, the term was politicized and, in some contexts, used to criticize political correctness. The meaning of such expressions therefore vary, depending on who's using it.

[2] Another term for this is "mass psychosis", a phenomenon where a large group of people lose touch with reality, often driven by fear, propaganda, or social pressure. It leads to irrational beliefs, behaviours, or delusions that spread collectively, sometimes resulting in hysteria, moral panic, or totalitarian control.

sole agenda of many an emperor and despot of old, and in the 21st century it became that of a relatively small group of globalists. Competing for the upper-hand, powerful entities initiated the various 20th and 21st century conflicts and economic disruptions, and after about a century of these, a handful of powerful players emerged.[1]

Among the various mind-influencing programs that incorporated morality-affecting propaganda, were the idealistic concepts of communism, socialism and the various 'isms' in-between. That all these systems failed over time was inevitable due to them lacking compassion, sensitivity and creativity. Meritorious based systems[2] were also attempted, but these became subject to democracy which, in reality, became just another system that was easy to manipulate and corrupt.

With the rise of technology- backed capitalism[3], the resultant technocracy is destined to become the next master of power in the contemporary world. With its addictive gadgetry and sensationalised services, technology has become the primary tool through which total control and influence can be obtained over the flow and content of information. Naturally, with the rise of Artificial Intelligence, its value among the authoritarian entities has grown exponentially. This is because, with their control over it, these entities can literally sway the beliefs and subsequent morals of people, at the stroke of a key. With this, and its ability to rewrite history and the power to enforce its assimilation into the minds of its subjects, there is also the belief that anything is possible and can be gotten away with. The consequence is that we are witness to unprecedented levels of often interconnected corruption in almost every center of power in the world.

And ever since this occurred, whatever reason and logic that was present among the morals of contemporary people of old, has in some quarters turned to erratic and utterly unpredictable Chaos.

The Opposing but Occult Political and Geopolitical Logic

When we observe the opposing sides of the political and geopolitical arenas, we note how *reason and logic* are applied to customized sets of morals. These

---

[1] As an example of the globalists' dominance of the media: In the United States, the five mainstream media companies (Comcast, Disney, AT&T, Paramount and Sony) control an estimated 85-90% of the media landscape, whilst in Europe, five media corporations (Bertelsmann, Vivendi, BBC, Sky, and RTL Group) control around 70-85%. Of these media giants, Institutional Investors Vanguard Group, BlackRock and State Street play a dominant role in the ownership of these media companies in both regions, whilst a handful of significant families and the UK government exercise controlling influence.

[2] Meritocracy emphasizes achievement and capability as the key drivers of success and social mobility.

[3] Technocracy advocates for rule by experts in technology and AI, with an emphasis on data, science, and efficiency in governance.

are usually cunningly founded on the *reason and logic* of comparative and historical observations that were suitably selected to motivate a desired agenda[1]. Another feature that is observed in whatever new morals are established on either of such opposing sides, is that they will largely be absent of *the metaphysical aspects and spiritual context of the individual man*.

These 'metaphysical aspects' do not merely refer to forms of philosophy or psychology. This is because philosophical or psychological reason does not find much root in the minds of those unfamiliar with such advanced logic. These 'metaphysical aspects' refer to the higher dimensional or vibratory nature of man, being the field of energy that forms *the greater part* of what he is[2]. It is referred to as the 'greater part' as it manifests and thus dominates the physical realm, being the realm that is detected by the five physical senses, and in a lesser context it also dominates the realm of his thoughts. That said, by ignoring the metaphysical aspects of man, one denies the very existence of his higher vibratory or higher dimensional being – this is akin to acknowledging the shadow but ignoring that which casts it, let alone what caused its illumination.

In addition, by ignoring man's 'spiritual context' one *removes* the most contributory part of what is necessary for him to liberate that which is referred to by some as the *essential man*, and by others as his *soul*.

We may now note how the removal of the 'spiritual context' is often not unintentional or accidental – especially when we consider that more than 80% of the world's population believes in a god, higher power, or spiritual force.[3] This is when we observe, within the *reason and logic* behind such an intentional removal, how an opposing and intelligent metaphysical entity is seen to be active. On further inspection, we can see how this same entity or Possession manipulates the psyche of those who control the political and geopolitical arenas. The use of esotericism, including that of symbols, ceremonial rites and *dark occultism* is very much and visibly active here, as is its primary aim; which is to distort the psyche of the contemporary public. It does this by influencing and redirecting systems of belief by having them

---

[1] As an example; according to political scientists, the CIA was involved in the overthrow of around 50–80 governments between 1947 and the early 2000s. These are not denied but often justified as necessary to "contain communism" or "preserve democracy", but they remain controversial due to their consequences on democracy, human rights, and the fact that these coups were in the service of corporations (See *War is a Racket* by Smedley D. Butler, a US Marine Corps major general).

[2] Depending on who one asks, this field of energy is also referred to as the Aether, Akashic Field, Zero Point Field or in science as the Primordial Energetic Field or Quantum Field. It is a unified energy field or field of consciousness that underlies and shapes the material world. It is non-physical, intelligent, and interconnected, out of which the three-dimensional world emerges as a kind of projection or crystallization. As energy precedes matter, physical reality is seen as a dynamic manifestation of deeper, invisible forces or metaphysical fields.

[3] Approximately 84% according to Pew Research and other global surveys.

accept the morals of others, including those of the state and religious dogma. The power attained from the effects of these is veritable, and in certain occult circles, it is considered as none other than sorcery or black magic.

Morality as Defined by Those who Speak, and Those that Act

If we are to consider the presence of duality in all things, then we must also consider its presence in morality. If we then apply *reason and logic* in the moral consideration of Compassion and Truth, such as in an action or thought (as in asking *Why* and considering *How*), we would discover that the only decisions where the morality cannot be debated are those which are selfless. For example, if a man only speaks of the morally correct way of doing this or that, but never acts accordingly, then he will likely be found debating the probable pros and cons with others who are equally inactive but who see it otherwise. A form of reality-altering 'magic' occurs at the moment of such a debate. By defending untested but now challenged thoughts or ideas causes them to change in their intended meaning. In other words; when ideas or thoughts *that are untested* are debated between a proponent and opponent, both of whom are equally inactive and unconscious, then the actual debate-process will cause a mutation of their opinions, to become part of their identified egos. When this occurs on their principles of morality, which to each are considered fundamental, they will change as well, *automatically*. The debate on such morals will thereby have adapted their original intention, by which they unknowingly experienced a change in their perceived reality.

It is at this point that the original meaning behind their verbal claim of what they would do, and upon which their respective principles were based, will begin to fade like shadows, and soon to be forgotten. For example, a guard in a prison where political prisoners are kept is initially motivated by the morally absent and criminal nature of his prisoners. Then, upon a change in government or public opinion where such prisoners are exonerated, any debate around their previous acts will automatically alter[1]. This change becomes evident when the proponent and opponent now focus on defending their opinions, instead of the consequences of such opinions.

When we direct this phenomenon to principle-imposed but *passive* societies, who do nothing but talk about things, we begin to see why or how it is that they entertain such constantly changing morals. In contrast to them however, are the activists who *actively*, selflessly and diligently work to expose and implement their view of Truth. This is especially prevalent when it concerns the lies and false intentions of authoritarian individuals and entities. The activist's appeal is seldom served, as he is usually outnumbered by the

---

[1] Consider the examples of terrorists becoming freedom fighters, or when patriots are seen as criminals or as traitors only to become heroes, and when victorious invaders are labelled as liberators.

inactive but opinionated, many of whom are under the influence of rule or order based organizations that seek to defend their belief in what is morally accepted. Consequently, whether we like it or not, the reality will continuously change in the presence of expressed morality.

All that said, being active does not make the activist immune from this feature of morality. Even those who actively expose what is verified as Truth may eventually become lost in what they choose to expose. This occurs when they unwittingly become biased about not only what and what not to expose, but also why they chose to do so, and how.

Fact and Rule based Morality

As mentioned earlier, morality will always be on a slippery slope, even when it is based on factual or intellectual truth. In such a case, it is simply facts which are expressed in Information Technology as 'data'. Therefore, information that has not been thought about, or practiced as such, regardless of whether it is true or false, has no reality that is tangible. Just as we cannot 'eat' what are considered as our 'good intentions', we cannot expect to be married to someone or own something, simply because we have a piece of paper that says so. To consider something as our own, it requires a certain degree of compassion, combined with levels of self-sacrifice and physical care. Such care or compassion is also not something we can simply lay claim to either. For it to be sincere and true requires a certain level of understanding and, in turn, this understanding requires us to be familiar and know the subject or subject matter.

Thus, if one wanted to fully understand another's morals in order to interact without bias or judgement, then the consideration of such would have to be executed equally on *their Thinking, Feeling and Physical Centers*. It must, for example;

- be fully researched, understood and thought through;
- come from a place of compassion and unreserved acceptance;
- contain actionable intentions and consequences.

Naturally, even with such in depth consideration, there will still be some who will disagree and claim that something should be otherwise, but these opinions will be found resting on predominantly one of these base-centers. It will be overwhelmed by physical conditions, or kept emotionally aflame, or stuck in intellectual stubbornness. From our side, if we have observed and studied the subject or subject matter, and explored the sincerity of our feelings for it, which include our willingness to accept accountability for the action we may take, then our reality will supersede whatever reality-changing energy is released by those who merely rendered their opinion – even if that opinion was more factually true.

To apply this thought in an example; one may choose to not assist certain people who find themselves in a deplorable condition because one has come to understand that by doing so one only postpones an inevitable outcome. One may have concluded that such assistance would likely weaken these ones by creating forms of dependency. In the same way, one may choose to not educate or render an opinion where it serves no purpose in the environment or the nature of the individual. On the other hand, one may opt to render assistance or support, or offer an act of kindness, when that was not one's responsibility or required by one's society, but simply because one considered it important to do so.

Of course, in all cases of one's morality-based responses, keen awareness is necessary to ensure one is not enticed subconsciously, and that one has ensured that one is able to take account in the event of unexpected negative consequences.

The Purpose of Morality

As with all things in the life of a conscious being, Truth can only be considered Truth if it can accept and sustain the sincere challenge. The morals of a person who relentlessly and continuously persevere to be sincere, and upon those morals he builds his sense of *reason and logic*, are most likely to be morals that are truthful.

In this person, if his consequent actions are found to lose their validity or no longer be truthful, and as a result he immediately ceases its execution, then such circumstances applied to his revised morals will enhance a higher sense of awareness in him. This is especially so if by chance he becomes aware of an element within his ego-self, that wants to persist in preserving certain corrupted or polluted morals – morals which are stained by *biased* reason and logic – and then commences to dissolve them.

The awareness of the existence and nature of our morality, *defined by experiential reason and logic*, can therefore be seen as a threshold towards our self-realization. It is from here that we can begin to observe Truth by all its applicable dimensional components, and not by a belief that was conditioned or coerced.

Chapter 15
THE POWER AND PURPOSE OF PRAYER AND MEDITATION

The Lotus Flower – a representation of beauty, purity, and knowledge in various cultures, that thrives in muddy

**Where some seek Prayer for the wellbeing of Self and Soul,
in *fear* of the Unknown, or *hope* of Salvation,
others speak to God, His Saints, Prophets or Angels,
for their Comfort and Peace.**

**Where some Pray for *physical* Wellness *and material* Security,
or for the sake of Empowerment,
others seek to expose and convey the Light,
as a Channel to those lost and forgotten.**

**Where some access the Metaphysical to conjure the Occult,
to *embody* and *possess* the Forces of Darkness,
others practise to oppose and take dark entities to task,
disabling their lies and deceit, with the Light of the Sun.**

**… and then there is the Meditator,
who simply seeks the silence in Body, Heart and Mind.
Seeing Intuitive Portals begin to open,
his perception of Space-time dissolves.**

The Flow

When we observe the tree, we note how it gets its mineral and water uptake through the process of absorption through its roots. These essentials travel up its stem in a particular predestined design, from where they give life to branches with leaves, flowers and fruit. Simultaneous to this process we note how the crown in the canopy of the tree receives its life-force and pattern of growth from the Sun.

While both forms of energy are equally vital for the tree's existence, what they have in common is that both originate from the surrounding and permeating Cosmos. But Cosmos is not just a thing or a space. It is also the name for that which the ancient teacher known as Thoth, Hermes, Enoch or Mercury, referred to as "the Son of God"[1]. We can relate to this by observing how each of the said forms of energy play their role in every life-form on Earth, including that of man. Unlike the tree though, in the body of man not all energy is filtered, reformatted and directed into him through the living Earth for the Earth's own purposes. In him there is also the energy which enters through his crown to serve a purpose that is of a higher dimensional nature than that of Life itself.

Many forms of devotion and spirituality profess that it is through the crown that, at Death, the enlightened spirit or soul of man leaves the body. In some of these religions the crown is a part that is protected by a specific spiritual cover[2], and in some the crown – especially in children – is something that may not be touched by another's hand[3]. The point is that there are often very specific considerations surrounding the crown, including the direction it is pointed towards during burial[4]. Even the tradition of crown-wearing originated as a symbol of divine favor, power, and leadership, serving both a practical and ceremonial purpose in marking the status of the wearer. Hence, according to most forms of belief, and across the millennia, the crown is decidedly the portal through which Spirit enters man, and through which an enlightened Spirit eventually departs.

While the base-chakra[5] is considered the portal through which, or from which, physical life is made manifest, the crown-chakra is the birth canal of the higher being. Its venerated consideration forms part of the journey of the spiritual man, which ultimately also involves a form of parturition and what this necessitates.

---

[1] Hermes Trismegistus (Trice-reborn) is a legendary Atlantean, also known as the Egyptian god Thoth and characterized in the biblical Enoch (from the Book of Enoch). He is credited as the author of the Corpus Hermeticum, a collection of mystical, philosophical, and alchemical texts.

[2] Such as the Hebrew yarmulke and the Arab kufi.

[3] The taboo of touching the crown of children, who are seen as spiritually pure, comes from deep spiritual or cultural beliefs regarding the crown as sacred, linked to the passage to Soul, Spirit, or Higher Consciousness. These beliefs are particularly strong in Hinduism, Buddhism, and Shintoism, but also in the religions of Islam, Judaism and Taoism.

[4] In Islam an interred body is placed in alignment with the Qibla, which is the direction of the Kaaba in Mecca, Saudi Arabia.

[5] The Root Chakra is the first of the seven primary chakras in the body located at the base of the spine, between the anus and the genitals, at the perineum..

Defining the Purpose of Prayer

As was determined in earlier chapters, the nature of all things in the reality of man is defined by *how* they are perceived. As the perception of most consists of dimensions that are either consecutively layered or separately sphered[1], the perspective of Divinity or Higher Dimensions will be equally so to each observer.

For most people who pray, their process is one of recitation and repetition. Although the content of prayer naturally differs, what is similar is that the subject matter is usually based on *topics of importance*, that relate to themselves. Regardless of whether these *topics of importance* are to do with health, happiness or the prospect of wealth, they come with an applied expectation or 'hope', which usually entails a one-dimensional path with a two-dimensional 'picture-like' outcome in mind. This implies that these one- and two-dimensional forms of prayer, when placed on the diagram of the 'Opposing Pyramids of Reality', indicate the path of either the *Follower of Order* or the *Follower of Faith*[2].

This observation referred to the duality of Order and Faith, but does not imply that such forms of prayer do not serve a higher purpose. They naturally do as they can be very powerful, even though this power is largely psychological and thus, *psyche-based*. For example, we can see how there is a very distinct energetic effect of such rhythmic repetition, especially when it is done in large numbers, such as in chanting crowds. This is discussed in more detail below, but of emphasis here is that the effect of prayer in such collectives does not necessarily always serve the individual. A prayer's benefit is ultimately dependent on the *inner awareness* that is maintained by the individual during such routines. And this inner awareness is, in turn, dependent on his or her purpose behind it. In other words, whichever level of being the prayer's purpose is meant to serve, is dependent on what it was that the individual intended.

Observing the Power of Prayer

While a repetitive prayer with a strong intention may lead us to higher levels of awareness, its physical effects become noticeably more enhanced when groups of one- and two-dimensional followers pray together[3]. Such gatherings generally serve to resonate and enhance the collective psychic energy, especially if the individuals are like-minded, in which case the effect on the individual self can be greatly enhanced. As mentioned above though, when

---

[1] See Chapter 6.

[2] As defined in *The Way of the Pilgrim*, and as per Diagram A at the beginning of this book

[3] The enhanced effects do not necessarily benefit such groups when they are perceived as a threat to authoritarian entities.

joining such a group one must remain aware of the fact that when one works as a group the outcome may, and likely will, be different. This is because the energy in a group generally follows a one-directional aim with a picture-like outcome. It may still enhance the inner state of an individual participant, but this effect will be second to its primary effect, being the redirection of whatever the group's collective energy seeks to enhance.

The individual who does find himself individually enhanced in such gatherings may, along with this discovery, find himself motivated to seek his individual independence of mind – free of the influenced and directed paths of the group. In such a case, the now mentally liberated individual is more likely to combine the traditional practice of prayer with forms of meditation and lifestyle changes.

On the other hand, the individual who does not wish for, or experience, such individual enhancement is more likely to be identified with and within the strength of the group. Such groups will consequently form named entities of their own, and found their own church or temple as a central entity, incorporating the groups preferred discipline and *rule-based order*.

Where the organizations of these rule-based orders naturally serve many a good-hearted Follower, the down-side becomes evident when the organizations become *rule-dependent*. What commonly occurs then is that the leading elements in them will expect or demand its devotees to remain loyal to its rules. This may then be enforced through various punishment and reward methods, which may not necessarily be considerate or harmonious to the inner-wellbeing of the individual participant, or, for that matter, that of other groups who follow a different set of rules.

The pursuit of individual independence within these environments, is therefore seldom supported.

To summarize this, we may consider that the Power of Prayer can work in various ways, but, if we remain unaware of its effects on our psyche, we are more likely to become subjected by its collective power, when wielded through an organization. What then follows is a type of docility, where one begins to support dogma for its own sake, whilst the state of one's inner life is left behind. If we now reconsider the Inverted Pyramid displayed at the beginning of this book, we can see how such docility to organized prayer can easily lead a follower to the slippery slope of false prophets and charlatans. This becomes more evident when we observe how, in the Inverted Pyramid, the conscious way of life makes way to the regimented and sensory based one. To put this in other words; it is when our emotional consideration takes priority over what is necessary which, in turn, begins to determine our thoughts and subsequent beliefs. Where this may appear of little consequence, the larger effect is that in this dimensionally downward spiral, where thoughtfulness becomes subject to the physical and sensory demands, the intuitive influence from higher dimensions remains out of reach.

Defining the Power of Meditation

Most forms of *group*-meditation are rooted in religious or spiritual disciplines, within which many will promote the power of prayer. Such groups may then advocate prayer routines that consist in part or in full, of recitation and repetition. Characteristically this will comfort the fearful and hopeful contemporary man, but such emotion oriented practices seldom promote much for him in the long term, except perhaps the practice in itself. In such a case, when the individual undertakes to practice in solitude, he is likely to have an experience that differs from when he practices in a group. Seeing the limitation of orchestrated practices he contemplates, and gradually his now contemplative prayers begin to blend with periods of silent meditation.

It is within the silent comfort and calm composure that the meditator's mind begins to find new depths. If he can persist in maintaining his quiet state of mind for a mere few minutes, he may notice how he experiences a new level of being. It is one that can be described as a state where he is neither in the dream-state of sleep nor one where he actively pursues his thoughts. In-between these two opposing states the meditator begins to observe his life separately from himself, as if from a distant horizon, and see how his thoughts follow patterns, akin to children at play.

As such he may see himself and the world objectively, as is and no longer biased by external influences. The result is that, although he cannot change the world or the things that touch him, he can influence them by how he perceives them. Hence, from the meditator's understanding and unopinionated perspective, all that he observes responds in kind[1].

Observing the Purpose of Meditation

While the vitality of water, nutrients and gasses for the animate cannot be understated, they are not the source of life. This resides in the Earth's biosphere, which obtains its Life-force energy from the Sun and the surrounding Cosmos. In man, the natural flow of Life-force follows a path that flows through the Earth and enters him first and foremost through his base center known as the earlier described Root or Kundalini Chakra, from where it empowers his higher centers.

The Meditator becomes conscious of these same cosmic or 'Sacred Earth' energy flows through him, but begins to notice a separate flow of a more

---

[1] It is well known that at both quantum and psychic levels, the act of observation influences both living beings and inanimate objects, suggesting that the observer plays an active role in shaping the behavior or state of what is being observed.

refined and lighter influence. It enters him through the top of his head, or Crown Chakra, from where it flows top-down. He notices how this 'Divine' energy illuminates his higher Intuitive and Thinking Centers first, whereafter it flows along a path of conscious awareness, into the lower centers.

If we now consider these two flows, and what it is that enhances them, it can be reasoned that Prayer enhances the *physical* identity and Meditation enhances the *metaphysical non-identified* self. Where Prayer tends to enhance the identified self, in Meditation the various identified personalities become subject to the Observer's illumination, causing them to dissolve like shadows before the rising sun. Thus, while both serve their purpose, the way of the Meditator enables man to pursue his journey through life as the Master intended, and not as intended by any particular ego.

The Meditator will also encounter others who are like him. But, where the devotee to Prayer tends to focus on matters to do with life and what it can provide him with, the silent mind of the Meditator seeks to enhance the Whole. To the experienced Meditator's mind, every moment in the life of all beings is equally precious and, whilst he is in a state of Meditation, he does not consider the practise in itself for, at that moment in Time, the Soul or Higher-self is merged with that of others.

Thus said, among both the Meditator and those who Pray, most will prefer to practise in a church, a temple, in natural surroundings or somewhere in quiet solitude. Any of these will naturally serve as ultimately, all that is done by these practitioners, in the conscious observation of what is true and in harmony with the elements, will enhance to some degree or other, all and everything their intentions touch.

The Synergy in Prayer and Meditation

Earlier in this chapter, we observed how the Sacred Earth's natural energies, in service of Great Nature, flow from the base or root upwards, and how Life-force – that simultaneously services man's Essence – enters him top-down, through or via his crown. While these two influences appear to flow in opposite directions, their existent duality forms part of the whole. Combined in man, they serve a combination of purposes, some of which may seem obvious or natural, and others that can only be discovered experientially.

In the tree we see how, for its physical growth, water and nutrients flow along its genetic code in one direction. At the same time, from an opposite direction, the Sun's rays energize the tree's overall life-force and directs its growth across Time[1]. The same phenomena would occur within man, were it not for

---

[1] What is inferred here is that a tree's growth follows the genetic code within its seed. Its further growth, however, including the distribution of its branches, the shape of its canopy, and its time-relative function and place within the forest, follow a higher dimensional design that is encoded in

interference from his ego. When looking at the vast majority of people, it is not difficult to note the glaring imbalances in their respective gene-encoded growth due to chemicals and electromagnetic interference. The same occurs with their time-related development, which becomes subjected to more of the same[1], but also external interference on his psyche. As a result, we often see how the attention of most people is dominated by their focus on only one form of growth or energy center, which often, in time, leads to immune disorders and chronic health issues, but also to a severe limitation in spiritual awareness.

The tree generally does not encounter these problems, but then the tree does not consider the illusory one- and two-dimensional facets that distract the attention of most men and women. People differ from the tree in many aspects of course, but especially when considering that the Universe's Grand Architect or Creator designed and created man for a different purpose. Unlike any other animate form, man has the ability to become aware of his dimensional make-up, and with that he is able to become conscious, grow a soul and attain higher dimensions.

Hence for man, it is necessary to focus his attention on both flows in the realm of his or her spiritual practices. Where prayer can be envisioned as that which supports and organizes his physical and social life fruitfully, meditation can guide him out of the dense, material and social identifications. *Thus, if prayer is the road and vessel, then Meditation is the journey.* The attainment of higher dimensions will therefore require the co-existence and harmonious application of both.

---

the Light.

[1] Referring to polluted air and water, genetically modified food, drugs, electro-magnetic interference, etc.

Chapter 16
CONTEMPLATING TAT SVAM ASI; "THOU ART THAT"

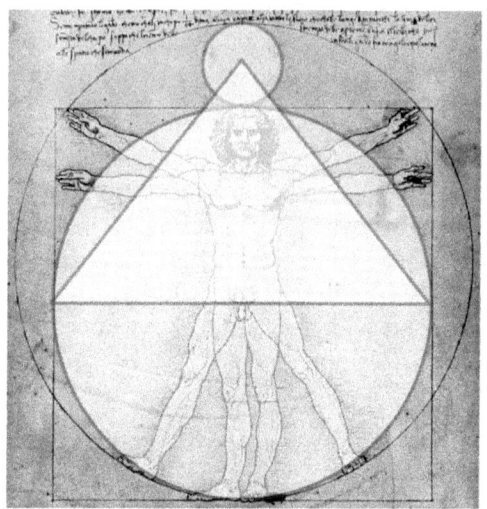

Da Vinci's Vitruvian Man's perfect integral ratio with the dimensions of the Earth, Moon and the Great Pyramid.

"That" is the Sacred Space,
made manifest solely for love of the beautiful,
with conscious consideration of all things and elements,
to influence and guide the spiritual essence of man,
when he can accept it as is, without judgement or opinion,
regardless of its history or state, without the need to change.

"Thou" is that Space,
where the Light shines like a million trillion suns for all who seek it,
where the lost may find release, unconditional love and acceptance,
and where the Darkness finds its nemesis in Time and non-existence.

And whether it is made of steel and stone or flesh and bone,
it is Thou art That is where God rests.

What Art Thou?

Wherein lies the beauty of man?

- The *Creationist and Spiritualist* believe beauty is found in the spiritual journey of man, in his ability to become at-one with the Saviour, Guru, Prophet or Creator in the form of God or the Universal Mother.

- The *Evolutionary Theorist* will see his physical and mental prowess as how he got to be on top of Earth's food chain. Of these, some may believe it is his established civilization that enables him to recognise beauty in music, poetry and the arts, whilst others claim it is found in the depths of an accomplished intellect.

- The *Naturalist* will find beauty in Great Nature and in particular in the human body. Being a miracle of cellular compositions that formed tissue, bones, organs, brains and a nervous system, he sees in man an evolving organism that is in synchronicity with a living planet.

- Then there are the *self-proclaimed Leaders of the collectives of man*, ranging from those who rule small countries and organizations, to the globalists who consider humanity as a mechanism they must control. These will see beauty and perfection in their collective ability to build and create, reach the stars and, in Time, attain a technological form of immortality.

Of course, every-one of these perspectives on 'the beauty of man' carry a measure of merit, but also degrees of naiveté. This is because, if we *sincerely* wished to explore the beauty of man further, we would also need to consider the beauty in *Logic*. Consider, for example, the logic in the law of Cause and Effect and the law of Correspondence. These laws dictate how all things are observably connected, through a number of links or forms. Consider, for example, when looking at the emblem at the beginning of this chapter, the corresponding beauty of man portrayed within the Great Pyramid on the Giza Plateau, and the earth-moon dimensions:

The *Creationist and Spiritualist* may prefer to believe the Pyramids were built by gods or some other form of interdimensional cosmic beings, and the *Evolutionary Theorist* will prefer an explanation along the lines of a preceding civilization's evolution and natural selection[1]. The latter's views are often politicised by the *Leaders*, who see little value in such origins, but more value in being able to claim that these Pyramids were created by their predecessors. Last but not least there is the *Naturalist*, who believes he will find his answer in man's supranatural abilities.

The observation of such differing views is not aimed at dispute or ridicule of any of these perspectives because, as mentioned earlier, they all contain elements of truth – even though many of such 'truths' factually contradict one another. What all will likely agree on though is that it is hard for us to envision the vast scope of building structures such as the Great Pyramid. For example, consider that it consists of more than two million blocks of stone, each weighing several tonnes and differing in size, yet as a whole assembled

---

[1] The process in nature by which, according to Darwin's theory of evolution, organisms that are better adapted to their environment tend to survive longer and transmit more of their genetic characteristics to succeeding generations than do those that are less well adapted.

with the highest levels of precision, alignment and grouping, incorporating geometric, cosmological and magical elements that are veritable and intentional. The accepted theory, according to a politicised Egyptologist-academia[1], is that the Great Pyramid was built by the hard working Egyptian citizens and farmers over a period of 20 years, during the months of the Nile's floods. Of course, when common sense and *Logic* is inserted into this theory, a paradox occurs[2].

The point of this example is that, without firsthand knowledge of these things, these details are just that; theoretical details. Whatever the theoretical narrative that is considered as true today will likely be indicated as otherwise in the future, only to be disputed again when the old narrative no longer has the desired effect. Such hypothetical details are therefore not things we must ponder on excessively. For example, we cannot reliably consider the official narratives 'fundamental' enough to build an enduring thesis on the origins of the Giza Plateau. And the same can be said of the Beauty of Man. But let us expand this view, as there is a lot more to the biological and psychological miracles that the human body incorporates:

The correlation between the Sun, Earth and Moon is well known and was previously written about. Their dimensions and ratios are also found in the architecture of the Great Pyramid referred to above. But further correlations are observed in the complete man himself[3]. Depending on one's perspective, these would be considered as:

>Illusory and imagined; or
>Coincidental and thus accidental; or
>Mechanical and artificial; or
>Divinely integral and thus intentional.

Whichever way you prefer, each of such views as well as others that exist, will likely be equally debated and substantiated. Ultimately though, to the observer, it is only *That what it is*. However, the one view that cannot be debated is the fact that *it is*, which is therefore just *That*.

---

[1] The field of Egyptology is heavily politicized to bolster national pride through historical, institutional, racial, and economic forces. Like any academic discipline tied to identity, nationhood, and history, Egyptology reflects broader societal and geopolitical currents.

[2] For example – ignoring the precision cutting of each stone, the over-all design and supposedly primitive technologies – this claim would entail the cutting, transport and placement of roughly 50 blocks per hour; that is if armies of many thousands of stonemasons were able to work simultaneously non-stop, 24 hours per day.

[3] For example; the Golden Ratio (1: 1.618) can be found in the Earth to Moon diameters, the Sun to Moon size and distance ratios, many of the Great Pyramid's dimensions, and the division of the human body. As such it is seen as a bridge between nature, design, and beauty, linking the macrocosm (architecture) and the microcosm (human body).

Who Art Thou?

"Who am I?" is the question that, in one form or another, occupies most contemplative minds, and has done so across the ages. As a result, it sparked the journey of countless Seekers to become Pilgrims. To these Pilgrims, the answers that they may find at an unknown point of their journey, will likely be of a nature that is not comprehended by those who did not undertake this path. This inability would be even more so if they tried to rationalize the Pilgrim's path with an emotion-oriented intellect.

As was reviewed earlier, such feeling-based thinking is usually stimulated by either fear or hope, and with the expectation of a picture-like outcome. Similarly we can see how a person who merely tries to rationalize such self-exploratory path, without doing the work of observing himself, exists in a turbulent reality of ego-based opinions[1].

For example, to try and understand something like the existence of a mathematically, geodetically and cosmically perfect Giza Plateau, or the beauty of the Whole-of-Man analytically, is not realistically possible. This becomes more evident when we observe the ever increasing complexities man encounters in his attempt to re-create the biological features of man, using artificial intelligence and in a severe defiance of Natural Law.

In the *'The Way of the Pilgrim' trilogy*[2], we reviewed the context of man at considerable length. In this we concluded that this 'context' – *individually or collectively* – cannot be found in any of its component parts or in its sum total. Not even the physical merger of all *the known parts* will establish much, except perhaps combinations of rudimentary mechanical and reactive patterns. Without an absolute awareness of the present, the NOW that overrides the past or future, an understanding of who or what the Beauty of Man is, cannot be attained.

Thou Art That

The beauty of anything can only be discovered within a realization of the Whole. This also applies with the understanding of a person or a collectives purpose. Varying theories aside, most people who are limited to only one of the disciplines, such as academia, science or spirituality have, as yet, not been able to substantially understand *the meaning* of something like, for example, the Giza Plateau, at least not with an answer that can withstand other theories and opinions. Perhaps sites and structures like those of Giza contain and represent many things, but ultimately whatever it is, to most what they see is a

---

[1] Another term for this is to "Know thyself", as inscribed at the Temple of Apollo at Delphi, a major religious site in ancient Greece.

[2] *The Inner Evolution of Man; The Outer World of Man;* and *Merging the Inner and Outer Word of Man*

mere façade of that which they are.

A similar view corresponds with the unique, miraculous, magical and phenomenal man. While almost every component part of men and women, including the metaphysical ones, are deemed fraught with faults and irregularities, of which there are ample and numerous examples, each of these remains an inextricable and integral component-part of him or her. And none of these even remotely replicate the Whole.

It can be said therefore that the *Beauty that is Man* can only be realized through a process of discovery. It is, however, something that can only be found when one is not looking for an 'outcome' as such. Hence, where the Seeker commences his journey, the Knower observes, and upon becoming at-one, knows that he, she and *Thou art That*.

AN INTRODUCTION INTO THE CLOSING CHAPTERS OF THIS BOOK

Metatron's Cube, also considered as the Divine Blueprint of the Universe

The Value of Knowledge

Once we can accept the Possession of Man in our reality, the question that arises next is what to do with this information? As it is with all things, information on its own has little value unless it is combined with other things – holistically so to speak[1]. Only when information is applied in life can it become the kind of 'knowledge' that leads to our understanding and acceptance of what is.

Naturally, for the information to exist in the world, the presence of *an intention of truth and sincerity* is essential. After all, falsehood does not exist, except in the minds of the deceitful and ignorant egos of man. Because the application of information is not an outcome based science that can be tested and repeated, such as one would in chemistry or mechanics, and because the

---

[1] Information is considered the functional substance of the (masculine) left-brain, where-as the (feminine) right-brain provides the projected whole or 'holistic' view. Iain McGilchrist - *The Master and His Emissary: The Divided Brain and the Making of the Western World*.

Possession can be cunning and deceptive, it (the application) is an art that is seldom applied overtly. In most of us, outside of the Possession's ubiquitous influences, our true and realized aims in life are usually practiced covertly. To say this in other words: our awareness of something that is publicly accepted on the basis of hearsay or mere repetition, but which is an obvious lie, is not acknowledged or applied in life.[1]

If, instead, we overtly applied an acknowledged understanding of the Possession, it would not only be of considerable value to our individual selves, but it could also benefit our community or society, the world at large, *and one could even say the possessing entity itself.*

The dominant benefit of such an understanding is that its application can lead to the dissolution of that most common of all causes of humanity's collective 'misbehaviour': that of Fear. Of course we must be aware of the dangers in the world, and apply caution and common sense, but we must also acknowledge the reality that a possessive influence should not be the cause of fear. We do not need to fear 'becoming possessed' or prone to absurd and fanatical behavior like that of an intoxicated or drugged person, or become malicious by taking from others that which was not rightfully earned. We just need to be aware of our vulnerability to a possession's effects, just as we would be to the effects of addictive substances.

Remember that although effects, like those of misbehaviour, may have a Possession as their cause, underlying all their influences we have:

- the ability to inform ourselves,
- our self-awareness, and
- the power of Choice.

To Know the Future by Knowing Ourselves

A conscious life begins with us knowing when we are informing ourselves, and when we are being informed. Because our ability to be aware of ourselves depends largely on us knowing ourselves, we need to be aware of *what* influences our thoughts, feelings and our re-active doing of things, and *why* it does so. If we can do this, then we can 'mindfully' observe *how* these influences reach the various parts of us, and only then can we apply our focused attention on the task of countering it.

To further assist the reader in this awareness we will, in the closing chapters of this book, take a hypothetical look at the indomitable and energetic causes

---

[1] For example: Consider a voter's acceptance of the rhetoric of his popular candidate; a warlord's claims of a now vanquished enemy's former brutality or inhuman nature; the idea that human beings have a Sun-overruling influence on the planet's climate; the belief in one's group of people being exceptional and more favoured by God over others; or the contemporary belief of having control over one's psyche, and being immune to external influences!

that drive human society – unlike those that guide the natural world. By taking these into consideration, we may be able to see what direction the future of humanity may take, and how we can find our individual place, *or Purpose*, on its veritable roller-coaster.

The first of these chapters looks at one of the mechanisms that, *hypothetically,* 'drives' or empowers the known Cosmos. It bypasses the known forms of energy such as chemistry, electricity, gravity, quantum consideration, or even the science to do with fractals and holograms. Whereas these are all verified and well-studied disciplines, the problem we encounter occurs when we try to determine their respective causes, or to combine them. For example, when one group chooses to believe that the Cosmos was formed out of a Big Bang and is expanding, with the phenomenon of gravity as its primary driving influence, another group will claim that there was no Big Bang event, that the Cosmos is eternal, timeless, constantly changing and that its primary driving energy is electrical. Where some spiritualists will consider human beings as spirits or souls having a human experience, other equally unsubstantiated views will consider that the purpose of the human being is to grow a soul by combining the ego with a form of permeating spirit. Where some see life on Earth as a privilege that they wish to reincarnate in some form or other whereas others see life in the flesh as a trap or training ground from which only enlightened humans can escape or transcend. Perhaps we must consider that all are right, and that their opposing and differing realities are simply facets of the same gem, such as one symbolized in Metatron's Cube above[1].

The second and last chapter looks at the place the individual person occupies within the great cycles of civilization. In this we consider how the Possessions influence across the Great Mechanism of Time must also follow very specific laws or principles. In this we have to consider how these act on the individual ego as an eternal centrifuge, through which the enriched and mature soul can transcend.

We will review that whilst we collectively experience this cyclic process individually, the nature of civilizations is not just one that rises and then falls. It seemingly sits atop a greater spiraling mechanism, being our Solar System's journey through the galaxy. By this we mean that our consecutive civilizations are not just separated by Time, they must differ in type and nature across the eons as well.

---

[1]Metatron's Cube encompasses all five Platonic solids (the fundamental shapes considered as the foundation of all matter and energy, including the Tetrahedron (Fire), Hexahedron (Earth), Octahedron (Air), Icosahedron (Water) and Dodecahedron Aether). As it contains the thirteen circles symbolic in the Kabala's Tree of Life, it was named after the archangel Metatron. As such the symbol represents the underlying patterns of creation, embodying balance, harmony, and the interconnectedness of life.

The purpose of these hypotheses is therefore not to offer the author's opinion or pipe-dream. It is simply to elucidate an understanding of the divine nature in the seemingly inexplicable chaos, the entropy of which surrounds humanity on almost every level.

Chapter 17
THE GREAT MECHANISM THAT DRIVES THE POSSESSION OF MAN
(A HYPOTHESIS)

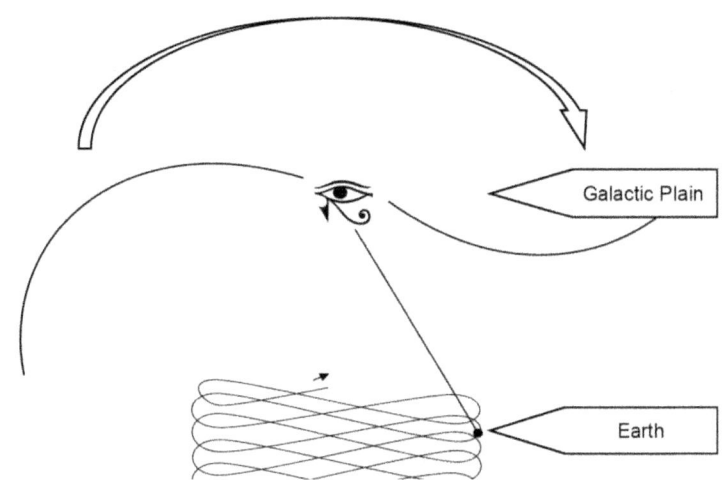

A Schematic Perspective on Eternity, represented as a perpetual pendulum that swings on the spiral trajectory of the Great Mechanism.

The Causal Force of Influence behind the Possession

So far in this book, we determined that mind-possessing entities or influences are present and conscious in every aspect of biological life. In humanity we note that they are particularly virulent in people who are not only not conscious of the influence of these entities, but who actively identify with the effects on them. These people will claim that the entities' doing is of their own 'will', even when the relevant acts make no practical or logical sense. Consequently, we noted that the duly possessed person is typically unbalanced across his or her three base centers, and seen as mechanically reactive in their doing, feeling and thinking. This causes them to remain asleep to the presence of their own Essence or inner-being, and their life subjected.

We further determined that a possessing entity is highly infectious and, depending on its core interest, it will form, influence and empower man's societies and collectives. We also saw how that, from within these collectives, the Possession goes to work on the minds of its individual participants, and mutates these to serve itself first and foremost – regardless of the human and material cost.

It was also determined that, until such time as a person becomes aware of his higher dimensional potential, and begins to observe himself, he remains an automaton. Everything this automaton does is mechanical and caused by, or related to preceding effects; nothing he does, feels, thinks or speaks is his own. However, besides the Law of Causality that the automaton is subject to, there is another force that determines or influences how he does, feels, thinks or speaks. Whereas we identified the phenomenon referred to as the Possession of Man as active and responsible for these influences on him, what we have as yet to determine is *why* it is that this possessing force functions *this way*. The reason is because 'this way' is, after all, destructive to both its host and thereafter, ultimately, itself.

Realizing the Divine Mechanism or Great Cycle

As we all know, the Earth is not a stationary object. Relative to our star the Sun and our Milky Way galaxy, it moves in at least five ways:

- It spins on its axis, making a full rotation every 24 hours that we call a Day.
- It rotates around the Sun in cycles of approximately 365.25 days that we call the Solar Year.
- It spins around its axis like a spinning top, a cycle that takes approximately 25,920 Solar Years, and that we call a Great Year[1].
- We then note how the Earth, as part of the Solar System, moves around the center of our Milky Way galaxy and,
- When we zoom out even further, we can note the movement of our galaxy as a whole, relative to other galaxies, within the Great Cosmos.

When we consider the impact of the effects of our planet's movements on our existence and lives, we see that they are reduced along this same order. For example, we all experience our movement from day into night, and back into day, to the extent that we schedule and plan most aspects of our lives around it. We naturally note the Solar Year as well, but this to a lesser extent than the day-to-day one. The last two movements also have an effect on us, but they have such little impact that, besides those who follow or practise astrology, in this contemplation we do not consider them in the physical and psychic existence of man.

However, the Great Year that occupies the middle of these five Earth movements, is one that very few people are ever aware of. Even fewer will

---

[1] The Great Year is also known as the Precession of the Equinoxes, a Platonic Year or a Precessional Year.

consider the Great Year's mathematical integral status with man[1]. Still, for those who are interested, much has been written about humanity's observance of the Precessional Cycle[2]. From its correlation in how we design structures and the timing of events, to its incorporation in the temples and pyramids of Ancient Egypt many thousands of years before the time of Plato[3] who supposedly first introduced it, but this is not what this chapter is about. What is important and relevant is that this cycle exists and that, although it may not have a physical or noticeable impact on man or the existence of his societies, it has a most dominant influence on the characteristics of the Possession of Man.

The Design of the Great Mechanism

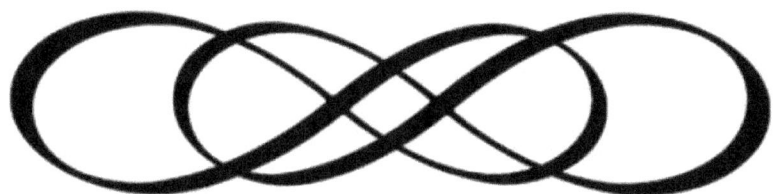

Like any type of clock-like mechanism, the design of the Great Year's Mechanism correlates in that it also determines cycles with a particular functional aim or purpose. With regards to the Great Year and the general perspective of the human being, we note that it has a multi-dimensional purpose:

- From a one-dimensional perspective, we see how it swings pendulum-like, from one end to the other and as such, it appears to act like the driving weight of a grandfather clock. To most one-dimensional perspectives, this to-and-fro action will be its only observed movement.
- From a two-dimensional perspective, we will note a rotation of sort that indicates a two-dimensional cyclic pattern. It is one that resembles a lemniscate (also referred to as the 'infinity' or figure-eight symbol).
- From a three-dimensional perspective, we begin to incorporate the knowledge of our planet's existing physical and time-related pattern. To our contemporary academia and cosmologists, this cycle

---

[1] There are many but, for example, consider that the life of the average male human being's existence lasts about 1 degree of a 360 year Great Year, or 72 Solar Years.
[2] See: https://grahamhancock.com/fordr3/
[3] 428 – 348 BCE

is considered as an interesting and mechanical feature, but one that has a limited influence on the Biosphere.
- From a four-dimensional perspective, we begin to discover that the only part of planet Earth that is *not* subject to the movement of the Great Year's precessional cycle, is the spiritual journey of man. In fact, it is one that can only be realized when one has experienced an awakening of the Essential Self, which self is *separate* of the biologically dependent and mortal Ego. This is because, among those whose realities are dominated by their ego, which ego was largely formed by their external-world, few will notice that it is their ego's inherent psychic nature to seek its enhancement through physical, material and artificial means.
- From a five-dimensional perspective, the precessional Great Year is considered illusory, and thus separate from the Essential Self that arose and matured on the spiritual path. From here, the Great Year's cycle is analysed independent of the Ego's conditioned bias. It is observed as influencing the Possession of Man which then influences the collective psyche of people which, in turn, influences the individual psyche.
- The six- and higher dimensional perspectives become complex as we try to understand the mind of the Creator or God. However, when we take note of the hierarchical nature of the preceding dimensions, we begin to imagine it as Divine Intention or Purpose.

The Laws or Principles of the Great Mechanism:

The Principle of Motion

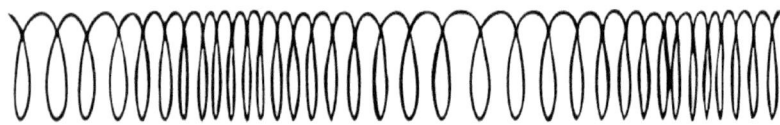

When a one- and two-dimension oriented person perceives the trajectory of a precessional Great Year, all he sees is a repetitive pattern that has little or no form. The three-dimensional person's understanding expands from here to incorporate the element of Time, but aside from this, it only begins to retain 'form' for him when he incorporates the Earth's movement on the galactic plain. But still, even if he ignores the hypothesis of a Big Bang beginning and a similar end all the three-dimensional person sees, at best, is a mechanism.

If the three-dimensionally oriented person realizes that this motion is perpetual or time-less, he may begin to see that there is more to this mechanism than just 'motion'. He may now begin to realize that it is an integral part of the Earth's 'life'[1]. In fact, he may now consider that the precessional cycle is comparable to the body's circulatory system that distributes heat, nutrients and waste accordingly, except in this case, *it distributes things of a metaphysical nature*. If he can understand this, and consider it a possibility, he may attain a dimensionally expanded perspective.

The outcome of this consequent four or higher dimensional perspective is the realization that the cycle of the Great Year is, in fact, not cyclic at all. Instead, its Great Mechanism represents a spiral that flows across the eons. This means that the Earth is never in the same place twice, and that whatever Solar and Cosmic influences the Earth is subjected to, will always be unique for that moment in Time.

The Principle of Trajectory or Shape

As mentioned, although the movement of the Precessional Cycle, when isolated from the other Earth-movements, appears circular, it is not when we consider this movement in combination with others. This is why many ancient cultures saw time as cyclic or even spheric, not linear[2], and expressed it as

---

[1] According to mystics and cosmologists alike, the life of a planet is part of a cosmic cycle of evolution and devolution. Philosophers will view this akin to an ongoing process of becoming and decaying, with everything, from human beings to celestial bodies, as everything exists in states of transformation and change. Planets, stars, and galaxies experience cyclical periods of existence, beginning, flourishing, and eventually decaying or transforming.

[2] When considered from a one or two dimensional view Time is linear; but from three dimensional

such in the lemniscate or figure-eight symbol. This is not without further foundation. When we graph the precessional motion of the Earth's equinox[1] across the zodiac as a function of Time, and project it onto a symbolic plane, it is visualized as looping – rising and falling, or ascending and descending. This led many of the esoteric traditions of Alchemy, Hermeticism and Vedic schools[2], to relate this cycle to the rise and fall of ages, which, in turn, relates to human consciousness, echoing the ebb and flow of the lemniscate.

To visualize the Great Year's mechanism as a spiralling lemniscate, try to imagine the precessional movement as a three-dimensional double spiral or even a figure-eight *path,* and incorporate the Solar System's movement through the galaxy. If Earth and the Sun are spiraling through space, the motion may trace a looping form, suggesting a shaped trajectory over vast scales of Time.

The Principle of Magnetism

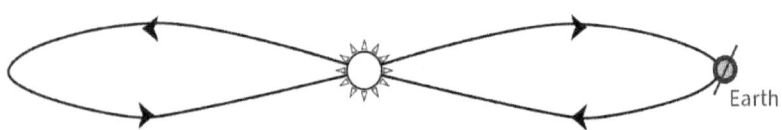

Where we reviewed the Great Mechanism along the principles of perpetual motion, its form or shape, and its hypothesized purpose, we may now also consider that there is a point of magnetism positioned at its center – like gravity's pull on the weight of a grandfather clock[3]. While accepting that the Moon naturally has an influence, it should not be too difficult to envision that the Sun takes the central place. After all, it is relative to the Sun that we define and measure the Precessional Cycle. If we can envision this, with the Sun located at the center of the lemniscate, it becomes evident that the Earth is either moving toward the Light or away from it. When considering the diagram above, one could envision a measurable period where the Earth sits in or near to the middle; and if there was to be a high point representing a Golden Age, this would probably be it. However, in reality, the Earth always moves, and of emphasis here is that this is either toward or away from the Light.

---

views, it is a series of cycles that repeat and transform as they evolve, and from four dimensional perspectives it becomes spherical, encompassing the past, present and future in one.

[1] The precession of the equinoxes refers to the slow westward shift of the equinoxes along the ecliptic over a cycle of approximately 25,920 years.

[2] Also, in Hindu cosmology, the Yuga cycles (Satya, Treta, Dvapara, Kali) form part of the Great Year, moving eternally from golden to dark ages, and back again.

[3] A grandfather clock is a tall, freestanding, weight-driven pendulum clock, with the pendulum held inside the tower or waist of the case.

Where this becomes monumental in our hypothesis is when we consider that:

- When something moves away from something like Light, it has an effect that differs from when it moves toward it, and,
- As everything in the Great Cosmos has a purpose and nothing is without reason, we must assume that this too has its purpose.

The Anomalies of our Civilization, that are Fruitless and Destructive to People and Society:

According to this hypothesis, it seems that for the past six thousand years the Earth has been moving away from the Sun's higher dimensional Life-emitting Light. If we look at this motion according to the shape of the lemniscate, we see how the effects of the motion away from the Light begin to gradually increase. Perhaps we can consider what kind of things or tendencies in humanity would be seen as typical, when its actions are hidden by a fading light, and also if there is evidence of such occult activities in the present era:

1. Consider the perverting and falsifying of verified history by the state, their academia and state sponsored historians[1].
2. Consider the rewriting of archeologically verified narratives related to the existence and state of consciousness in ancient civilizations by authoritarian entities[2].
3. Consider the failure by contemporary science to acknowledge the influence of metaphysics on matter and the principles of Relativity[3].
4. The acceptance of acts of cruelty and barbarism by contemporary societies worldwide, in both their entertainment and actual events in geopolitical spheres[4].
5. The subtle but evident altering of the psyche of the contemporary masses, through falsified and propagandised information, with its

---

[1] The ongoing practice of historical revisionism by state authorities to shape public perception and legitimize current political agendas is well known and documented.

[2] For example; authoritarian claims on a descendance from ancient empires like Rome, Babylon, or Egypt, to assert historical supremacy and territorial claims. This includes distorting archaeology around findings or sponsoring biased research to support ideologically driven narratives.

[3] Initially Albert Einstein, (who coined the equation E=mc2) openly acknowledged metaphysical implications, but later emphasized only measurable phenomena, sidelining deeper philosophical questions. Relativity's materialist bias is also evident in the prevailing scientific worldview, which often assumes matter is primary and consciousness or metaphysical aspects are byproducts, dismissing holistic or dual-aspect theories that suggest a more integrated reality.

[4] This acceptance reflects a deeper erosion of empathy, fuelled by a sponsored media, ideological tribalism, and a detachment from the human cost of both virtual and real-world violence.

aim to influence the majority of the public's perspective on the world of economics, and realpolitik[1].
6. The falsification or general non-disclosure by authoritarian entities of scientific and cosmological facts about the Sun's influence on the Earth's climate, and the miracle that is the Biosphere[2].
7. The non-acknowledgement of the Creator's metaphysical, spiritual and higher dimensional influences, and the pursuit of an artificial creator in the form of technology, artificial intelligence, and virtual realities.

The first six examples mentioned above can be related to rudimentary greed, power, sex or acts of desperation. As such, their presence is complex to relate to the so-called Great Mechanism, but not their degree or intensity. This relationship is not so with the seventh example, the tendency of which is difficult to explain except perhaps in terms of mass-psychosis[3]. But even that simply describes *what* it is, and not *why*.

The gradual departure of the contemporary masses from any form of spiritual path, being a recognition of a higher than human authority such as a Creator God or Divine Being, is hard to justify in terms of wisdom or intelligence. When we look at the past hundred and fifty years we see that this trend has been especially so, and has accelerated over the past few decades.

The dark acts of state and corporate globalist entities indicate a total absence of soul accountability, and we haven't even considered the murky realm of severe physical abuse. To these entities, as long as it is:

- cloaked in secrecy (anonymity), or
- justified to shareholders (profit), or
- along political and propagandized narratives (power),

it is simply accepted as 'a societal or psychological malady'. 'Accepted' as such at least by the lazy, ignorant and complacent contemporary observer, who simply follows these trends along with his forms of entertainment. That this path is abnormal, has no harmonious outcome and is potentially

---

[1] Realpolitik is the approach of conducting diplomatic or political policies based primarily on considerations of given circumstances and factors, rather than strictly following ideological, moral, or ethical premises.

[2] For example; It is widely acknowledged that the Sun plays a major role in Earth's climate. However, state sponsored climate scientists lay claim to the alleged phenomena that global warming is primarily due to human-caused greenhouse gas emissions, not solar variability – largely to strengthen political agendas on carbon taxes and energy policies.

[3] Mass psychosis is a phenomenon where a large group of people loses touch with reality, often driven by fear, propaganda, or 'groupthink'; the synergy in a collection of emotionally erratic people. It can lead to irrational beliefs, behaviours, or social movements that override individual reasoning.

catastrophic to humanity's civilization as a whole, is not considered.

It seems that this is because these contemporary masses have decided that God either does not exist, or does not care, as He does not intervene. Hence, the path we are on and bear witness to seems to lead us collectively into unprecedented and unknown territory. The question is just, is this an unprecedented cliff, or is it simply the end of the pendulum's swing, or is it both?

Turning points that Link Events with Precessional Time

The non-acknowledgment of a Creator God, Divine Being, or Higher Dimensional Influence is not something new or unique; there are numerous examples of such in both scripture[1] and myth[2]. However, as both scripture and myth are consecutive copies of earlier testaments, they are exceedingly difficult to date. For example, the incident of Noah and the Great Flood is paralleled by a similar story of Mithras[3]. In this we are told both Noah and Mithras lived somewhere between 2,800 BC and 1,500 BC. But the 'Great Flood' or 'Deluge' they refer to, we now know occurred at the end of the Pleistocene era. It was caused by the extraordinary and sudden melting of the northern icecap, heralding the end of the Ice Age, which occurred about 11,700 years ago.

When we consider the myths surrounding Noah and Mithras, we must also take into account that myths generally contain elements of truth, whether historical, natural, psychological, or cultural. Subsequently, if we correlate the Great Flood with the reported sudden demise of Atlantis 9,000 years before the time of Solon[4] or around 11,600 years ago, we see that these earth-changing events are almost certainly the same.

We then note the vast and megalithic temple complexes, such as those of Gobekli Tepe in South-eastern Türkiye, which date to at least this same era or even older, as does the Giza Plateau. Where the formers date was established by carbon dating, the monolithic Great Sphinx is now dated to at least a similar time[5], as was the Great Pyramid. There are numerous such examples

---

[1] There are numerous examples of the Israelites rebelling against God, from the times of Moses (1260 BC) to those of Solomon (931 BC).

[2] See Glossary and End Notes: *The Lament of Hermes*, where Hermes Trismegistus, the Atlantean scribe (See *Emerald Tablets* by Doreal) who established a new civilization in Egypt around 10,948 BC or about 12,960 years ago, lamented about the imminent departure of the gods from Egypt.

[3] Mithras featured in both ancient Persian (Zoroastrian) and Vedic (Indian) traditions.

[4] A Greek statesman who visited Egypt in 570 BC, as per Plato's *Timaeus* and *Critias*

[5] According to Dr. Robert Schoch, a geologist and professor, geological weathering patterns, especially water erosion on the body of the Sphinx, date it back to possibly as early as 9,000 BC or older.

on almost all continents[1], but what stands out amongst most of these is that there is a noticeable decline in their number and quality, until around 5,000 years ago when, for example, the Egyptian Kingdoms[2] *recommenced* with the building of megalithic structures in vast temple complexes.

The Anomalies in Ancient Civilizations, that were in harmony with People, Society and the Earth:

Although we do not know what happened to builders of the ancient structures that we still see everywhere, or who they were built for, we can tell a lot by both what they left behind, and what they did not. We have already reviewed the various documented and visible structures, but to list some examples of what is not visible, and not left behind:

1. There is no legacy of these ancients, if they were even human, or where they went.
2. They did not leave us with the kind of written testimony or instructions, that our contemporary academia and historians would accept without dispute[3].
3. There is no sign or description of the techniques or tools that were used to accomplish these obviously extraordinary feats.
4. There is no explanation as to the design or purpose, even though such feats and ideas would (if they belonged to the present civilisation) want to be acclaimed[4].
5. There is no explanation or teaching on the energies that were captured, channelled and redirected in these structures, even though these may have been cleaner and more sustainable than the limited soil, water, and air polluting forms that humanity employs currently.

---

[1] See the published works of Robert Schoch, Graham Hancock, Robert Bauval and John Anthony West.

[2] Between 2686 BC and 250 BC.

[3] There are of course many, such as the Pyramid texts, the Sumerian tablets, the Emerald tablets, and the testimony in eastern and western scripture, but as these are not often politically acceptable, or in conflict with current forms of belief, they are seldom acknowledged as 'historical'.

[4] The fact that these designs and purposes are (to the keen and in-depth observer), multi-purpose, multi-layered and multi-dimensional, makes any such explanation as complex to understand. This is why it is the opinion of some who have studied these for decades, that these structures' existence through time makes for their own testimony.

Observing a Turn of the Tide, a Return to the Light:

The Phenomenon of Population-growth

From around 1960 the Earth's human population increased from around three billion people by about one billion every twelve and a half years, or figure about 300% over roughly 60 years, to the present eight-plus billion inhabitants[1]. Now:

- If we were to envision the human race's collective psyche or spirit as a kind of matter, we'd most definitely see how this increase in density would substantially affect this matter. For example, compare it to increasing the gas in a hermetic system by 300%.

- If we add the effects on human activity *because* of this increase, along the lines of their productivity, intensity, psychically, and by both genders, we will see this number increases cumulatively and exponentially. For example, when the number of people in a certain space increases, like in a city, their levels of consumption and activity increases.

The formulation of these increases would be a factor that would likely differ from one theoretical mathematician to another[2], but it would certainly be very high. However, if we were to compare the resultant effects with those of matter, we can imagine how such an increase in density and activity, within the hermetically sealed space of our Earth's Biosphere, would lead to a monumental increase in heat!

Now, while the Earth's population increase can be explained in *logical terms* such as food-production, medical facilities, increased life expectancy and a drop in infant mortality, the presence of these 'logical terms' can also be explained by not looking at them as causes, but as effects. In other words; the consequences of an artificially increased and overheating population. If we pursue this line of thought, perhaps we must next ask why this would be so, by what design, and by whom?

The Phenomenon of changes in Right and Left-brain Perception

We should next consider the changes that (hypothetically) occurred since the period around 4468 BC, especially those to do with the ability to design and build megalithic structures. It suggests that humans of that time either had some influential external sources, or that notable changes occurred in their ability to think and perceive things analytically. As mentioned in earlier chapters, there is a relative volume of evidence that indicates advanced

---

[1] https://ourworldindata.org

[2] A theoretical mathematician would formulate the exponential increase as a function where the rate of change is proportional to current values, which values would change due to their being reflected when the quantity grows.

civilizations that preceded our current one. However, even for such advanced people to transfer their knowledge and abilities to the relatively primitive beings they encountered, these primitive ones would have had to undergo neurological, psychological and intellectual evolution. In general, this could have occurred if their brain function, or perception, shifted from the right-brain to the left brain. Where these differ predominantly is that:

- The right-brain (lobe or hemisphere) is considered the feminine side, and one that considers things multi-dimensional holistically.
- The left-brain (lobe or hemisphere) is considered the masculine side, and one that functions along the physical one, two or three dimensions analytically.

In the science of BioGeometry, it is suggested that early (primitive) humans primarily operated with right-brain perception, which is intuitive, holistic, and deeply connected to nature and energy fields. This mode allowed them to experience reality in a more spiritual, symbolic, and instinctive way, and they were closely tied to survival, nature, and subtle energies.

At a certain point that appears to aim at around this same shift, roughly 6,000 years ago, the human intellect or cognitive consciousness began to evolve. It indicated a shift toward left-brain perception, which is more analytical, rational, linear, and language-based. This shift marked the development of civilization, structure, and technology, but it also led to a separation from the intuitive, energetic understanding of life.

That something like this occurred is evident but what is not evident is what caused this shift (or swing). Of interest here is that a similar shift occurred roughly 12,000 years ago, that coincided with the demise of the Atlantean civilization, said to contain the legacy of Ancient Egypt's pyramid and temple builders.

Either way, it is realistic to hypothesize that a similar shift is underway at present. There is an evident awakening among the majority of the mature masses (being those older than 28 years), to the deceptive nature of the Possession in almost every quarter of authority. The only component that still resists this awakening is the very small sector that controls the elements of global finance, media and political power. But their continued restriction of the masses is only causing their resistance to grow exponentially, in number and activity.

Hence there are substantiated views that the current rate of conflict and absurdity is a necessary transitional stage in human development. According to these views humanity is entering an era of true or natural balance, where the advanced understanding of the natural energies, such as those present in both the Possession and Purpose, comes from the integration of both hemispheres.

The Phenomenon of Desperate Times and Desperate Men

In continuation of the preceding view, when we observe the men and women who control the political and geopolitical activities of large and many small and relatively insignificant entities (states, agencies, armies, corporations, etc.), it is clear that something very unusual and unprecedented takes place in them. In many cases, shortly after they attain control, their sense of reason and logic takes a complete about turn; their moral threshold takes shades of grey, and their policies, at times, are destructive to both themselves and their subjects.

Some may blame the existence of certain cults and sects such as those that embrace philosophies of redemption through sin and satanism[1]. Although there are many of these in the halls of power, their numbers on a global scale are relatively minor but despite that they are not necessarily insignificant. What is not insignificant, however, is the tolerance of an exponential increase in degree and number of authoritarian abuse[2], by an educated and yet exceedingly ignorant populace.

What makes this ignorance worse today is that the most inhumane and devastating acts are no longer covert, justified or denied, they are openly admitted and even glorified.

The Phenomenon of Reincarnation for non-transcended Souls

Perhaps we can relate this abnormal population-growth with the process of transcendence of illuminated souls, or rather, the reduction of transcendence due to the absence of consciousness, or Light?

If we were to pursue this author's view that the purpose of human life is for an immortal Spirit[3] to realize itself by merging, for the duration of a full and harmonious life, with a sincere and awakened ego, then the phenomenon of a reduced amount of transcendences would make sense. One can imagine that a life filled with insincere thoughts, feelings and actions is not one that carries sufficient substance, from a Higher Dimensional perspective. The metaphorical Chalice of Truth, in other words, would carry insufficient content for a complete soul to transcend.

The Phenomenon of Resource and Energy Depletion

Our civilization is depleting its non-replaceable planetary resources at an

---

[1] The followers of the 17th century Ottoman Jew Sabbatai Zevi, a self-proclaimed Jewish Messiah, whose teachings included the belief that acts traditionally considered sinful would transform into righteous ones.

[2] Over the past decade there's been a significant global decline in judiciary strength and rule of law which, according to Transparency International, is tied to the rise of authoritarianism.

[3] For clarity on the use of the term "Spirit", see the opening diagram in Chapter 10.

unsustainable and accelerating pace[1]. Naturally this observation is linked to the level of our consumption and the fact that we have not yet applied any realistic form of renewable energy. Also linked to this phenomenon is the fact that other forms of energy have been pursued but are suppressed for reasons that make little sense; reasons beyond those of control over supply and profit margins. There are many examples to substantiate these views, but the point here is that we remain dependent on hydrocarbons and combustible-type engines to create electricity; all of which are tied to very real and known limits.

But, besides paying lip-service and making token gestures, the majority of our population continues to pursue a quantitative lifestyle. This is not the fault of any consumer, and neither can it be blamed on corporations that were realized to supply the consumers' demand. However, it is clear that something 'has to give'. This is because most of these 'issues' are inherently causal, mechanical and unavoidable. As such they are as unstoppable as the Solar cycles that lead to climatic changes, that cause crop failures, famine, disease, disharmony, and revolution, which catastrophic period will be followed by a grand revival and reconstruction. It is not pessimistic or optimistic to think so, it is simply nature[2].

The Picture that Emerges from the Collation of Phenomena

We can add more examples, from Solar induced climatic changes, stages of Mass Extinction, Singularity[3], or the effects of Electro-magnetism on life itself, but it is not feasible to go into all of these here. This is even more so as many of these conditions and predictions are influenced by authoritarian entities, who entertain preferred narratives. Whatever the cause, it is clear that these various trends and phenomena are not only unsustainable, they are also as unstoppable as the Sun rising in the morning. Even the increase in artificial divides between people, such as the gender-bias and woke phenomenon, seem to have the destructive power of a wrecking-ball, swinging through various societies like a gigantic pendulum.

When we then turn our attention to the topic of this book, namely The Possession of Man, we can see how its highly influential possessing force is

---

[1] Supposedly, humanity is consuming 1.7 Earths worth of resources annually, and at the current pace, without major behavior, policy, and economic shifts, will head into a resource crisis by 2060. However, this date is being negatively affected by the exponentially increasing rate of ecosystem collapse (soil, forests, biodiversity).

[2] Consider the Black Plague (ca 1350 AD) was preceded by the Great Famine (1315-1317 AD), which was caused by a mini Ice Age that began in 1300 AD. Then consider that this coincided with the Hundred Years War of 1337 – 1453 AD, which coincided with the Italian and Northern Renaissance, that brought a new wave of prosperity into the 15th and 16th century.

[3] In general terms considered as the merger of an ego with Artificial Intelligence, and the biological person with a machine.

prevalent within every aspect of humanity, *like water is to aquatic life*. Over the past century or two, as we moved ever further from the Light, the environ our planet entered got colder, denser, and more adverse to humanity's purpose of Being.

As such we must wonder how much further we can go, what will the turn of events look like, and what will be the final straw? Consider that it (the collection of phenomena) cannot only get more unrealistic, it is in fact quite surreal. It is almost as if humanity has lost its sense of gravity, its ups-and-downs so to speak. Therefore, if it is no longer real, perhaps we are on that U-turn back towards the Light, perhaps we have already passed it! Of course, even if we have, it seems logical that the righting of wrong, or the re-establishing of up and down is not going to be an overnight event, it may take centuries! But if we follow this narrative, it is not where its logic leads us. If we have made that turn, it also means that we did so as a global family. Consequently, we are all moving toward the Light within which everything that was previously hidden by shadows, is now openly visible, and displayed for all to see. Again, this may not be an instant occurrence and much of what was done will automatically, and even desperately resist becoming undone. As such, what was false and wrong but hidden, now exposed becomes brazen. Applying the last of its now rapidly evaporating power, the Possession will likely throw in all it has to keep what it so cunningly accumulated.

However, the same logic points to a conclusion that this final phase of the remaining darkness will pass relatively quick. The reason for this is the obvious presence of an increase in 'illumination' of the contemporary masses, being their ability to discern up from down, right from false, and logic from illogic. In addition, the Possession itself, being a low dimensional and re-active force, will inevitably find its own 'illumination'! Being a force that is equally subject to the earlier described Great Mechanism, as all sentient beings on planet Earth, it too will be powered and enhanced by the same Light we are now moving towards.

The process of 'illumination' in other words, will be as exponential as our recent path into the murky darkness was.

Chapter 18
THE PURPOSE OF MAN

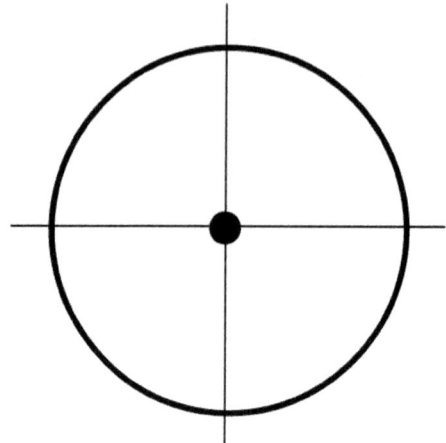

The Circumpunct:
- Ra, the Sun God in Ancient Egypt
- The Divine Spark or Spirit,
- The Philosopher's Stone
- Axis Mundi, the Portal to Higher Dimensions, beyond Space-time.

Purpose

If we can acknowledge the Possession as a *natural* phenomenon, and envision it as a *natural* force that manifests the collation of humanities countless and vastly differing realities, we should be able to recognize the Divine Purpose in it. Understanding this can be of great value to us, as it can substantially ease the suffering of our respective individual journeys in and through life. After all, we do not have to be part of that larger component of mankind that seems to be inescapably and addictively infected by one or a number of Possessions.

It is regrettable that of those who are infected, most are irrevocably unaware that the thoughts, feelings, words and choices they give rise to are not their own. This is largely because, unlike influenza or other infection, the Possession customizes itself uniquely around the archetype and ego of the individual host, who then embraces it as their own. Subsequently, their lives are defined by the world that surrounds them and its Possessions that they surrendered their thinking, feeling and physical beings to.

As a result, the Possession is present when a civilization or agency needs to be founded for a populace to build, grow and thrive, and this would be ok, were it not for the inherent underlying laziness of man. For example, in a newly established and thriving civilization we see how, within a few generations, the successors of the original builders, who did not experience the hardships or necessities of old, become complacent. Basing their reign believing that they know when they do not, all sense of creativity evaporates. In its place they build mere shells of what once was, and fill these with a perpetuation of modified copies that increase in absurdity. In this too the Possession learns, accommodates and grows. Blinded by sex, greed, ignorance and stupidity, the complacent man inevitably turns to conflict, never realizing the unintended consequences.

We now realize that the resultant and periodic collapse or 'fall' is almost certainly a part of Great Nature's design, especially when we see how it often coincides with natural events[1]. When we look into our distant past, beyond our recorded history, we find dateable evidence on almost every continent that this occurred. Whether it was by solar-induced climatic changes or meteor impact, via resultant floods, earthquakes, famine, disease or forms of mass-psychosis that drove men and women mad, the resultant fall was the same.

This means that there is actually very little that we can do to save humanity from itself. As such, we may be better off using our time here to pursue a good, conscious, and harmonious life for ourselves, our families, and the tribe we have chosen to make our home with. If we can accomplish this, then it does not really matter whether we live on the rise, crest, fall or trough of any particular social structure. After all, our higher dimensional Essence or Soul is unaffected by these lower dimensional events, as is its successive or transcendent journey.

The state of our 'civilized' world in general, and the Possession that controls the majority of its authoritarian systems, is what it is. These 'systems' may think that they control the fate of people, but in reality they do not. This is because every man and woman is born in pure innocence and goodness, and regardless of what parents, priests, peers or society as a whole may say, *at the time of birth there is no debt to settle*. The only debt we have is to ourselves, to our Purpose, and this is a debt we can settle by living an ordinary but harmonious, sincere and purpose-filled life. As such, it is possible for all of us to attain, within a single life, the transcendence of our consciousness to Higher Dimensions.

The previous chapter contemplated the Great Mechanism of our three-dimensional experiential reality. In this we hypothesized how, since 4468 BC[2]

---

[1] See previous chapter, under *The Phenomenon of Resource and Energy Depletion*.

[2] This era can be correlated to a phase of worldwide temple and pyramid building by the priesthoods and initiated who carried the knowledge, art and magic of their time. Among the various and numerous purposes of these accomplishments, their intent was to preserve their knowledge during the millennia of darkness they knew would follow.

mankind moved from the Light, until it reached the widely acknowledged turning point in 2012 AD. In this chapter we consider the existence of a 'force' opposite to the Possession, one that enables and guides the journey of the transcending Soul. It is a force that is influenced, energized and synergized with the intent, passion and harmony of man, but one which has largely been suppressed. Kept preserved in the temples, monasteries and sacred or consecrated places of all kinds, including the sincere hearts of people, it has no name except perhaps, to call it by what it is: The Purpose of Man.

Possession versus Purpose

We experience reality in an *orderly* Cosmos. As the concept of order is in defiance of entropy, or Chaos, there must be a particular point of magnetism that makes it so. If we can see this beyond the limited spectrum of physics, we may discover that it was purposely created and even encoded[1] with certain irrefutable principles or laws. These are best summarized as follow[2]:

Hermetic Principles	**Cosmic Law**
Mentalism	Unity in Diversity
Correspondence	Change
Vibration	Perpetual Motion
Polarity	Opposites
Rhythm	Periodicity
Cause and Effect	Causality
Gender	Balance

Where each of these can be reviewed in great detail, of relevance here is the Principle of Polarity, also known as the Law of Opposites. In previous chapters we described and deliberated about the Possession in considerable detail. And whether one likes it or if one prefers to use another name or description, the existence of a force or presence that captures and takes over the mind, feelings and actions of people – individually and collectively – is undeniable. However, what is incontestable is when there is a dark side, there must also be a light side, and where one was described as the Possession of Man, its opposite would be the Purpose of Man[3].

---

[1] We see the presence of these intelligent codes wherever we look, from the movements of our star the Sun and whole galaxies, down to the existence of Life in the Earth's Biosphere, including our DNA.

[2] William Walker Atkinson; *The Kybalion*.

[3] These can also be considered as opposites when we see how the Possession of man dominates his reality of free will, and when the Purpose of Man enables him to define his intention by which he adapts his way of life, by which he may dominate his free will.

Thus, opposite to the Possession of Man stands the Purpose of Man, and this becomes clear when, for example, we see how the contemporary man responds or reacts relative to the Light – as described in the Great Mechanism. Without a clear and visible or 'illuminated' definition of what to do or how to behave, especially when they are part of a collective or organization, the contemporary man is easily misled and made dependent on a sort of possessing agency. However, when people move towards and into an era of illumination or Light, regardless of whether this is voluntary or involuntary, their Purpose made visible is what reigns in influence. Of course, it is very difficult to define this phenomenon because *the nature of humanity* has seemingly not changed in our recorded past, or roughly 6,000 years. By this 'nature of humanity' we refer to the perpetual pursuit of people to form ever larger agencies, kingdoms and empires, only to see these fall without fail, through their descent into war, social unhappiness, and the consequent economic decline.

We have no precedents of this, as all we have of civilizations that existed prior to our 'recorded history', which is also the last time that humanity was on our hypothesized trajectory toward the light, are its monuments. As was elucidated earlier and as is commonly known, these monuments are not mere symbolic structures like the majority of monuments erected in cities today. However, the mystery that surrounds the origin and purpose of these thousands of structures found worldwide remains largely unanswered. The reason why we do not understand how our forebears accomplished what they did, or why, is because we believe that they - as human beings - were like us. We cannot envision that people could be so 'other and opposite' in their motivations, fears, abilities and physical-energy based technologies. Even when we consider the hypothesis of non-terrestrial visitors or panspermia[1], most believe that such beings would likely be as aggressive and invasive as our present civilization's human beings are. This is because the contemporary left-brain physics-oriented minds are formatted to think along the way of physical matter and energy only, and thus struggle to envision this otherwise[2]. The exception here is when people awaken from their mechanicalness and stop re-actively following these physical influences. Only then can we return our focus inwards, and begin to note our essence, or inner being.

In other words, we can and will evolve, but not in any physical sense.

As an example, consider how many believe their evolution relates to material or intellectual growth, or how their life's physical purpose evolves. However, if one considers this across a life, one may note that in their higher awareness, such as that of the essential self, nothing has really changed. We may

---

[1] Panspermia is the hypothesis that suggests life on Earth originated from outer space.

[2] See Chapter 17, under "The Phenomenon of changes in Right and Left-brain Perception"

remember what we dreamt of becoming as little children, and how this was often related to what we thought our parents wanted or would like. This childish but *internal or right-brain* thinking naturally altered during our dreamy adolescent years, largely due to *external or left-brain* logic from peers, parents, and teachers. In some young adults, this external influence was overruled by choice or necessity, but in most cases, they stay on course and study or learn to become what their life's influences caused them to be. Most people will stay on their selected course; for example, they may change companies but continue with their respective allocated careers. To most of these, it no longer matters whether they had studied for them, liked them, and whether they made them happy, or not. Around the mid-life, some become aware of their unhappy state and begin to make changes. Of these, some act when they realize their dream-jobs do not match their expected standard, or when external considerations force them to make changes. Again, to these, their decisions were dominated by the effects of external causes; from a world that was moving away from an illuminated higher Purpose, and into a world that became increasingly darker, denser and rule based.

Of course there are some who make changes on their own initiative, often intuitively, and often at considerable cost or risk. But either way, whatever name or description one prefers to give it, with every change in the way we think, feel or do, there are always invisible forces at work. These forces are either external or internal, and often even the so-called internal ones are external, simply because we don't really understand the difference.[1] However, it should be evident that these external forces originated from the magnetic or repulsive influences of an external Possession, and the internal ones were stimulated by our inner beings Purpose. These in turn affected the egos dominance by either left or right brain lobe or hemisphere.

The Power of Purpose

The struggle between Possession and Purpose describes their subconscious influence that we are all subject to. The only exception is when some of us begin to recognize this because we have started to observe ourselves. Because most people believe their thoughts are their own, and that they are in charge of their decisions, they never question them and, as such, they remain oblivious of these influences.

However, whatever these attracting or repulsive influences may be, they may determine *what* we do, but not *how*. This 'how' is not something we often have much choice in, with the exception being our awareness of these forces, in both their presence as well as their conscious nature.

If we do notice them we may find that a Possession has entities that will

---

[1] As examples one can consider religious, political or ideological motivations.

actively, and if need be forcefully, prevent liberating or exposing forces from entering its domain. Consequently, a Purpose that is true will equally have guarding entities of its own. Thus, a Purpose's guarding entities, our intention and our relative degree of sincerity are what will determine our fate. If our motivation was oriented around just another type of Possession, then any fortune or glory that comes with it will be controlled by the Possession's entity, and unlikely to last. However, if the Purpose was founded intentionally, by the sincere and aware man, then, regardless of what occurs in the physical realm, the guardians of Purpose will serve those who observe their Essence within their heart.

The Purpose of Guardians

The existence of metaphysical beings referred to as 'Helpers' or 'Guardians' is nothing new, and there are many different types with as many names[1]. For now, we'll simply refer to them by what they do, which is to guide, help or guard the Purpose of Man in his germination and growth of an immortal soul.

Guardians are described in all forms of religion, spirituality, mythology, folklore and, at present, in much of our entertainment. Where scripture and myth tell of a time when these 'other-dimensional' or 'other-vibrational' beings existed amongst mankind[2], during the increasing darkness of the past few millennia, testimony of them gradually subsided. As a result, much of our understanding of them has been replaced by an orderly and heavily sponsored dogma, under the watchful eyes of statist entities, who use it as a means to better contain and control their subjects.

Besides the manipulation of the lives and livelihoods of people, the greater travesty of these dominating controls is that the remaining physical senses cannot detect these higher vibrational or dimensional beings. For this a certain higher sensory development must be in place, which entails an enhanced conscious awareness that is supported by a knowledge-based understanding. This is not something that develops naturally, like teeth and puberty, it can only be attained through a strong intention and a particular approach to self-awareness, or self-observation. Consequently, as this is not commonly possible within a one or two-dimensional reality-perspective, a large part of

---

[1] i.e. Angels, Archangels, Cherubim / Seraphim, Nephilim, Messengers, Celestials, Spirits, Guides, Light beings, Ethereals, Watchers, Protectors, Sentinels, Wards, as well as Neters (in Ancient Egypt) and Devas (in Hinduism).

[2] For example: in Christian scripture, see Genesis 6:1-4, Exodus 33:11, Hebrews 13:2, Acts 14:11-13. In Islam angels and divine messengers interact with humans by God's command, and usually in direct form; and in Hinduism – the oldest of religions – gods walking among men is a fully embraced theological truth, especially in the doctrine of avatars. Vishnu, Shiva, and other deities routinely interact directly with the human world, often taking on human or semi-human forms to do so.

humanity must proceed by the tragically fallible element of faith alone[1].

But as we now know, all this is natural and integral in the Greater Purpose of the Cosmos, where nothing true is ever lost or wasted. Hence, if this is the path of many, then there must be a supportive reason, which forms part of the Purpose of Guardians.

Perhaps these beings are the omnipresent lifesavers of mankind, and all we have to do is ask!

In Closing

Although much of what was deliberated in this book was accompanied by footnotes, the path that was followed originated in a holistic understanding of the presence of both the Possession and the Purpose. This was then analyzed and gradually filled with logic, history, and relatively easy-to-confirm anthropological, psychological, sociological and philosophical observations. It also followed a line of understanding of religion, spirituality and mythology.

From this perspective then, it is my conclusion that the most important tools or mechanisms that our Creator instilled in each and every one of us, are:

The Power of Compassion
The Power of Prayer
The Power of Belief

---

[1] The fallibility of "Faith", see Chapter 8: *Truth and its Inevitable Nemesis called Hope.*

EPILOGUE

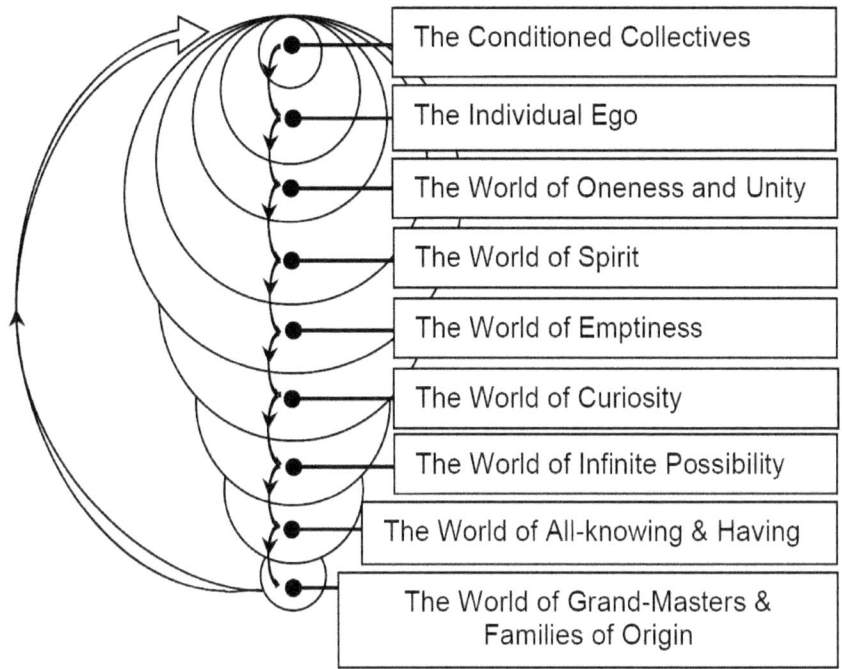

With the veils and layers of the Observer's conditioned reality removed, his vision is unimpeded. Free from the distracting draw of his Collectives magnetism, his struggle with many is now reduced to One.

Within the consequent Interconnectedness of his now Unified State, he enters that Endless Ocean and drifts harmoniously, amalgamated in Divine Emptiness.

Descending into forgetfulness, he is in a world of mystery and wonder. Contemplating how he came to be, he realizes that to know, he must again divide; reinserting new veils and layers,
he forms new realities.

He discovers once more how the Structure's Whole is dependent on the definition of all its possible, integral and component parts.

And as the Great Machine re-starts he is again challenged to escape from his unconscious state of doing, feeling and thinking.
He begins to live and discover anew,
while his Soul awaits his re-awakening;

patiently, lovingly, ultimately and infinitely.
Transcending the Structure of Reality

From within the rhythm of a cyclic centrifugal Cosmos, the Soul of Man is brought into existence. Tested and tried under all possible and impossible conditions, he arises as a Being of Divine Magnificence; one that embraces both finite and infinite qualities, through physical and metaphysical elements.

This was its Purpose, as it is written:

"Throw it upon earth, and earth will separate from fire. The impalpable separated from the palpable. Through wisdom it rises slowly from the world to heaven. Then it descends to the world combining the power of the upper and the lower. Thus, you will have illumination of all the world, and darkness will disappear."[1]

As such the Soul of Man traverses out of the dense rudimentary earth, into the heavens and beyond. Upon his illumination, free from all that binds and possesses, including the constraints of his body of suffering, the journey-eternal commences.

---

[1] Excerpt from *The Emerald Tablet of Hermes*, by Hermes Trismegistus, as translated by Idries Abutahir Shah, a great Sufi Master (1924 – 1996).

APPENDIX A
CONTEMPLATING THE RISE AND FALL OF CIVILIZATIONS

To conspire is part of human nature, but the idea of a *functional global* conspiracy, such as that which entertains secret meetings and collaboration, with as its aim the enslavement, control or destruction of humanity, is unrealistic. Humanity is simply too diverse and divided to sustain any such power and profit-based collusion.

There is however an invisible force or presence that is metaphysical and undetectable, except by its effects. These effects possess a part of life itself, and are therefore inevitable, cyclic, and observably present in both the individual and the collective being.

As such it correlates its forces, with as its purpose the survival and enhancement of itself, at any cost.

The Opposites of Man

In the Duality of Creation, man, is divided in the opposites of masculine and feminine gender, but mankind as a whole also has its opposite. This is the feature of the individual being against that of the Collectives[1] he forms with others. These are in complete opposition to each other. One can even consider that the nature of the individual being is *inherently* good and yet his collective undertakings are *inherently* bad, as these inevitably only serve the collective – not the individual. However, it seems that in Creation, this was purposely designed as such and connected as Light and Darkness, where neither can exist without the other!

We may therefore consider ourselves wise because we believe we know ourselves, and believe we know how to guard our minds. But, if we do not know or realize the opposite nature of our Collectives to our individual self, then we have only discovered one of mankind's two divisions in Creation's design. This is unfortunate for most who consider themselves Believers, as these are predominantly conditioned to be integrated with only one of the many and various Collectives. Consequently, the Believer does not necessarily see how this makes them shadow reflections of something much greater and more complex, or that this affects them in every way as individual beings directly and indirectly. Accordingly, they will not easily acknowledge when the Collectives of man have created an artificial world that serves its own interests first and foremost. Within the Collective's artificial world little or no

---

[1] In this section, Collectives is capitalized due to it being referred to as an Entity.

energy (consideration) is given for the journey of individual realization, being the inner and spiritual transcendence of the true conscious 'Self'.

Because of the absence of this 'inner awareness', the human ego[1] is often referred to by some as something unholy and even the Demiurge, and yet, the personality remains an essential part of us, as it is within this identity that the Self is enabled to grow and realize Itself. It is only when the ego is left empowered and unencumbered, that it can at times go bad, or become the 'root of evil'. We can observe how this potential emerges in us all when we become identified with things, feelings, or with our Collectives. The realization of the ego's powerful presence within the Self is usually only made when the mind is stilled, but this stillness is not something that can be attained consciously. Usually it occurs during meditative, spiritual practices, or forms of yoga[2], combined with a sincere wish to know. It is through the continuation of such practices that the individual can begin to pacify this ego and activate his Intuitive Center through which a realization of awareness of his individual path-to-purpose can occur.

Whilst the individual must, in the daily function of life, engage with his ego, the Collectives will create the physical, emotional and intellectual reality within which the individual is conceived, born and conditioned, and within which he must mature to find this path-to-purpose. However, seldom during this daily function does the individual realize how infected the 'true-self' has become by his surrounding world.

Defining the Demonic Possession of Man

In these writings I have chosen to use the term Possession, but others have referred to the same as the Capture, Demon or Logismoi, and others. The reason for these names is because it is more than just a classification of evil or mere sadistic, barbaric, psychotic, psychopathic or sociopathic behavior; as these are all merely effects of an underlying cause. Where, for example, psychopathy is considered a genetic disorder, it does not lead to a person automatically taking pleasure from causing harm, as even such 'pleasure' is a feeling that the psychopath cannot theoretically sense. Most observers of these effects are rather contemporary[3] in their ability to consider this, and skeptical of the idea of a demonic existence. Most likely this is because to them, the reality of a demon's ability to possess even the strongest and wisest among them, scares them. Hence the Possession is seldom acknowledged for what it is: *a cognitive, conscious and self-aware entity, that transmits itself from mind to mind, along both parallel and consecutive strands.*

---

[1] In this, Ego, Personality, and Personal Identity are used synonymously.

[2] Yoga in this case refers to activities designed to harmonize body, mind and feelings.

[3] In these writings, the term 'contemporary' describes a person who is limited to perceiving things one or two dimensionally.

At present, with its flames fanned by a viral network in a globally connected world, the Possession has changed much of its influencing modus operandi. Where before it remained hidden in the shadows of secrecy, of late it came out into the open and drew much attention to itself. Although this caused a considerable reaction among those who remained awake and aware, its powerful influence continues to dominate the perception of the contemporary masses. In this it continues to harvest their attention-energy, which enables it to endure. This effect not only boosts the Possessions confidence and empowers its servants; it also increases its subjects. Today we can see how it has accumulated and gathered formidable financial and military forces around it. These are represented by those who are easily corrupted, or ignorant of its effects, as well as *those who have donned uniform or suit, and who serve its rules and dogma knowingly and without hesitation.* This could be a perfectly acceptable state of existence for some of the contemporary masses, except that the vast majority of them are stuck in unawareness – as in various states and degrees of hypnosis and unaware of Life's higher purpose and possibilities.

To an unbiased observer, it should be fairly obvious that the Possession's destructive and energy-consuming way is, in every way, in direct opposition to the constructive and energy-enhancing path of the individual who is conscious. However, we must consider the Possession as a feature that enhances or amplifies both growth and decay. In addition, being integral with Creation, we must consider the Possession as more than just a psychological phenomenon or an organism. *In fact, as an organism the Possession is comparable to an insatiable and infectious virus, that is conscious of itself.*

If we consider the Possession as an organism, and if we were to imagine its metaphysical shape as we would with the physical senses, we will find that it manifests a multitude of equally metaphysical tentacles. It does this at will, and yet only its effects are ever observed. We would 'see' that these 'tentacles' penetrate the auric fields of the emotionally unstable and usually unaware Follower (of Faith and/or Order[1]). From here, these 'tentacles' artificially stimulate the Emotional Center of the individual, which convinces him to adopt the applied effect as his own, and as an entity he is responsible for. At times they may consider the phenomenon as something divine-like or supernatural which they consequently believe they need to defend or nurse. When the Follower of Faith or Order does so, he simultaneously feeds the Possession by 'paying' it with his attention, by which he empowers it with his very vitality or life force. In the process, the host's resolve on absurd and unrelated things will noticeably weaken, especially as he becomes increasingly subjective to the Possession.

---

[1] See Diagram 1 at the beginning of this book.

In both those who are corrupted and those who are subjected, the Possession will enhance their emotional states to levels that are often inexplicable in terms of humanitarian reason and logic. For example, one sees how, among both the abuser and the abused, it is only when one of them awakens and begins to observe its possessing nature within him- or herself, that the Possessions metaphysical tentacles evaporate, like a shadow before the light, often leaving a somewhat disorientated host to wonder if it ever existed.

Hence we may note that, be it for whatever reason, the Possession only exists whilst its hosts enable it, and how it thrives off their life force.

The Mark of the Possession, in Signs and Symbols

If the preceding perspective on the Possession can be grasped, then it may become easier to recognize and understand the ancient symbolism that is often found in public use. Although it is usually hidden or disguised by the very entities that host it, their mastery over it is often somewhat arrogantly placed in plain sight. In many cases one can identify dragon and serpent-like resemblances, and in others the clever use or incorporation of geometric shapes and mathematical sequences, often with no obvious reason or related logic. In some instances, these symbols are so openly displayed or engraved, and used over multiple decades and even centuries, that few will question them as anything unusual, let alone supranatural or abnormal. However, when we investigate the origin, meaning and inherent energy[1] of some of these designs, we may find ourselves peeling the layers off an underlying disguise. With their cores consequently exposed, we may begin to see various forms and degrees of darkness in them. These include the offshoot of Saturn-worship, also known as satanism, within which we find related and interconnecting symbolism, ranging from hexagons to cubes, to rings and the all-seeing eye[2].

When observing the use of signs and symbols we can begin to see them as dots connecting nations, organizations, corporations, religions, old families, customs and traditions, as well as the centers of global finance and governance. By connecting these dots, one may see how they take the shape of an ancient organism; one that is often represented in the shape of an octagon or octopus, and which has influenced the ruling powers for millennia.

To envision the Possession's influence and infectious nature through its effects, we can see how it resembles one of Great Nature's other inherent forces, that of Earth's gravity. It is also invisible as only its causal effects can

---

[1] Like sound and light, these energies are real and quite measurable. For more information see https://www.biogeometry.ca/

[2] Although such dark and often inciteful cults, organizations and nations will be found using these symbols, and often because of their inherent energy, the symbols naturally predate their use, and often by many millennia.

be detected, and similarly, when anything subconsciously enters the Earth's magnetic influence, *it automatically becomes a part of it.*

The Effects and Purpose of the Possession

In the public arena, the nature of the Possession's various entities has of recent times changed quite substantially, especially since the onset of the 2020 Covid narrative. When influenza, as ancient as man himself, was psychologically inserted into the minds of a contemporary public and portrayed as a deadly pandemic, it affected the psyche of the vast majority of people[1] worldwide. It had already taken a giant leap into controlling the same public's fear-based awareness with the 911 affair in 2001, the 7/7 bombing in London in 2005, the grave injustices through military conflict and the overthrow of government that accompanied them, and even the 'Sub-prime' financial crisis of 2008[2]. The objectives in these agendas were dual:

- The first was the attainment of public acquiescence. Through this it was able to expand its ability to capture their Emotional Centers and mutate these into pseudo-thinking centers. As these would function off programmable feelings, the fearful publics pursuit of truth through reason and logic would come second.
- The second objective entailed a form of gradual gene manipulation. This one is even more sinister in nature as it affects the body's energy portals or chakras, and in particular the third eye and crown chakra. These two represent the energy portals that enable man's spiritual (or right-brain) activation and the consequent higher dimensional inflow from the Intuitive Center.

With this well-developed ability, the Possession's numerous and various interconnected worldwide entities commenced with an orchestrated effort to actively conquer all threats to its existence and growth[3]. The merger of science and spirituality, in lieu of a suppressed science opposite to a dogmatic religion, was considered as one of such threats. Another was the harmonious merger of any masculine and feminine features, and not just in those of relationships and family values, where the masculine and feminine roles were now close to becoming interchangeable. The Possession's interference to disrupt reason, logic and truth entered every sector of life. The reason for this was (and still is) the creation and distribution of confusion and fear. The

---

[1] According to WHO statistics, around 70 % of people worldwide took at least one COVID-19 vaccine dose.

[2] While these events are different in nature, they form a chain of predictable, controllable and provable geopolitical and economic cause-and-effect, with each one setting conditions that contributed to the next.

[3] Consider as an example, the U.S. doctrine of unipolar dominance, otherwise known as the Defense Planning Guidance, aimed at preventing the rise of any rival power that could challenge U.S. global dominance, whether in Europe, Asia, or elsewhere. Although written in 1992, its presence in the geostrategic world cannot be missed.

Possession feeds off such low vibrational and low dimensional emotions, and at the same time, it convinces the subservient public of its necessity – regardless of truth.

To the Possession, the threat of exposure is further amplified by the profound, miraculous emergent effects arising from *the merger of opposites-in-Truth. As an example of such 'opposites-in-Truth', consider the miraculous that can emerge through the merger of the feminine with the masculine, or science with spirituality.* Not only does the merger between opposites *not* lead to their respective neutralizing; among humans it also leads its participants to a phenomena that was referred to by Rosicrucian alchemists as the 'Alchemical Wedding'. This 'wedding' depicts the spiritual transformation and inner union of opposites that leads to the emergence of purer or higher dimensional, intuitive intelligent and Transcended Beings.

To the Possession this represents a clear and present danger. The reason is that it represents a deleting or dissolving kind of force; a type of light-exposed shadow 'annihilation' if you will. This makes the Possession consider such emergent processes as its mortal enemy. The truth in this observation (from the Possession's perspective) cannot be denied of course, but then, neither can the harmless perspective of a Transcended Being. Being akin to the Light, the Transcended Being will still *unreservedly* love and accept the inevitable reality of the Possession, as a part of itself. Hence:

As unjust and horrifying as many events in the world are,
or as heartless and senseless the actions of many of its possessed
organizations, corporations and uniform-orientated structures;
they remain a natural part of the world of man. Thus;

No force or new set of rules and laws will ever rectify this, on the contrary.
The more of these one applies, the more powerful the influence of a
Possession grows, and the denser it gets.

A view on Co-existing with the Possession

Just as Ghandi observed that 'an eye for an eye would make the whole world go blind', the same applies when we believe in fighting violence with violence, as this only leads to more violence. In fact, most acts of violence are physically or emotionally reactive, which means that the making of decisions does not originate from the Thinking Center but the Emotional Center. Consequently, they are void of considered or contemplated reason and harmony-based logic. The result of is that no matter the threat or arena the Possession wishes to address. the duly possessed minds begin to seek more of their own or similar kind. This inadvertently leads to an exponential increase in dis-order and chaos. Consequently, at present, with the escalation in technology enabling the relentless pursuit for authoritarian control on a global scale, these may indeed be interesting times.

With the majority of people on both sides of the 'for' or 'against' spectrum living within the illusion of one and two-dimensional realities, the absence of a deeper understanding will likely lead many of them into a descending spiral of a physical and potentially violent nature. With the present civilization moving ever further away from Order and more towards Chaos, its fate across the various dimensions is complex to predict[1]. This is even more so when we consider that whatever modern or innovative ideas the Possession's entities establish to try to fix or to improve things, are all aimed at the sensory elements and untested.

However, in an intelligent and conscious Creation, we may assume that the next cycle of civilization is unlikely to be more destructive than the current one. This is because a more destructive one would likely erase the very possibility of any *re*-established or *re*-set civilization. Within this, Creation would lose the purpose of its eon old existence; being the miraculous phenomenon of conscious and intelligent human life. In this purposely Created Universe that we perceive, such a self-destructive design would be absurd as every element in its construct, including both microcosm and macrocosm, was made manifest to complete harmonious and flawless perfection.

To summarize:

Although the Possession referred to herein, is a lower dimensional but still factual part of the construct in man's experiential Creation, the possibility of it causing a higher dimensional or conscious life-ending cataclysm, is non-existant. This is because the higher dimensional nature of Creation is defunct of Space-time and, as such, cannot allow for such an unmanifest outcome. If it were allowed or possible it would mean It never was.

In other words, as an alternative explanation:
'That which purposely gives cause to Itself to realize and be aware of Itself, whilst being omnipotent, cannot undo Itself.'

When we are able to realize the fundamental ubiquitous co-existence of opposing features within our day-to-day surrounds, we may begin to recognize that this is meant to be. Between this and the fingerprints of Creation that are found everywhere in Great Nature, we cannot but note the invisible but conscious and intelligent influence on our day-to-day experience of occurring

---

[1] This view may be debated by saying that the establishment of a global rule-based order will prevent such chaos, but if we consider that this artificial order is dependent on technology, a stable global economy and an unchanging Cosmos, we can recognize the extreme fragility of this policy.

and re-occurring life. To add to this feature of reality, consider the untold interactive and miraculous experiences by a great many, in forms that are physical, astral, inner-thought or other. These include the profound phenomena of insight by numerous seers into Creation's omniscient matrix of all-knowing, also known as the Akashic Records. To consider all these as mere coincidence or luck would be both naïve and ignorant of what should be evident to the unbiased eye. Any so-called inevitable or disastrous 'end' to what was purposely brought about would therefore be paradoxical in the order of Divine Impossibility.

> *Hence, by law, an immortal Possession exists eternally,*
> *but only as a shadow cast off Consciousness.*
> *Its degree of darkness and its shape therefore,*
> *is determined by the brightness and purpose of Light.*

Of course, the term Consciousness that we refer to here is that All-and-Everything or Oneness, which is impervious to that known as the fundament of Space-time. It is impervious because both Space and Time can only exist in the awareness of the three-dimensional man, for which he must intelligently apply his five physical senses. For example, this explains why plants and animals, like the unconscious and oblivious man, do not have a realized concept of Time or its passage. In fact, one could add to this that the reality of Time, to the intelligent and aware human being, is *dependent on his or her certainty of death*.

As neither the plant nor the animal have a human-like awareness, being one that is based on sets of stored and sequential memories, they do not observe Death as an ending. To these, every form of life merely represents food or fuel for the next lifeform or 'cycle', that the consumed one then becomes one with. Consider how the life-force of millions of shrimps and small fish become part of the enormous whale that consumes them, or the plant that is consumed by other plants or animals. Thus said, when we look at entities that exist within the existing life-force of plants and animals, and which are passed from one form to another, we can then see how such entities can be considered as eternal. In correspondence with plant and animal life, we can then see how the existence of the Possession, as an entity that is equally one-dimensional in its nature, is equally eternal.

Seeing that a human being is in-part an animal, the life-force entity in him is also eternal, like that of the plant and animal. It is only from the perspective of our ego that we see ourselves as mortal. As such, it should be evident by now that the Possession has an ego as well, and a very powerful one. Unlike man however, the existence of the Possession's ego is one that can transcend the life-span of a physical organism, and one that is not limited to a single organism at a time. Consequently, it can be said that the Possession is both eternal and immortal.

From this we can conclude that, for an eternal and immortal entity such as the Possession, Time has no substance and from its perspective both the past and future are not time-related. This explains why the Possession is unable to realize compassion. *To a one-dimensional eternal and immortal entity, the past is only relative for the food or lessons it contains, and the future is only considered from a perspective of things that can feed it or end it.* Thus, to an eternal and immortal entity, anything that cannot be seen, counted, measured, and controlled has neither meaning nor value.

Containing and Limiting the Possession

If we are able to realize the Possession as an ever-changing, shape-shifting and adapting shadow of Consciousness, we may find that, in the perceived reality of the one- and two-dimensional man, it will appear as both eternal and immortal. However, as an entity the Possession remains metaphysical, and thus, we can only ever observe its effects. Residing with and within the equally metaphysical ego of contemporary individuals, the Possession exists by feeding off their low-vibrational life-force. This means that any physical power that the Possession is ever able to exert, is always channelled through its subjected and often unconscious servants and followers. As it is not affected by the human concept of accountability, the Possession is not hampered by elections or selections, and therefore is able to continue to wield its power of influence on its entities across generations, and in some cases centuries or even millennia. The evidence of this is easily found in the recorded history of kingdoms, empires, religions, corporations, and forms of collective gangsterism that caused the exploitation, suffering and destruction of countless people. If we review these acts among the world's differing ethnicities and other categories of division, we note that – political bias aside – there is very little differentiation between the groups it targets. In fact, we see how opposing parties, such as with suppressor and suppressed, will continuously change sides. However, there has historically been a preference to suppress and even destroy or wipe out certain minorities that included Earth's natural-energy aware and spiritually awakened people. For example, we note the fate of the native and animist tribes of the Americas and Australasia, or the spiritualist Bogomils and Cathars of Europe. The motivations behind almost inexplicably bizarre and equally grotesque and barbaric atrocities that were committed stand as a case in point. At times, the applied brutality by some entities even included the sacrifice of their own people which, besides the attainment of minor societal and geopolitical influences, this brutality seemed to have little measurable benefit.

The Possession's desperation to feed itself and expand, in a hermetically sealed and thus limited environment, has caused it to become brazen. Despite the internet-based global audience and institutions of justice, which continue to bear witness to wrongdoing and intentionally falsified detail, organized incidents of genocide continue to occur, and under a variety of guises. However, in this inter-connected world it has become considerably more complex to undertake demonic actions, such as those of genocide, without accountability, as this interconnectedness has caused a considerable public awakening or awareness. Atrocities that were previously occult and disguised are now no longer hidden, and often undertaken by various of the Possession's entities in plain view. In addition, we note that very few of these actions were incidental, and that most are indirectly or even directly spawned and sponsored by state, corporate and secretive agencies.

We also note how the Possession applied active measures[1] to maintain its dominance over an unaware public. We note how the described public awakening has led directly to the Possession countering this awakening trend by controlling, altering and censoring the information the public is exposed to. This move was then countered by entities that provided alternative sources of information which seemed to mushroom out of nowhere. These alternative sources, in turn, became subjected to new laws and directives to regulate them, often under banners of so-called 'peace and safety'. We can go along with this back-and-forth line of reasoning ad-infinitum, but seldom does the contemporary public note the presence of the perpetual pendulum. The results of this are highly technological forms of psychological and social brainwashing operations on an unprecedented scale. They range from staged pandemics and pseudo-wars, to the division of citizens along political or religious divides, all of which are driven by equally fake politicians and priests, who resolutely remain above the law. To a normal and logical reasoning mind, the absurdity of this theatre is obvious, yet throughout the ages, the majority of citizens remain mesmerized by its carefully scripted antics.

Today, the Possession has gathered more minds into its following than ever before, but in this lies its ultimate failure. Besides the consequence of insatiability, in its pursuit to grow it also becomes exceedingly 'top-heavy'. Historically, in empires, religions and all forms of organizations, its growth lead to an escalation of inner-division, and this is still so today. We can easily see how such inner-division is followed by a form of controlled disorder that is firstly disadvantageous to its subjects. Then, when a corrupted collective's decay begins, it does so from within and becomes impossible to stop without major implications. If we observe our so-called civilized world of today, we can see that this decay is well underway, and it is only a matter of time before

---

[1] Active measures refer to covert political operations used by statist agencies that include surveillance, espionage, propaganda, and the spread of dis- and mis-information. These tactics are employed to manipulate public opinion in support of political movements and corporate interests.

its current form as a functional entity implodes. The *natural, mechanical and traditional trend* in such instances is that the old behemoth is replaced by two or three lesser but still influential entities[1], which in time are respectively overturned by various smaller competing ones. The effect of this downward spiral in itself will also mutate, as it can only continue until its residual entities reach an elementary level. Like we see with elements on the periodic table, it is at this elementary level that the entity (or element) loses its ability to function as the substance from which it came. For example, when an empire is broken down to a collection of petty-kingdoms and feuding warlords. It is only then, at the elementary level, that the natural environment is ready to recommence the hosting of a new cycle. This occurs through the gradual merger or intensification towards a unified and single entity. As another example, consider the violent break-away of the American colonies from their 'Crown-entity', followed by an era of genocide, lawlessness and civil war, to the bloodstained birth of the entity called the United States of America.

But a civilizations rise and fall occurs separately from the inner growth or decline of the individual. In fact, when we consider the fate of an individual within these revolving cycles, we see that the individual's position in the cycle makes little or no difference. Just as some may find their purpose or awakening as a result of the up- or downward motion, the unawakened one- and two-dimensional individual will likely succumb into his preferred state of 'convenient forgetfulness'. This state, in turn, is rooted in man's inherent laziness which, as insufferable as it is, still forms part of the biological nature of the earth-bound man. It subsequently leads the easily distracted and mesmerized individual into successive forms of enslavement, with centers of magnetism or attraction that, in reality, comply to the newly perceived cycle. This 'new' reality in other words, will again consist of egos which are subservient to the Possession, and whose purpose includes the pursuit of forms of identification. For example, we can envision this when a group of people change their alliance to a political party or religious sect. If we were to compare their previous egos to that which is now attached to the newly entity they have joined, we will likely note a change in their individual egos character and perspective. But we may also note that behind the nature of their new ego the same overpowering and mind-possessing entity remains.

That this phenomenon occurs repeatedly follows both logical and evident reason, especially among one- and two-dimensionally oriented people who are unable to envision the parallel or multi-dimensional strategies they are subjected to. This feature of humanity is further substantiated when we observe another phenomenon of Great Nature; that of *Morphic Resonance:*

---

[1] Consider the divisions of the various empires, churches and religions as examples.

Morphic Resonance was first coined by Rupert Sheldrake, an English author and parapsychology researcher[1]. It describes the collective learning that takes place across a species, without the presence of physical contact, and as Sheldrake indicates, that occurs in man and the animal and plant kingdoms as well. Where Morphic Resonance may apply to a civilization's decline is when this phenomenon can be seen working in reverse as well, through the feature of popular un-learning. For example, consider the reduced complexity in the use of language or the feature of declining knowledge, logic or intellect. These are exacerbated when an ignorant public becomes dependent on electronic gadgetry to do their thinking and remembering for them, and in addition begins to justify and even reward poor performance. This is more visible in a socialist populace where we see how the phenomenon of coerced unlearning correlates to a decline in compassion. This loss is especially evident when we consider those that are not related or affiliated with us, and often in numbers that are hard for our logic to envision, such as the death, suffering and displacement of millions.

Because the beginning of a civilization's decline is gradual, it is seldom noticed, largely because a simultaneous 'dumbing-down' of its complacent societies occurs. As the latter accelerates, the former rate of descent will increase exponentially. When it then inevitably and irreversibly spins out of control, a state of Chaos emerges, naturally. After the 'fall' of a civilization, the ability to rebuild itself will depend on the height to which its artificial growth was enabled. For example, the more dependent a complacent citizenry had become on its Possession's entities or organisms, makes their ability to exist as individual minds much more complex. It must also not be forgotten how such states of dependency become the trigger-events for other factors, such as easy food and energy supply, as well as the presence of a decent state to oversee the function of infrastructure and general welfare. But there are even more vital requirements that are not as obvious, such as the feature of a safe haven to which one can turn. Without a so-called 'homebase' where basic physical safety and respect for life resides, the absence of reason, logic and knowledge are unlikely to stimulate the creative spirit that was surrendered and lost.

The circumstances that emerge following the end of a civilization are therefore complex to predict, but what is predictable is that they will be subject to the laws of Duality and Causality. What this means is that, like the succession of seasons, the scale of decline and the degree of chaos, will determine the period that must pass before the soil is sufficiently fertile for a

---

[1] For in-depth understanding, read Rupert Sheldrake's book: *A New Science of Life* (US) or *Morphic Resonance* (UK)

new civilization to put down its roots, and what its shape and character will be.

As a result, one can conclude it likely that a civilization that rises out of entropy or Chaos, will be one that differs substantially from anything that preceded it.

The Consequence of Restraining the Possession

To actively 'fight' the Possession has never done much good, as either the activist is overwhelmed by the persistent and multifaceted influence of its entities, or the activist becomes part of one of them. These and the abovementioned views may therefore appear pessimistic from a selected perspective, but that would only be from the dimensionally limited views of egos that are fixated to a solitary physical realm, absent of a metaphysical causal one. Additionally, such views are likely to be encountered among people who instinctively (automatically) resist any change in the opinions they identify with, which, in many cases, resides within an already chaotic existence of fluctuating beliefs.

However, this does not necessarily affect the lives of individuals who realize that they have a choice. They can either allow themselves to be subjected to the reality of the re-creating 'machine' by serving as a part of it, or they can use their 'new' surroundings to enhance their re-awakening as individuals.

Of course, such individual awakenings are not popular among the Possession's entities because they tend to represent the very nemesis that places checks and limits on its authority. In fact, evidence of the consequence of such can be seen in both corporate environments and geopolitical spheres[1].

Unlike biological life, the Possession can exist in the absence of Light because its existence endures within the psyche of the *un-awakened or un-realized* individual egos of man. Its causal influences are therefore technically not always the fault of the Possession's entities because often, the non-awakening or non-realization of an individual's ego is due to the quality of the choices that were made. But, regardless of the consequence of these choices, or the subsequent state of their civilization, individuals will continue to 'incarnate' in them, perhaps repeatedly, to mature into conscious and realized beings. This may result in vast amounts of still un-awakened beings being stuck in various states of darkness but still, amongst these, the beckoning Lights that also and inevitably will exist among them will shine so much the brighter – like veritable beacons!

---

[1] Consider the historical fate of breakaway republics, or challengers of so-called 'traditional ways of government', or countries that challenged US dominance on the global financial system - like the Petrodollar.

To Conclude:

The process of cycles of the individual man and his civilizations are both inevitable and ever-present, but these ultimately are what enables his realization or awakening. This seemingly automated mechanism of Order out of a perpetual Chaos is therefore not without its Higher Purpose. In it, even the deepest of cogs is exposed from time to time to the Light. As such it can be deduced that:

Once the individual becomes aware of his being aware,
of a higher existence within his surrounds, then he will realize,
that as co-creators, all are at-one with Consciousness.

At that point, for the observer,
what exists and occurs in the three-dimensional world,
is little more than the illusory construct it is.

APPENDIX B

EVADING THE POSSESSION THROUGH GOVERNANCE BY THE PRINCIPLES OF TWELVES

The number twelve is a symbol of natural order. It orders the field of number itself, and past civilizations have made it the basis for ordering time, both greater and lesser cycles, for theology, psychology and political constitutions. The dodecahedron with its twelve pentagonal faces was Plato's symbol for the ideal earth, and it is a model for the tradition of twelve races and psychological types. In classical Greece each nation with its own cult and sanctuary was divided into twelve tribes, three to each of the four quarters, in imitation of the zodiac. This same cosmological pattern has been known at different times throughout the world. Associated with this pattern is the form of religion which recognizes a council of twelve gods, the Olympians, and draws its teachings from science and philosophy rather than beliefs and dogma. *Its worthy followers are initiated in the Mysteries and led towards justice and understanding.*[1]

Purpose

The purpose of this appendix is to suggest a ground-up and integral structure of organization or governance, that aims at enhancing the awareness of all the people it serves, whilst it distributes its authority and accountability to all who consciously choose to participate in them.

It follows the *Principles of Twelves* and structures the division of the collectives of humanity in *Nine Layers of Participation*. It does not seek to undermine sovereignty, ethnicity, or other forms of separatism. Instead, its multidimensional structure has within its design the potential for all forms of collectives to govern their own environment and interact with others only where they need to. Although the structure described herein is applied to the collective humanity, it is made up of smaller components, each of which resembles the whole in appearance and function, such as one experiences in holography[2].

---

[1] John Michell and Christine Rhone: *Twelve-Tribe Nations*
[2] Holography is the method of generating three-dimensional images from a two-dimensional source, which technique has a wide range of uses, including data storage and microscopy. This

As a ground-up, rather than a top-down governed structure, it distributes forms of power along a paradigm that balances authority with accountability. It does this along plains that have height, width, breadth, and depth[1]. As it places potentially chaotic (human) components into states of natural and harmonious order, it can be considered as a blueprint for veritable representative democracy[2]. However, as it is not aimed at centralizing wealth, power, and control, and as it is unlikely to be as profitable as the present systems, it would be naïve to assume that it will be popular amongst profit-motivated entities. But its key ingredient is and will remain the presence of consciousness. However, in its design the collective flow towards such consciousness will be natural (and thus, intuitive).

Introduction

To the contemporary observer, the world of people is seen as divided along lines of relativity. There are those of gender, race, religion and nationality, but also physical things, such as what they have and who they know. This is of course an illusion within an already illusory reality. After all, these divisions only exist by stimulus of the senses, which are imperfect, temporal, and easily influenced.

To explore the division of people we must understand that the Created Cosmos was made manifest from Oneness to one of duality in opposites. In this, for every part and thought, an opposite must exist. It is therefore important and ultimately necessary that every man, woman, and child first defines what is true for him- or herself, and only afterwards look outwards to see what is true for the other. This way, if we first define what is true for ourselves and then discover the views of the other, we can better determine whether that which we considered was true for us at first, is verifiably so.

But, the contemporary[3] person seldom notices when or how their truth was changed and will likely deny that this is even possible. As a result, most will trust their external sources like little children who follow a promissory one-dimensional path to an outcome based two-dimensional goal.

Of those who recognize this trend and know to remain outside of this group of followers, by law of division, half will actively engage the contemporary ones,

---

concept can be expanded on by considering that the three-dimensional idea or form that is holographically generated, produces within its projection, its own two-dimensional images, which can, in turn, be regenerated into three-dimensional copies of the original form.

[1] A term also used in the New Testament, Ephesians 3:18

[2] A policy under the rule of people acting on the behalf of and, to a lesser extent, in the interests of the voting blocs by which they were elected.

[3] The term 'contemporary' in these writings, refers to that part of humanity whose awareness is limited to the first and second dimensions. This 'bulk' follows the Pareto Principle that divides humanity and its effects along a division of around 80 / 20. This group is not defined by social status, intellect, or demographic classification; the contemporary one will be represented by both the followers and their leaders.

be it for fame, profit, or a form of controlling influence. The other half who does not remains passive, and does not care to engage or subject themselves to such influences. Of these, some will become conscious of causality and reality, and the influence of choice that makes them relative.

The conclusion of this is the observation that the division of man is not by birth, belief, or physicality. It is not by intellect, possession, or *what* it is they did or did not do. It is *why* they did or did not, and *how* they made that choice.

Part I
The Principles of a Sustainable Pyramidical System

If we consider that humanity is fundamentally divided by how its people perceive reality[1], we can categorize their perspectives in dimensions, similar to the first four dimensions in geometry. This method of division relates to an individual's awakening to Higher Dimensions, call it Consciousness if you will, and is harmonious with the multi-dimensional, physical and metaphysical design of man[2]. When we subsequently consider this natural division of people, we can understand how only a relatively small portion of people ever realize how integrated we are with an Indivisible and Timeless Consciousness[3].

The majority of people do not attain a higher and multi-dimensional level of awareness, even though many believe they do. As a result, those who don't know but believe they know are unable to realize the limitation their various forms of belief represent to their world, and the one that surrounds them. Most value the purpose of life on the quantification of qualifications, most of which have important sounding names, titles, decorations, and things that money can purchase. This low-dimensional fixation is made worse when they expansively teach others their perspective on three-dimensional logic; being one that exists of illusory one- and two-dimensional constructs, but that cannot see the holistic or multidimensional whole. As a result, their perceived reality will not acknowledge the influence of Higher Dimensions – except perhaps in mathematical theory. This is a considerable limitation as, by itself and without an external influence, their thoughts are unable to create anything original. We can see this when they repeatedly try to solve their problems by using the same kind of thinking that created them[4]. Their one and two-dimensional perspective on creativity is therefore limited to results that their

---

[1] See *The Inner Evolution of Man*, Chapter 1: *The Transcending and Descending Dimensions of Man*
[2] In these writings, the masculine referral such as man, him or his throughout these writings, unless otherwise described, does not refer to gender but humankind or humanity.
[3] Timeless Consciousness or consciousness by itself are capitalized to indicate the Divine.
[4] "We cannot solve our problems with the same thinking we used when we created them": A. Einstein

minds obtain from an odds ratio[1], being a combination of things that were already known. Therefore, within their three-dimensional world all occurs as it has before, following mechanical and mathematically predictable laws.

We can see how this is very evident in the governance of people by selected groups of individuals, especially when no consideration is given to authentic spirituality[2]. This has historically led to repeated periods of fear-based misery that were followed by processes of self-destruction, and not just of the subjected contemporary masses, but also inevitably, of their equally contemporary rulers.

> *If, therefore, humankind as a civilization, opted to avoid these destructive cycles and enter an age of harmony, it would have to change its established structures of governance, in a way that is opposite to what it is at present.*

To better understand the inevitability of these *destructive cycles*, we must consider the 'Law of Octaves' that exists and applies to everything that is subject to Time-related change in the known Cosmos[3]. This includes the patterns-of-repetition that an unaware, reactive and suggestible individual experiences throughout his life. For example, we can observe this law at work in the actions of individuals when they set off with the best of intentions, but then gradually change their views and principles on even their most devout beliefs, from one opposing pole to another, and often without noticing that they have done so.

> *Hence, even the most sincere and correct individual who is unaware of this phenomenon, and who does not contemplate on how or why he does things, cannot ever be trusted to govern effectively – naturally.*

This cyclic rhythm or pattern is also present in the concepts and evolutions of the collectives of man, and why history is largely made up of representations of this.[4] But it even extends into the fabric of Creation itself.[5]

---

[1] An odds ratio is a statistic that quantifies the strength of the association between two events, A and B. The odds ratio is defined as the ratio of the odds of A in the presence of B and the odds of A in the absence of B, or equivalently, the ratio of the odds of B in the presence of A and the odds of B in the absence of A. (Wikipedia)

[2] Authentic spirituality is in opposition to its inauthentic version, which uses dogma, fear, institutional objectives, and a hierarchy of leaders.

[3] The Law of Seven also Law of Octaves, as described by GI Gurdjieff, relates to the vibratory nature of all things that increases or decreases at certain intervals by a particular frequency. This law indicates how there are specific breaks where this particular frequency change differs, which causes the increase or decrease to not follow a straight line but a curved one. This curve causes the general direction of increase or decrease, if continued without other interference, to eventually find itself going in an opposite direction.

[4] As an example, one sees how Christ's teachings on compassion and forgiveness evolved into crusades, inquisitions, and acts of barbarism, or where the Prophet Muhammad's work to unify the Arabs under Islam led to their sectarian division, or where a liberating force becomes a dictating one.

[5] The Law of Octaves is seen throughout Great Nature and the Cosmos, including, for example, the Periodic Table, where the increase of atomic weight of elements, in every eighth element

Hence, *among the contemporary collectives of man*, the idea of 'free will' is entirely imaginary. We can see how this extends into the belief in man's ability to govern outside of these cyclic mechanisms, when all he does is pursue a quantitative increase of power. The effects of such ultimate power upon those elected to govern will, without exception, eventually and inevitably, corrupt them. One of the first signs that this occurs is when rulers become protective of their power and deceptive in their nature, such as when they begin to seek ways in which they can continue to govern. In time, the longer their exposure to such power, the stronger their addiction to the darkness that grants it, and the more desperate and brutal their actions become.

Therefore, regardless of the circumstances[1], for an individual or collection of individuals to govern fairly and effectively, the residual effects of such power upon them must always be accounted for. For this to be possible, the design or structure of every component of governance must be verifiably transparent, and include a system of accountability to every part of the authority it governs. This accountability must then be proportionately placed on those who accepted such authority.

Part II
Defining a Harmonious System of Governance

For an organization of governance to function in a harmonious and sustainable system, free from the cycles of growth and decay, it must be:

1. *In harmony with the Essence of Man.*
2. *In harmony with the Cosmos, Earth and Great Nature.*
3. *Internally sustainable, by its component or affiliated parts.*

1. In Harmony with the Essence of Man

The Essence[2] of man is attained when individual people discover the effects of their physical, emotional, and psychological or psychic influences on themselves, others, and the very fabric of their perceived reality. For this attainment to be possible in a society or an organization of people, everyone who is subject to, or affiliated with it, must be integrated through degrees of individual authority, which degree is balanced against an equal accountability.

(representing the 'Do'), has similar properties as the first one.

[1] Consider how martial law is connected to an incident caused by the same forces that implement it, to maintain authoritarian control by overriding democratic or constitutional processes.

[2] 'Essence' referred to herein, is that state of being within which the individual attains his or her highest state of being, beyond the physical, emotional and psychological or mental realms. It is considered as the state within which man functions intuitively and flawlessly as either a human being on its own, or as part of a small or large collective of people.

For example, let's say we wish to express an opinion within an organization, but our social status is at the base level of a pyramidical structure. In this situation we will see no effect on the audience we address. Without such an effect we will soon give up or seek an alternate means of persuasion which, of course, could lead to unintended consequences. If we were to compare this to a view expressed by a celebrity of sort, or one of a higher social ranking, then this would automatically overrule any 'lesser' one's ability to be heard. There is perhaps a sense of logic to such an order, but often these more popular individuals are actors and unable to do much else. The consequence of this is the misuse of misplaced authority combined with the absence of accountability on one end, and the degrees of obliviousness and docility on the other.

To prevent this and enhance the individual participant or stakeholder's awareness, the authority over a collective or organization of people must, from it's very inception, be accompanied by accountability; no matter how small or large. For this to be possible and irrefutable, governance at every level of an organization's structure must be by individuals who are personally known by those upon whom they see the effect of their voice, action, or other influence.

As it is not realistically possible for the average person to have more than a dozen non-familial individuals whom he or she personally knows well, including their personalities and affiliations, and by whom he or she is equally well known, this number is both limited and special. Besides the number twelve and its multiples surrounding it being relative to many elements in man's general organization, and being more divisible than the number ten, it also corresponds with macrocosmic features such as the Zodiac, the Earth's axial precession[1], and its movement around the Sun. Even traditionally, in myth, legend, and scripture, governance of societies was often arranged in groups of twelve[2]. Hence, to stimulate the essence in the individual man and woman in a collective or an organization of sorts, a feeling of individual worth must be induced. This must simultaneously be brought into synchronicity with a harmoniously balanced collective, which will – in turn – stimulate and enhance a feeling of individual worth. For this process of mutually beneficial support to be feasible, the collective's organization must maintain an order by twelves, such as presented in Part III below.

---

[1] Earth's axial precession is the change in the orientation of its rotational axis. Being a cycle of approximately 25,920 years, it correlates to 12 Platonic years, which number forms part of the canonical numbers that interlink the microcosm with the macrocosm, which governs Nature in the Cosmos.

[2] Christ's Apostles, the Greek Titans, the tribes of Israel, the Twelvers in Shi'ism, the knights around King Arthur's Round Table, etc, and even the assembly of most military units are multiplications of 12.

2. In Harmony with the Cosmos, Earth, and Great Nature

Harmony is attained by working within, and in concert with, criteria that precede the dawn of man, and which occur *naturally*. It is therefore necessary to observe both the natural order of things as well as the elemental and repeating ratios, shapes, and the numerical orders observed in all forms of creativity and interference. This includes the making of artificial physical or social-metaphysical structures similar to those which occur naturally in the Cosmos and Great Nature, because such designs are in sync with the creative energies of the Cosmos itself. As examples of this, we need but observe the magnificence of structures like pyramids, temples, and cathedrals[1], as well as special buildings where important decisions are made[2]. One need but enter such spaces to sense the entwined energies of the Cosmos and Great Nature, with the loving and devoted psyche of untold generations that built and frequented them.

The immensely complex, and highly accurate use of very specific ratios, angles, alignments, and numbers is often lost to the contemporary observer, as is how their critical ingredients were often incorporated with extraordinary effort and at great cost.

To some such efforts may seem excessive, and the result of enlarged egos, but the fact is that serious and conscious observation was incorporated into every component. This included its social, physical, metaphysical and spiritual elements. The importance of the resultant psychic energy will, when applied lovingly and harmoniously, add synergy to every individual effort and collective effect it serves

3. The Internal Sustainability, by its Component or Affiliated Parts

The sustainability of any organization is only assured when it is entirely and independently supported by its internal components or affiliated parts. This means that its structure must have incorporated elements that encapsulate its operational liabilities, without these needing to take or use more than what their presence and influence contribute. It could be stated that it must aim and persevere to leave the organization's 'holistic whole' more enriched and enhanced than its sum-total, being that which it was without its organizational structure. Besides the physical ability to support such general sustainability, this condition also relates to the subject of responsibility; where *all forms of authority must be with accountability*.

---

[1] i.e. The Giza Plateau in Egypt, the Pantheon in Rome, and numerous Gothic Cathedrals.
[2] Consider the masonic designs incorporated in the governing structures of dominant cities like London, Paris, Washington DC, New York, San Francisco, etc.

DIAGRAM 3

The Nine Layers of Participation for Governance of Public Affairs

The Household Circle
= 4 - 12 Adults

The Street Circle
= 12 Households = Up to 144 Adults

The Block Circle
= 12 Streets = 144 Households = Up to 1 728 Adults

The District Circle
= 12 Blocks = 144 Streets = 1 728 Households = Up to 20 736 Adults

The Town Circle
= 12 Districts = 144 Blocks = 1 728 Streets = 20 736 Households
= Up to 248 832 Adults

The State Circle
= 12 Towns = 144 Districts = 1 728 Blocks = 20 736 Streets
= 248 832 Households = Up to 2 985 984 Adults

The Country Circle
= 12 States = 144 Towns = 1 728 Districts = 20 736 Blocks
= 248 832 Streets = 2 985 984 Households = Up to 35 831 808 Adults

The Federation Circle
= 12 Countries = 144 States = 1 728 Towns = 20 736 Districts
= 248 831 Blocks = 2 985 984 Streets = 35 831 808 Households
= Up to 429 981 696 Adults

The Civilization Circle
= 12 Federations = 144 Countries = 1 728 States = 20 736 Towns
= 248 831 Districts = 2 985 984 Blocks = 35 831 808 Streets
= 429 981 696 Households = Up to 5 159 780 352 Adults*

* This number happens to correspond with the approximate 'Adult' Population at present, but differences would be absorbed at 'Household' Level.

Part III
The Principles of Governance by Twelves

Traditionally, a leader's plan of succession was deemed as most important, especially if he was loved and respected as a strong but fair and correct leader. This was because, without a unifying plan or purpose to subject him to, his subjects would inevitably succumb to their contemporary nature, and divide. Still, after two or three successive generations, neither the subjects nor their leaders will understand or remember the origin of their strength, wisdom, and guidance, out of which they rose. Subsequently, their land or structure will become corrupt and fall, regardless of its wealth and power.

As an alternative, man invented many isms[1], but without a correct and unifying purpose, their rule is driven by greed and ambition, and is not long-lived. This is why the existence of an organization's structure, can only survive if it follows the laws of nature, and is sourced and resourced from the ground up.

The Structure

The following organizational structure is described in one and two dimensional concepts, but its functionality will be seen to be multidimensional and complex in nature. It outlines a hierarchical division of layers comprising interconnected 'circles', with each circle being attended to by twelve members. Each of these members is the representative of a circle of twelve members positioned in circles at the preceding or lower level. Thus, as per the diagram below, with exception to the "Household" circle, any one circle of twelve will represent one-hundred and forty-four members of the twelve preceding or lower circles. In other words; each circle either represents or is represented, by a circle of twelves. The purpose of this structure, as is elucidated further down, is to create an order of accountable authority, that is both practical and sustainable in its functionality, as well as the organizational purpose as a whole.

As the primary purpose of this structure is to sustain the organizational whole, the rules at its core are described in the 'Constitutional Principles' below. These aim at:

- sustaining the structure's overall hierarchy, and
- ensuring that, regardless of what occurs within any one circle, such as in the event of its internal senility and subsequent demise, the structure can internally re-establish itself without affecting the holistic 'whole'.

---

[1] 'isms' refers to political ideologies or doctrines for a form of governance that contemporary people identify themselves as subject to, such as Capitalism, Communism, Socialism, Meritocratism, Technocracism, Gerontocracism, etc.

The Constitutional Principles in Circles of Twelve:

1. Any circle of governance comprises a maximum of twelve members.
2. One cannot be a member in more than one circle of a particular Layer.
3. One's Household circle can quit its Street circle, and become a member of another 'Street', provided the members of that Street circle are less than twelve and can accommodate it, and that they approve of this Household joining their Street by majority vote. One cannot change ones place in a successive or 'higher' circle without also changing all the way down to Street circle.
4. The twelve members of a circle must select their representing 'head' by majority vote. The eleven members that are governed by their selected head, shall be able to supplant him or her by a majority vote among all eleven members).
5. If, during a meeting of all twelve members, a number of members choose to abstain from decision making, which then results in an even division between opposing sides, then from those who voted and did not abstain:
   - Either the vote of the most recently joined member in the circle is to be withdrawn, or,
   - the youngest member (by age) must abstain.
6. Upon a member's departure from a circle – be it for whatever reason – then his or her replacement is selected and brought into the circle, under the following conditions;
   - He or she must be from the same circle as the departing member, but,
   - He or she does not have to be the head of that preceding circle.
   - The placement must be with the free will of this new member,
   - The new member must be approved by a majority vote of the remaining eleven members and,
   - The departing member is not eligible to vote.
7. Each circle will select from their twelve members, one member to serve the next successive level's *Circle of Governance*. In this:
   - The selected member must be willing and able to do so.
   - The selected member does not have to be the head of the preceding circle.
   - The selected member does not have to be charged with the duties of governance of the hierarchically preceding *circle* or *circles*.
   - The age of the selected member in circles at Household to District level, must be an adult of at least 18 years of age[1].

---

[1] An adult is considered one who is at least 18 years old. This minimum is based on the age at which a person reaches full growth and is regarded as being self-sufficient and responsible. This

- The age of the selected member must, in circles from Town level and up, must be at least 56 years old[1].
8. In the organization that is governed by the Principles of Twelves, *the same principles of governance must be applied in its subordinate forms, divisions, or departments*, which will include its associated and affiliated collectives, entities, or organisms, on any scale.
9. To avoid the possibility of forms of corruption or favouritism, by or among the members of the successive senior and more influential circles, being circles *from Town-level and up*:
    - Its members are to be remunerated sufficiently to be able to adequately commit themselves (if need be) on a full-time basis, to the execution of their circle's tasks. This remuneration is determined within their respective circle which, in turn and by proxy, will be subject to consent by the twelve circles it represents.
    - The members of these senior circles who are remunerated can continue to own or control property or business outside their functions in their circle if they wish, but to avoid any sense of hypocrisy, these properties and businesses must now also be managed by the Principles of Twelves.
    - The same principles of governance or management by Twelves will be required from entities, organizations, and persons, who are employed or affiliated with the execution of the circle's functions. However, this does not have to apply to its third parties such as suppliers and contractors. When, for example, anyone or anything related to circles of Town-level and up owns or controls[2] an entity that involves a collective of people, and that entity has more than twelve persons in it, then the validation of such a collective entity, in its operational self, requires it to be organized and managed along the Principles of Governance by Twelves.
    - In all cases, if a remunerated member of a circle from Town-level and up does not wish to restructure their property or business, the remaining members of their circle can, by majority vote, choose to overrule this condition. In the same vein, they can also vote to have such a non-compliant member replaced.
    - Accountability at all levels is the glue that will keep the organizational structure sustainable throughout. This accountability will, due to the

---

may differ regionally and can be increased as determined within each respective circle, but not decreased.
[1] The definition of a person who is considered emotionally and intellectually fully matured, and sufficiently so to commence intelligent and intuitive functioning.
[2] be it owned as an individual, an association, an organization, a corporation, or government,

system of twelves, be almost automatic. However, actions and transactions must remain transparent enough for the affected adjacent, successive and preceding circles to understand. This kind of transparency must be present throughout, including its associates and all who participate in the execution of its respective functions and overall purpose. Caution must be observed to prevent excessive administrative bureaucracy processes throughout.
- Accountability must be observably relative. When a member is deemed responsible for whatever went wrong, then such accountability must be fair and relative, and not punitive or retaliatory.

Part IV
The Philosophy behind the System of Twelve's Multidimensional and Natural Structure

To understand the philosophy behind the design of this system of Twelves, we must first understand the contemporary man's patterns of reactive thought. Most Freudians believe that sensuality is what drives the greed and fear which fuel man's system, but these claims are only partially true. Whereas these are veritable tools that direct and manipulate the contemporary man's patterns of behaviour, what ultimately fuels them, is his existential desire for control, offset by his inherent laziness. These weaknesses are commonly suppressed through rules and forms of conditioning, but which are then, by the same means, easily circumvented.

If one structures and governs an organization or a society of collectives along the principles of Twelves, it establishes a veritable ground-up order, within which its respective collectives cannot but accept or waive accountability of their function in it. As such there would be no separate set of rules about right or wrong in what one chooses, as long as it complies to that which one agreed to within one's circles of Twelves, which circle was appointed and enabled to fulfil that role.

From here, the consequent results will thereby be transparent to all those in the selected, affected, and responsible circles. This means that in this arrangement one may opt to defer one's responsibility as a member of one's organization or society, but then as a participant or stakeholder one's circle, one will remain accountable to its effects.

Comparing a Top-down with Bottom-up Governance

For any public participation to be effective, especially in the governing of a collective of free people, the *division of representation*[1] must be all-inclusive and transparent. This is generally speaking the official agenda of most democracies, but as these are structured to *independently* govern from the top of the pyramid, the definitions of Truth and Reality become distorted as they traverse down the layers of distributed or diluted authority, and deferred accountability.

When we observe the layered and opposing forms of awareness, such as displayed in the Pyramids of Opposite Reality[2], we can see how Truth is increasingly diluted with fiction, as one goes down the inverted pyramid. This dilution increases to the extent that reality or fact becomes opposite to what it was at the apex. This confusing distortion is often intentional, as it enables those in charge of the upside-down pyramid, to alter reality, behind which they can act without accountability. The consequence of this will be left to those who inhabit their worker- and middle-class levels, and who are unaware. These lesser aware levels are generally brainwashed[3] from birth to believe it is 'their duty' to carry their masters' burden, pay their taxes, fight their wars, and afterward, rebuild their cities.

A realistic perspective on the behaviour of societies will show how this is and has historically always been present – especially once their controlling elements attain a certain level of authority. It becomes especially evident when societies experience a poor outcome in their economics or foreign relations. In these, the democratically elected who were directly responsible, are seldom held proportionally accountable.

It is unfortunate that the rise in Information Technology, that created such unprecedented access to a wealth of information and ability, simultaneously does as much harm as good. For example, consider how almost every system of government uses this technology to maintain certain predetermined, usually fear-oriented narratives. To reverse this is no longer possible, but what can be done is to establish a parallel approach that is opposite in its structure. Instead of the enhancement of greed for profit and power, it must incorporate the elements of truth, compassion, and realization, with an ever-present freedom of choice to engage or not, for everyone.

To implement such a system that is opposite in its societal structure, the principles of how it is organized and governed must be different in almost every conceivable way. However, this does not refer to ownership, as the capitalist component angle remains an integral part as well. Consider how the

---

[1] Representation in government, is the method or process of enabling the citizenry, *or some of them*, to participate in the shaping of legislation and governmental policy through deputies chosen by them.
[2] See Diagram 1: The Pyramids of Opposite Realities
[3] Brainwashing, also known as mind control, menticide, coercive persuasion, thought control, thought reform, and forced re-education, is the altering of the human mind, against a person's will by manipulative information manipulation and psychological techniques

systems at present aim at controlling the minds, bodies, and resources, but whose resultant product is prioritized to empower and grow the authoritarian entities, be it a government, a corporation or any organized group of people. Instead, an organization that is governed by the Principles of Twelves applies its focus on competent authority, that resides abreast with accountability.

The Momentary Problem of Productivity

Of course, the factor of unpredictable changes in leadership and subsequent accountability will cause considerable hindrance in progress and productivity. This will especially be visible in idealistic and long-term projects, but besides this being natural, it can even be considered necessary. This is because, in the case of such changes in leadership, the consequential burdens would be carried by the circle that made the change. This burden would further be noted by the twelve circles which that implementing circle's members represent, as each of them represents a circle of twelve members (including themselves), to whom they must answer. Thus the effects of such changes would be like growing pains, as within this order Cause and Effect becomes a considered element, and the unintended consequences would thereafter be detected and corrected faster.

Most political and other forms of government, including those of capitalist, communist, and socialist orientation, function along one-dimensional conditions with two-dimensional outcomes. This is why, in this illusory and conceptual world, we see leaders displayed like celebrities, elevated on illuminated pedestals and thrones, the height of which being relative to their incompetence. What makes matters worse is when we see how these leaders and their selected 'nobles' are little but façades, controlled by clever, cunning and equally unstable and unsustainable entities.

Contrary to these democratic and socialist systems of central control, an organization that is governed by Principles of Twelves will, in time and by its very natural design, draw only those who are *creditable, virtuous, and scrupulous* into its folds. These are not qualities that are easily faked or schooled and will only be found among ones who are sincere. In addition, because every member of a circle is known to the other eleven, as well as the group of circles that appointed him or her to represent them, one who acts against the will of their circle, or any of their preceding ones, will rapidly find him or herself supplanted by a majority vote in any one of these.

Consequently, instead of having one corrupted leader replaced by another through one-dimensional elections, where both sides are orchestrated by the same entity, a candidate's sincerity in his or her circle of twelve will always be subject to its members' appeal.

The Automated Effects of the System's Natural Structure

An insincere person can only remain so in seclusion. Members who serve in a ground-up structured organization will always be accountable for that for which they accept responsibility. As each of the members of an applicable circle are similarly accountable to those who placed them there, it is only logical and natural that they will contemplatively observe the decisions and actions of all, including their own.

Hence, contrary to a person being elected by a large volume of voters whom he or she does not know, and who do not know him or her, the Circle of Twelves does know and will observe those who it appointed.

This order will naturally also illuminate and dissolve the psyche possessing traditions of secretive 'old guards', who selectively maintain their inner circles of power. In addition, no collective of people, as a whole, can ever be forced involuntarily into a conflict. For example, any approval for an action of enforcement of a militant nature, or of taxation, would need to have a definite (and not perceived) majority across the system. Any implementation, such as an increased tax for a particular purpose, would also not be able to be continued indefinitely, once its purpose has been served.

Part V
The Formation and Functional Structure of Circles

1. The Household Circle

Although its name infers a household, which suggests a related family, it can also be a selection of adult[1] individuals that wish to form a circle, separate from their relatives.

a. The Household Circle consists of a minimum of four and a maximum of twelve adult individuals.
b. For a selection of Household Circles to make up the twelve that can form its successive Street Circle, some of the applicable Household Circles can merge with other Household circles or divide into two or three smaller Household circles. When necessary this can happen provided the minimum of four and a maximum of twelve adult individuals is maintained.
c. Any individual can only serve in one Circle at Household-level. He or she is free to leave his or her Circle should they choose to do so, but if they thereafter wish to return, then this would only be with the consent by the majority vote of the members of their former circle.
d. If a member wishes to join another circle, then this too must be with the

---

[1] The definition of an adult person herein, is considered one who is at least 18 years old.

consent (by majority vote), of such a preferred circle.
e. If a member wishes to appeal his or her Household Circle's decision surrounding his or her membership position, then he or she can appeal to the Street Circle that resides atop for counsel. Such an appeal would be limited to obtaining counsel as the successive Circle cannot overrule the preceding Circle's decision to do with its internal management.
f. The overall role of each Household Circle is to:
  - Select a representative to join and monitor the successive Street Circle.
  - To make arrangements and take decisions that only affect the represented households.
g. In each Household Circle a representative is selected, by majority vote, to represent it as one of twelve members of the successive Street Circle.

2. The Street Circle

The Street circle is formed by selected members of twelve Household Circles, that are within same geographical area. It is naturally possible that, due to the geographic situation or its subsequent population distribution, an area does not enable the formation of another Street Circle, or has insufficient Household Circles to complete a Street Circle. In such cases, to ensure that it complies with the Principles specified below, the formation of a Street Circle in the 'same geographical area' must be relative.

a. The Street Circle fulfils its primary purpose, within the organization of Twelves, by selecting one member to represent the circle on the succeeding Block Circle.
b. To do this, the Street Circle must contain twelve Household Circle representatives. If there are insufficient Household circles, and its existing Households are not able to divide as described (in 1. b) above, in that case, it must consider merging with another Street circle, even if this is temporary and not favorable.
c. If it cannot divide its Household Circles to make up for the required twelve representatives, and there is no other Street Circle to merge with that is equally incomplete, then one of the adjacent Street Circles that is complete, must consider dividing some of its Household Circles, and transfer these to complete the said Street Circle. This would be purely an administrative transfer, and not require any of its members to physically relocate.
d. If no adjacent Street Circles will or can be accessed to accommodate this particular Street Circle, then its Household Circle representatives will have no choice but to temporarily or permanently dissolve it. This is because, without its ability to function within the organization's structure,

including its representation in a successive Block Circle, will have no other purpose.
e. These guidelines are very important, as the formation of a fully represented Street Circle from preceding Household Circles forms the heart of the system of Twelves' pyramidical structure. The abovementioned guidelines also serve to coerce and motivate the applicable representatives to merge or transfer to form the required Household and Street Circles.
f. From the resultantly completed Street Circle, one representative is selected by a majority vote, to represent it as one of twelve members of the successive Block Circle.

3. The Block Circle

A Block Circle is formed by selected members of twelve Street Circles, that are within the relatively same geographical area. The formation of a Block Circle follows a similar arrangement as the preceding level of circles, and thus represents:

a. 12 Street circles or 144 Household circles, and
b. manages the structure that governs between 576 and 1,728 adults.

4. The District Circle

The formation and purpose of a District Circle follows a similar arrangement as the preceding level of circles, and thus represents:

a. 12 Block Circles, 144 Street Circles, or 1,728 Household Circles,
b. and manages the structure that governs between 6,912 and 20,736 adults.

5. The Town Circle

The formation and purpose of a Town Circle follows a similar arrangement as the preceding level of circles, and as a Town Circle it represents:

a. 12 District Circles, 144 Block Circles, 1,728 Street Circles, or 20,736 Household Circles,
b. and manages the structure that governs the activities of between 82,944 and 248,832 adults.

6. The State Circle

The formation and purpose of a State Circle follows a similar arrangement as the preceding level of circles, and represents:

a. 12 Town Circles, 144 District Circles, 1,728 Block Circles, 20,736 Street Circles, or 248,832 Household Circles,
b. and manages the structure that governs the activities of between 995,328 and 2,985,984 adults.

7. The Country Circle

The formation and purpose of a Country Circle follows a similar arrangement as the preceding level of circles, and represents:

a. 12 State Circles, 144 Town Circles, 1,728 District Circles, 20,736 Block Circles, 248,832 Street Circles, or 2,985,984 Household Circles,
b. and manages the structure that governs the activities of between 11,943,936 and 35,831,808 adults.

8. The Federation Circle

The formation and purpose of a Federation Circle follows a similar arrangement as the preceding level of circles, and represents:

a. 12 Country Circles, 144 State Circles, 1,728 Town Circles, 20,736 District Circles, 248,832 Block Circles, 2,985,984 Street Circles, or 35,831,808 Household Circles,
b. and manages the structure that governs the activities of between 143,327,232 and 429,981,696 adults.

9. The Civilization Circle

The apex circle aptly named the Civilization Circle has a formation and purpose that follows that of the preceding level of circles. As a 'Civilization' it represents:

a. 12 Federations, 144 Countries, 1,728 States, 20,736 Towns, 248,832 Districts, 2,985,984 Blocks, 35,831,808 Streets, or 429,981,696 Households,
b. and manages the structure that governs the activities of between 1,719,926,784 and 5,159,780,352 adults.

Part VI
The Nature of an Inherent Limitation on Power

The Civilization Circle outlined above comprises twelve Federation Circles, each of which comprises 12 Country Circles, of which each again reports to the next circle down the scale, in this case being 12 State Circles, and so forth. Although it represents, across the nine levels, millions of circles, one may envision how, within this system, each representative member in every circle maintains a line of direct and indirect responsibility and accountability. We can even observe that the person who heads the ninth level or Civilization Circle, can actively be removed on any of the preceding levels, all the way down to his or her Household Circle. The selected head of the world's civilization could, in other words, be deposed by the majority vote in a Block, Street, or Household Circle, he or she was appointed from.

This scenario would be unthinkable in the present world, as it would pose a veritable and ongoing political, geopolitical, and geostrategic threat to the continuation of its rule-based system of governance. However, when we study the cycles of past civilizations, empires, nations, dynasties, and tribes over the recorded millennia, we will find that there has been little that was ever stable, fair, and uncorrupted for very long. Even empires that ruled for centuries did so by means of force and perpetual conflict (or money backed by military power). It is the same within most of the world's democracies, whose elected governments continue to fall subject to the same dark powers of their deep states and affiliated entities. Their relentless and often ferocious drive to protect and maintain their power over all forms of exchange, including finance, information, military, and resources, is usually justified in the name of 'progress'.

However, the definition of progress can be considered from a quantitative point of view, and a qualitative one. Subsequently, progress is relative, and its methods and morals cannot be considered as having experienced such, if it was at the cost of Truth, or a ruling representative's *meritorious, creditable, virtuous, and scrupulous* state of being.

In an organization that is governed by the Principles of Twelves, any quantitative progress would automatically fall subject to the qualitative one, but within a truthful, effective, and trusted system of management and leadership, the quantitative progress would soon be on par. Furthermore, any progress made would be more sustainable within a qualitative system, where its management or leadership is relative to the accountability of the ones tasked with such, and who are observed to be physically, emotionally, and mentally able to do so.

The Effects of the Principles of Twelves in the Environs of Geo-politics

In the geo-political world, this bottom-up governed by Twelves structure would naturally pose veritable administrative challenges. They would lead to disruptions and potential for conflict between States, Countries, and Federations, were it not that each of these States, Countries, and Federations would be aware of the conduct of the other's representatives. The *consequential accountability of bad governance,* therefore, by a person or group of persons in a circle, would *be limited to that particular circle and the circles that selected it*. Where, for example, a State Circle causes a certain crisis, then its effects would remain within that State and the representatives of the twelve Town Circles that it represents. As these would all be directly and indirectly accountable for approving the responsible scheme or selecting person that led to that scheme, these would internally and automatically, commence towards correcting it. The other States on that level, for example, would only be affected if:

- Their respective twelve Town Circles chose to get involved.
- Their successive Country Circle suggested it.

The Effects of the Principles of Twelves in the Environs of Politics

In the political world, the constant and unpredictable replacement of senior representatives would pose equally great complexities. This would primarily be due to the lack and loss of knowledge and experience of relations between statesmen and bureaucracy. However, this phenomenal effect would be the same in such cases on all levels and circles. If representatives of such circles are ignorant of proper conduct or protocol, they would be ineffective and rapidly replaced with a more capable one by their fellow and supporting representatives. In fact, in the system of Twelves, the replacement of representatives with more able and effective ones would be more favourable than in a democratic system that is tied to terms, rather than performance. Furthermore, in the systems of Twelves, peers who knew but did nothing, would be equally accountable for their colleague's deterioration of things.

The Effects of the Principles of Twelves in the Environs of Finance

In the worlds of finance, as with those of technocracy, the appointment of unskilled and without-ability representatives will lead to a lack of qualitative and quantitative progress. Besides the direct damage that incompetent individuals cause, the indirect effects, such as the lack of suitable funding caused by insufficient profits or taxes, would exacerbate this. This would obstruct supposed societal 'improvements', but then, artificially stimulated or accelerated advances in this area are seldom without side-effects. Consider, for example, how the creation of FIAT money and its creation out of nothing through systems of credit, leads to the inevitable deterioration of economic stability that only affects its middle and worker class people, including their future generations.

If we now consider that the applicable decision-making representatives of the successive circles in these *'Nine Layers of Participation'* are directly accountable, and under the structured review by those they represent, their peers, and their successive circle. The natural internal organization of a society that governs by the Principles of Twelves is such, that subversive trends would be identified long before they attained a possessing life of their own. Corrective action would therefore, almost automatically, be taken that would revert a society to common sense and the consideration of all factors and persons affected. This would include the implementation of systems of finance and technology that benefit society as a whole, and not just a selected handful.

On Taxation and Contribution

Most of the world's democracies and other authoritarian states govern from behind charades of bias, being either political or ideologic in their design. They create the appearance of being considerate to public best interest and free will, but in reality are steered by their puppeteers; the old-boy networks known as the deep state.[1] It must be recognized that the deep-state's perspective on what is best suits little but their own purposes, which includes the survival and expansion of their authority. This they do by manipulating the public's will through control over information content and distribution, and by maintaining absolute control over powerful armed forces.

To maintain control over these entities and forces naturally requires vast funding. As mentioned in the earlier example of finance, this funding is enabled through systems of credit, but these systems in turn, base their power on the ability to raise and levy taxes, combined with having exorbitant privilege.[2] Either way, the scope of this tax collection system directly relates to the amount of power the state can gather and wield. Subsequently, the taxes it applies to its citizens often have very little to do with reality. Seldom is any conscientious consideration given to what is truly in the citizens interest, or how harmful excessive taxation is, and that taxes are seldom, if ever, decreased or eradicated.

If we then consider the part on how these taxes are spent. The politically appointed are very good at appearances and making speeches, but as limited in intelligence as their accountability. Thus, when it comes to the task of governance by those without ability, they simply defer the complex matters of finance and expenditure to their puppeteers; the bankers and selected corporations who, in turn, fund their political campaigns.

In an organization that is subject to the Principles of Governance by Twelves, the system of decision-making across the *Nine Layers of Participation* will not experience such weaknesses or benefit. This is, of course, unless those they represent, their peers, and their successive circle accept it. If such campaigns or active measures were accepted and implemented, then the consequential accountability would not just reside with the circle in authority, but also those circles that supported and are supported by that particular circle.

The Inevitable Cycles of Order and Chaos

An organization that is subject to the Principles of Governance by Twelves, as an entity of which its psychic components are controlled by the continuous

---

[1] An exclusive informal network linking members of a social class or profession or organization in order to provide connections and information and favours (especially in business or politics).

[2] Exorbitant Privilege refers to the benefits that the US Federal Reserve Bank has due to its own currency being the international reserve currency. For example, it cannot ever face a balance of payments crisis because their imports are purchased in currency they can create in any amount.

presence of independent individual and collective consciousnesses, can and will manifest a harmonious and even utopian coexistence. It would not be affected by differences of class, race, ethnicity, ideology and dimensions of awareness, and may likely have a very long life expectancy. However, although the above-described Principles with its *Nine Layers of Participation* offer a universal blueprint for a popular and sustainable state, and perhaps, a true example of representative democracy[1], it would be naïve to assume that this utopian state could remain as such forever. This is because parallel to any societal pyramid, including one that is internally sustained, there is the ever-present reality of the dark side of the human mind; its ego of varying identifications. As is evident and easily visible everywhere, the ego establishes realities that have a life of their own, and that shape their primary purpose and function around the continuation of its own illusory one and two-dimensional existence. It does this by increasing the complexity of things it knows in lieu of exploring an unknown, which it fears may end it.

These trends are particularly powerful when an ego or entity believes it can improve its environment's existing systems[2] without having to undergo a form of change. Within such a pursuit, the ego-entity will persevere to find ways to make things more efficient, cheaper, faster, or more popular, but, due to the innate nature of its desire, will remain blind to the inevitable law of unintended consequences.

In an organization that is subject to the Principles of Governance by Twelves, the inevitable and costly disruption of projects and programs caused by the unscheduled replacement of senior circle representatives will occur. This in turn will, in time, give rise to more permanent and independent shadow entities that are programmed to circumvent or even avoid this. Following their nature, these shadow entities will reactively work towards the establishment of more permanent structures to stabilize succession. As such, they will reform the Deep State[3]. Even if such structures were to then act transparently and overtly, in time they would rally to compete with the succeeding circle representatives and, in one form or another, replace their authority.

This view may appear pessimistic but, *in the absence of Consciousness among the majority of people*, the described cause-and-effect is simply the observation of a foregone conclusion. In the absence of a creative and

---

[1] A political system in which citizens vote for representatives to handle legislation and otherwise rule that entity on their behalf. The elected representatives are in turn accountable to the electorate for their actions.
[2] Consider, as examples, a system such as the very outdated SWIFT payment system that is still in use for making international payments; or the use of internal combustion engines and hydrocarbons (fossil fuels) as a source of energy; the ever-expanding system of laws and rules in civilized societies, including our systems of compulsory education.
[3] The Deep State, also referred to as a shadow government, entails a network of especially nonelected government officials and private entities, that operate extralegally to influence and enact government policy.

conscious presence, the manifestation of such an overruling force would therefore be quite natural. However, once societies become familiar with the simple but mutually beneficial workings of governance under the Principles of Twelves, it will be equally likely that some will, in time, displace such 'deep state' structures and return to these principles.

We could also explore the causes behind the *'absence of Consciousness'*, that lead to states of chaos. Consciousness on its own is complex to define. It can be considered as something not subject to the laws of Great Nature or the Cosmos, and yet, it permeates and defines everything in Creation. For example, it is the degree of awareness of Consciousness that defines the mineral, plant, animal, human, and enlightened being. This has nothing to do with the intellect because, regardless of any so-called intelligence, when the degree of an organism's awareness drops below a certain vibratory level, its nature will become like that of the lower vibratory one. It's the same as when a civilized person or society reverts to acts of barbarism. Without a sense of conscious awareness in its Group Feeling[1], its very purpose as such a group would wane, and without purpose it will, eventually, by one cause or another, cease to exist.

This theory on the inevitability of cycles of Order and Chaos is therefore not a pessimistic one, but an observation of the consequence of a distracted civilization. We may even consider that this causal and integral design is intentional. Perhaps its purpose is to do just that, and through that fulfil a higher Purpose: To restart the magnificent cycle of civilization-building over again. After all, it is within these infinite cycles of growth and decline, that the Soul of Man has the opportunity to reinvent or rediscover Itself, individually and collectively, and how in time, some will again discover the same observations on the nature of events and cycles, as those that were recorded herein.

> Time I am, destroyer of the worlds,
> and I have come to engage all people.
> With the exception of you [the Pandavas],
> all the soldiers here on both sides will be slain[2].

---

[1] A term coined by Ibn Khaldun (1332 – 1406) in The Muqaddimah, that refers to the establishment and decline of dynasties and civilizations around a collective identification.

[2] Spoken by Lord Krishna in Bhagavad Gita (11:32), where he reveals his divine and universal form to Arjuna. Speaking of his cosmic role in creation and destruction, he is identified with Brahma (the Creator), Vishnu (the Preserver) and Shiva (the Destroyer); which deities represent the cyclical nature of the Universe in Hindu philosophy.

LAST WORD

In contemplation, be still.
Silence opens the door to Eternity,
Eternity is the place of All-being.
All-being is Unity.

Rise with the sun,
but meditate before.
Do not heed the emptiness,
that suggests otherwise.

Rest the Mind of all that is not necessary,
but be vigilant, and do not sleep.
Apply the body with life and joy,
but do not let it think or seek.

And the Heart, oh that Heart,
preserve it as that most precious,
from those that seek and covet
its attentive and purest light.

A SUGGESTED BIBLIOGRAPHY

Hermes Trismegistus:	Corpus Hermeticum
Hermes Trismegistus:	The Emerald Tablets
Maurice Doreal:	The Emerald Tablets of Thoth the Atlantean
William Walker Atkinson:	The Kybalion
G.I. Gurdjieff:	In Search of Being
	The Herald of Coming Good
	Beelzebub's tales to his Grandson
P.D. Ouspensky:	In Search of the Miraculous
	A New Model of the Universe
	Tertium Organum
Maurice Nicoll:	Psychological Commentaries on the teachings of Gurdjieff and Ouspensky
	The Blue Germ
Ibn Khaldûn:	The Muqaddimah
Graham Hancock:	Fingerprints of the Gods
Robert Bauval:	The Orion Mystery
	The Egypt Code
Hancock and Bauval:	The Keeper of Genisis
	The Master Game
John Anthony West:	Serpent in the Sky
Bruce Lipton	The Biology of Belief
Ibrahim Karim	Hidden Reality, the BioGeometry Physics of Quality
Iain McGilchrist:	The Master and His Emissary: The Divided Brain and the Making of the Western World
Eckhart Schmitz:	The Great Pyramid of Giza
Gerry Spence:	Perpetual War for Perpetual Peace
Smedley D. Butler:	War Is a Racket
Herman Hesse	Siddhartha
Rudolf Steiner	Theosophy
Edward Bulwer Lytton	Zanoni
Jason Louv	John Dee and the Empire of Angels: Enochian Magick and the Occult Roots of the modern world

The general works in writing and recorded talks or teachings of

Jiddu Krishnamurti	Sri Swami Venkatesananda	Alan Watts
Eckhart Tolle	Carl Gustav Jung	Ayn Rand
Charles Eisenstein	David Icke	The Gospels

and of course, the open minds of the Hellenic thinkers of ancient Greece and India.

The Way of the Pilgrim: Book I
The Inner Evolution of Man

In the ancient Greek precinct of Delphi, at the entrance of its Temple of Apollo, the words "KNOW THYSELF" were inscribed. This was not a suggestion but a requirement for all who wished to understand its sage's counsel, its meaning was simple:

TO KNOW THE WORLD OF DUALITY AND CONTRADICTION, WE MUST FIRST LEARN TO KNOW ONESELF.

The contemporary human being is stuck in a one and two-dimensional world of fear and desire for food, wealth, sex, recognition, and immortality. Unaware of their illusory identifications, or that their perception of these manifest their reality, many remain oblivious of their hybrid state as both *physical and metaphysical beings.* This does not serve them well, neither in life nor for their attainment of higher dimensions – which's attainment does not come naturally. It requires an awareness of the conceptual world and the recognition of our mechanicalness within it.

The observations and contemplations in this book aim to offer such awareness, and to enhance the seeker of Truth with the means to discover, understand and accept his or her *divided* Self.

It reviews the reality of our inner world philosophically but logically. By applying contemplated thought on humanity's various forms of belief and ideology, this book observes the psychology and sociology of contemporary ways. It does so in the present and historical arenas of politics, geopolitics and corporatism; not just factually, but also through the lens of spirituality and magic.

It defines the supernatural wonders for which the seeker must cross his or her own threshold. Of course, the answer to the mystery of human existence will not be found in any of the selected subjects or even the sum of their parts; it is only in the understanding of the Whole of the Self that complete and unreserved acceptance can emerge.

The Way of the Pilgrim, Book II
The Outer World of Man

THE WORLD THAT SHAPES US, WAS FIRST SHAPED BY US. THUS, TO UNDERSTAND THE WORLD, WE MUST STUDY IT FROM THE BASIS OF KNOWING OUR SELF, OUR ORIGIN AND OUR ULTIMATE PURPOSE.

As seekers of Truth we choose to discover and become aware of our Essential Self separate of our personality or ego. To understand this we must apply ourselves in life, but in order to avoid the world's harmful nature we must look upon humanity and try to understand the perceived reality of others that they are willing to sacrifice or do harm and die for.

To understand this, we must apply an unbiased and open-mind, and choose to not follow the words and claims of a selected few, but to understand the reason and logic, in their structures and history.

From the source and the firm-ground of knowing our Self, we can learn to understand *The Outer World of Man*, and enter the mind of the technocrat, politician, elitist and scientist, the atheist and dogmatic priest, but also that of a contemporary man.

In order to accomplish this, and not lose track of the 'greater whole', we must also zoom out, in scope and in Time, to the beginning of all things.

This book addresses these observations, by considering *who* did *what*, and contemplate the *WHY* and *HOW*.

Ultimately, we may believe we know ourselves, but to understand our worlds of form and formless we must also realize the constant influence their multiple dimensions have on the various parts of us. This includes our physical and sensory bodies as well as our thinking-mind and psyche, and learn how our civilized order's ever-expanding and evolving tentacles, reach for the heart to drain the soul.

The Outer World of Man offers seeds for the truth-seeking contemplative-mind, and to guide its journey.

The Way of the Pilgrim, Book III
Merging the Inner and Outer World of Man

THE ALCHEMICAL MAGIC EMERGES WITHIN THE CONSCIOUS MERGER OF OPPOSITES

The primary elements for the alchemical merger of opposites are fire and water, but these must be applied through processes of friction and non-attachment. In addition, for the magical or miraculous emergence to occur, this merger must be done in a medium of conscious harmony, immersed in care and grounded on Truth.

The surreal existence of the hybrid-human being is the product of this: a physical, sentient, mindful, yet also psychic and spiritual entity, whose reality seems improbable, yet somehow it is.

If we consider that this enigma is of a finite and temporal form, yet with an acknowledged ability to understand the existant reality of infinity within a timeless construct known as the Cosmos, its wondrous mystery can take us to the next level.

In humanity's collective organism called Civilization, with its beauty, innovation and achievement balanced against fear-based greed and destructive barbarism, then certainly, by rights none of it should exist, and yet it does. And it gets better:

The microscopic individual human being, who exists for only a flash of Time, within the absurdly complex yet magnificent, endless and eternal Universe, can – within that single spark of Time – become aware of the whole:
The All and Everything!

By *merging our Inner and Outer Worlds* we will find that nothing is random and that everything has purpose; the good and bad, the beautiful and ugly. This book contemplates *WHY* this is so as knowing this enables us to understand *HOW* to live, love and accept, unconditionally.

www.ingramcontent.com/pod-product-compliance
Lightning Source LLC
Chambersburg PA
CBHW050209240426
43671CB00013B/2265